T0389075

Theory and Method of Evolutionary Political Economy

The world is in turmoil, the dynamics of political economy seem to have entered a phase where a 'return to normal' cannot be expected. Since the financial crisis, conventional economic theory has proven itself to be rather helpless and political decision makers have become suspicious about this type of economic consultancy. This book offers a different approach. It promises to describe political and economic dynamics as interwoven as they are in real life and it adds to that an evolutionary perspective. The latter allows for a long-run view, which makes it possible to discuss the emergence and exit of social institutions.

The essays in this volume explore the theoretical and methodological aspects of evolutionary political economy. In part one, the authors consider the foundational contributions of some of the great economists of the past, while the second part demonstrates the benefits of adopting the methods of computer simulation and agent-based modelling. Together, the contributions to this volume demonstrate the richness, diversity and great explanatory potential of evolutionary political economy.

This volume is extremely useful for social scientists in the fields of economics, politics, and sociology who are interested to learn what evolutionary political economy is, how it proceeds and what it can provide.

Hardy Hanappi is ad personam chair for Political Economy of European Integration at the European Commission and professorial research associate at SOAS, University of London. He is also president of the Vienna Institute for Political Economy Research (VIPER), Austria.

Savvas Katsikides is University Professor and Jean Monnet Chair at the University of Cyprus.

Manuel Scholz-Wäckerle is Senior Lecturer at the Department of Socio-economics, Vienna University of Economics and Business, Austria.

Routledge Advances in Heterodox Economics

Edited by Mark Setterfield
Trinity College, USA
and
Peter Kriesler
University of New South Wales

Over the past two decades, the intellectual agendas of heterodox economists have taken a decidedly pluralist turn. Leading thinkers have begun to move beyond the established paradigms of Austrian, feminist, Institutional-evolutionary, Marxian, Post Keynesian, radical, social and Sraffian economics, opening up new lines of analysis, criticism and dialogue among dissenting schools of thought. This cross-fertilisation of ideas is creating a new generation of scholarship in which novel combinations of heterodox ideas are being brought to bear on important contemporary and historical problems.

Routledge Advances in Heterodox Economics aims to promote this new scholarship by publishing innovative books in heterodox economic theory, policy, philosophy, intellectual history, institutional history and pedagogy. Syntheses or critical engagement of two or more heterodox traditions are especially encouraged.

For a full list of titles in this series, please visit www.routledge.com/series/RAHE

29. Varieties of Economic Inequality
Edited by Sebastiano Fadda and Pasquale Tridico

30. Reclaiming Pluralism in Economics
Edited by Jerry Courvisanos, Jamie Doughney and Alex Millmow

31. Policy Implications of Evolutionary and Institutional Economics
Edited by Claudius Gräbner, Torsten Heinrich and Henning Schwardt

32. The Financialization of GDP
Implications for economic theory and policy
Jacob Assa

33. Evolutionary Political Economy in Action
A Cyprus Symposium
Edited by Hardy Hanappi, Savvas Katsikides and Manuel Scholz-Wäckerle

34. Theory and Method of Evolutionary Political Economy
A Cyprus Symposium
Edited by Hardy Hanappi, Savvas Katsikides and Manuel Scholz-Wäckerle

Theory and Method of Evolutionary Political Economy

A Cyprus Symposium

Edited by
Hardy Hanappi, Savvas Katsikides and Manuel Scholz-Wäckerle

LONDON AND NEW YORK

First published 2017
by Routledge
2 Park Square, Milton Park, Abingdon, Oxon OX14 4RN

and by Routledge
711 Third Avenue, New York, NY 10017

Routledge is an imprint of the Taylor & Francis Group, an informa business

British Library Cataloguing in Publication Data
A catalogue record for this book is available from the British Library

Library of Congress Cataloging in Publication Data
A catalog record for this book has been requested

ISBN: 978-1-138-20409-6 (hbk)
ISBN: 978-1-315-47021-4 (ebk)

Typeset in Times New Roman
by Swales & Willis, Exeter, Devon, UK

Printed and bound in Great Britain by
TJ International Ltd, Padstow, Cornwall

Contents

Figures

Tables

Contributors

Philippe Bouquillion is Professor of Information and Communication Sciences at the University Paris 13, a member of the Laboratory for Information and Communication Sciences (LabSic) (http://labsic.univ-paris13.fr/En/index.php/bouquillion-philippe). His research focuses on the Political Economy of Communication and Cultural Industries. He has led various research programmes funded by various institutions.

Silvano Cincotti (ME 1990, PhD 1994) is Professor of Economics and Finance at the University of Genoa, Italy. His current research topics are agent-based macroeconomics, energy economics, financial stability and sustainable growth and corporate social responsibility. He is the author of more than 180 scientific articles. Silvano Cincotti is Coordinator of EU FP7 GSS Project SYMPHONY (2013-16).

Carlo D'Ippoliti is Associate Professor of Political Economy at Sapienza University of Rome, Italy. He is author of *Economics and Diversity* (Routledge, 2011, winner of the 2012 EAEPE-Myrdal Prize), and assistant editor of the open-access journals *PSL Quarterly Review* (formerly known as *Banca Nazionale del Lavoro Quarterly Review*) and of *Moneta e Credito.*

Wilfred Dolfsma, trained as an economist and a philosopher, is professor of Innovation and Entrepreneurship and Associate Dean (Teaching) at Loughborough University London, UK. He recently guest-edited a special issue of the *Journal of Product Innovation Management*, and published *Innovation Networks* (with R. Aalbers; Routledge, 2015).

Ismail Ertürk is Senior Lecturer in Banking at Alliance Manchester Business School, the University of Manchester, UK. His research interests include financialisation, banking, corporate governance and cultural economy. He advised the United Nations Conference on Trade and Development on their creative economy report on Istanbul. He co-edited *Routledge Companion to Banking Regulation and Reform* (Routledge, 2016 forthcoming), and *Financialisation at Work* (Routledge, 2008) and co-authored *After the Great Complacence* (OUP, 2011).

Giorgio Fagiolo is Associate Professor of Economics at Sant'Anna School of Advanced Studies, Pisa, Italy, where he holds a tenured position in the Laboratory of Economics and Management. He holds a bachelor's degree in mathematical statistics from the University of Rome La Sapienza and a PhD in economics from the European University Institute (Florence, Italy). His main areas of scientific interest include agent-based computational economics, complex networks, evolutionary games, industrial dynamics and economic methodology (with particular emphasis on the scientific status of agent-based computational economics; empirical validation of economic models; and their policy-related implications). His papers have been published, among others, in *Science*, *Journal of Economic Geography*, *Journal of Applied Econometrics*, *PLoS ONE*, *Journal of Economics Dynamics and Control*, *Computational Economics*, *New Journal of Physics*, *Physical Review E* and *Journal of Economic Behavior and Organization*.

Claudius Gräbner is a research associate at the Institute of Institutional and Innovation Economics in Bremen. His research covers economic complexity, development economics, game theory, the evolution of social institutions and the methodology of social sciences. His recent work was published in the *Journal of Institutional Economics*, *Journal of Economic Issues* and the *Handbook of Heterodox Economics*.

Edeltraud Hanappi-Egger completed her doctorate in information technologies at the Vienna University of Technology (TU Vienna) in 1990. She has been a visiting researcher in Stockholm, Toronto and Oslo, among others, and was the recipient of an Austrian Academy of Sciences grant from 1993 to 1996. In 1996, she received her venia docendi in applied information technologies from TU Vienna, where she worked as an associate professor until 2001. She has been Professor for Gender and Diversity in Organizations at the Vienna University of Economics and Business (WU) since 2002. Hanappi-Egger has published over 350 papers on gender and diversity in organizations, has spent time at numerous international research institutions (most recently at the London School of Economics and McGill University), and currently holds an EU Jean Monnet Chair. She sat on the University Board of Graz University of Technology from 2008 to 2013. Edeltraud Hanappi-Egger was Chair of the WU Senate from 2006 to 2009, and Head of the Department of Management from 2012 to 2014. She has been Rector of WU since 1 October 2015, and is the first woman ever to hold this position.

Ernst Hollander is a sustainability economist affiliated to the University of Gaevle, Sweden. In the 1970s he worked on the shop floor of the engineering company Sandvik and in the research department of a blue-collar union in the 'LO-family' (Swedish confederation of trade unions). He has an MBA from the Stockholm School of Economics and Dr Tech. At Harvard he worked with the Union for Radical Political Economics. Most of his research has dealt with user-initiated sustainable innovation.

Svetlana Kirdina is Head of Sub-Division, the Institute of Economics, Russian Academy of Sciences, Moscow, Russia. She is the author of five books and over 180 articles in academic journals and books. She is the recipient of the 2014 Clarence Ayres Visiting Scholar Award (Association for Evolutionary Economics). Her principal fields of academic interest include institutional economics, the methodology of economics and the history of economic thought.

Gloria Kutscher is Research and Teaching Associate at the Institute for Gender and Diversity in Organizations, Vienna University of Economics and Business (WU). Gloria Kutscher completed psychology studies with specialisation in economic, work and organizational psychology. Following a critical gender and diversity approach, she especially focuses in her research on social class, (in)equality, identity and consciousness in groups and industrial relations. Gloria Kutscher received the Dr. Maria Schaumayer Thesis Prize in 2012 and WU Excellent Teaching Award in 2015.

George Liagouras is Associate Professor of Economic Analysis in the Department of Financial and Management Engineering at the University of the Aegean, Chios, Greece. His research interests include evolutionary and institutional economics, methodology and history of economic analysis, and political economy of post-industrial capitalism.

Killian McCarthy is an Assistant Professor at the University of Groningen, the Netherlands. An economist, his research focuses on the performance of mergers and acquisitions, and in this he increasingly considers geographic factors in explaining post-acquisition innovation-based performance. He has also published on the economics of money laundering.

Pierre Mœglin is a professor in communication sciences at the University Paris 13 (LabSic), and a member of the Institut Universitaire de France. As a specialist in the socio-economic aspects of cultural, creative and educational industries, he is the author of numerous publications and talks, in France and abroad.

Asjad Naqvi is currently a post-doc at the Institute for Ecological Economics at the Vienna University of Economics and Business, where he works on issues of growth, migration, unemployment, distribution and climate change. He received his PhD in Economics from the New School for Social Research in New York.

Reynold Christian Nathanael is a PhD graduate in Computational Economics and Finance from the University of Genoa, Italy. He has expertise in agent-based macroeconomic modelling with heterogeneous and interacting agents. Prior to macroeconomic research, he has experience in business project and application support at Australia New Zealand Bank.

Bulent Ozel holds a PhD in Organization Studies, an MSc in Computer Science and a BSc in Electrical-Electronics Engineering. His recent research interests are agent-based modelling, social network analysis, data mining, qualitative aspects of processes on collaboration in sciences and open-source projects. He is the author of many scientific articles published in international journals.

Pascal Petit is an economist and Centre National de la Recherche Scientifique director of research emeritus, attached to the Centre d'Economie de Paris Nord. He has published books and articles on institutional economics of economic growth and structural changes and comparative analyses of national trajectories of modern developed economies, stressing the diversity of capitalist growth regimes and their crises. Recent co-edited publications include *The Hardship of Nations: Exploring the Paths of Modern Capitalism* (Edward Elgar, 2006), *L'économie mondiale en 2030: ruptures et continuités* (Economica, 2013) and *Challenges for Europe in the World, 2030* (Ashgate, 2014).

Marco Raberto (MS 1999, PhD 2003) is Associate Professor in Business and Management Engineering at the University of Genoa, Italy. He is author of more than 50 scientific contributions in books and journals on the topics of agent-based modelling in economics and finance, financial stability and financial time series analysis.

Marco Ranaldi is a PhD student and teaching assistant at the Paris School of Economics and the University of Paris 1 Panthéon-Sorbonne. His research interests range from the dynamics of functional income distribution to the political business cycle.

Miriam Rehm holds a PhD in Economics from the New School for Social Research, New York. She has been with several multinational organisations, and taught at universities in New York and Vienna. She is currently an economist at the Austrian Federal Chamber of Labour (AK Wien) responsible for macroeconomics and distribution.

Bernhard Rengs is a post-doc researcher at the Wittgenstein Centre for Demography and Global Human Capital and the Vienna Institute of Demography. He has an interdisciplinary background in computer sciences and economics and received his degrees from the Vienna University of Technology in Austria. His past research focused on computational social simulation, computational economics, evolutionary economics, applied game theory and information visualisation. His current research mainly focuses on the application of computational agent-based modelling and mixed methods in demography, population economics and political economy.

Andrea Roventini (male) is Associate Professor at the Institute of Economics, Scuola Superiore Sant'Anna, Pisa, Italy. His main research interests include complex system analysis, agent-based computational economics, business cycles and the study of the effects of monetary, fiscal, technology and climate policies. He has participated in several projects financed by the European Commission (FP7 and Horizon2020) and the U.S. National Science Foundation. He is advisory editor for the *Journal of Evolutionary Economics*. His work has been published in *Journal of Evolutionary Economics*, *Journal of Applied Econometrics*, *Journal of Economic Dynamics and Control*, *Environmental Modelling and Software* and *Macroeconomic Dynamics*.

Manuel Scholz-Wäckerle holds a position as Senior Lecturer at the Department of Socioeconomics at Vienna University of Economics and Business. Manuel is trained in economics and computer science and received a doctorate in social and economic science at the Vienna University of Technology in 2010. His research interests involve evolutionary political economy, institutional economics, agent-based modelling (micro-meso-macro) as well as the social ecological transformation.

Andrea Teglio holds a PhD in Electronic Engineering and a PhD in Economics. He is Associate Professor at the Economic Department of University Jaume I of Castellón, Spain. His main research interests are agent-based modelling, macroeconomics and complex systems. He is the author of many scientific articles published in international journals, and has also directed several research projects.

Introduction

Cyprus is a very special place. It has been a hotbed of cultural development for more than 3,000 years and its – not only geographical – position at the crossroad of different empires and their traditions still is a fundamental advantage for the conquest of new territory. To mix different perspectives, to soften worn-out attitudes and get rid of obsolete prejudices, to merge core issues of seemingly unrelated scientific disciplines, all these practices are particularly well embedded in a place like Cyprus.

A *symposium*, as it was understood in ancient Greece, was a drinking party. The underlying motive for supporting a social gathering of philosophers and their friends with substances – mainly alcohol – that seduce to more uncontrolled expression of opinions and more extroverted behaviour in general is very interesting: in spelling out more daring hypotheses, in expressing wild emotional feelings of love and hate with respect to the views of other participants of the symposium, in showing deep despair in one moment and unfounded excessive joy in the next, in being hard to understand and slowly falling into speechless meditation, in all these exceptional developments well-respected authorities tacitly escaped authority in the course of an ongoing symposium. Giving up on exerting one's authority makes it easier to pay deference to other participants' authority, or more precisely, to pay attention to the content of what they are saying.

Nowadays a scientific symposium is just a kind of workshop meeting of scientists; the ancient spirit has been replaced by the vague intention of behaving cooperatively and following a mutually constructive style of exchanging knowledge. When we planned to organize a conference of the European Association for Evolutionary Political Economy (EAEPE) in Cyprus and to call it the *Cyprus Symposium*, we had this type of modern scientific event in our minds. But in the course of this EAEPE conference the ancient meaning of a symposium did strike back. The exceptional landscape in which the wonderful conference location was embedded as well as the many side-attractions – including a wine-drinking party – opened up an atmosphere of general friendship among all participants. Contrary to the standard of eager self-marketing of competitors in a world of A-journal publication that prevails at so many international conferences. the Cyprus Symposium became a kind of friendly discussion club; an event where starting points for interventions into the real political process were discussed – mostly replacing the usual sequence of displays of individual greatness in conference sessions. The distinctions between the different streams of thought and preferred objects of investigations within EAEPE – a fact that has haunted this organization since its foundation – these distinctions started to become realized as fruitful interfaces rather than as probable lines of breakage of the organization. Scholars from agent-based simulation modelling discussed with economic historians, debates between hard-core post-Keynesians, Schumpetereans and Marxists mixed with those of pragmatic political activists, seemingly detached topics like the formalization of dialectic reasoning coalesced with mundane views about the design of EU institutions.

After this experience the three editors of the two books covering the most important contributions to this Cyprus Symposium really had a hard time structuring all this wealth of ideas. The sheer amount of work presented led to the conclusion that two volumes were needed to transmit the manifold content and thus the spirit of this conference. We finally came up with the decision to have four parts, two in volume 1 and two in volume 2. The first volume would focus more on the special focus of the event while the second volume would be more in line with event-independent usual distinction between theory and method.

Volume 1 therefore has the title *Evolutionary Political Economy in Action* – this is what we did and discussed in Cyprus. Scholars in political economy necessarily are themselves part of the political process; in times of radical transformation of Europe this is becoming more evident every day. While in the long period after World War II it often seemed to be sufficient to point at important topics (e.g. the importance of an economic meso-level), to criticize wrong methodologies (e.g. the preferred enemy of neo-classical economics) or to interpret what a great economist of the past *really* intended to say (e.g. Darwin, Marx, Keynes, Schumpeter), in the process of European metamorphosis we are now forced to propose quick and not-too-dirty action plans on what to do next. The strange scientific tribe of academic economists traditionally is not very good at that. Today academic careers in the field are made of mathematical versatility and membership in the club of politically untouchables. Political passion hurts. The experiences at the Cyprus symposium, the hotly debated policy issues that were of immediate importance for European citizens in the next few years, these motives for our scientific work, they pointed in the opposite direction: passion is needed, it is at the core of the intrinsic motivation of a scientist, our theory building has to return to address the grand problems of practice in Europe's political economy. This is what the chapters in volume 1 aim for.

The first part covers a broad range of topics concerning selected problems and how to change them for the better. This ranges from the danger of military conflicts at Europe's eastern border via several aspects of welfare decline and vanishing growth prospects to questions on how to form resistance against obviously destructive political forces. The second part of volume 1 provides spotlights on the very special situation of the crisis in Greece and Cyprus. This part of Europe had often been accused of being the origin of the problems of European unification; even today several scholars in political economy refuse to consider Greece as just another member state of the EU; for them it is an exceptional type of state with an extraordinarily corrupt bureaucracy and population, which just has to be forced to correct its behaviour. This is the background of the set of so-called austerity measures that are prescribed by certain EU politicians and supported by economists treating Greece as a singular problem of a population with a general tendency towards unethical and economically unsustainable behaviour.

The contributions in the second part of volume 1 do not share this perspective but instead propose to take a much more detailed look at the processes that took place in Greece and Cyprus in the last 10 years. Replacing the mono-causal and highly ignorant view just described by insightful analysis of what really happened in certain policy areas often enables the authors to come up with much more useful proposals for improvements. As a common feature of emphasis, they consider the crisis in these states not simply as a local failure based on national misbehaviour but dig deeper into the relationship between European partner countries. Despite the evident need to reconsider local political and bureaucratic structures, there certainly is the need to modify Europe's economic policy, in particular its banking system and financial architecture too. As in the first part of volume 1, the emphasis is on using theory to solve practical problems, a maxim too often missing in the neo-classical paradigm but pivotal for evolutionary political economy.

The second volume, with the title *Theory and Method of Evolutionary Political Economy*, is structured more conventionally into a part on recent theoretical achievements in the area of evolutionary political economy and a part on the new set of methods which this approach has acquired and produced. Theory building in evolutionary political economy by the very nature of its aspirations is a very wide field. Not only in biological systems the emergence of a large variety out of which new forms, new combinations, emerge, a similar drive towards a diverse set of evolutionary theory fragments occurs in theoretical contributions of our discipline. In the selected chapters topics like the role of creative industries, conceptual boundaries between biology and political economy, a reappraisal of classical forerunners of evolutionary political economy (Polanyi, Goodwin, Marx), the role of unions, a study of a country-specific emergence of evolutionary thought (Russia), and finally an evolutionary investigation into the market of corporate control are dealt with. Each of these chapters follows a unique line of research under the common umbrella of evolutionary political economy. The purpose of part 1 of the second volume is to stimulate researchers in specific lines of research in evolutionary political economy to take a look at other scientists' findings – across the wide and rich area that we cover. It appears to be a most innovative strategy to learn with conclusions by analogy,[1] a forbidden theoretical territory for most neo-classical economic theory, which works by making deductions from axioms. For evolutionary political economy conclusion by analogy is a major tool for innovative theoretical breakthroughs.

The last part in volume 2 is devoted to the particular attention that evolutionary political economy has to pay to its methodological toolbox. Contrary to neo-classical economic theory, which more or less just adopted the standard mathematical apparatus of classical mechanics of the early 19th century, our discipline still is struggling to develop its own take on methodological issues. What can be said so far is that computer simulation techniques certainly will play a major role. Of course, the historical fact that the same mathematical genius who developed the computer, John von Neumann, also was the one who set out to develop a new formal language for the social sciences, i.e. game theory, is remarkable.[2] For many decades now a radical change in the methods to be used in the social sciences seems to be in the air. For evolutionary political economy one of the major kick-offs came in 1982 when Richard Nelson and Sidney Winter published their book on evolutionary economics; their central method was the use of computer programs for firm behaviour.

The papers selected for this part of the book are meant to provide examples for the simulation approach in evolutionary political economy; they also should throw a light on some meta-issues to enable the reader to explore advantages and limits of the newly emerging essential methods of our research field. Macroeconomic policy is influenced by economic models; traditionally these models were dynamic stochastic general equilibrium (DSGE) models. However, during the Great Recession critique has grown concerning DSGE models from several directions. In the second part of the second volume the methodological pitfalls of DSGE are discussed (Chapter 9) and contrasted with the potential and promise made by agent-based modelling (ABM). ABM has become an alternative on macroeconomic scale (Chapter 10) today and computational simulation allows the implementation of complex models with, for instance, endogenous credit-driven business cycles (Chapter 11). Otherwise ABM allows multi-country economies (e.g. artificial monetary unions) to be simulated and different fiscal policy settings to be tested (Chapter 12). This bottom-up computational method works particularly well for testing policy experiments, even in very specific regional environments. It is shown how the method can be used to study the socioeconomic impact of natural disasters and potential policy responses to them (Chapter 13). Thereby we highlight the versatile application area of ABM for different economic policy settings and the strong interdependences between micro-, meso- and macro-level dynamics. We have indicated that evolutionary political economy places the scientist at the centre of the political process. To this extent it is necessary to discuss the implications of this for formal modelling (Chapter 14). This important scientific effort is often neglected in the economic mainstream, as shown in the example of the Transatlantic Trade and Investment Partnership (TTIP).

In sum, these two volumes contain an extremely rich and widespread collection of innovative ideas. In doing so they provide an example of an evolutionary process, more precisely, of the stage of this process when material is organized as a wide variety from which the following selection process will then select and recombine the most promising ones. No other stage of theory evolution is as challenging – but also as intellectually rewarding – as this stage. We are glad to invite the readers of these two volumes to share with us this exciting experience.

Vienna 2016
Hardy Hanappi, Savvas Katsikides,
Manuel Scholz-Wäckerle

Notes

1 See Ribeiro (2014).
2 Compare Hanappi (2013, pp. 3–26).

References

Hanappi H. (ed.) (2013) *Game Theory Relaunched.* New York: Intech Publishers.

Nelson R. and Winter S. (1982) *An Evolutionary Theory of Economic Change.* Cambridge, MA: Belknap Press.

Ribeiro H.J. (ed.) (2014) *Systematic Approaches to Argument by Analogy.* Heidelberg: Springer Publishers.

Part I

Evolutionary political economy – theory

1 Creative economy as a resource for specific local developments

Ismail Ertürk and Pascal Petit

This paper will critically discuss the emergence of the concept and practice of creative economy as an economic growth model to be applied across the board of all contemporary economies and will investigate the relevance of the notion of creative activities for the development of local areas which are relatively isolated and deprived of tradable natural resources.

First, a genealogy of the concept of creative economy through definitions and measurements in various national and international examples will be constructed, with special references to the debates on cultural and creative industries at international institutions like United Nations Educational, Scientific and Cultural Organization (UNESCO) and United Nations Conference on Trade and Development (UNCTAD).

Second, policies regarding creative industries will be assessed based on the type of international interventions under examination (be it foreign direct investment or migration flows) and the kind of cultural and human capital these areas have benefited from (including digital literacy). The performativity of such policies may have to consider a more comprehensive accounting of economic development, taking on board the dimensions of well-being that are stressed in the "Beyond GDP" debates.

Third, the performativity of cultural and creative industries in some areas that are isolated and deprived from natural resources but enjoying touristic appeal and good migration flows with remittances from diaspora (as is the case with most Caribbean countries) will be analysed.

International origins of creative economy as a development model

The international origins of the concept of creative economy as a feasible economic development model in the developing world can be traced back to the UNCTAD XI Ministerial Conference in 2004 (UNCTAD 2008, p. 3). Four years after the XI Ministerial Conference, UNCTAD produced a milestone report on creative economy that defined and measured creative industries that make up creative economy for policy purposes in the developing world. This 2008 report was a collaborative work among five UN institutions – UNCTAD,

United Nations Development Programme (UNDP), UNESCO, World Intellectual Property Organization (WIPO) and International Trade Centre (ITC) – that had been involved in policy formulation and implementation in and statistical expressions of various aspects of cultural and creative industries in the world. The 2008 report that was entitled *The Challenge of Assessing the Creative Economy: Towards Informed Policy-Making* was a milestone policy document because (a) it expanded the earlier familiar narrower cultural industries concept of UNESCO to include economic categories like innovation, knowledge and information that have animated the policy debates in post-industrial economies in the 1990s and (b) it produced comprehensive statistics that authoritatively showed the size and growth of creative industries in the global economy. Critical academic work on creative industries too acknowledged the performative significance of this 2008 report at the international level (see, for example, Flew and Cunningham 2010; Tremblay 2011; Dubina *et al.* 2012). Although the policy initiatives and debates regarding cultural and creative industries have taken place at national, regional and city level before the UNCTAD report in 2008, an international framework with trade and Global South focus did not exist. The 2008 report has been updated bi-annually since then and two more reports were published in 2010 and 2013 (UNCTAD 2010; UNDP and UNESCO 2013).

The 2008 report announced creative economy as a "new development paradigm" and aimed at encouraging and informing policy on creative industries in the developing world. The UNCTAD 2008 report acknowledges the differences in various previous academic and policy discussions, from Adorno's cultural industries concept to the Australian and UK governments' creative industries policies in 1994 and 1997, in defining what creative economy is, and introduces the following definition of its own:

> – The creative economy is an evolving concept based on creative assets potentially generating economic growth and development;
> – It can foster income generation, job creation and export earnings while promoting social inclusion, cultural diversity and human development;
> – It embraces economic, cultural and social aspects interacting with technology, intellectual property and tourism objectives;
> – It is a set of knowledge-based economic activities with a development dimension and cross-cutting linkages at macro and micro levels to the overall economy;
> – It is a feasible development option calling for innovative multidisciplinary policy responses and interministerial action;
> – At the heart of the creative economy are the creative industries.
>
> (UNCTAD 2008, p. 4)

This definition of creative economy is then supported by a classification system for creative industries that was developed by UNCTAD experts and forms the backbone of measuring creative economy globally. UNCTAD's classification system (Figure 1.1) differs from other well-known academic and policy-oriented

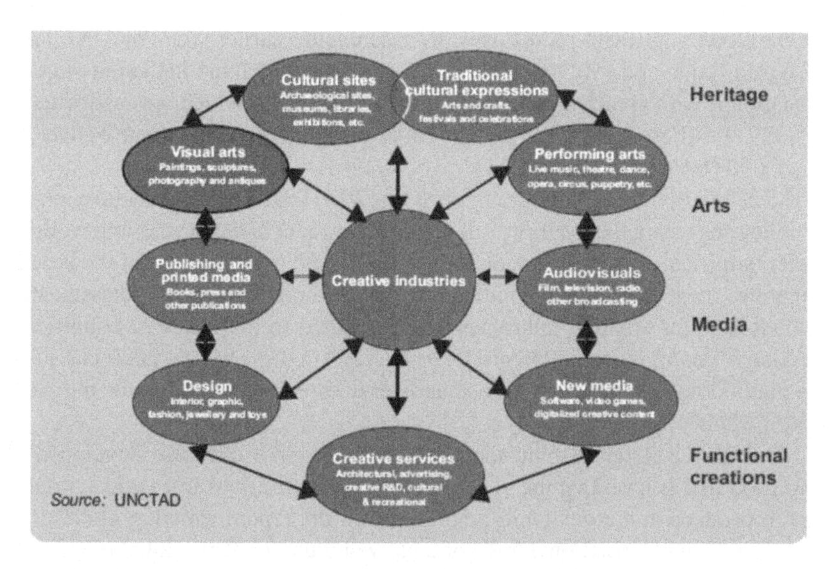

Figure 1.1 UNCTAD's classification of creative industries

Source: UNCTAD (2008, p. 14)

classification systems for creative industries primarily for aiming (a) for statistical robustness and consistency in collecting data and (b) not to exclude the developing world's non-market cultural and creative assets like heritage and traditional arts from quantification of creative economy. As such, UNCTAD's classification of creative industries puts human creativity in the developing world qualitatively on an equal footing with innovation in knowledge economies of the developed world. Creativity in cultural activities then becomes a universal upstream economic foundation for the production and distribution of innovation-driven technological goods and services in the nexus of creative economy.

What makes the 2008 UNCTAD report especially relevant for policy, however, is the statistical content that maps creative economy globally, highlighting its significant share in gross domestic product (GDP) and its above-average growth in international trade and industry. The message to the national economic policy makers is very clear: this is an industry that requires specific policies for its nourishment and management. In this respect the UNCTAD report seems to be building on the earlier UNESCO publications on cultural goods and services in 1992, 2000 and 2005 that had aimed to measure the size and growth of cultural goods and services in the world. Of these earlier UNESCO reports, the 2005 one was much more ambitious in scope and concept as it aimed to define and categorize cultural output in a more robust way and measure it more comprehensively. It also emphasized the growing impact of internet and digital technology on the creation, distribution and consumption of cultural products by highlighting the rise of e-books and downloadable music. This 2005 UNESCO report, which is entitled *International Flows of Selected Cultural Goods and Services 1994–2003*, shows that cultural and creative economies constitute 7% of world GDP. Other statistics that the 2005 UNESCO report uses, by referencing earlier work by UNCTAD, the World Bank, and PwC to prove its case, are the global market value of goods and services with creative industry and cultural content, which was estimated to be US$ 1.3 trillion in 2005 and had grown at an annual compound rate of over 7% since 2000 (UNESCO 2005, p. 11).

The 2008 UNCTAD report transforms this 2005 UNESCO report into a manual for policy for creative economy as development model in the developing world by further empirical sophistication on the definition and measurement of the broader economic category of creative industries. Furthermore UNCTAD's classification methodology for creative industries is more suited to the needs of countries in the Global South, whereas, according to UNCTAD, UNESCO's 2009 classification methodology for cultural goods and services is more suitable for the North (UNCTAD 2010, p. 111).

The UNCTAD reports introduce a comprehensive database developed by UNCTAD that is based on the classifications and definitions in Figure 1.1 and is used to produce numerous tables and graphs in the report, showing globally the size, growth and international trade of creative industries. This global mapping of creative industries by UNCTAD reveals growth rates that are higher than average GDP rates both in the developed and the developing world. This mapping exercise also produces comparative performances of countries by product category. There are also case studies of countries and cities to highlight policy initiatives. For example, according to UNCTAD calculations, the share of creative industries in some European countries is bigger than both computer and related activities, and manufacture of food, beverages and tobacco (Table 1.1).

Table 1.1 UNCTAD calculations of the share of creative industries in selected European countries

Proportion of GDP contributed by:				
Country	*Cultural and creative sector**	*Manufacture of food, beverages, tobacco*	*Real-estate activities*	*Computer and related activities*
Denmark	2.6	2.1	1.0	1.2
Finland	3.1	2.6	5.1	1.5
Latvia	3.1	1.5	1.8	1.5
Lithuania	3.4	1.9	1.8	1.3
Netherlands	2.5	1.6	2.6	1.4
Poland	2.7	2.2	2.3	1.4
Sweden	3.2	1.7	2.7	1.3
United Kingdom	3.0	1.9	2.1	2.7

*Industries included in cultural and creative sector vary among countries. For qualifications to the interpretation of these data, refer to source.

Source: UNCTAD (2010)

Such selected statistics conveniently support UNCTAD's general message that creative economy is too important to ignore. Another statistic from the report shows that developing economies have higher share of exports of creative goods in arts and crafts, design and new media in world trade. Although the higher share of arts and crafts is expected, the shares of developing countries in design and new media may surprise the uninformed (Figure 1.2).

The second creative economy report by UNCTAD in 2010 updates data but also introduces conceptual elaborations such as creative ecology, creative commons, collaborative creation, experience economy and soft innovation. The financial crisis of 2008 influenced the policy part of the 2010 report, as the trust in market mechanism in developing creative industries had been severely damaged. After the great recession of 2008, the 2010 UNCTAD report expressed firmer confidence in creative economy as a development model and saw it as a holistic approach to economic development where social inclusion and sustainability could be achieved together with GDP growth in post-crisis global economy. The south–south trade then became more vital for the developing world as the demand in advanced industrial economies slowed down after the crisis. The 2010 report also offers a progressive vision of economic development through creative industries by linking the successes of the green economy to the deepening and widening of the creative economy.

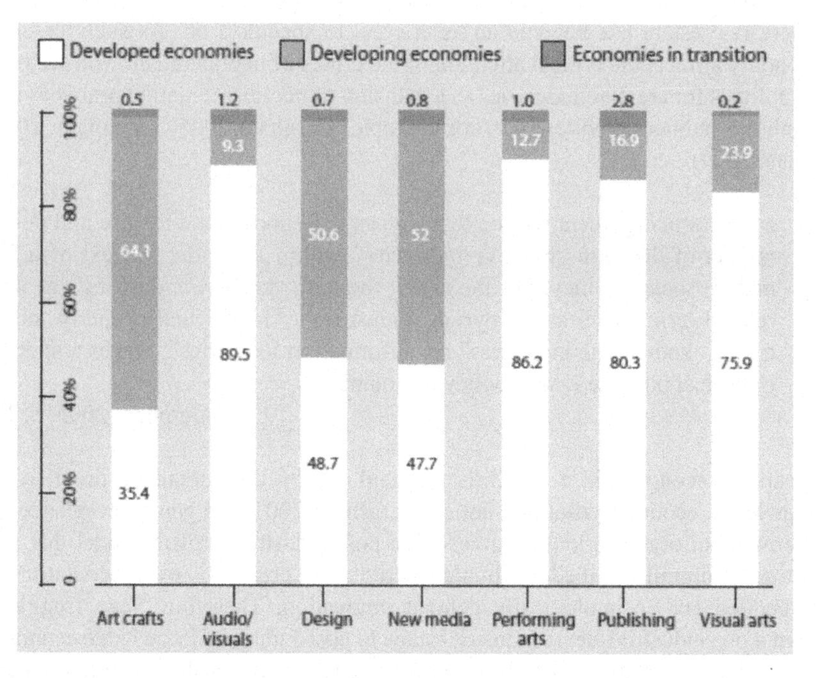

Figure 1.2 Share of economic groups in world exports of creative goods, 2008 (%)

Source: UNCTAD (2010, p. 130)

> In this context, the creative economy and the so-called green economy can reinforce each other, since they share the objective of promoting development that is more sustainable and inclusive. Many creative industries are already offering solutions to the environmental, social and economic problems and are experiencing success.
>
> (UNCTAD 2010, p. 65)

From creative industries to creative models of local development

Questioning the relevant level of policies

As well as the previous work by other UN institutions like UNESCO, the influential policy-oriented works by Richard Florida on creative class and clusters, Charles Landry on creative cities and John Howkins on creative economy inform the UNCTAD's creative economy reports. These works by such celebrity thinkers and consultants also provide a clearly identifiable spatial visibility for creative economy because creative clusters of Florida, creative cities of Landry and creative economic activities of Howkins have urban postcodes, competitive indices and urban planning that crowd the election programmes of most local politicians. Unlike a mining shaft or off-shore oil rig the creative economy is almost exclusively an urban real-estate project that fits in well in financialized capitalism where real estate has become an asset class to speculate on. As such, creative economy attracts the critical attention of the critics of neoliberalism who see public policies for creative industries as expansion of neoliberal market practices into symbolic human activities (see, for example, Garnham 2005; McGuigan 2005; Evans 2009).

> My central argument will be that we can only understand the use and policy impact of the term "creative industries" within the wider context of information society policy. For the use of the term "creative industries", as with related terms such as "copyright industries", "intellectual property industries", "knowledge industries" or "information industries", serves a specific rhetorical purpose within policy discourse.
>
> (Garnham 2005, p. 15)

Creativity economy in a way fills the void left by the unrealized promises of knowledge economy after the dot.com crash of 2001 and gains acceptance by international organizations as a desirable post-industrial growth model that prioritizes culturally embedded human activity of creativity over economically embedded and technologically defined innovation. Therefore "leap frogging" from a pre-industrial, semi-industrial stage to post-industrial knowledge economy can be imagined to be possible (UNCTAD 2008, p. 6). In the EU too, after the disappointing outcome of the Lisbon Strategy where knowledge-based economy (KBE) would bring competitive prosperity to the EU, it became clear that the KBE model was not that straightforward. The activities under view had a global scope in a liberalized world economy and no nation states were in a position to implement any industrial policy that would have contributed to construct in the EU the best KBE in the world. The EU itself, had it overcome its despising of industrial policy, could not have achieved this objective. The KBE remained a buzz word, except that the poor result in terms of employment of this Lisbon agenda led the EU to play it down by the mid-2000s and turn to standard, poorly effective policies. Somehow references to creative industries appeared as a leftover of this "big plan", but with a policy that had shifted to a more down-to-earth objective of creating growth and jobs through cultural and creative industries (European Commission 2012). Indeed, this concept of artistic creativity and scientific innovation having mutually beneficial commonalities in societal and economic development was argued much earlier by UNESCO in the World Conference of Science in 1999 and now seems to be adopted by the EU. The concept of creative industries as an economic development model has been around for quite some time now without being definitively discarded or validated. In 2013 Nesta, the UK innovation charity, produced a manifesto calling for a refreshing of ideas about creative economy in both the UK and the world.

> But I hope the analysis set out here will also be of interest in many other parts of the world which also want to make more of a living out of creativity. A previous generation of ideas and policies – many of which spread across the world over the last two decades – has run its course. It's now time for a refresh. This manifesto shows how.
>
> (Bakhshi *et al.* 2013, p. 6)

In effect this perspective, whereby one searches more for local models of development in a new global context, marked by the development of information and communication technologies (ICTs), of multiple international transactions and of the so-called creative industries, does constitute a new promising basis for local development studies.

On the conditions of emergence of creative local models of development

In this section we list some of the conditions likely to preside over the successes or failures of local patterns of development trying to get the most out of the global context provided by creative industries and their environment. Somehow our objective is a preliminary investigation on the ecology of creative local economies.

Isolated territories in our modern globalized world

By isolated territory we mean a territory with a community the integration of which is not straightforward in the present highly competitive and widespread world economy. It has no natural resources that are readily tradable or competitive developed industries with an open future in this world economy. Its integration is therefore a questionable issue. However, isolated territory does not mean no link to the rest of the world. Part of our hypothesis is that some links have diffused around the world, opening new opportunities from internet connections to media diffusion of information and knowledge, notwithstanding the links with distant communities through migration and tourism flows. All these links are effectively or potentially changing the behaviours and expectations of the members of the community under view. For isolated territories these links create opportunities that may or not be taken advantage of. Often the territory under view is of agricultural origin and local agriculture is at the roots of its culture, but it could also be places where culture has been associated with other trade, such as old mining or manufacturing activities. A major implication of this isolation is that the territory will have to count mainly on a dynamics of its own to take advantage of these opportunities. Diffusion of the products of creative activities, as defined in the first section of this chapter, constitutes major components of these links with the outer world. It is obvious for the productions of *creative content providers* (radio, television, music, games, films, books, fashion), but also for the productions of *creative service providers* (design, architecture, new media, advertising) and those of *creative experience* (*original*) *providers* (performing and visual arts) to retain the three creative providers of the typology retained by UK Technology Strategy Board (2009) (Figure 1.1).

Local cultures as potential bases of redevelopment

Local cultures broadly shape the behaviours and ways of thinking of the members of communities. Still, they should not be seen as fixed codes of conduct. These rules are more or less strictly followed and one tends to speak accordingly of strong or weak local cultures. Chiefly these references evolve. They are influenced by external contacts and/or by local experiences, be they happy events or dramatic ones. Local cultures have thus histories of their own which may lead either to consecrate new practices or revisit some roots.[1] An example of such waves of change in local cultures can be seen in the turn taken by regional cultures in France following the progressive industrialization of the country. It led at the beginning of the 20th century to fancy revivals of supposedly long-lost traditions such as the celebration of the Celtic link in Brittany or the Viking heritage in Normandy (see Hobsbawm and Ranger 1983).

The actions of small groups can lead to such changes if communities are somehow open to them, meaning they perceive these changes as strengthening their community links, e.g. boosting trust within the group. The plasticity of these local cultures is therefore a potential to be considered when investigating how to improve the economic activities of these communities and their external relations. This improvement tends to be thought of in terms of market activities generating income increases, although the primary objective, and the one likely to be more promising, is to improve the well-being of these communities. Such objective is manifold, being culturally idiosyncratic.

Enlarging the objective to well-being enhancement gives more room for selecting the trajectories to be followed to make the best of the previously mentioned connections with the creative activities of the outer world. Some processes of such interactions are rather straightforward. The diffusion of ICTs and media channels new ideas that may change the relative weight and form of some cultural practices. In turn some traditional activities such as cooking, craftwork or leisure can acquire new status and lead reflexively to initiatives conveyed by ICTs and media. The creation of new platforms is a case in point of such evolution which consolidates and expands social links.[2] Also important is the new status given to craftsmanship with the growing attention paid to the notion of design which both confirms the tradition and contributes to its evolution.

The same move of consolidation and renewing can concern all traditional activities. These integrations of traditional activities in new settings can open the way to radically new creative activities. An important issue in these developments is whether they are market-oriented or directly concern improvements in community well-being. If the experience of market economy is relatively weak and the average income of the community rather low, improving well-being directly and in specific ways can be both innovative and substantial. It can thus be turned in terms of creation and/or developments of new commons, which could have in turn cumulative effects on the creativity of the community in their use of the connections with the outer world.

The expansion in the form of increasing market activities has its own more classical merits. The diffusion of the effects is straightforwardly turned into income increases that diffuse through the whole community. The evidence of this income effect fuels the attractiveness of market-oriented developments while their vulnerability to external changes in market conditions reduces it. There are clearly trade-offs between the two orientations (market or non-market-led developments) that deserve to be investigated, putting into use the cultural heritage. Both can be combined and/or alternated. The whole process is likely to be an evolutionary dynamic with communities learning how to adjust and enrich their structure of well-being and income, remembering that well-being is itself a multidimensional notion, thus allowing various arbitrages. It remains an issue whether the variety of local cultures can accommodate more or less successfully market or non-market-oriented processes of adaptation. There has been a clear overall trend to privilege market-oriented adaptation processes. The nature of contemporary challenges may favour a more non-market orientation.

On the contemporary challenges to the revival of territories

We have already stressed that overall changes in local cultures often followed major broad challenges to previous ways of life. We referred above to the changes induced by the diffusion of industrialization. Similar broad challenges occurred when major changes of governments (such as moving from kingdoms to republics) or of religions (with the diffusion of Christianity then Islamism) took place in Europe, the Middle East and North Africa. We are witnessing somehow a change of similar magnitude with the threat to the environment. The globally diffused message is that the world has reached a point where major changes in our way of life have to occur, if we want to set the world back on a sustainable path. The message has been widely received and local experiences are now interpreted through this broad frame. The echoes and policies coming from the successive international meetings following the Intergovernmental Panel on Climate Change (IPCC)[3] reports, from Rio 1992 to Paris 2015, are making ever more precise the threats of climate changes and of their local impacts.

Any policy aiming to set the world on the path of sustainable development implies tremendous adjustments. Such changes cannot be imposed top-down; people have to be clearly directly concerned and mobilized to achieve such ambitious objectives. Bottom-up changes, e.g. changes formatted at local levels, are the only chances to meet the targets. An illustration of such a challenge can be given by the factor 4 objective, implying to divide by four 1990 per capita emission of CO_2 by 2050 in order to avoid an increase in global warming of more than 2 degrees, which IPCC experts consider as a limit above which climate change would lead to dangerous chaos. All these policy debates and their mediatization are raising concerns at local levels and inducing some ill-defined quest for solidarity. It may lead to different behaviours. Associations rallying communities around objectives improving well-being or helping them to take part in broad movements on climate action may be welcome. But one should not omit the fact that an atmosphere of more or less defined fears can also boost reactionary populist movements, blaming everything on past politics and pretending that they can solve (or ignore) the broad threats that are announced.

The challenges of these forthcoming changes and how to face them are all the more important because communities are locally exposed to major climate perturbations, be it violent typhoons, long droughts or large floods. One specificity of the current threats on ways of life is to favour creative non-market activities. The need to foster community links and mutual trust boosts the organization of festivals and other forms of celebration of community spirit. A good example of such reactions can be found in the experience of some mining regions (like Loos en Gohelle in the north of France[4]), where the shock of the mines closure was overcome with the creation of an annual festival celebrating the traditions of the mining country together with information and involvement in climate actions. Such an example of resilience can also be seen in localities after dramatic experiences, such as Minamata in Japan.[5] These dramatic experiences are telling about the reactions of communities, adjusting their codes of conduct in more or less creative ways, to face the various threats on their ways of life. Still. even if we have stressed the endogenous dimension of such responses, communities are not alone in formatting these reactions and the tutelage of higher authorities has also to be taken into account. The study of the resilience factors of communities is important but the hierarchical contexts and the structure of external links in which local communities are *de facto* placed also matter.

We have mainly stressed above the impacts of global threats of climate change and how they may impact local cultures in the ways they shape the norms and behaviours of local communities. Still, the issues linked with environmental changes are even broader and have to include all the safety risks linked to the pollutions that human activities induce. These safety risks are manifold. Our knowledge of these pollutions is progressing step by step, following scientific discoveries and the exhaustion of the controversies on the effectiveness of their impact. The case of the detrimental effects of asbestos is a good example of the length of such processes and of the hazards of their mediatization. Similar issues can be raised on more recent discoveries such as the risks tied to endocrine disruptors. A lot of pollutants are still being investigated that may turn out to harm specific groups of the population (pregnant women, children and aged persons being often first in line). The above examples are general cases of pollution. In some cases of pollution tied to productive activities, the impacts are rather localized. Such were the cases for instance, of the devastation caused in Minamata, Japan, by the refuse of a factory or in the French West Indies by overdoses of pesticides in agriculture. Taking into account the occurrence of such dramatic events, the analysis of the determinants of resilience of the populations under view becomes a major issue and connections with the outside world may then be crucial for relatively isolated populations.

Safety issues seem then to require some permanent local watch. In other words, the contemporary structure of risks calls for local mobilization and actions with continuous access to information and knowledge, which is an incentive to pay attention to the connections with the outer world that we stressed above. While often a creative economy in poor isolated places is seen as a means of accessing product markets and increasing local incomes, more and more importance should be given to the capacities it conveys to meet the growing bulk of safety risks. Local isolated communities are more and more conscious of such risks and therefore open to organize themselves to meet them. A growing literature rightly insists, after Sen (2010), on the importance of building up capabilities of resilience within communities (see CGDD 2015).

Towards a typology of creative models of local development

The previous section featured the general conditions under which relatively isolated territories can forge some pattern of local development, making use of links with the outside world provided by creative industries and of the capital of trust that a lightly challenged culture gives to a community. The project in its early phase is, in the above context, created by a small innovative group. Beyond this general feature of an endogenous impulse, one has to take into account a certain context of external support, more or less crucial for the success of the local initiative. The support of local authorities, that represent a remote central power, often seems crucial to legitimate and bring some modest financial support to the initiative at its early stage.[6] Then the diasporas, when they exist in metropolis or foreign countries (as is often the case for insular economies) may constitute meaningful support in the phase of taking off. At the same time as the action is gaining some recognition, it may be opportune to structure its organization or to ally with existing civil society organizations (CSOs). The support of CSOs helps to consolidate and enlarge the base of the model of development. It then reaches a stage when international firms may see some marketable aspects in the process. Similarly, international institutions may become involved in supporting the activities under view if the communities are threatened by either safety or security risks. Supports may thus seem to loosely depend from the stage and size of development of the new pattern, whether market-oriented or not. The characteristics of the project and the timing and strength of the supports help to form a typology of these creative local development models, as shown in Table 1.2.

The first column of Table 1.2 lists a few characteristics of the local projects as designed by the small group leading the initiative under view. Four elements are retained: LP1, the entrepreneurial dynamism of the innovators; LP2, the cohesion and trust of the community concerned; LP3, the challenges motivating the initiative; and LP4, the digital dimension of the project, taking into account the specific capacity to broaden the scope and the reach of the initial project that this digitalization allows, as stressed in Dahlman *et al.* (2016). The second column in Table 1.2 lists the potential supports that a project, initiated in an "isolated" community, can get at different phases of its development. The third column finally details in a couple of words the drivers and likely timing of such supports. Local authorities

Table 1.2 Nature and supports of local creative development models

Characteristics of local projects (LP)	*Potential external supports*	*Main drivers of supports*
LP1 Entrepreneurial spirit of the innovators	Local authorities	LP1 Supports social innovators to reduce the pressure on public expenditures
LP2 Cohesion, trust and cultural heritage of the community		LP3 Risks coverage
		LP2 Cultural heritage matters
LP3 Challenges to be met: whether security risks or safety risks	Diaspora	LP4 User-friendly
		LP3 Priority given to deep security crises, more diffuse support for safety risks
LP4 Digital dimension of the project	International institutions	LP1 Entrepreneurial spirit for marketable projects
	International firms	LP4 User-friendly
		LP3 Solidarity with safety and security risks
	Civil society organizations	LP2 Cohesion and trust matter

acting at an early phase of the project are attentive to the entrepreneurial spirit (LP1) of the group of innovators and to the reckoned social usefulness of the project (LP3). Diasporas can support the project at a more mature phase, when its links with the core of a local lively culture become clear in LP2. The digitalization dimension also matters as it facilitates the links with the diasporas and the diversity of the forms of action and contacts. International institutions can intervene if the project appears congruent with their own action plans regarding various security or safety risks in LP3. Their support occurs most often for communities in developing countries and the projects have to reach a certain stage of development to be easily identifiable, beyond the specificities of local cultures. The supports of international firms most often intervene also at some mature stage of the project and the main identifiers are then the entrepreneurial spirit of the leaders (LP1) and the operability of projects making use of digital facilities (LP4). Finally, the support of other CSOs will either follow the same signals as international institutions for projects in developing countries but may also occur in developing countries, where the density of CSOs is important, at an early phase and following criteria similar to those retained by diasporas, e.g. cultural feelings of LP2, to which one could add proximity of objectives.

Beyond the analytical advantages of the grid deployed in Table 1.2, which displays the diversity of local development models, many questions remain on the trajectories of these projects. Creative industries produce dynamics of their own, leading to more or less successful outcomes. Balance sheets have to take into account externalities fuelling or inhibiting, for instance, the development of sharing or collaborative practices in education, health, housing or leisure. In other words the market and non-market dimensions of the effects of these local models have to be jointly considered. Many studies are calling for inventories of all the local new deals that such local creative development patterns present (see, for instance, most EC and UNCTAD reports in the references). It is clearly vital to elaborate the policy guides that are needed to plan the support mechanisms. At a time when the need for more social justice and greater community resilience to face rising security and safety risks is rapidly increasing, proactive policies are most welcome, providing they pay special attention to the impact on the well-being of the communities and are not too restrictively impressed by the hazardous results in terms of market incomes. In effect, it is most likely that the diffusion of such local models may have decreasing returns in terms of market outcomes but increasing returns in terms of well-being improvements. The inventories of local creative models of development, that are rightly called for, have to take into account this dual effect.

Notes

1 Part of these evolutions in local cultures includes local behaviours regarding old buildings and landscapes that could be considered as cultural heritages, thus more or less valorized. In that sense cultural heritages are potential assets that can be valued in different ways by the local communities under view.

2 Collective Awareness Platforms for Sustainability and Social Innovation (CAPS) are ICT systems leveraging the emerging "network effect" by combining open online social media, distributed knowledge creation and data from real environments ("Internet of Things") in order to create awareness of problems and possible solutions requesting collective efforts, enabling new forms of social innovation. See http://caps2020.eu/about-caps/.
3 The IPCC is the international body for assessing the science related to climate change. The IPCC was set up in 1988 by the World Meteorological Organization (WMO) and UNEP to provide policymakers with regular assessments of the scientific basis of climate change, its impacts and future risks, and options for adaptation and mitigation. The Fifth Assessment Report (AR5) was released in four parts between September 2013 and November 2014.
4 See (in French) to what extent this small mining town has used the climate change concern in its revival policy: http://www.loos-en-gohelle.fr/wp-content/uploads/2014/11/2014-10_re%CC%81cit-v5.pdf.
5 See Kusagoand and Miyamoto (2014).
6 A lesson that can be illustrated, for example, by two of the examples we mentioned, Minamata in Japan and Loos en Gohelle in France.

References

Bakhshi, H., Hargreaves, I., and Mateos-Garcia, J. (2013) *A manifesto for the creative economy*, Nesta, London.

CGDD. (2015) *Société résiliente, transition écologique et cohésion sociale: études de quelques initiatives de transition en France, premiers enseignements*, Collection Etudes et Documents N°124, Commissariat Général au développement durable, Paris.

Dahlman, C., Mealy, S., Tang, J., and Wermelinger, M. (2016) *Harnessing the digital economy for inclusive development*, OECD, Development Centre, Paris.

Dubina, I. N., Carayann, E. G., and Campbell, D. E. J. (2012) "Creativity economy and a crisis of the economy? Coevolution of knowledge, innovation, and creativity, and of the knowledge economy and knowledge society", *Journal of Knowledge Economy*, 3, 1–24.

European Commission. (2012) *Promoting cultural and creative sectors for growth and jobs in the EU,* European Commission, Brussels.

Evans, G. (2009) "Creative cities, creative spaces and urban policy", *Urban Studies*, 46(5&6), 1003–1040.

Flew, T., and Cunningham, S. (2010) "Creative industries after the first decade of debate", *The Information Society: An International Journal*, 26(2), 113–123.

Garnham, N. (2005) "From cultural to creative industries", *International Journal of Cultural Policy*, 11(1), 15–29.

Hobsbawm, E., and Ranger, T. (1983) *The invention of tradition*, Cambridge University Press, Cambridge.

Kusago, T., and Miyamoto, T. (2014) "The potential for community based action research for area studies: a process evaluation method for the improvement of community life", *Psychologia*, 57, 275–294.

McGuigan, J. (2005) "Neo-liberalism, culture and policy", *International Journal of Cultural Policy*, 11(3), 229–241.

Sen, A. (2010) *The idea of justice*, Harvard University Press, Cambridge, MA.

Tremblay, G. (2011) "Creative statistics to support creative economy politics", *Media, Culture & Society*, 33(2), 289–298.

UNCTAD. (2008) *Creative economy report 2008: the challenge of assessing the creative economy: towards informed policy-making,* UNCTAD, Geneva.

UNCTAD. (2010) *Creative economy report 2010: creative economy: a feasible development option,* UNCTAD, Geneva.

UNDP and UNESCO. (2013) *Creative economy report 2013 special edition: widening local development pathways.*

UNESCO. (2005) *International flows of selected cultural goods and services, 1994–2003,* UNESCO, Paris.

UK Technology Strategy Board. (2009) *Annual report B and accounts 2008–2009,* The Stationery Office, London.

2 Creative industries between "living labs" and "robinsonade"

Philippe Bouquillion and Pierre Mœglin

Introduction

The notion of creative industries emerged in the United Kingdom during the 1990s within the Think Tanks of the Labour Party. The official definition of the creative industries given in 2001 by the British authorities identifies three main and common characteristics: "those industries which have their origin in individual creativity, skill and talent and which have a potential for wealth and job creation through the generation and exploitation of intellectual property" (Department for Culture, Media and Sport, United Kingdom, 2001).

Thus the notion of creative industries includes in the same category activities in which creation plays a central role. Thirteen domains are concerned: (1) advertising; (2) architecture; (3) art and antiques; (4) small-business sector; (5) design; (6) mode; (7) cinema and video; (8) interactive leisure software; (9) music; (10) performing arts; (11) publishing; (12) IT services and software; and (13) television and radio. For its part, in 2004, UNCTAD defined the creative industries as: "Activities producing symbolic products with a heavy reliance on intellectual property for a market as wide as possible" (p. 4).

Before long, this notion became very important in academic work, in urban planning and also in public policy toward culture as well as economic development. Then, after Tony Blair came to power, this notion of creative industries tended to replace the notion of cultural industries in public speeches and policies. The notion of creative industries came from the world of consultancy, especially the work of urban planners, including Charles Landry (Landry and Bianchini, 1995; Landry, 2000), and from the political sphere. This particular origin explains why the notion spread so quickly and strongly. In contrast, the concept of cultural industries originated in the academic sphere from the 1940s and public authorities referred to this concept much later. For example, in France, the notion of cultural industries became a category of public policy only at the beginning of the 1980s. During the 2000s, the notion of creative industries spread on a very large scale (in Europe, South America, Asia and Pacific), supported and developed by national authorities (which commissioned official reports written by consultants or academics) and by supranational institutions, including the European Union, United Nations Conference on Trade and Development (UNCTAD) and United Nations

Educational, Scientific and Cultural Organization (UNESCO). In addition to the concept of creative industries the notion of creative economy appeared (Howkins, 2001; Throsby, 2001). This term refers to the increasing importance of creation and creativity in the overall economy, beyond the creative industries. In April 2008, UNCTAD published a paper attempting to measure the degree of development of the creative economy worldwide. A second report was published in 2010, and a third report in 2013.

A central question is: what development can creative industries offer to remote places and are the local populations and cultures at the centre of the development process or on the periphery?

The objective of this contribution is to present hypotheses rather than results of completed research. However, these hypotheses are backed by researches we have already done or supervised, for example in India, especially in remote places in Gujarat, and in Mauritius.

We will confront the promises of the promoters of the creative industries (Chapter 1) with the pitfalls already identified by our initial investigations or by critical researchers, especially in remote areas. Three issues will be raised and presented in three successive chapters. They refer to employment in the creative industries, the process of valuation and rationalization of production, and the general political and economic issues that weigh on the players of the creative economy active in remote areas.

The promises

Proponents of the notion of creative industries highlight the industrial and financial performances of creative industries in terms of contribution to gross domestic product (GDP), growth and job creation. In Britain, this sector has grown faster than others and has gained a significant position in the economy. Therefore, according to the author of an official report on creative industries (Smith, 2008), "Creative industries must move from the margins to the heart of British economic policy". Likewise, an official Australian report on creative industries, in 2008–2009 concluded that creative industries have made a larger contribution to GDP than a number of traditional industries, such as agriculture, forestry and fishing; electricity, gas, water and waste services; accommodation and food services (Ministry for the Arts, 2011). In Germany, "The share of culture and creative industries enterprises in the overall economy amounts to almost 7.4% of all enterprises, 2.5% of turnovers, 2.8% of employees and 3.3% of overall employment (including self-employment)" (Federal Ministry, p. 41).

There are three main reasons why creative industries create more jobs than other industries for the same contribution to value added. First, microenterprises are predominant in this sector. The second reason is linked to the particular characteristics of labour in these industries and more precisely to the importance of self-employment. For example, in Germany, "16% of all persons employed in the core area of the culture and creative industries (a total of 219,376 persons) are self-employed" (Federal Ministry, p. 50). Besides, "if the number of marginally employed persons (at least 12% or 162,000 persons, according to Micro Census data) is added to this number, the share of self-employed persons increases to almost 28% of all persons employed in the culture and creative industries" (Federal Ministry, p. 50) In comparison, "the total share of self-employed persons in the overall economy amounts to approximately 11%" (Federal Ministry, p. 51) Thirdly, creative industries are low-capital-intensity industries. This is why, according to the proponents of the notion, they can be developed without significant initial financial investment and, thus, they offer an opportunity for remote and underdeveloped areas.

The theme of creative industries took on great importance in emerging and developing countries, including remote places, and especially in developing assistance programmes managed by supranational institutions from the mid-2000s. Creative industries are presented as a panacea for those countries and areas. For example, the authors of the two official reports published by UNCTAD describe a world in which social difficulties could be removed or at least greatly reduced because of creativity and creative activities. A holistic and optimistic vision of development is then promoted.

> Another important social aspect of the creative industries relates to their role in fostering social inclusion. . . . the creative economy includes cultural activities that can be important in linking social groups in communities and contributing to social cohesion. Communities that are plagued by social tensions and conflicts of various sorts can often be brought together through shared participation in cultural rituals. Initiatives such as community arts programmes build social capital by boosting the ability and motivation of people to become engaged in community life and inculcating skills that can be usefully employed in local creative industries. Furthermore, creative activity can be shown to be important for individual health and psychological well-being.
>
> (UNCTAD, 2010, p. 54)

This development, moreover, would be environmentally friendly and sustainable. Creative industries are considered to be integrated in a special territory and as difficult to relocate. Local resources are valuable on national and international markets:

> The transformation of traditional knowledge into creative goods and services reflects the cultural values of a country and its people. At the same time, these products also have economic potential; they may be in demand by local consumers or they may enter international marketing channels to satisfy demand from consumers in other countries. The essential feature of the creative industries, which link the traditional knowledge at one end of the value chain with the ultimate consumer at the other end, is their capacity to serve both cultural and economic objectives in the development process.
>
> (UNCTAD, 2010, p. 38)

Individuals are directly involved; the basic entity of creative industries is not large companies but small ones and even individuals. According to the discourses, creative industries help to foster social and economic inclusion and local territories are the pertinent scale:

> A more holistic approach to development is needed. It is time to take a step back from the global and look more deeply at the local, identifying specificities and identities of countries and recognizing their cultural and economical differences in order to capture their real needs and surrounding environment. It seems crucial to explore the linkages between creative capacities, trade, investment and technology, and see how this can translate into a vibrant creative economy able to contribute to economic prosperity and poverty reduction.
>
> (UNCTAD, 2010, p. XX)

In the same time, creative industries help to open the local territories to global market. According to UNCTAD, creative industries have already increased the role of developing countries in global trade. In north–south as well as south–south trade, creative goods have growing importance:

> South–South regional trade and investments have been vital to mitigating the effects of the global recession. While the traditional manufacturing industries were seriously hit, the more knowledge-based creative sectors were more resilient to external shocks. In 2008, despite the 12 per cent decline in global trade, world trade of creative goods and services continued its expansion, reaching $592 billion and reflecting an annual growth rate of 14 per cent during the period 2002–2008. This reconfirms that the creative industries have been one of the most dynamic sectors of the world economy throughout this decade.
>
> (UNCTAD, 2010, p. XX)

In order to increase the role of creative products from the south in global trade, two issues are raised. First, development plans of creative industries may be an opportunity to influence public policies in order to liberalize trade and financial flows in emerging countries. For instance, according to UNCTAD (2010), "Developing countries are therefore encouraged to include creative goods in their lists of products as they conduct their negotiations under the Global System of Trade Preferences" (p. XX.) Second, the issue of intellectual property rights (IPR) is also at the top of the agenda. Developing countries need to respect IPR but at the same time, according to these discourses, a balance has to be found between the interests of rights holders and the interests of valorization:

> A major challenge for shaping policies for the creative economy is related to intellectual property rights . . . The evolution of multimedia created an open market for the distribution and sharing of digitized creative content.

. . . The time has come for governments to review the limitations of current IPR regimes and adapt them to new realities by ensuring a competitive environment.

(UNCTAD, 2010, p. XXIV)

Gaëtan Tremblay notes the international extension of the theme of the creative industries:

> beyond the good feelings, this initiative also has for objective to extend and to strengthen the intellectual property laws. A strategy of inclusion to enforce rules of the game, including by the countries which reproduce more than they create.
>
> (Tremblay, 2008, p. 80)

Thus, according to this conception, thanks to the creative industries, the future looks bright for developing countries, including remote areas. But this future is under the auspices of market globalization. The critical conceptions of the north–south relationship are now banned by such representations. Discourses on economic or cultural imperialism seem to be no longer appropriate.

However, our surveys in remote areas lead us to criticize the perspectives put forward by the proponents of creative industries.

The types of production: a growth driven by culture and creative industries?

Much of the production exemplified in the official reports as well as the cases we have studied are based on heritage or intangible heritage, including handicrafts. In the cases we have studied in remote places, these products aim at either the tourist visiting the area or more distant consumers located in urban centres of the country of production or abroad. In some cases, production may target both types of market. In the first case the products are sold directly to tourists or sometimes they are also part of a distinction strategy of the touristic supply on the scale of a whole territory or for an organization. For example, in Mauritius, hotel companies have supported programmes for craft developments (sometimes by creating a "tradition" that did not exist). Handicraft products are usually sold in specialized shops in these hotels. Likewise, hotel companies have often rehabilitated historical places and produced musical shows in hotels (Peghini, 2016).

In all cases, the products of these isolated territories are put in relation to external consumers. Likewise, it is true that these activities rely more on labour input than capital input. However, a question arises: to what extent can these products generate employment and growth in these territories?

It is difficult to give reliable and quantitative answers to this question. Access to information is extremely difficult. Official statistics are often not available or they do not evaluate what share of the added value remains in the territories of production nor how many people are employed and for what hourly volume.

Similarly, organizations that oversee production generally try to prevent researchers observing the conditions of production of goods. It is therefore difficult to know what are the precise conditions in which the workforce is employed, and in particular the time spent producing goods, the ratio of labour input to capital input and the conditions of workers' compensation. Similarly, for example, in India or Madagascar, we found objects for tourists which were claimed to be produced by local artisans but which were actually industrially produced in China.

Nevertheless, our investigations have brought some answers. In rural areas, the workforce is employed part time. In rural areas of Gujarat, for example, artisans and peasants divide their time between working the land and handicrafts. The more the work of artisans is framed by a well-organized organization, a non-governmental organization (NGO), for example, the more time spent at work is important. In urban areas, for example in the slums of Mumbai in which we investigated, the workforce is employed with extreme flexibility.

In almost all cases we observed workers are poorly paid. The remuneration of artisans is comparable to the remuneration of other low-skilled workers. When production is supervised by an NGO, it is possible that health services for workers and education for their children are added to the main salary. This situation is due to several reasons. First, generally, artisans are in an extremely dominated social position. This domination is linked to poverty, illiteracy, to their origin (for example, the caste system in India), religion or gender (women are often paid less than men). It is also increased by the fact that these workers live in an isolated territory. Usually, local people do not have the skills and, even less, the relation networks that could allow them to produce creative products by themselves and to disseminate and promote these products outside their territory.

Second, low wages of workers, including skilled and specialized craftsmen, are linked to the fact that the value of handicraft products is not based on their specificities or on the "personality" of workers. In almost all cases we observed, even the name of the craftsman was unknown. Thus, handicrafts strongly differ from artistic products for which the fame of known artists is central to building value. In the case of handicrafts other strategies are at work to build the value of the products. These strategies are conduct by the organizations which are supervising the production. We will look more precisely at these strategies below. But already we can highlight that the value of the creative product is mostly based on the designers' work (these designers are working within organizations overseeing production). Also, the value of creative products relies on the reputation of the production area. Thus, the "star" is not the craftsman but the territory. Artisans are interchangeable. Therefore, they have no chance of creating a favourable balance of power when it comes to determining their remuneration. Remuneration is then linked to the goodwill of organizations employing craftsmen.

In India, we have seen cases where such fees were higher than usual. In fact, increasing the income of artisans helps to increase the value of products. For example, organizations that present themselves as NGOs wanted to distinguish their products from those of their competitors by emphasizing that their artisans were well paid and thus the products had a charitable dimension and were part of a sustainable development process.

Note that this inability of workers to influence their remuneration is not unique to the craft. For example, in Mauritius, musical performances in hotels provide only low wages to musicians (Peghini, 2016). The music that is played in hotels is assumed to be typically Mauritian and the result of interbreeding of the various ethnic cultures in Mauritius. Therefore, the economic value of this music is not primarily related to the quality of interpretation but to its background. Interpreters are interchangeable. The value of music comes from its territorial origin.

In sum, the potential impact of creative industries on the development of isolated areas is even lower when the organizations governing these productions are able to capture most of the value added. If they are able to do so, it is because they have a grip on the various stages of the product lifecycle, from creation to sale.

The process of rationalization and valuation of production

In the cases we observed, the process of rationalization and commodification of production gave the organizations managing production the ability to produce and extract to their profit the value added. The process of rationalization and commodification takes place mostly through design and digital infrastructure and networks.

Creative activities involved the availability of networks and digital infrastructure. However, the existence of digital networks, including broadband networks, does not automatically create development based on creative industries. These digital networks link the intermediaries, buyers and those responsible with artisans, vendors and various services (including investors). They also link the diffusion or distribution structures and outlets and fans or experts who authenticate and carry on the discourse of authenticity. Digital networks thus materialize (and confirm) the central position of intermediaries. Their reliability determines the quality of coordination between actors; the reactivity of the industry and the extent of product distribution. The problem is that, often, the implementation of these systems is hindered by the weakness of the existing infrastructure.

It is therefore interesting to examine the strategies of these intermediaries to access reliable networks and the policies towards digital infrastructure. For example, the intermediaries can gather on free zones separated from the rest of the country where high-quality infrastructure are implemented and used by the creative industry players as well as, among others, players in the tourism economy or the financial system.

The rationalization of crafts usually occurs nowadays through design. Surveys were conducted in Delhi, Mumbai, Jaipur and especially Gujarat, particularly in Ahmedabad and Bhuj area on activities of non-automated weaving (handloom), which were supervised by NGOs. Since the 1990s, these organizations have introduced deep transformations in craft, in particular by taking into account the design. Design is understood here both as a set of practices to design products and as a way of constructing their symbolic value.

In the cases we have studied, designers and socio-economic players which have integrated design are not only intermediaries that would link one existing supply and demand. But through design these players can structure the main stages of the industrial process, from creation, upstream, to dissemination and construction of value, downstream. They are at the heart of the commodification of handicrafts. However, NGOs claim that their actions articulate economic efficiency and social progress. We will not examine all aspects of the work of NGOs. We only emphasize how their intervention contradicts the discourse of empowerment.

First, the artisan should definitely not be "creative". Upstream, NGOs order products to craftsmen: artisans do not take the initiative. The designers of these organizations are involved very early in the economic process. They determine the product's main characteristics (form, content, material used) and also the main characteristics of the process of production and reproduction, including fragmentation and by-product, manufacturing techniques of each component, the division of labour and remuneration of artisans. Of course, NGOs claim that their actions help to train artisans in new skills and techniques, in particular to lower costs, producing in series (no prototype) at a constant level of quality, and controlled quantities in a limited time. Anyway, NGOs control the whole process. They take advantage of this situation, for example, by transferring to artisans the achievement tasks and financial risks. NGOs can also provide financial aid, including loans and advances or even raw materials. Artisans can be paid by the piece, time or in a fixed way. Their pay is often linked to the cost of the various components (if these components are purchased by artisans) and standard manufacturing time. Production can be carried out in small factories belonging to NGOs but generally it takes place in villages.

Second, in order to allow commodification of products, the designers reinvent a tradition disconnected from its local base. The involvement of NGOs enables dissemination of handicrafts outside communities. Patterns and colours are less specific to communities or individuals and designated status. These products are suitable for consumers from the Indian middle class or foreign consumers. In the cases we have studied, foreigners were previously dominant but Indian consumers are now more numerous and more strategic. NGO action can also periodically renew the offer, unlike many traditional productions from the circuit of the emporium or middlemen.

However, the symbolic value of crafts is partly due to the fact that products are supposed to be made in isolated communities. For this purpose, communities are often described (incorrectly) as living in total isolation. But actually most of the specificities of the products linked to the community in which they are produced are hidden because these specificities are the markers, sometimes stigmatizing, of a very specific social group. Local anchoring must strengthen the capacity of products to sell well in domestic and international markets and not hinder. Moreover, in the Indian case, the very fact that products aimed at a global or national and not just local market helps to increase their value to Indian consumers. Integration into the market system, whether Indian or international (versus self-consumption by local producers) proves that these products are of high quality.

The reinvention of tradition must lead consumers to believe that the goods are characteristic of a particular territory, but at the same time designers have to show that these products carry symbolic value not only locally but also nationally and globally. The art of the designers is therefore to reconcile these two conflicting requirements. To do this, they present these products as an expression of Indian culture. In fact, the notion of Indian culture is very blurred. Indeed, the differences between regions, historical periods and types of populations are strong. Thus generally, designers highlight, especially in product promotion campaigns, the fact that these products reflect an India that is modern and open to the world but which draws its strength from its history and cultural traditions. Craft is therefore described as an essential component of this history and culture. The task of NGOs and especially their designers is, from these local and different traditions, to build and defend Indianness. In this perspective, these products are compared to or assimilated with artistic products. NGO leaders are referring here to culture in the anthropological sense. Thus, the emphasis is not placed on the personality of the creators (artisans or designers) but on the fact that these products reflect "traditional" Indian culture. Because of design, tradition, now adapted to modernity, would be defended and preserved and these products help to protect and promote Indian tradition. In other words, local products are mainly a component of a broader set, the national culture.

Thirdly, the symbolic value of handicrafts also relies on the fact that the whole production process is supposed to comply with the requirements of sustainable development and especially the conditions of employment and remuneration of labour are claimed to be good. Designers or those who wish to promote their work, including NGO leaders, build an important discourse about the relationship between designers and artisans. They also emphasize the figure of designers as defenders of crafts and artisans. However, as said before, our observations show that wages remain very low. But the low wages and the representation of artisans as socially dominated are important for the construction of the value of crafts. The members of the Indian middle class or high class are socially distinguished by purchasing crafts: they provide assistance to artisans. The former appear as socially dominant and the latter as dominated. Thus, the construction of the symbolic value occurs by highlighting the phenomenon of social domination.

In sum, in the cases we studied, the process of rationalization and production of commodification totally escape the local people and organizations. They require high skills and significant resources. In addition, the specific cultural forms of remote areas do not really matter. What matters is their ability to integrate into the construction of a national culture.

The different players and their interest in creative industries: between charity and economic, political or religious issues

The isolation of these areas can facilitate the mobilization of the different players involved and of the local population. Actually implementation of development plans can be facilitated. However to better understand the real interests of the different players it is necessary to look at them more closely. In the cases we have studied, the players involved in the development of creative industries usually claim to be NGOs. But these NGOs are backed by very different social actors: national or international public organizations; players specialized in the charity business, including domestic and foreign actors articulating a charitable and commercial dimension (for example, Fabindia is in connexion with 80,000 producers); religious groups or industrial players in the field of cultural and creative industries or in any other economic sector. Of course, NGO activities are supposed to articulate economic efficiency and social progress. However their involvement in these activities can also be explained by other economic, political or religious considerations.

First, let us focus on the economic issues when NGOs are linked to industrial interests. In different cases we have studied, we found that the geographical areas of intervention of NGOs correspond to areas of intervention of the economic players linked to NGOs. For example, the association Shrujan was created after the earthquake that occurred in Gujarat in 1969, at the initiative of the Shroff family. The Shroff family is a family of industrialists now based in Gujarat and Mumbai and very active in Budj, an isolate part of Gujarat close to the Pakistan border. This family owns a factory producing and selling fertilizers to farmers in this region. These fertilizers have generated significant soil pollution; some soils are now wastelands. Crafts produced in the Shrujan association provide work to the farmers who can no longer cultivate their land. In this example, it appears that the appearance of the NGO charity covers a desire to preserve the social and economic domination of the company in an isolated area.

Second, NGOs can be built on religious or community bases.This is, for example, the case of Qasab, a Muslim NGO in Bhuj whose stated core objective is the empowerment of women in Muslim communities (1,200 women in 52 villages in a survey in January 2012). Note that very sharp community tensions between Muslims and Hindus have occurred in recent years in this border region of Pakistan. Some NGOs are of foreign origin. For instance, Kala Raksha is the association founded in 1993 in Kutch (Bhuj region) by an American, Judy Frater: 1,000 women from six communities work with Kala Raksha. But in our study area, these foreign NGOs are relatively few. When NGOs are built on religious or community bases this can raise important policy issues. For instance, the objective can be to preserve the Indian government's influence on partly nomadic populations, or to preserve the religious or caste organization of society in these areas. It can help reduce religious tensions in areas close to the Pakistan border or, on the contrary, it can reinforce these religious and community-based conflicts.

In sum, in the observed cases, organizations that govern these activities can be integrated into economic and geopolitical issues that go far beyond the objective of development of isolated territories in which they are located.

Conclusion

We had initially asked a question: what development can creative industries offer to remote places and are the local populations and cultures at the centre of the development process or on the periphery?

In conclusion, it is clear that the answer is generally negative, at least on the limited scale of the cases that we have observed. In isolated territories, these so-called creative activities offer local workers mostly relatively low-paid and low-skilled jobs. Local cultures are essentially an element of commercial distinction of the products made locally. And on national and international markets, local cultural traits partly disappear in favour of aesthetic characteristics considered as more universal or reflecting Indianness. Organizations that manage these activities rarely originate in the isolated territories. These organizations are engaged in economic and political issues that go far beyond the single issue of the development of isolated areas. Organizations, more than the local creative workers, are the real instances of creation and innovation, from the point of view of the shape of goods as economic processes. Networks and digital infrastructure that play an important role in these processes hardly allow local actors to take control of their destiny by reversing the trends we have just presented.

More fundamentally, the activities we studied seem very compartmentalized. Usually, the various projects are not linked, even the ones belonging to the same sectors, craft for instance. Likewise, the links between different sectors are even rarer. Thus, in a given territory, these activities, without synergies, can hardly generate significant growth. For example, in Mauritius, musical performances in hotels provide only low wages to musicians and have generated almost no development of the musical industry outside the hotels. This relates to a more general conclusion: policy towards creative industries is often based on artificial aggregation of disparate industries. Synergies and training effects across disparate sectors (crafts, music industry, information and communication technology, tourism) are often weak.

References

Department for Culture, Media and Sport, United Kingdom. (2001): "Creative Industries Mapping Document 2001", http://webarchive.nationalarchives.gov.uk/+/http://www.culture.gov.uk/global/publications/archive_2001/ci_mapping_doc_2001.htm (accessed September 17, 2016).

Federal Ministry of Economics and Technology and Federal Government Commissioner for Culture and the Media. (2009): "Culture and Creative Industries in Germany", Research Report, http://www.kulturwirtschaft.de/wp-content/uploads/2009/03/german_cci_en_summary_0903231.pdf (accessed September 17, 2016).

Howkins, J. (2001): *The Creative Economy: How People Make Money from Ideas*, London, Penguin.

Landry, C. (2000): *Creative City: A Toolkit for Urban Innovators*, London, Earthscan.

Landry, C., Bianchini, F. (1995): *The Creative City*, London, Demos.

Ministry for the Arts. (2011): *Creative Industries, A Strategy for 21st Century Australia.* Retrieved from http://arts.gov.au/sites/default/files/creative-industries/sdip/strategic-digital-industry-plan.pdf.

Peghini, J. (2016): *À la recherche de l'Île Maurice, entre île réelle et île rêvée*, Paris, Presses Universitaires de Vincennes, to be published.

Smith, C. (2008): "New Talents for the New Economy", Department for Culture, Media and Sport, page 4, http://webarchive.nationalarchives.gov.uk/+/http:/www.culture.gov.uk/images/publications/CEPFeb2008.pdf (accessed September 30, 2016).

Throsby, D. (2001): *Economics and Culture*, Cambridge, Cambridge University Press.
Tremblay, G. (2008): "Industries culturelles, économie créative et société de l'information", *Global Media Journal, Canadian Edition*, 1(1), 65–88.
United Nations. (2013): "Economy Report 2013: Widening Local Development Pathways", http://www.unesco.org/culture/pdf/creative-economy-report-2013.pdf (accessed September 30, 2016).
United Nations Conference on Trade and Development. (2004): "Creative Industries and Development", 4 June, http://unctad.org/en/Docs/tdxibpd13_en.pdf
United Nations Conference on Trade and Development. (2008): "Creative Economy Report 2008", http://unctad.org/fr/docs/ditc20082ceroverview_fr.pdf (accessed September 30, 2016).
United Nations Conference on Trade and Development. (2010): "Creative Economy Report 2010: A Feasible Development Option", http://archive.unctad.org/Templates/WebFlyer.asp?intItemID=5763&lang=1 (accessed September 30, 2016).

3 Population thinking vs. essentialism in biology and evolutionary economics

George Liagouras

Introduction

The approach in terms of population thinking is the cornerstone of Darwinian biology. As a matter of fact, modern evolutionary economics is based *from the outset* on population thinking. This has been done in an implicit way, as in the case of Nelson and Winter (1982), who focus on the diversity of firms without referring explicitly to population thinking. But this has also been done in an explicit way by the scholarship, openly claiming the revolutionary implications of population thinking for life and social sciences (e.g., Metcalfe, 1989; Hodgson, 1993). Could population thinking be the Mecca of evolutionary economist and social scientists? I will argue throughout this chapter that things are far more complicated. Even in biology and in its philosophy the notion of population thinking has led to important tensions that have been underplayed by evolutionary economists.

The canonical view of population thinking derives from a narrative that was dominant during the latter period of neo-Darwinian synthesis. Roughly speaking, this was the synthesis between Darwinian natural selection and Mendelian genetics that dominated biology throughout a considerable part of the 20th century. More specifically, in 1959 Ernest Mayr, a major proponent of neo-Darwinian synthesis, claimed that "Darwin introduced a new way of thinking into the scientific literature, 'population thinking'" (Mayr, 1959/1976, p. 27). According to Mayr, the former scientific way was the typological thinking that had its roots in Plato's idealistic philosophy, where reality was the blurry reflection of perfect ideas or forms (types). Echoing Plato, modern "typologists" focused their attention on ideal types or statistical means and considered variation an accidental phenomenon. On the contrary, "populationists" privileged the diversity of individuals, "or any kind of organic entities," within populations. In a nutshell: "For the typologist, the type (eidos) is real and the variation an illusion, while for the populationist the type (average) is an abstraction and only variation is real" (Mayr, 1959/1976, p. 28).[1]

Then in 1965 David Hull, who later became one of the most influential philosophers of biology, advanced a similar argument against Aristotelian essences. His intervention criticizing the static definitions of the species category was influenced by Karl Popper's attack on "methodological essentialism." In order to define essentialism, Hull (1965) cited the following fragment from Popper's *The Open Society and its Enemies*:

> I use the name methodological essentialism to characterize the view held by Plato and many of his followers, that it is the task of pure knowledge or "science" to discover and to describe the true nature of things; i.e. their hidden reality or essence. It was Plato's peculiar belief that the essence of sensible things can be found in other more real things – in the primogenitors or Forms. Many of the later methodological essentialists, for instance Aristotle, did not altogether follow him in determining this; but they all agreed with him in determining the task of pure knowledge as the discovery of the hidden nature or Form or essence of things.
>
> (Popper, 1950, p. 34)

The excessive approaching between Plato and Aristotle made by Popper proved very helpful for a synthesis between Mayr's and Hull's arguments. Some years later, Mayr (1969) used "essentialism" and "typological thinking" synonymously. From a philosophical point of view this does not make sense. Essentialists are typologists, but the opposite is not necessarily true. Humean empiricists and Lockean nominalists are both typologists, but they are not essentialists. Nevertheless, the opposition between population thinking and essentialism (typological thinking) was repeated in Mayr's later publications and it became famous not only in biology but also in other disciplines like economics and anthropology.

Over the last years a revisionist history of biology has evolved that refutes the claim that taxonomists before Darwin were mired in Aristotle's or Plato's essentialism (Winsor, 2006).[2] It seems, however, that most of the above revisionist accounts do not dispute the pivotal role of population thinking in biology. What they do call into question is the narrative which presumes it was Darwin who put an end to "two thousand years of stasis" (Hull, 1965) in Western science and philosophy. From a *conceptual* or *methodological* point of view what is more important is the advent of a new literature that re-evaluates the opposition between population thinking and essentialism. In plain words, population thinking is no longer considered the quintessence of the biological approach, and essentialism in biology becomes a subject of serious debate.

Consequently, the first objective of the present chapter is to review the existent, disparate literature on the topic and as such inform the evolutionary economist as to the complications inherent in population thinking which have been inferred by the recent debates in biology and the philosophy of biology. Then the second objective is to show that the anomalies accumulated by population thinking within biology are very helpful to understand the limits to population thinking in the economic and social realm. The chapter is divided into five sections. The following (second) section discusses the tensions raised in the initial and strong version of population thinking implying a full-blooded anti-essentialism. The third section examines a more reasonable version of population thinking that tries to find also a place for essentialism under the notion of "proximate causes." The fourth section is dedicated to the limits to population thinking in economics. After recognizing its successful application in the sub-disciplines of industrial dynamics and economic anthropology the case for an (essentialist) "evolutionary political economy" is briefly made. Finally, the last section provides concluding remarks.

Population thinking as strong anti-essentialism: are species mere mental constructions?

The strong version of population thinking popularized by Mayr (1959/1976) leads to explosive tensions regarding the ontological status of species. The initial question is rather simple: if population thinking is the opposite of essentialism, and the notions of "type" and "essence" must be banished from biology, how would species then be defined? Traditionally, the species were considered "natural kinds," but this term has been subject to very different interpretations. The most fundamental opposition has been between the Aristotelian and Lockean conceptions of species (Ayres, 1981).

In the Aristotelian metaphysics, each species possesses its own specific nature or essence that provides the *telos* (ultimate goal) of its existence. For example, what distinguishes the human species from other animals is the faculty of speech (*logos*), which includes what the Latin authors called later *ratio* (rationality). Certainly, human species can also be recognized and identified by superficial features or properties (featherless biped, etc.). Nevertheless, for Aristotle only the knowledge of the specific essence of each species can provide its scientific definition.

In the third book of his *An Essay Concerning Human Understanding*, Locke (1690/1975) distinguished between the nominal and the real essence of kinds. The real essence was the underlying microstructure that explains the very nature of kinds. Still, according to Locke the human mind cannot gain access to the hidden structure of particles forming the real essence of things. Our mind only has access to the superficial characteristics, that is, to the nominal essence of kinds. Such an empiricist view of the world leads directly to nominalism. If we are condemned to ignore real essences, then our classification schemes would necessarily be conventional or even arbitrary. Species therefore do not correspond to collections of entities with a reality beyond us, but are fabrications of the mind.

Mayr's endless troubles with the "basic unit of biology"

We can now better localize the challenge facing the theorist of population thinking. Obviously, species are not eternal natural kinds. On this point, Darwinian evolutionism has undeniably been validated by modern science. But does the ubiquity of variation implied by population thinking mean that the "basic unit of evolutionary biology" (Mayr, 1982, p. 296) is simply a matter of subjective classification? This seems counter-intuitive to our proper experience. We have been able to distinguish dogs from cats in different places and times since we were children. And, even if we argue that this folk biology is no more than a false impression, how is it then possible for primitive people to have roughly the same species classification as "Western university-trained scientists" (Gould, 1980, p. 207)?

Mayr (1982, pp. 267–269) acknowledged that Darwin's *Origins* took a nominalist stance. And since the beginning of the 20th century an important nominalist camp has existed within Darwinian scholarship. But Mayr never adhered to it. He always maintained that, whatever the difficulties in defining species may be, the latter correspond to real discontinuities in nature, not simple constructions of the human mind. Ironically enough, his strong opposition to nominalist ideas sometimes compelled him to make curious essentialist declarations like the following: "In spite of the variability caused by the genetic uniqueness of every individual, there is a species-specific unity to the genetic program (DNA) of nearly every species" (Mayr, 1982, p. 297). Such a hesitation between nominalism and essentialism hints to a very open-minded scientist, but it can hardly be considered proof of coherence.

The "Species as Individuals" thesis: anti-essentialism pushed to the absurd

The thesis of "Species as Individuals" (hereafter S-a-I) developed by Ghiselin (1974) and Hull (1976, 1978) attempted to extract the anti-essentialist camp from its impasse though semantic innovation. It claims that the debate between essentialism and nominalism in biology is based on a false postulate. It presupposes that species are classes (or sets or natural kinds). Yet species are actually *individuals* and not *classes*. A class is defined by the common properties (nominal and/or real essences) of its members. All members in the class of the element "gold" bear the atomic number 79. With the organism as their paradigm, individuals do not have members but parts. California is a part of the USA in the same way that the heart, kidneys, and lungs are vital parts of the same organism. Even though both classes and individuals are *real*, they are totally different in the following respects:

- a The different parts of the individual do not have common properties that can define them. Because it is impossible to list the properties that are necessary and sufficient to define their names, the latter are proper names (General Motors, USA, Charles Darwin) provided by a simple act of baptism.
- b The class concept implies the existence of intrinsic properties in all places and at all times. Gold has its place on the periodic table regardless of the time and place of its formation. Individuals, on the contrary, are space- and history-bound. Just as all individuals undergo birth and death, and remain globally consistent for the duration of their lives in spite of continuous evolution, species are defined as "spatiotemporally localized lineages" or "particular chunks of the genealogical nexus."
- c Given that individuals have no intrinsic properties and are spatiotemporally restricted (points a and b, above), they are not eligible for analysis by scientific laws. Explanations about the evolution of particular species have the status of "historical narratives" concerning "unique sequences of events"

> (Hull, 1976, p. 188). Still, evolutionary theory is a scientific one because it refers to the evolution of life *in general* and not to the evolution of a particular species or the transition from one species to another.

Subtle as the whole argument is, the identification of species with individuals still presents two main shortcomings.

Firstly, the crux of the argument is based on the postulate that "(t)he relation which an organ has to an organism is the same as the relation which an organism has to its species" (Hull, 1976, p. 181). This is far from convincing. General Motors is an individual because its parts are (hierarchically) structured and cooperate to realize a particular goal. A species is not like General Motors but like the automobile industry, where autonomous and quasi-similar individual firms are struggling for survival. Similarly, the relationships sustained between heart, kidneys, and lungs within the same organism have little to do with the (direct or indirect) struggle for existence between members belonging to the same species. We have here a strange conflation of cooperation with natural selection. And as Ruse (1987, p. 235) so aptly put it: "If you take Darwinian selection seriously, you must simply reject the S-a-I thesis." Stated otherwise, from a Darwinian point of view you have to pay too high a price to consider species as individuals.

Secondly, the effort to exorcise the essences from evolutionary biology through class–individual opposition leads to curious, if not to say extreme, statements. If species are individuals then they cannot be studied by scientific laws. Hull (1978, pp. 357–358) is very clear on this point:

> Learning may be species specific, but if learning theory is to be a genuine scientific theory, it cannot be limited *necessarily* to a single species the way that Freud's and Piaget's theories are. As important as descriptions are in science, they are not theories.

Following the same logic one should include in humankind-specific narratives not only all the social sciences (Ruse, 1987, p. 237) but medicine as well! By the same token, given that the earth is an entity from the class of planets, geology should not be regarded as a genuine scientific theory. Underlying these odd assertions, we find the same controversial postulate, presuming a rigid opposition between scientific laws (classes) and historical narratives (individuals). Scientific laws address eternal natural kinds or "timeless regularities in nature," whereas historical descriptions concern "unique sequences of events."[3]

The major drawback of such a sticky opposition is that it excludes *a priori* the existence of time- and/or space-bound regularities and their intrinsic properties. However, the very fact that individuals are "historical entities persisting while changing indefinitely through time" (Hull, 1978, p. 341) implies that the persisting features are spatiotemporally bound regularities. And these regularities could be explained by the corresponding theoretical mechanisms. I will return to this shortly, in R.N. Boyd's redefinition of natural kinds.

Farewell to positivism: the consequences of the new essentialism for the philosophy of biology

Hull's rejection of essentialism in his 1965 paper had been informed by a wider positivistic consensus in the philosophy of science from that period. Real essences and their corollaries (causal powers, hidden structures, underlying mechanisms) were "unobservables," and therefore metaphysical entities that should be banned from modern science. By the 1970s this positivistic consensus had disintegrated due partly to the seminal works of Kripke (1980) and Putnam (1975).

The new essentialism advocated by Kripke (1980) and Putnam (1975) can be summarized in two points. The first point is that the major task of science is not to discover correlations at the level of observable phenomena but to find the essential properties or the hidden structures that explain the observed correlations. In other words, the progress made by modern science rejected Locke's fear that there is no access to the true essences of things. The second point of the new essentialism is that the classification of our world is not arbitrary. The possibility of knowing real essences implies that the objects inhabiting our world constitute natural kinds. Thus, reality exists independently of us. Furthermore, even if we don't know the essence of a thing, we can anticipate its existence from the observable features or the manifest properties of this thing. And this is enough to ensure that the meaning of a term remains constant over the centuries. For example, what we call "gold" today in English is no different from the χρυσός of the Ancient Greeks. And according to Putnam:

> when Archimedes asserted that something was gold (χρυσός) he was not saying that it had the superficial characteristics of gold . . .; he was saying that it had the same general hidden structure (the same "essence", so to speak) as any normal piece of gold.
>
> (Putnam, 1975, p. 235)

It should be noted however that the ascent of modern essentialist philosophy is far from just a simple revival of Aristotle's essentialism. Aristotelian science starts from the approximate knowledge of common sense (*doxa*) and proceeds speculatively, through rhetoric, dialectics, and logic, to discover the real nature of things. Modern science is experimental. Essences can be anticipated from their empirical manifestations but their existence must be assessed experimentally. Therefore, the definitions of natural kinds are *a posteriori* categories. Besides, their adoption by the scientific community does not imply that they cease to be subject to epistemic doubt. As Putnam (1975, p. 225) points out, "future investigation might reverse even the most 'certain' example."

In the continuity of the road opened by Kripke and Putnam, the most decisive contribution for reconciling biology with essentialism comes from the philosopher Richard N. Boyd (1991, 1999). Boyd's general project is to elaborate a more sophisticated version of realism and a more flexible notion of natural kinds that would be appropriate for both biology and social sciences. Especially for biology, he suggests that the rejection of the idea that species have essential properties relies on an outdated notion about natural kinds. Such a notion implies at least three *sine qua non* conditions for natural kinds:

1 They are defined by the necessary and sufficient properties shared by all their members.
2 They are universal in the sense that their essential properties are not historically restricted.
3 They can be explained by universal laws.

According to Boyd, the above received wisdom about natural kinds has its roots not in Aristotle but primarily in modern empiricism and secondarily in "physics envy." Therefore, examples such as "water = H_2O," used by Kripke, Putnam, and their followers, "misleads us about what is essential to the essentialist critique of Lockean nominalism about kinds."

> What is essential is that the kinds of successful scientific (and everyday) practice cannot be defined by purely conventional a priori "nominal essences". Instead, they must be understood as defined a posteriori real essences that reflect the necessity of our deferring, in our classificatory practices, to facts about causal structures of the world.
>
> (Boyd, 1999, p. 146)

Thus, Boyd's notion of *homeostatic property cluster* (HPC) kinds violates the empiricist conditions prescribed for natural kinds while respecting what he regards as essential to essentialism.[4] From this perspective, biological species are the paradigmatic HPC kinds. On the surface, a species is presented to us as a cluster of concurring similarities. These similarities are too vague to be *sine qua non* conditions, but stable enough to allow us to distinguish one species from another. For example, whatever the differences in the external appearance of dogs, no one could mistake a dog for a cat. Such a coexistence of phenotypic properties is caused by homeostatic mechanisms (gene exchange through interbreeding, developmental constraints, niches, etc.). The latter "act to establish the patterns of evolutionary stasis that we recognize as manifestations of biological species" (Boyd, 1999, p. 165). Certainly, the "evolutionary stasis"[5] cannot pertain indefinitely, but this only means that species are "historically delimited natural kinds." Most importantly, similar remarks apply to the social realm. No one can say exactly when feudalism finished or when capitalism started, but it would be quite difficult to contest the existence of capitalism and feudalism as historically bound kinds (Boyd, 1999, p. 155).

Population thinking as soft anti-essentialism: the opposition between ultimate and proximate causes

An important precision about the place of population thinking in biology has been provided by Mayr (1961) himself in another seminal paper arguing for the specificity and independence of biology *vis-à-vis* physics and chemistry. In a nutshell, Mayr's thesis implies that essentialism is a dead issue in *evolutionary* biology, but a legitimate, even though "simplistic" approach (p. 1502), in *structural* biology.

From Mayr's "backward-looking" ultimate causation . . .

Mayr (1961) distinguishes between two large biological fields, structural ("functional" in the text) and evolutionary biology. The former category lumps together three different biological sub-disciplines (Ariew, 2003, p. 556; Laland et al., 2011, p. 1512):

1. physiology or anatomy;
2. developmental biology (the study of organic development from the embryo to the adult);
3. molecular biology (the study of the genetic material of different species and higher taxa).

These biological sub-disciplines deal with the structural elements of *representative entities*, ranging from cells to whole organisms. And their typological thinking is essentially the same as the experimental methods of physicists and chemists. Evolutionary biology, on the contrary, addresses the enormous *diversity* and *continuous change* in the organic world.

From the definition of the two biological fields, Mayr hastens to minimize the status of structural biology. He insists that structural biology answers the question of "How?," whereas the fundamental question in evolutionary biology is "Why?" In other terms, the structural biologist provides the *proximate causes* of biological phenomena, while the evolutionary biologist uncovers their *ultimate causes*. The distinction between "How?" (proximate causes) and "Why?" (ultimate causes) sounds more or less artificial. Is it plausible, for example, to suggest that the scientists trying to decode the DNA structure don't pose the question "Why"? On the other hand, Mayr himself explains that when evolutionary biologists ask the question "Why?," what they really mean is "How come?" Such an artificial distinction was hard to swallow, at least for philosophers informed by the new essentialism.

In his plea for realistic pluralism in biology, Kitcher (1984) argued against Mayr's distinction between proximate and ultimate causes. He proposed instead to distinguish between *structural* and *historical* explanations: "There are indeed two kinds of biological investigation that can be carried out relatively independently of one another, neither of which has priority over the other. These kinds of investigation demand different concepts of species" (p. 320). According to Kitcher, what unifies the two types of investigation is a common scientific methodology presupposing different levels of reality. Both approaches start from surface patterns in the morphology and physiology of organisms and seek to unveil the deeper causes of these patterns. The historical investigation focuses on the genealogy of species, while the structural approach concentrates on their underlying structures and mechanisms.

Devitt (2008, 2010) further developed and substantially updated Kitcher's distinction between structural and historical explanations. He argues that all biological generalizations – say, for example, the fact that Indian and African rhinoceroses don't have the same number of horns – require two distinct explanations. The historical one addresses the question of the "evolutionary history that *led to* the generalization being true" (Devitt, 2008, p. 352) while the structural one seeks to explain "*what makes* the generalization true": "Regardless of the history of its coming to be true, in virtue of what is it now true?" (Devitt, 2008, p. 352).

Finally, regarding the motives behind Mayr's "disciplinary chauvinism" (Dewsbury, 1999), they range from philosophical to purely materialistic. As he reports in his correspondence, he saw in developmental biologists the followers of Plato under whose influence he had suffered throughout his school and college career (Amundson, 2005, pp. 207–208). On the other side, the upsurge of molecular biology was perceived by him as a major threat that "required constant vigilance to prevent that all financial resources and new positions would be given to this new field" (Mayr, reported in Beatty, 1994, p. 348). Still, whatever Mayr's motives, his underestimation of developmental and molecular biology is today out of momentum. Molecular biology succeeded *inter alia* in decoding the entire human genome and then advanced to comparisons between the genomes of *Homo sapiens*, her relatives (e.g., Neanderthal), and chimpanzees. Such comparisons provide groundbreaking information about the genealogical evolution of humankind. On the other hand, the rising "evolutionary developmental biology," known also as "evo-devo," effectuated a paradigmatic shift that challenges the monopoly of the Darwinian paradigm in explaining biological evolution (Amundson, 2005).[6]

. . . to population genetics' "forward-looking" ultimate causation

Ex post we can say that Mayr has lost all the big battles he entered into. Not only have molecular and developmental biology triumphed during the last decades, but also the ahistorical vision of population genetics, his interior enemy (Amundson, 2005, p. 203), marginalized his own historical or backward-looking conception of ultimate causation.

A first, albeit indirect, questioning of Mayr's dichotomy came from Tinbergen's (1963) alternative classification in terms of four questions, namely:

1 causation (mechanisms analyzing the adult organisms);
2 ontogeny (developmental mechanisms);
3 survival value (present and future evolution);
4 (past) evolution.

Tinbergen never regrouped his four equally important questions into a hierarchy between ultimate and proximate causes. Most importantly, he was clear that the survival value of a trait in the present is logically independent from its evolution in the past. Both questions have in common the explanatory primacy of natural selection, but only survival value, because of focusing on the present, is able to study selective processes experimentally. Nevertheless, most neo-Darwinians felt confident in regrouping "causation" and "ontogeny" to proximate causes and "survival value" and "evolution" to ultimate causes.

But the worst was still to come. For Mayr, as well as for Darwin, evolutionary biology was a historical science. Mayr (1961) argued that evolutionary biology, at the opposite extreme of classical mechanics, deals with unique phenomena that are characterized by a high degree of indeterminacy, complexity, and *unpredictability*. Nonetheless, the success of population genetics promulgated an ahistorical conception of the mechanisms at work in natural selection. The domination of population genetics within neo-Darwinism transformed the latter to a probabilistic science that, contrary to Mayr, aims to supply reliable predictions (e.g., Endler and McLellan, 1988; Ariew, 2003; Griffiths, 2009). Thus, in searching to predict the "survival value" of a trait in the future, its past history is more or less irrelevant. Nowadays, as the evo-devo researcher G. Wagner (2007, p. 147) nicely put it, "one can be a successful population geneticist without knowing much of life's history on earth." To be sure, neo-Darwinians still address historical material, but they do it in the same way that New Economic History addresses history. The debate on "adaptationism" that opened with Gould and Lewontin (1979) and is still flourishing today is the major symptom of this anti-historical tendency.

In the end, it is not sure that the forward-looking version of ultimate causation provided a better argument than Mayr's initial thesis. On the contrary, the final outcome has been a far more confusing use of the terms ultimate and proximate. Most biologists seem to follow the forward-looking version. Still, even in this case the simultaneous reference to Tinbergen and Mayr makes the notion fuzzy. Certainly, Mayr and population genetics have in common the underestimation of structural or essentialist biology. But, this does not constitute sufficient grounds for conflating the naturalists' historical perspective with the geneticists' probabilistic point of view.[7]

Population thinking and anti-essentialism in economics: who's afraid of 'evolutionary political economy'?

Having analyzed the major anomalies accumulated by population thinking in biology we can now turn our attention to its adoption by evolutionary economics.

The first wave of population thinking in economics: neo-Schumpeterian industrial dynamics

The first wave of population thinking in economics refers to the literature on market processes and innovation that followed the breakthrough realized by Nelson and Winter (1982). In the important literature accumulated on these topics the evil of essentialism or typological thinking is represented by the neoclassical representative firm. Hence the metaphorical use of population thinking from biology enabled evolutionary economists to model and study competition as an evolving process based upon the ever-rejuvenated variety of firms.

The achievements of the neo-Schumpeterian literature are now so well established and recognized that they don't need further presentation. The question is if this form of evolutionary analysis can claim to cover the whole subject matter of economics. Even though the major reference from biology is the population genetics' version of population thinking, the distinction between ultimate and proximate causes is not used at all. Therefore, we are faced with a strong version of population thinking that wants to ban every form of typological thinking, even the non-essentialist ones.

Such an imperialistic attitude is not convincing even at the micro level, which constitutes the predilection of neo-Schumpeterian economics. The Marshallian representative firm provides the most problematic version of essentialism. You cannot use it as a straw man to beat Adam Smith's manufacture of pins in the 18th century, Marx's big industry in the 19th century, Berle and Means' modern corporation or Alfred Chandler's multiunit corporation in the 20th century, and Lazonick and O'Sullivan's "maximizing shareholder value" corporation in contemporary finance-led capitalism. Obviously, the aforementioned authors recognize the enormous variety of firms in the different periods of capitalism they study. But behind the impressive variety of firms they see a dominant form and its deep structures. Firms here correspond to Boyd's conception of species as HPC kinds. A consistent population thinker should reject these important works as typological or essentialist because they are based on *representative* corporations. But in this case we would have lost precious knowledge about the (time- and space-bound) organizational species operating *above* the competitive game between the individual firms of each industry.

At the macro level, the imperialistic claims of population thinking are even more problematic. In the beginning (Nelson and Winter, 1982), the neo-Schumpeterian project bet that the evolutionary approach would provide the right microfoundations for macroeconomics. Today we can conclude that this is far from the case. Neo-Schumpeterian approaches have been concentrated on the micro–meso level. And sporadic efforts to combine macroeconomics with population thinking have reached deadlock (Liagouras, 2016). The final outcome is hardly surprising. Genuine macroeconomic analysis from Ricardo and Marx to Keynes, Schumpeter, and Minsky tries to analyze the deep structures (essences) explaining the stylized facts or "semi-regularities" (Lawson, 1997) of a capitalist economy. If population thinking could provide microfoundations for macroeconomic analysis then all the heterodox macroeconomic thought would have very little explanatory value.

The second wave of population thinking: economic anthropology or foraging economics

A second wave of research inspired by Darwinian population thinking seeks to explain the human capacity to cooperate and to follow moral rules (e.g., Bowles and Gintis, 2011; Hodgson, 2013; Pagano, 2013; Witt and Schwesinger, 2013). The study of the making of the cooperative and moral species we call humankind is valuable *per se*, as a question of economic anthropology. But what is at stake here is far more important. For most of the economists participating in this stream of research, the study on the origins of human nature is expected to provide a realistic alternative to the overwhelming domination of *Homo economicus* in the dismal science. The central hypothesis, first launched by evolutionary psychology, is that all types of human societies and institutions are contingent on the hardwired elements of human nature. The latter have been formed in the long process of hominization, mainly during the Pleistocene and Holocene periods.

This hypothesis openly contradicts traditional social theory (e.g., Marx, Sombart, Weber, Schumpeter), which explicitly or implicitly postulates that human nature is too flexible to provide an account for social evolution. But it also goes against more circumspect Darwinian biologists who argue about the inadequacy of the Darwinian paradigm to comprehend human history. As remarked by Gould (1980, pp. 83–84):

> Darwinian evolution continues in *Homo sapiens*, but at rates so slow that it no longer has impact on our history. This crux in the earth's history has been reached because Lamarckian processes have finally been unleashed upon it. Human cultural evolution, in strong opposition to our biological history, is Lamarckian in character.

Given the trade-off between Darwinian and Lamarckian processes, a possible way to defend the adequacy of the Darwinian paradigm for social sciences is to stick to the hominization process and claim that the resulting human nature (instincts, proclivities, and so on) provides the ultimate cause for the analysis of human societies.

The recent adoption of the ultimate/proximate distinction (Wilson and Gowdy, 2013) enables evolutionary economists to sustain a more convincing position than the simple rejection of structural explanations. Structural or synchronic analysis is tolerated as proximate cause. What is less clear is the meaning of ultimate cause in evolutionary economics. Sometimes the conflation between Mayr's backward-looking perspective, Tinbergen's non-hierarchical set of four questions, and population genetics' forward-looking causation is more pronounced than in biological literature. But, by the use made of the ultimate/proximate distinction we can infer that what the majority of evolutionary economists have in mind is a very specific version of Mayr's backward-looking ultimate causation. In accordance with Mayr, they assert that the evolutionary history of human cooperation or morality addresses the "Why?" (ultimate cause) of economic and social organization, whilst the workings of specific socio-economic systems inform us about the "How?" (proximate cause). But then they part company with Mayr and the other neo-Darwinian scholars (e.g., Dobzhansky, Hull, Sober) whose conception of species implies that there is no such thing as human nature.

The major question is, however, if the progress made in foraging economics can help us to understand the capitalist society we live in, or (for the historians) the civilized societies of the past. This could be the case only if the human mind had the limited plasticity of other animals. Or, even the eusocial animals have never witnessed such a tremendous evolution in social organization going from tribal to modern societies.[8] It is quite probable that, in the same way that Chomsky found a universal grammar common to all human languages, social scientists will one day explore a universal moral grammar. Nevertheless, as Chomsky's universal grammar is of little help in understanding the grammatical and syntactical differences between Ancient Greek and Modern English, the hardwired elements of human nature are of little help in understanding the economic and political differences between ancient Athens and modern America. If we adopt Mayr's terminology, this means that the so-called proximate causes are far more important than the "ultimate" ones. Incidentally, the "ultimate" lesson we learn from some versions of the burgeoning literature on foraging economics is that humans are both self-interested and moral beings, and/or that all social systems combine competition with cooperation in different degrees. These lessons have great value against the unidimensional notions of *Homo economicus* and economic efficiency promoted by mainstream economics. But, from an analytical point of view, they seem too general to be relevant.

Is something missing? The case for 'evolutionary political economy'

In their effort to apply Darwinian population thinking in the economic realm the two aforementioned strands of evolutionary economics put aside the structural analysis of capitalism, its eras (e.g., finance-led capitalism), and its geographical varieties. The neo-Schumpeterian branch avoids structural analysis by focusing on the micro–meso level and short-run evolution. The resulting vacuum regarding long-run evolution (Witt, 2008) has been recently completed by the ascending current of foraging economics, which makes the analysis of modern capitalism a byproduct of investigations about the the hominization process that took place a long time ago.

This tendency to exorcise structural analysis is exemplified at the philosophical level by the silence of evolutionary economists regarding the species problem in biology.[9] Such a gap seems very strange for heterodox economists who militate in favour of a history-friendly approach in the discipline. The reason is that, given their concentrations, both strands of evolutionary economics don't need to address the fundamental questions about history and theory underlying the species debate. But the exorcism of structural analysis has above all important practical consequences. The 2008 crisis of modern finance-led capitalism provides an excellent test for assessing the relevance of modern evolutionary economics. Not surprisingly, evolutionary scholars have had a lot to say about the mainstream assumptions adopted by policy makers, but too little about the crisis itself and the structures that were "responsible" for it. Shedding light on the causes of the crisis presupposes discerning the stylized facts of finance-led capitalism (typological thinking) and exploring the deep-seated structures – and their contradictions – that underlie the persistence of those stylized facts (essentialism). But all this is beyond the scope of population thinking.

On the contrary, this is the predilection domain of evolutionary political economy. The latter is *evolutionary* in a totally different way than the approaches in terms of population thinking. Its objects of study are what Hull and Ghiselin wrongly called individuals, and R.N. Boyd designated as historically bound kinds. Unavoidably, its epistemological background is not the obsolete "logical empiricism" adopted by Hull and his followers but the new essentialism which vindicates the methodological stance of the heterodox economists working with representative entities.

At the same time, the focus on structural analysis does not mean that evolutionary political economy is dismissive of questions of history and origins. It simply addresses these questions through a radically different methodology. As I explained elsewhere (Liagouras, 2015), Darwinian analogies could explain the survival of certain institutions, or technologies opposed to others in a fictitious stateless world. But, they cannot apprehend the creation of *complementarities* and *synergies* between different institutions and technologies to form a system (Freeman, 1991; Crouch et al., 2005), that is, an *internally related whole*. The issue here is not the selection of one institution (or a technology) against its quasi-similar competitors, but the creation of a division of labor between interrelated institutions/technologies. That's why social systems change mainly *from within* (Schumpeter), through the interplay of their *internal* relationships and contradictions.

Finally, evolutionary political economy is *political* in the sense that it does not limit itself to restating in a sophisticated manner – through the biological jargon of natural selection and struggle of existence – the managers' vision of the economic world. It seeks instead to go beyond the "surface" of capitalist phenomena and to critically analyze their underlying social structures and power relationships.[10]

Concluding remarks

In guise of conclusion let me make two sketchy comments. First, it becomes more and more clear that the promoters of biological imperialism in social sciences try to create a complex of inferiority to their colleagues. According to their intimidating strategy, evolutionary theory in biology stands far beyond social sciences, and the latter should precipitate to cover their lag if they want to make progress. The discussion of the insurmountable contradictions created by population thinking within biology showed that this position is not warranted. On the contrary, in many issues concerning history and theory, biology would have many things to learn from social sciences. As the developmental biologists Depew and Weber (1995, p. 495) argued long before: "Perhaps it is not too much to say that what we need is an evolutionary theory worthy of the best social theory, not a social theory trimmed to fit a rapidly receding, overly simplistic evolutionary theory."

Second, it must be also clear that there is no problem with applying population thinking in economics. On the contrary, population thinking led to a scientific revolution at the micro–meso level, and very probably it will do the same in economic anthropology. The problem is rather the imperialistic claims suggesting to apply population thinking to the totality of economic or social phenomena. If these claims are taken seriously, a large part of economic, social, and psychological thought of the two or three last centuries would be either wrong or redundant. Are we facing such a radical breakthrough in modern thought? Waiting for a definitive answer, it is not without importance to note that Darwinian imperialism in social sciences takes place at the same time that neo-Darwinian synthesis loses momentum within evolutionary biology.

Notes

1 Certainly, if you take the word "real" *à la lettre*, then Ariew (2008, p. 65) is justified in speaking of "silly metaphysics." For example, the mean of a population is no less real than the individual values it represents. It seems however that what Mayr means here by "real" is to dispose of explanatory power or "causal efficacy" (Sober, 1980, p. 371).
2 This turn in the history and methodology of biology is aptly summarized by Wagner's (2007, p. 151) rhetorical question: "Was everyone before Darwin an idiot?"
3 We can find in this postulate the intellectual roots of D. Hull's later major works, like his strictly genealogical conception of scientific evolution (Hull, 1988) as well as his attempt to provide a general account of selection in biology, immunology, and behavior (Hull et al., 2001).
4 Regarding the argumentation of the Darwinian orthodoxy against the new biological essentialism, see mainly Ereshefsky (2010).
5 Boyd's notions of "evolutionary stasis" and "homeostatic mechanisms" have already been used by punctuated equilibria theorists (Eldredge and Gould, 1972). Obviously, the evolutionary theory that corresponds perfectly to the rehabilitation of essentialism in evolutionary biology is the "punctuated equilibria" approach.
6 Regarding the revolutionary implications of evo-devo for evolutionary economics, see Martin and Sunley (2015) and Liagouras (2016). See also Wagner (2001) and Amundson (2005) on the close relationship between evo-devo and Boyd's essentialism.
7 To the best of my knowledge, D. Haig (2013) is the only scholar who insists on the fuzziness implied by the notion of the ultimate causation. Note that this problem is distinct from the question of the blurring frontiers *between* ultimate and proximate causation (e.g., Vromen, 2009; Laland et al., 2011).
8 Veblen (1914/1994) was the first major author who reconstructed human history by departing from a bundle of instincts. In order to fulfill his project he postulated that under exogenous conditions an instinct can be transformed to its contrary. Such a tautological strategy can *ex post* accommodate all possible change, but it is poorly informative. Witt and Schwesinger (2013) provide a more consistent and convincing account on the same subject matter. Still, as they correctly remark, what remained in capitalism from the initial cooperative endowment is just "footprints."
9 Pagano (2011) provides an outstanding exception to the above trend.
10 For elaborated accounts on the relationship between political economy and evolutionary economics, see MacKinnon et al., (2009) and Martin and Sunley (2015).

References

Amundson, R. (2005). *The changing role of the embryo in evolutionary thought. Roots of Evo-Devo.* Cambridge: Cambridge University Press.

Ariew, A. (2003). Ernst Mayr's 'ultimate/proximate' distinction reconsidered and reconstructed. *Biology and Philosophy*, 18(4), 553–565.

Ariew, A. (2008). Population thinking. In M. Ruse (Ed.), *The Oxford handbook of philosophy of biology* (pp. 64–86). Oxford: Oxford University Press.
Ayres, M.R. (1981). Locke versus Aristotle on natural kinds. *Journal of Philosophy*, 78(5), 247–272.
Beatty, J. (1994). The proximate/ultimate distinction in the multiple careers of Ernst Mayr. *Biology and Philosophy*, 9(3), 333–356.
Bowles, S., & Gintis, H. (2011). *A cooperative species: human reciprocity and its evolution*. Princeton: Princeton University Press.
Boyd, R.N. (1991). Realism, anti-foundationalism and the enthusiasm for natural kinds. *Philosophical Studies*, 61(1), 127–148.
Boyd, R.N. (1999). Homeostasis, species, and higher taxa. In R.A. Wilson (Ed.), *Species: new interdisciplinary essays* (pp. 141–185). Cambridge, MA: MIT Press.
Crouch, C., Streeck, W., Boyer, R., Amable, B., Hall, P., & Jackson, G. (2005). Dialogue on 'institutional complementarity and political economy. *Socio-Economic Review*, 3(3), 359–382.
Depew, D.J., & Weber, B.R. (1995). The fate of Darwinism: evolution after the modern synthesis. *Biological Theory*, 6(1), 89–102.
Devitt, M. (2008). Resurrecting biological essentialism. *Philosophy of Science*, 75(3), 344–382.
Devitt, M. (2010). Species have (partly) intrinsic essences. *Philosophy of Science*, 77(5), 648–661.
Dewsbury, D.A. (1999). The proximate and the ultimate: past, present, and future. *Behavioural Processes*, 46(3), 189–199.
Eldredge, N., & Gould, S.J. (1972). Punctuated equilibria: an alternative to phyletic gradualism. In T. Schopf (Ed.), *Models in paleobiology* (pp. 82–115). San Francisco: Freeman Cooper.
Endler, J.A., & McLellan, T. (1988). The process of evolution: towards a newer synthesis. *Annual Review of Ecology and Systematics*, 19, 395–421.
Ereshefsky, M. (2010). What's wrong with the new biological essentialism? *Philosophy of Science*, 77(5), 674–685.
Freeman, C. (1991). Innovation, changes of techno-economic paradigm and biological analogies in economics. *Revue Économique*, 42(2), 211–231.
Ghiselin, M.T. (1974). A radical solution to the species problem. *Systematic Zoology*, 23(4), 536–544.
Gould, S.J. (1980). *The panda's thumb: more reflections in natural history*. New York: Norton.
Gould, S.J., & Lewontin, R.C. (1979). The spandrels of San Marco and the Panglossian paradigm: a critique of the adaptationist programme. *Proceedings of the Royal Society of London B: Biological Sciences*, 205(1161), 581–598.
Griffiths, P.E. (2009). In what sense does "Nothing make sense except in the light of evolution?" *Acta Biotheoretica*, 57(1–2), 11–32.
Haig, D. (2013). Proximate and ultimate causes: how come? and what for? *Biology and Philosophy*, 28(5), 781–786.
Hodgson, G.M. (1993). *Economics and evolution: bringing life back to economics*. Cambridge: Polity Press.
Hodgson, G.M. (2013). *From pleasure machines to moral communities. An evolutionary economics without Homo economicus*. Chicago: The University of Chicago Press.
Hull, D.L. (1965). The effect of essentialism on taxonomy: two thousand years of stasis (I and II). *British Journal for the Philosophy of Science*, I: 15, 314–326; II: 16, 1–18.

Hull, D.L. (1976). Are species really individuals? *Systematic Zoology*, 25(2), 174–191.

Hull, D.L. (1978). A matter of individuality. *Philosophy of Science*, 45(3), 335–360.

Hull, D.L. (1988). *Science as a process: an evolutionary account of the social and conceptual development of science*. Chicago: University of Chicago Press.

Hull, D.L., Langman, R.E., & Glenn, S.S. (2001). A general account of selection: biology, immunology and behaviour. *Behavioral and Brain Sciences,* 24(3), 511–573.

Kitcher, P. (1984). Species. *Philosophy of Science*, 51(2), 308–333.

Kripke, S. (1980). *Naming and necessity*. Cambridge, MA: Harvard University Press.

Laland, K.N., Sterenly, K., Odling-Smee, J., Hoppitt, W., & Uller, T. (2011). Cause and effect in biology revisited: is Mayr's proximate-ultimate dichotomy useful? *Science*, 334(1512), 1512–1516.

Lawson, T. (1997). *Economics and reality*. Abingdon: Routledge.

Liagouras, G. (2015). From heterodox political economy to generalized Darwinism: Geoffrey Hodgson's tensions in retrospect. *Review of Radical Political Economics*. doi:10.1177/0486613415594161.

Liagouras, G. (2016). The challenge of Evo-Devo: implications for evolutionary economists. *Journal of Evolutionary Economics* (under review).

Locke, J. (1690/1975). *An essay concerning human understanding*. In P.H. Nidditch (Ed.), Oxford: Oxford University Press.

MacKinnon, D., Cumbers, A., Pike, A, Birch, K., & McMaster, R. (2009). Evolution in economic geography: institutions, political economy, and adaptation. *Economic Geography*, 85(2), 129–150.

Martin, R., & Sunley, P. (2015). Towards a developmental turn in evolutionary economic geography? *Regional Studies*, 49(5), 712–732.

Mayr, E. (1959/1976). Darwin and the evolutionary theory in biology. Reprinted as: Typological versus population thinking. In E. Mayr (Ed.), *Evolution and the diversity of life. Selected essays* (pp. 26–29). Cambridge, MA: The Belknap Press of Harvard University Press.

Mayr, E. (1961). Cause and effect in biology. *Science*, 134(3489), 1501–1506.

Mayr, E. (1969). Footnotes on the philosophy of biology. *Philosophy of Science*, 36(2), 197–202.

Mayr, E. (1982). *The growth of biological thought*. Cambridge, MA: Harvard University Press.

Metcalfe, J.S. (1989). Evolution and economic change. In A. Silberston (Ed.), *Technology and economic progress* (pp. 54–85). Basingstoke: MacMillan.

Nelson, R.R., & Winter S.W. (1982). *An evolutionary theory of economic change*. Cambridge, MA: The Belknap Press of Harvard University Press.

Pagano, U. (2011). Interlocking complementarities and institutional change. *Journal of Institutional Economics,* 7(3), 373–392.

Pagano, U. (2013). Love, war and cultures: an institutional approach to human evolution. *Journal of Bioeconomics*, 15(1), 41–66.

Popper, K.R. (1950). *The open society and its enemies*. Princeton: Princeton University Press.

Putnam, H. (1975). Mind, language and reality. In *Philosophical papers* (Vol. 2, pp. 215–271). Cambridge, MA: Cambridge University Press.

Ruse, M. (1987). Biological species: natural kinds, individuals, or what? *British Journal for the Philosophy of Science*, 38(2), 225–242.

Sober, E. (1980). Evolution, population thinking, and essentialism. *Philosophy of Science,* 47(3), 350–383.

Tinbergen, N. (1963). On aims and methods of ethology. *Zeitschrift für Tierpsychologie* 20(4), 410–433.

Veblen, T. (1914/1994). *The instinct of workmanship and the state of the industrial arts*. London: Routledge/Thoemmes Press.

Vromen, J.J. (2009). Advancing evolutionary explanations in economics: the limited usefulness of Tinbergen's four-question classification. In H. Kincaid & D. Ross (Eds), *The Oxford handbook of philosophy of economics* (pp. 337–368). Oxford: Oxford University Press.

Wagner, G.P. (2001). Characters, units and natural kinds. In G.P. Wagner (Ed.), *The character concept in evolutionary biology* (pp. 1–10). San Diego: Academic Press.

Wagner, G.P. (2007). How wide and how deep is the divide between population genetics and developmental evolution? *Biology and Philosophy*, 22(1), 145–153.

Wilson, D.S., & Gowdy J.M. (2013). Evolution as a general theoretical framework for economics and public policy. *Journal of Economic Behavior and Organization*, 90, S3–S10.

Winsor, M.P. (2006). The creation of the essentialism story: an exercise in metahistory. *History and Philosophy of the Life Sciences*, 28(2), 149–174.

Witt, U. (2008). What is specific about evolutionary economics? *Journal of Evolutionary Economics*, 18(5), 547–575.

Witt, U., & Schwesinger, G. (2013). Phylogenetic footprints in organizational behavior. *Journal of Economic Behavior & Organization*, 90, S33–S44.

4 The contemporary relevance of Karl Polanyi – a Swedish case

Ernst Hollander
Special support from Maria Malama

Introduction

Open-minded social scientists often are surprised when their predictions turn out to be correct. Some are even elated. Elation over accurate predictions, however, cannot be expected from present-day scholars inspired by Karl Polanyi (1886–1964). The last 40 years have seen what Karl Polanyi could have called 'disembedding on a global scale'.

The Polanyian concept of disembedding focuses on three elements which must be transformed into *(fictitious) commodities* when attempts are made to *create a self-regulating market.*[1] They are land, labour and money. But in the attempts to do so the very web of life is undermined. This is key in Polanyi's analysis (in 1944) of the greatest breakdown in modern civilisation before the one to which we are presently heading. The period leading up to the breakdown of the 1930s–1940s was called the *laissez-faire* era.

After the Second World War there was widespread scepticism – even in elites – of a renewed attempt to create a self-regulating market. Finance was *re-embedded* and in what we today call the Global North, welfare states were created whereby i.a. labour was partially re-embedded. In the Global South came a development towards decolonisation and later on attempts to create national economies.

But in the 1970s global finance re-emerged and we entered *a neoliberal era* which paralleled the *laissez-faire* era in the overreaching dream of a self-regulating market. In the Global North welfare gains have been reversed, governments have been weakened and labour unions undermined. In the Global South land and water grabbing on a massive scale illustrate the intensified commodification of 'land' in the Polanyian sense.

With the concepts of Rio 92, we can today talk of the undermining of three categories of sustainability: economic, social and ecological. In spite of great advances in measured GDP and technology many of the dystopian predictions referred to initially have been proven correct.

Among those predictions only two will be mentioned here. On the financial scene we are watching the most serious crisis since Polanyi's days. And when it comes to right-wing authoritarianism, those who already in the 1990s saw the gathering clouds have been far too correct for their own liking.

This chapter relates to the Cyprus conference. The focus there was the crisis in Southern Europe. Here I complement those images by looking at what has happened in Sweden. Together with a number of other countries in Northern Europe Sweden has been viewed as exemplary in adapting to changes in the world economy. In this it has been contrasted to Southern Europe. By more closely studying the Swedish case I simultaneously wish to illustrate how a Polanyian lens can be used and question the long-term resilience of the way in which Sweden has adapted during the last three decades.

Building on tensions

Sweden is the largest of the Nordic countries and is outside the Euro zone. We are many who believe that 'a Swedish model' has been abandoned. When the abandonment took place is more contested. Politico-economic arguments could be given for the early 1970s, the period leading up to the Swedish decision in the early 1990s to join the EU, or the ascendance to power of 'the Alliance' in 2006. 'The Alliance' is the centre-right coalition which governed Sweden between 2006 and 2014.

The idea that the Swedish welfare state, labour market and corporatist model continues to be resilient in the face of challenging global circumstances is, however, also widespread.

In this chapter I will methodologically start from a number of tensions.[2]:

The *first tension* is the one between an image where a 'reinvented model' is applauded and a more critical interpretation of the developments. Early in 2013 *The Economist* carried a special report called *Northern Lights*. The subtitle was *The Nordic Countries are Reinventing their Model of Capitalism*.[3] The rosy pictures represented by *The Economist* are contrasted with images largely coming from the *Nordic centre-left* where dire socioeconomic tendencies parallel to those in other parts of the West are stressed.

The Economist's description is useful since it can represent a whole set of analyses which underestimate the risks of disembedding. To me the traditional strength of the Nordic models must be understood in relation to the relative strength of non-elite forces in development. Those forces are weakened when there is an over-emphasis on *markets as a societal form of coordination.*

A *second tension* is between external and internal forces. The *embedded liberalism* of the period up to the early 1970s was dependent on a specific international environment but had deep roots in Swedish history (Blyth 2002).[4]

I also stress a 'Polanyian triangle' which – to my mind – is often neglected by economists. I am referring to the three forms of economic coordination discussed by Polanyi et al. (1957). While market and redistribution are discussed a lot, reciprocity – the oldest form of human coordination for wellbeing – is mostly left to anthropologists. This sad state of affairs is slowly changing in discourses on development economics and social capital. But when it comes to mainstream economists' accounts there is still a major dearth. In discussing this triangle I look at a whole family of relations between market and state, non-governmental organisations and the state, but I refer to them as a *third tension.*

In this chapter I sketch arguments rather than finish them. When trying to think about ways out of 'the triple crises' – social, ecological and economic – exercises of such a nature are important. I hope to contribute to a discourse on which Swedish experiences can be used and which ought to be avoided when working for multidimensional sustainability. I also want to explore how the *re-emergence of global finance* seems to have undermined even some of the most resilient kinds of embedded liberalism.[5]

Long-term explanations for Swedish socioeconomic resilience

Oft-neglected factors behind the creation and the resilience of 'the Swedish model' are the wealth of *social capital* accumulated since at least the mid 19th century and the protection afforded to the Swedish form of embedded liberalism by the Bretton Woods system (1944).

Examples of phenomena related to the historical accumulation of social capital are:

- the old tradition of a strong small-holding peasantry and the weak feudal heritage;

plus 19th- and early-20th-century:

- surge in literacy and basic education;
- labour, temperance and other 'popular' movements plus an enlightened *bourgeoisie*;
- independent, movement-based education exemplified by study circles, folk high schools and libraries.[6]

Civil society also had a 'more benign' state to deal with. Rothstein and Trägårdh (2007) stress that the Swedish 19th-century state was less repressive compared to continental European states. Related to this was extensive local self-government, no legal hindrance of unions or strikes, a civil service that was relatively independent and uncorrupt. So the Swedish state was rather well integrated with civil society. The social formation which evolved has been termed 'democracy from below'. 'State institutions . . . and political processes . . . have played important roles . . . [But] equally important is the deliberative and inclusive democratic process that has occurred outside of these ordinary contexts ' (Rothstein and Trägårdh, 2007: 249–250).

de Vylder (1996) tries to explain the Swedish success story from 1870 to 1960 which was characterised by high growth in GDP and exports and noteworthy stability. He emphasises the 'very fortunate combination, or balance, of various forms of capital'. Those various forms of course include natural, financial and directly productive capital but also infrastructural and human capital. He specially underlines social capital: 'We have norms, institutions, networks, organisations, traditions and attitudes which together constitute a society's social capital'.

Yet others stress the massive Swedish emigration around the 1900 turn of the century. This exodus created a shortage in labour supply which forced Swedish employers to take a more cooperative stance.

After these hints about the historical accumulation of social capital I move on to a more speculative factor for resilience. The idea is that the Swedish model in a more narrow economic sense was dependent on *the capitals control regime* of the early post World War II period.[7] To political economists the Swedish model is often focused on the *Rehn–Meidner* plan presented in the 1950s.[8] The idea was that unions, together with the Social Democratic government, should pursue a strategy that simultaneously aimed to equalise wages, reduce inflation and improve productivity. The union's 'solidarity wage' policy initiated industrial restructuring towards higher-value-added economic sectors.

The model was important historically and could be important in the future. The model made possible a broader than usual endorsement of international economic transformation and state policies of flexible adjustment. During the first decades after World War II advanced social demands such as for more just wages could drive industrial restructuring towards economic sectors of the future. Under more benign conditions the mind set created by the model could today initiate ecologically driven restructuring in accordance with global sustainability needs.

The model, however, presupposes that the extra profits which result from the flat – solidaristic – wage structure are used to expand firms in the geographic space – Sweden in this case – where those profits are created. In periods of unregulated capital movements, such as *laissez-faire* before the 1930s or neoliberalism after the 1970s, the model will, however, not work. Under such conditions the super-profits of the firms which benefit from the model will be exported.

The argument is thus that Sweden could continue to build a strong international economic position during important post-war years – that is, until around 1970 – with the protection of the Bretton Woods system.

A factor for the relative resilience, even after the 'embedded liberalism' had been abandoned, is the vote 'no' to the euro in the 2003 Swedish referendum. Since a wide section of the Swedish elite argued for a 'yes' vote, this explanation is less discussed in Sweden than one might expect.[9]

A first glance at the contrasting images of the Swedish U-turn

The Economist's Special Report (2013: 3) is applauding that Sweden is a leader in slaughtering sacred cows. 'The streets of Stockholm are awash with the blood . . . [of sacred cows]'.

According to the report, the period 1970–1990 was a period of decline. Or maybe the decline started in 1960, when 'the middle way veered left'.

The positive trends after 1990 most applauded by *The Economist* are, i.a., the reduction of public spending as a percentage of GDP (from 67% to 49%), the scrapping of taxes on wealth and the cutting of corporate tax rates. Dramatic lowering of real-estate taxes – especially for the most wealthy – and Sweden's entry into the race to the bottom of corporate taxes are also saluted.

Some important developments go unmentioned. The dramatic worsening of the Gini coefficient is maybe the most obvious of the omissions. Even OECD reports make clear that Sweden has had one of the fastest rises in Gini (deterioration in equality) among developed countries in the 1985–2008 period (OECD, 2011: 24).

Developments in the educational sector are mentioned but the description is highly biased. Not mentioned is that the Swedish school system, which used to provide reasonably equal opportunities and a dramatic reshuffling of Swedish social hierarchies, has now turned into a deeply segregated system which is bringing back an ugly class society. One alarming development which might be a result of this is that a high proportion of early school leavers have become authoritarian in their values.

But *The Economist*'s Special Report (2013: 5) puts the blame on the growing diversity in Sweden rather than on growing inequality. 'The growing diversity of Nordic societies is generating social tensions'.[10] This is an argument which only the far right is using in Sweden. Up to the end of autumn 2015 Sweden was – with quantitative measures and on a per capita basis – the most welcoming country in Europe. The growing tensions in my analysis result from factors such as rising unemployment, dismantling of strong labour rights and a general weakening of social cohesion – not growing diversity *per se*.

Squeezing or challenging business?

In order to understand the contrasting images it is useful to look at both the economy at large and at specific sectors/companies.

According to *The Economist*'s Special Report, 'the new Nordic model begins with . . . fiscal responsibility rather than pump-priming' (2013: 4). In fact, a hallmark of the Rehn–Meidner model was that it aimed at stemming inflationary tendencies by combining restrictive fiscal policies with supply-side measures such as subsidies for retraining and resettling. It was decidedly anti-cyclical. The model was successful until the fall of the Bretton Woods system. The irresponsible fiscal policies of Sweden which eventually brought about a major crisis in the early 1990s were in fact initiated by the centre-right parties during their 1976–1982 reign (Blyth 2002: 219–220).

Another part of *The Economist*'s Special Report analysis of the fall of 'the old model' is that 'the Social Democrats . . . kept squeezing business'. To my mind this 'squeezing' posed healthy challenges to the elites. And challenges came from all kinds of non-elite forces. Solidaristic policies of the model were definitely problematic for unproductive firms in industries such as textiles. The concomitant demands for better work environments – both physical and psycho-social – were challenging for engineers and production designers who had to listen simultaneously to worker and productivity demands. Demands for less toxic environments were also challenging (Hollander 2003). All those challenges became seeds of innovation.

Also at the company level I would argue that 'the old model' had many benign effects. This can be illustrated by the very innovations mentioned in *The*

Economist's Special Report. Those innovations can be traced to the environment created by the model. Some examples follow.

The strong position which *Ericsson* continues to have has important roots in the historic cooperation with the Swedish Telecom Board, which was still state-owned at the time when the basis was laid for Ericsson's position as leader in telecom equipment. The telecom board was a sophisticated *demand shaper*.[11]

Likewise the strength of *Volvo* Trucks has a lot to do with traits of 'the old model'. Strong work environment demands were important when Volvo Trucks developed its leading edge in global markets.

The Economist's Special Report stresses *Sandvik's* obsession with promoting productivity. Maybe it would be useful to ponder the role of a strong and constructive Metal Workers' Union when looking for the roots of this.

The Economist's Special Report states that 'the compression of Swedish incomes . . . almost killed the goose that laid the golden eggs'. With this statement we come to the core of the controversy. We who appreciate the legacies can quite to the contrary think that, for instance, the advanced production systems which are the envy of so many engineers around the globe can be seen in relation to the solidarity wages policy which was a cornerstone of the old model (Sandberg 2013, i.a. chapters 2 and 5).

The root causes of the disintegration of the Nordic models should rather be looked for in international developments. The Swedish 'success story' from 1860 to 1960 included a balanced adaptation to the international environment and openness to trade. The companies – some of them mentioned above – which still dominate the Swedish economy tried their wings early on in international competition.

The Bretton Woods architecture reopened world trade after World War II. Swedish companies early on invested abroad in production capacity. What changed when Bretton Woods 'ended' was that Swedish big firms gradually got more choice of whether to adapt to internal Swedish challenges *or* focus more on expanding abroad. Earlier they could be counted on to pursue *both* those strategies simultaneously.

In the 1970s the international conditions for the model were thus changing dramatically. The real choice was already then between dismantling or developing the model.

Among sectors where there were attempts to develop rather than dismantle one can underline gender equality, ecological sustainability and workplace codetermination. To paraphrase *The Economist*'s Special Report, the Swedish centre-left *consciously* tried to make Swedish companies and other institutions 'reach the future first'.[12] Results in the three areas mentioned and in many others were impressive.

The logic behind the abandonment of the 'post-war Swedish model'

If we discard the idea that 'the old' Swedish model of 'embedded liberalism' was economically unsustainable, how can we understand that it was dismantled? And what was the role of Social Democracy in this?

We need to start in '*the Polanyian Period*' in order to understand the dramatic change from the Swedish socioeconomic formation that seemed so attractive to 'centre-left' observers 40 years ago.[13]

We single out five periods of importance for the story and *start with the inter-war period* after the First World War. Taking a Central European perspective, Polanyi referred – in an article from 1933 – to the time span ranging all the way back to 1918 as 'one single economic crisis' (Polanyi, 1933 [1999]: Ch. 31).

In Sweden the long period of uninterrupted Social Democratic domination of Swedish politics started in 1932. Initially, it built on a class alliance between workers and peasants and a labour movement compromise with the leading factions of capital. Those 'internal' compromises made possible continued economic growth and prevented fascist forces from gaining strength. The ideological basis for the crisis policies of the 1930s has been described by Ryner in terms of 'a Marxist-institutionalist synthesis represented by the coming together of the thought of Marxist-inspired activists . . . and Ernst Wigforss on the one hand and Gunnar Myrdal on the other'.[14]

Sweden then entered the post Second World War period with a more or less intact production system. The period up till the mid-1960s is *the second period we consider*. It was partly the booming early post-war years that formed the frame when the 'old model' was conceived. The first seeds of the coming demise of the model were, however, sown already during this period. The centralisation of wage bargaining was a prerequisite for Labour's ability to deliver on its promises in negotiations. But a tendential fall in mobilisation of the Labour movement was at the same time a threat to its cohesion and creativity.

Swedish democratic modernity – much admired at the time – has also been accused of developing insensitivity. The million dwelling units programme (1965–1975) has been quoted as *the* case in point. This programme was developed as an answer to a housing crisis in big cities following the 'structural rationalisation' of the 1950s. The programme and the spirit it represented are still contested.

As in the rest of the Global North, the year 1968 is a symbol for youth uprising in Sweden. Our *third period stretches from 1965 to 1982* and thus includes the period of the first centre-right government since 1932. In my tradition the '1968 uprisings' are seen as 'generated by *contradictions of Fordism*'. The tensions had the double effect of shaping on the one hand a 'Swedish New Left' within and outside Swedish Social Democracy and on the other a dawning Swedish neoliberalism.

The centre-right government's fiscal irresponsibility and parody of industrial policy in the late 1970s further delegitimised 'the Swedish model' in spite of the fact that those policies were pursued by centre-right governments. When the Social Democrats (SAP) returned to political power their political ambitions had changed compared to those of the early 1970s (Östberg 2012).

The centre of gravity in the Swedish state and in the labour movement had changed *in our fourth period* – from 1982 to 1994. Economic state managers wielded more power than hitherto and the policy pursued by the Social Democratic governments was 'compensatory neoliberalism' according to left critics.

In the fourth period Sweden opened up to international financial capital. The short-term background included a 'run on the Swedish krona (SEK)' and the SAP government abandoning its unconditional full employment commitment as well as announcing its intention to apply for EC membership (Lindberg & Ryner 2010: 36).

Before discussing *our fifth period (1994–2014)* we ought to point to definitions of *commodification* and *financialisation.* Since this is discussed elsewhere in this book we will just cite the Financialisation, Economy, Society and Sustainable Development (FESSUD) project – see below. According to FESSUD on Sweden (Stenfors 2014: 16), 'the processes of financialisation contain . . . de-regulation of the financial system itself and the economy more generally; . . . at a systemic level, the dominance of finance over industry'.

(Re-)commodification means that, for instance, social services are commodified. This is a prerequisite for financialisation.

We will divide the fifth period into periods 5a and 5b. During period 5a the (re-)commodification and financialisation of central societal areas were introduced on a tentative yet fateful scale. The areas include housing *as well as* health, child care, schooling and care for the elderly – HEW for short.[15]

The pension reform of the late 1990s also represented a paradigmatic shift to neoliberalism (Belfrage & Ryner 2009).

Cynically, period 5 in its entirety can be viewed as a time of preparation for, and realisation of, massive venture capital private profits in central societal areas. The HEW part of this process has been described in a book which will be used below as one starting point in a section which contrasts two images of Swedish (re)commodification/financialisation.

Period 5b (2006–2014), when a centre-right government led by Reinfeldt ruled, meant concerted efforts to undermine foundations of the socioeconomic formation built by the Social Democrats (SAP) from the 1930s to the 1970s. This formation from the 1930s to the 1970s has been described by Social Democrat economists as resting on *four pillars* (Carlén *et al.* 2014: 29–33).

(a) labour market characterised by high degree of unionisation, sophisticated partners and 'self-regulation of the labour market' by those partners;
(b) social insurance compensations covering a high percentage of the income before the time of the damage. The social insurance financed by levies proportional to income;
(c) central welfare services (HEW) paid by taxes and conducted by public authorities. The services distributed according to need and provided on equal terms to all citizens;
(d) taxes high enough to finance advanced public ambitions combined with a tax system which was *per se* redistributing.

This run-through of the pillars is very rough. But I now turn to 'the attacks' effected by the Reinfeldt government. These are briefly summarised as follows (Carlén *et al.* 2014: 208–212):

- Attack on pillar a – Labour market: rebalancing the Labour market in favour of employers through making union membership, as well as unemployment insurance, much more expensive. At the same time institutional reforms were passed which favoured employers in low-wage service sectors.
- Attack on pillar b – the social insurance system: drastic reductions in rate of income guarantee in the other social insurances – e.g. sick leave, parental leave. Less support for rehabilitation after hardship and for moving to other jobs.
- Growing subsidies for private insurance solutions.
- Attack on pillar c – the HEW system: marketisation, privatisation and financialisation of the Swedish HEW system.
- Attack on pillar d – the progressive tax system: general lowering of taxes. Weaker redistributive effect of taxes. Massive subsidies to low-wage service sector, making life easier for the wealthy.

An even bigger problem than the roughness of this run-through is that it is based on an account which puts all the 'blame' on the policies pursued during 2006–2014. The dismantling effected or prepared earlier is then underrated. Therefore the next section will contrast two accounts which have longer time perspectives. This is preceded by a paragraph on the end of period 5.

The results of the Swedish election in September 2014 meant an affirmation that Sweden had turned into a 'normal' European country. A Social Democratic–Green government was formed. If we, however, count the so-called Sweden Democrats – which gained almost 13% of the vote – as being a party of the extreme right, we see that the right wing in Sweden gained the upper hand in Parliament in the present decade (from 2010). Their advantage is now 10 percentage points. Since the 1930s there has only been one decade when the right wing had the upper hand and that was in the 1970s, when the advantage was only a few percentage points (Bengtsson 2014).

Contrasting images of commodification/financialisation

I will start the contrast with a section that is heavily influenced by a book, the title of which echoes Polanyi's most famous one. The English translation of the title could be *The Great Transformation – The Welfare Market Scrutinized.*[16]

The subsequent section is heavily influenced by a study which views Swedish financialisation with more sympathetic eyes.

A 'great transformation' of the provision of Swedish HEW

In *The Great Transformation – The Welfare Market Scrutinized,* Werne and Unsgaard (2014) described 'the financialisation of Swedish HEW'. From my point of view the most serious consequence of this 'great transformation' is that cohesive forces such as solidarity, voice and idealistic entrepreneurship have been undermined. This can also be phrased using the Polanyian concept 'reciprocity'.

We could call it 'forced reduction of reciprocity'. Below I use the phrase *social capital depreciation.*

A case in point is the Swedish version of the Friedmanian 'voucher plan' for schools – *skolpeng.*[17] When studying the consequences of the introduction of *skolpeng* and related developments Verdinelli (in Werne and Unsgaard 2014) looked i.a. at internet discussion threads dealing with how parents decide how to choose schools for their children.

'Ethnic Swedish' parents shy away from schools in 'immigrant-dense' areas. The concept 'immigrant-dense' is, however, in fact a signifier of an 'unfavourable class composition' in an area. Even though you – as a citizen – might be in favour of the old type of mixed schools you – as a parent – feel guilty if you don't choose 'the best' for your children. And 'the best' has to do with the networks you help your kids get into (Verdinelli in Werne and Unsgaard 2014: 173–196).

Sweden can thus be said to be a front-runner in extending the number of *Polanyian fictitious commodities*. Polanyi's traditional list of three fictitious commodities should maybe be extended with three *semi-fictitious commodities:* health, education and welfare. According to Werne and Unsgaard (2014), the financialised part of the Swedish HEW sector was in 2012 more than one-sixth of the total sector value. The commodified part – run according to the logic of price competition – is, however, much bigger since the private part of the sector exerts a strong influence on the publicly provided part. And it is all financed by tax payers' money.

The *commodification/financialisation* can be traced back to the 1970s – the third period discussed above – when Swedish neoliberals first sketched a counter-attack against what was perceived as a *Swedish way to serfdom.*[18] After a while the counter-attack got strong backing from the Swedish employers' association and in 1992 Sweden became the pioneer in the real-life use of the Friedmanian 'voucher plan' for schools.

An important aspect of Sweden becoming a front-runner in financialisation of HEW was the weak resistance from Swedish Social Democracy. Among the explanations suggested was the widespread criticism – also on the left – of the standardised methods applied when, for example, education went through a thorough-going expansion and modernisation from the 1960s onwards. The reluctance from municipal authorities to accept, let alone encourage, experiments with new pedagogic ideas *à la* Montessori or Freire is a case in point.

Some important early moves in the direction of commodification/financialisation of HEW were taken by a centre-right government in the early 1990s. But when the Social Democrats returned to power in 1994 the forces for continuing in the direction of HEW financialisation were already rather entrenched – also within parts of Social Democracy.

With historical hindsight the arguments used for introducing capitalist competition into the provision of schooling were rather insidious. The kind of schools which were to be given a (second) chance included parents' cooperatives, remote village schools threatened by closure and schools specialised in niche subjects.

After 'consolidation' of the private HEW sectors in the first decade of the 21st century, the markets were, however, dominated by a few huge corporations often domiciled in tax havens. The idealists of the 1980s did not stand a chance when confronted with giants who could profit from i.a.:

- expertise in presenting tenders adapted to public procurement rules, being able to 'pick and choose' the most 'profitable' students, patients, elders or other 'clients';
- secrecy when not under pressure from the openness rules for the public sector or openness expectations from the membership.

In 2011 the business-sponsored think tank SNS published an evaluation of the introduction of competition in the HEW sectors. Translated, the title could be *The Consequences of Competition – What's Happening to Swedish Welfare* and the report was written by a group of highly regarded researchers (Hartman 2011).

In a chapter on education the researcher mentions the risk that the actors will base their choice of schools on criteria such as 'generosity' in the grading of students, 'feel-good' factors and the socioeconomic composition of the parents. In another chapter – on elder care – a tentative conclusion is that competition has led to deterioration of quality in *both* public and private parts of the sector. Both parts now focus on lowering prices through reducing costs.

The editor of the report – Hartman – resigned from the think tank SNS when she wasn't allowed to respond to critique from the 'HEW financialisation lobby'. Since SNS was hitherto considered to be reasonably independent, a heated debate ensued after her resignation.

Commodification/financialisation of HEW remains a 'contested terrain' in Sweden. Public sentiment in this field has been changing. Mistrust against the public sector was common in the early 1990s. But in 2012, when asked about the idea of limiting profits in the welfare sector, most respondents were in favour. When answering a survey in 2012 altogether 62% considered it a good idea (42% strongly in favour, 20% in favour). Part of the background to the shift in public opinion was a number of scandals associated with large private risk capital HEW companies.

'The ideal country for financialisation'

The phrase 'ideal country for financialisation' comes from Stenfors (2014: 15). I can partially agree with this description of Sweden but not with Stenfors' arguments for it. I might with sadness call Sweden between the 1970s and now, the 'ideal country for social capital depreciation'.

My aim when using Stenfors (2014) is to show what you might see when viewing Swedish financialisation with sympathetic eyes. First a quote from his executive summary:

> the . . . transformation of . . . Swedish society . . . that began in the 1980s . . . can be summarised as follows:

> *First* – . . .
>
> *Fourth*, neoliberalism (as defined broadly) has penetrated the Swedish society profoundly, . . . the country has transformed itself from a role model for those wishing to implement reforms often associated with [Swedish Social Democracy] to a 'poster boy' for European parties on the Right
>
> . . .
>
> *Seventh*, the financialisation process has become highly visible in overall 'daily life', not least as market mechanisms have been encouraged to enter previously 'sacred' areas, such as housing, education, health care and pensions.
>
> (Stenfors 2014: 10–12)

Many of the features share traits with the pension reforms that turned 'working population (past, present and future) into investors and risk managers'.

On the new pension system itself Stenfors says i.a.:

> – In 2012 almost all adult Swedes are exposed to mutual funds directly or indirectly.
>
> Seen in comparison to the Swedish GDP, stock market turnover rapidly increased from less than 8% to over 200% (before the outbreak of the global financial crisis).
>
> (Stenfors 2014: 155, 128 and 29–30)

The financialisation of everyday life is also intensively sensed by all Swedes. A Swedish author reflects:

> The apartments in the house where I live are turned into individual private property. In the private school a lower proportion of the kids drop out.
>
> . . . Shall I then sacrifice myself? My son? My home? Of course not. And thus we all become parts of a system which we have not chosen ourselves – into which we have been forced.
>
> (Lundberg 2014: 14)

Swedes thus feel forced away from solidarity 'at gunpoint'. Returning to an academic socioeconomic language I quote from Stenfors' summary of Clark and Johnson (2009):

> structural changes in housing policies in the 1990s had significant consequences in a range of areas: a decline in new construction and a rise in vacancies; an increase [in] crowded housing conditions; an increase in privatisation and outsourcing of housing planning; an increasing segmentation in terms of gaps between different forms of tenure; the closing of municipal housing agencies and the abandonment of social housing commitments; . . . and a social polarisation manifested in growing 'supergentrification' and low-income filtering.[19]

The structural changes in housing policies combined with lowered ambitions regarding balanced regional growth had foreseeable effects on real-estate price developments – falling prices in peripheral areas and sky-rocketing prices in the centre. For instance, the real-estate price index for one- or two-dwelling buildings for permanent living in the three largest urban areas in Sweden rose from 100 in the early 1980s to between 700 and 800 in the second decade of the 21st century.

A precondition for financialisation is what Stenfors (2014) refers to as 'market-oriented reforms'.

> During the last few decades, a range of industries and services have been opened up to competition, either through direct privatisation of state-owned companies, or by allowing profit-maximising companies to enter the market. . . . with regards to areas such as taxi, mail, childcare and education, Sweden could be regarded as a 'front-runner' . . .

Other remarkable aspects of the Swedish financialisation process are less visible to all Swedes: 'Within the international foreign exchange markets, Sweden has evolved from being perceived as a volatile, unpredictable country during the late 1980s and early 1990s to gradually gaining a "safe-haven" status' (Stenfors 2014: 88 and 11).

A very important development – in fact, a cornerstone in the global transformation to *financialised capitalism* – is also very noteworthy in Sweden.[20] I am referring to a development where non-financial corporations derive more and more of their incomes from financial activities:

> throughout the period [1995–2011], property income . . . has increased significantly as a share of total resources . . . This trend has been driven by an increase in dividend payments and other financial incomes obtained by non-financial corporations, . . . The high proportion of property income obtained by Swedish non-financial corporations is fairly high compared to other countries.
>
> (Stenfors 2014: 10)

Before ending this section it is reasonable to give an account of some of the points where I diverge from Stenfors' (sometimes implicit) analysis. This task is made easier since there are important similarities between the way in which 'the old Swedish model' was understood in *The Economist*'s Special Report (2013), discussed above, and the way in which Stenfors implicitly interprets the old model. For instance, when Stenfors claims that 'the Rehn–Meidner model could . . . be seen as a "third way" – by rejecting monetarism and questioning Keynesianism' . . . (Stenfors 2014: 131), he is ahistorical since monetarism was not around when the Rehn–Meidner model was conceived. But more importantly, the Rehn–Meidner model should to my mind be seen as a development of Keynesianism through combining it with a Marxist legacy. This development of Keynesianism was possible partly because of the strength of the Swedish union movement. Just as the 'old model' had nothing to do with 'pump-priming', it also in no way was something in between monetarism and Keynesianism.

More generally I miss *agency* in Stenfors' account. The victories of the Swedish model in the early post Second World War years were certainly partially fruits of historical legacies from way back. But they were also fruits of a very astute strategy developed by Social Democracy during the first half of the 20th century. And when the model was abandoned from the 1970s onwards it was certainly a consequence of international developments such as the fall of the Bretton Woods system. But, as I see it, it was also due to conscious and semi-conscious actions by those opposed to the gradual transformation of Sweden into less of a class society. To me the economic and industrial policies from 1976 to 1982 amounted to semi-conscious undermining of the model. Blyth (2002 i.a. in Ch. 7) has argued forcefully for agency. Moving closer to today, the weakening of unions from 2006 to 2014 was definitely conscious.

Two more critical points concerning Stenfors' analysis will be briefly mentioned:

1 The very significant developments surrounding the Swedish financial crisis and the Swedish application for membership to the EEC/EU in the early 1990s are hardly discussed at all.
2 When discussing HEW commodification, Stenfors again dodges away from the politics of the developments. He writes about how the public sector has developed from 'an instrument of social transformation' to a kind of neutral service producer: 'A number of market-oriented reforms have been passed in order to increase efficiency in the public sector by allowing private initiatives to operate in parallel' (Stenfors 2014: 89).

To my mind the changes made are just as much instruments of social transformation, although, of course, with other political aims.

My criticisms, however, do not change the fact that the FESSUD project has done a great service to economics by supporting Stenfors in providing a uniquely comprehensive overview of a remarkable example of financialisation.

Finding contours of the next great transformation – are there still lessons to be learned from Northern legacies of reciprocity and redistribution?

The heading for my final section of this chapter replicates the name of the Cyprus Symposium Special Session on Polanyi as well as the contribution on which this chapter is constructed.

Here I will use the Swedish case to discuss the 'contemporary relevance of Karl Polanyi' using concepts introduced earlier in the chapter. After that I'll exemplify how the reduction of reciprocity and redistribution may have undermined the Swedish model, as well as whether there are still resilient features of the model which might be useful for the future. Finally I will point to three examples of ideas which can help us continue to hope in spite of all the lessons *not* to be learned from the many 'detours' of the last 40 years.

Contemporary relevance

The Swedish case underlines the centrality of finance. The financial policy changes of the late 1980s are central if you want to understand 'the Swedish U-turn'. Polanyi and the multi-faceted research community inspired by his works are rare in the 'sustainability sciences' in clearly identifying the economic sphere as central for the dangers of humanity's present course. Polanyi's analysis of *fictitious commodities* made clear that it is the very web of life that is at stake when money is converted into a (fictitious) commodity.[21]

The Swedish case is also especially poignant in calling forth the idea that Polanyi's list of fictitious commodities might have to be extended. This is because the financialisation of Swedish HEW has been so dramatic.

A key lesson from Polanyi's Great Transformation is that the *counter-movements* unleashed by *laissez-faire* (or today's counterpart, neoliberalism) may come from right-wing populists or even fascists. Forty years ago there were few social scientists who saw the risks of right-wing populists in a country like Sweden. Today the Swedish populist right party the Sweden Democrats has, according to reliable surveys, won ≈ 20% of electoral support (up from ≈3% in parliament elections in 2006 and ≈ 13% in parliamentary elections in 2014) and an MP of the party has got away with instigating mass acts of arson against buildings planned to be converted into housing for refugees.[22]

As suggested above (third tension), the concept of *reciprocity* points to yet another 'blind spot' – at least in important parts of the social science community. The importance and future relevance of reciprocity therefore remain 'under-explored'. But happily there are now – even among prominent economists – dissenting voices who suggest a 'coming age of reciprocity'. *Community governance* can serve as a description not only of 'peripheral' or traditional modes of cooperation but also of evolving patterns of the future.[23]

The Swedish case can nurture this idea that reciprocity – seriously suppressed during modernity – will re-emerge as an important principle.

Resilient features

This brings me over to some resilient features with roots in developments from the 1930s to the 1970s. Above I pointed to gender equality, ecological sustainability and workplace codetermination as areas where there were attempts to develop rather than dismantle 'the old model'. More generally I suggest that the traditions of 'democracy from below', transparency, reciprocity and equality can be revived and actually still show their promising faces on many occasions. Many innovations on which Sweden still builds much of its material fortunes are, as I argued above, a heritage from the times when there was more room than today for constructively challenging the elites.

Contours

The very era which *The Economist* calls a 'period of decline' (≈ 1965–1990) can actually be seen as one when seeds of a coming great transformation were first nurtured. Better *gender equality* has resulted in social innovations which can facilitate a balance not only between the genders but also between different spheres of life. A case in point is that the parental leave insurance system encourages sharing child care. *Workplace codetermination* laws may very well have paved the way for less cumbersome transitions to more horizontal ways of working together. One aspect in which reciprocity may re-emerge on a societal scale might thus be as *peer-to-peer-production*. And readiness to embrace *ecological sustainability* has opened up for many innovations.

The example of ecological sustainability as one harbinger leads to three very different books relevant for reflections on a 'possible Swedish/Nordic contribution' to finding contours of the next great transformation.

The 2016 yearbook of the Swedish Society for Nature Conservation has the theme 'Ägodela – köp mindre, . . .'; in English, something like 'OwnShare – Buy less, get access to more' (SNF 2016). The book features non-commercial examples of the sharing economy in fields such as mobility, housing, clothing and food. The social and material innovations point – at a practical level – far beyond our present society.

At a more systemic level Eric Helleiner is also visionary in his 20-year-old idea of re-embedding at many levels (Helleiner 1995). Above I stated that the Bretton Woods system created a partial re-embedding of global finance. I suggested that the environment created thereby was important for the Swedish Post Second World War model.[24] There were similar experiences in the other Nordic countries. When trying to revive 'democracy from below', but now on a global scale, the idea of multi-layered re-embedding should be considered. Then the Nordic experiences could be useful.

Finally, some ideas from Paul Mason's recent book could suggest that Sweden might be well prepared for the networked postcapitalist society he envisions. Swedish information and communications technology density is very high, collaborative work patterns are reasonably frequent and the academic and other white-collar unions are better organised than elsewhere. According to Mason, we might learn a lot about the future by looking at Wikipedia, which is organised 'in a decentralized and collaborative way, utilizing neither the market nor management hierarchy'.[25] So; there may still be a few things to learn from Sweden's long history of reciprocity on the tortuous 'road to freedom'.

Notes

1 I often use *italics* to signal that a certain concept comes from a discourse which I don't have the space to explain. In some instances I provide concept-explaining references in this text. I am of course happy to communicate with readers about concepts which remain unclarified here.

2 'Building on tensions' is a '*signifier*' of some of my methodological convictions. One account of those can be found in Hollander (2011, pp. 14–23).

3 Henceforth referred to as *The Economist*'s Special Report (2013).
4 This note on references has to do i.a. with my *Swedish '1968' background.* Sweden is 'a small country' and many with '1968' backgrounds know each other, specially if we consider those of us who aspired to *be movement intellectuals* of the diverse set of *1968 red-green movements.* Even so, we are too numerous for me to give 'due cred' to even a fraction of those whose accounts – written or verbal – inspired my image of the rise, fall and lessons from the 'Swedish model'. And a lot of inspiration also comes from those who do not have a *'1968' background.* Disregarding backgrounds, quite a few inspirations go unmentioned here. Some can be found in references in the works of authors to whom I refer in my text. A case in point is Blyth (2002). Other examples of overviews are Ryner (several years) and Sandberg (2013). An author who also provides an overview but who goes unmentioned in my text except here is Hort (2014). Besides those to whom I directly or indirectly refer I provide here a list of names that you as a reader can 'Google' (for instance, use the intersection of one of the <names> and <Swedish (or Nordic) (Welfare) Model>. One criterion for inclusion is that their texts are available in English. Another is that they cover areas where there is a special dearth in my own text. None of those principles are followed consistently: Klas Åmark, Irene Wennemo, Asbjørn Wahl, Claudius Riegler (mainly in German), Victor Pestoff, Rudolf Meidner (at least one book co-authored with Anna Hedborg), Andrew Martin, Rianne Mahon, Kurt Lundgren, Staffan I. Lindberg, Andrew Jamison, Annika Härenstam, Kaj Frick, Christian Berggren, Lars Bengtsson, Gösta Esping Andersen.
5 The phrase *re-emergence of global finance* is inspired by Helleiner (1994).
6 Sources for this 'intro to Swedish historical accumulation of social capital' include: Trägårdh (2007) and de Vylder (1996).
7 The capital control regime of the early post World War II period is discussed i.a. in Helleiner (1994, 1995).
8 See Erixon (2010), Haley and Hollander (2006) and Hollander (2011) as well as references therein.
9 Concerning the 'wide section of the Swedish elite' see Ingebritsen (1998, pp. 143 ff).
10 *The Economist*'s Special Report (2013: 5).
11 The concept *demand shaper* is presented in Hollander (2003). There you will also find more examples of innovations nurtured by sophisticated demands.
12 According to the *The Economist*'s Special Report, 'the Nordic countries have reached the future first'.
13 When I talk about 'the Polanyian period' it is based on the idea – mentioned above – that there are important parallels between the disembedding effected by the *laissez-faire* policies of the century leading up to World War I and those effected by the neoliberal policy period from ≈ 1975. 'The Polanyian period' also includes the period from 1918 to 1939 when all kinds of *countermovements* – left and right, democratic and authoritarian – emerged. Polanyi wrote *The Great Transformation* in 1944. I got inspiration for talking of a 'Polanyian period' and for exploring the parallels from Helleiner (1995, 1999).
14 Ryner (2004: 13). Also the following account is built extensively on Ryner (several years).
15 Concerning the phrase 'health, child care, schooling, care for the elderly' I will henceforth sometimes use the US acronym HEW (health, education and welfare). There are, of course, many differences between Swedish and Anglo 'welfare systems', but I will not go into them here.
16 Werne and Unsgaard (2014). Polanyi's book is Polanyi (1944).
17 See Friedman and Friedman (1979) for the original Friedmanian plan.
18 The 'way to serfdom' refers to Hayek's term. Swedish neoliberals were worried about a 'Swedish way to serfdom' and studied Hayek and his follower Milton Friedman intensively.

19 Stenfors (2014: 114), summarising Clark and Johnson (2009).
20 On the 'global transformation to financialised capitalism', see Orhangazi (2008).
21 See the introduction to this chapter as well as Hollander *et al.* (2015).
22 That a Polanyian framework might predict such a surge in right-wing populism was also mentioned in the introduction. Such a prediction could also be reached by an entirely different – quantitative – approach. This was recently demonstrated by Funke *et al.* (2015).
23 See my interpretations of some prominent economists in Hermele and Hollander (2008: 7–8).
24 A special thanks to Gary Dymski, who encouraged me to explore this aspect of Swedish history.
25 See Mason (2015 i.a. Ch. 5). Ideas related to the concept of *peer-to-peer-production* are presented there.

References

Belfrage, C. and Ryner, M. (2009) 'Renegotiating the Swedish Social Democratic Settlement – From Pension Fund Socialism to Neoliberalization' *Politics & Society* 37: 257–287.

Bengtsson, H. (2014) *Arena* #5. Stockholm: Bokförlaget Arena, pp. 17–18.

Blyth, M. (2002) *Great Transformations: Economic Ideas and Institutional Change in the Twentieth Century*. Cambridge: Cambridge University Press.

Carlén, S., Persson, C. and Suhonen, D. (2014) *Reinfeldtkoden* – . . . [in Swedish]. Stockholm: Ordfront.

Clark, E. and Johnson, K. (2009) 'Circumventing Circumscribed Neoliberalism: The System Switch in Swedish Housing' In: Glynn, S. (ed.) *Where the Other Half Lives: Lower Income Housing in a Neoliberal World.* London: Pluto, pp. 173–194.

de Vylder, S. (1996) '*The Rise and Fall of the Swedish Model*', UNDP Occasional Paper No. 26. New York: UNDP – Human Development Report Office.

Erixon, L. (2010) 'The Rehn-Meidner Model in Sweden: Its Rise, Challenges and Survival' *Journal of Economic Issues* 44: 677–715.

Friedman, M. and Friedman, R. (1979) *Free to Choose: A Personal Statement*. New York: Harcourt.

Funke, M., Schularick, M. and Trebesch, C. (2015) '*Going to Extremes: Politics after Financial Crises, 1870–2014*'. CEPR Discussion Paper No. DP10884. Munich: Centre for Economic Policy Research (CEPR).

Haley, B. and Hollander, E. (2006) 'Advanced Sustainability Demands from Labour: Re-embedding for Democracy and Ecology'. Unpublished book: manuscript is available from me/(EH).

Hartman, L. (ed.) (2011) *Konkurrensens konsekvenser: Vad händer med svensk välfärd?* [The Consequences of Competition: What's Happening to Swedish Welfare]. Stockholm: SNS Förlag.

Hayek, F.A. (2001) *The Road to Serfdom.* London: Routledge.

Helleiner, E. (1994) *States and the Reemergence of Global Finance.* Ithaca: Cornell University Press.

Helleiner, E. (1995) 'Great Transformations: A Polanyian Perspective on the Contemporary Global Financial Order' *Studies in Political Economy* (SPE) 48: 149–164.

Helleiner, E. (1999) 'Globalization and Haute Finance: Déja vu?' Reproduced in McRobbie, K. & Polanyi Levitt, K. (eds.) *Karl Polanyi in Vienna: The Contemporary Significance of the Great Transformation.* Montreal: Black Rose Books, Ch. 2, pp. 12–31.

Hermele, K. and Hollander, E. (2008) 'Taking Sustainability into Account' In: Frostell, B., et al. (eds.) (2008) *Science for Sustainable Development: The Social Challenge with Emphasis on the Conditions for Change*. Uppsala: VHU. (The full manuscript is available from me – EH.)

Hollander, E. (2003) 'The Noble Art of Demand Shaping: How the Tenacity of Sustainable Innovation can be Explained by it Being Radical in a New Sense', Contribution to 11th international GIN (GIN = Greening of Industry Network), conference in San Francisco. (Unpublished contribution which is available from me – EH.)

Hollander, E. (2011) *The Doll, the Globe and the Boomerang: Chemical Risks in the Future – Introduced by a Chinese Doll Coming to Sweden*. Research Report 2. Gävle: University of Gävle.

Hollander, E., Hermele, K., Negru, I. and Dymski G. (2015) *Using Polanyian Concepts to Bring Together Sustainability Discourses*. Special session at the 11th ESEE conference in Leeds.

Hort, S. E. O. (2014) *Social Policy, Welfare State, and Civil Society in Sweden, Volume II: The Lost World of Social Democracy 1988–2015*. Lund: Arkiv.

Ingebritsen, C. (1998) *The Nordic States and European Unity*. Ithaca: Cornell University Press.

Lindberg, I. and Ryner, M. (2010) 'Financial Crises and Organized Labour: Sweden 1990–94' *International Journal of Labour Research* 2(1): 25–41.

Lundberg, K. (2014) *Det här är inte mitt land* [in Swedish]. Stockholm: Atlas.

Mason, P. (2015) *Post Capitalism: A Guide to Our Future*. London: Allen Lane.

OECD (2011) *Divided we Stand: Why Inequality Keeps Rising*. Paris: OECD.

Orhangazi, Ö. (2008) 'Financialisation and Capital Accumulation in the Non-financial Corporate Sector – A Theoretical and Empirical Investigation on the US economy 1973–2003' *Cambridge Journal of Economics* 32: 863–886.

Östberg, K. (2012) 'Swedish Social Democracy after the Cold War', In: Schmidt, I. and Evans, B. (eds.) *Social Democracy after the Cold War*. Athabasca: Athabasca University Press.

Polanyi, K. (1933 [1999]) [translated to English]. In McRobbie, K. and Polanyi Levitt, K. (eds.), *Karl Polanyi in Vienna: The Contemporary Significance of the Great Transformation*. Montreal: Black Rose Books, Ch. 31. pp. 347–358.

Polanyi, K. (1944) *The Great Transformation*. Boston: Beacon Press.

Polanyi, K., Arensberg, C. M. and Pearson, H. W. (eds.) (1957) *Trade and Market in the Early Empires: Economies in History and Theory*. Illinois: The Free Press.

Rothstein, B. and Trägårdh, L. (2007) In: Trägårdh, L. (ed.), *State and Civil Society in Northern Europe – The Swedish Model Reconsidered*. Oxford: Berghahn Books, Ch. 8.

Ryner, M. (2004) 'Neoliberalization of Social Democracy: The Swedish Case', *Comparative European Politics* 2: 97–119.

Sandberg, Å. (ed.) (2013) *Nordic Lights: Work, Management and Welfare in Scandinavia*. Stockholm: SNS Förlag.

SNF (2016) '*Ägodela: Köp mindre – få tillgång till mer*' [OwnShare – Buy less, get access to more]. Stockholm: Svenska Naturskyddsföreningen (SNF).

Stenfors, A. (2014) 'FESSUD Studies on Financial Systems, No 13: The Swedish Financial System'. Available at: http://fessud.eu/deliverables/.

The Economist's Special Report. (2013, February 2) *Northern Lights: The Nordic Countries are Reinventing their Model of Capitalism*. London: The Economist.

Trägårdh, L. (ed.) (2007) *State and Civil Society in Northern Europe: The Swedish Model Reconsidered*. Oxford: Berghahn Books.

Werne, K. and Unsgaard, O. F. (eds.) (2014) *Den stora ovandlingen: En granskning av välfärdsmarknaden*. Stockholm: Leopard.

5 Marx through Goodwin

Carlo D'Ippoliti and Marco Ranaldi

As is well known, Goodwin (1955) determined a set of minimum conditions for aggregate activity, and specifically output growth, to present cyclical dynamics. In his seminal contribution (1967), significantly titled "A Growth Cycle," these conditions are represented through Volterra's model and relate in particular to occupational levels and distributive shares. With this model, Goodwin integrated the Marxian notion of class struggle for the distribution of income with Keynes' insight that potential output need not be constantly realized, but rather demand is a fundamental driver of economic activity.

In doing so, Goodwin (1985) himself informs us that he was following Harrod's intuition ("buried beneath is totally inept formalism") that "the economy is endogenously explosive, but endogenously constrained by full employment" (p. 11). Crucial inspiration for the model was Schumpeter's insight that "neither growth nor cycle would exist without the other" (Goodwin 1985, p. 10), whereas "Frisch misled a generation of investigators by resolving the problem with exogenous shocks" (Goodwin, 1990, p. 10).

Goodwin's model inspired a rich evolutionary and mostly post-Keynesian literature (recently reviewed by von Arnim and Barrales, 2015). Usually by modifying one of the seven foundational equations of his model, these authors focus on the impact of demand and functional income distribution on cyclical growth. Closest to our analysis is perhaps the recent contribution by Tavani and Zamparelli (2015), who investigate the impact of adding research and development (R&D) expenditure in the model. However, they do so within a framework of rational, optimizing agents, which Goodwin himself criticized: with chaotic dynamics, "a completely deterministic system produces unpredictable behavior. . . . Therefore the very basis empirically of rational prediction is destroyed" (Goodwin, 1990, p. vi).

Despite the success of his model, still in 1985 Goodwin considered it to be "unsatisfactory" (p. 10). The model was missing crucial Schumpeterian elements related to innovations, which Goodwin regarded as fundamental. These elements would be developed further when Goodwin's interests moved to chaotic models: "innovation is crucial to cycle theory because, in depression, with generalized excess capacity, there is no other basis for the new investment necessary to generate a new expansion" (Goodwin, 1990, p. 21). Thus, while Goodwin (1985) called himself a Keynesian, Hanappi (2014) rightly portrays him as Schumpeter's "assistant" (interestingly, Goodwin, 1990, in turn portrays Schumpeter as Marx's "most eccentric but important follower").

In his 1990 book, Goodwin introduces a third equation to better represent technical progress, adapting his original adoption of the Lotka–Volterra equations to fit Rössler's model. In this way, he developed a number of models aimed at representing short (Juglar's) and long (Kondratiev's) innovations-induced waves of economic activity, which were one of Schumpeter's main contributions to the history and theory of business cycles (Schumpeter, 1934).

In the book, Goodwin repeatedly affirms that there is "agreement" and "consensus" based on historical evidence for assuming that innovation comes in such short and long waves (which prompted him to use a logistic functional form to represent innovative investments); he only excluded the very short waves (Kitchin's) because they do not involve innovative activity. He followed Schumpeter almost fully on this point (with the only difference of assuming a "controlling" role for the state by means of income generating expenditure, in the most advanced models). So, when earlier describing the logic of his formalization of Schumpeter's intuition, he had even complained that mathematical terms might induce misunderstandings: "delivering a single pulse in response to a sufficient shock, the system is perhaps better called a pulsator rather than an oscillator" (Goodwin, 1985, p. 11).

In this work, we build on Goodwin's model, but we depart both from these later developments of his thought and from the above-mentioned post-Keynesian literature focusing on empirical applications of Goodwin's model or on specific variations of one or more of its hypotheses. Rather, we are interested here in investigating to what extent Goodwin's model can accommodate some crucial Marxian insights, considering how Marx was always one of its inspirations, and what are the consequences in terms of the model's predictions.

Specifically, when considering the relevance of technical progress, by then only unsatisfactorily considered within his model, Goodwin (1985) states: "surely Schumpeter was right to maintain that essential to the analysis is the reduction of inputs per unit of output, especially in the labour content of output" (p. 9). However, this intuition was well developed by Marx as well. Indeed, a frequently overlooked contribution by Marx is the treatment of growth and cycles within a unified conceptual framework. As is the case for Schumpeter, in Marx's analysis long-term and short-term dynamics are not independent, but rather the process of capitalist development exhibits cyclical oscillations. However, in Marx's treatment this is not a consequence of waves of innovations, but of dynamic substitution of capital for labor.

As already Ricardo hinted at, at the end of each business cycle, as a result of embodied technical progress, capitalists have at their disposal a more productive capital stock, which allows for more capital-intensive production techniques (Roncaglia, 2005). Such process implies that the initial conditions of each successive cycle are different from the previous one, implying an integration of cyclical developments in a growth framework.

We study the consequences of such a hypothesis – as well as the integration of some aspects of Marx's longer-term view, embedded in one of the laws of motion of the capitalist mode of production – on the main variables of Goodwin's model, i.e., employment and distributive shares. To do so, we employ the formulation of the model developed by Alfredo Medio in his 1979 Ph.D. thesis in economics, supervised in Cambridge by Kaldor and Goodwin himself.

Marx's theory of the business cycle and growth

A review of the economic and historical literature on Marx exceeds the scope of this work – and most probably the limits of any journal article (we refer the interested reader to the contributions and literature in Fine et al., 2012). Here we focus on a very specific aspect of Marx's thought that seems to have been often overlooked (Roncaglia, 2005). Marx's theory of the business cycle, or rather of cyclical development, stands out in the history of economic thought as one of the few attempts – along with Schumpeter's – to theorize aggregate fluctuations and economic growth not as separate analytical problems, but as interrelated aspects of the same economic phenomenon. Without any pretense to comprehensiveness or analytical profundity, it seems appropriate to very shortly recall it here.

As is well known, in Book II of *Das Kapital* [*Capital*], Marx introduced his schemes of reproduction. Among other things, these were aimed at showing that a capitalist economy does not occur as a problem of overproduction if the whole surplus is consumed for unproductive purposes (simple reproduction) or is invested in the creation of new capital (enlarged reproduction). Indeed, from the point of view of accumulation and creation of productive capacity, as well as technological progress, Marx held a favorable view of capitalism (e.g., in Marx and Engels, 1848) – not to mention the necessity of this stage of development in the dialectic historical process leading to socialism.

However, Marx identified a number of laws of motion of the capitalist mode of production, many of which imply an evidently bleak view of capitalism: growing income polarization accumulates as a consequence of the tendency to concentration and centralization of capital (which expels capitalists from the upper to the laboring class) and the proletarization of ever larger masses of people; crises become increasingly violent due to the tendency of the organic composition of capital to increase and of the rate of profit to fall. As is well known, these trends lay the "scientific ground" for predicting the inevitable substitution of capitalism with a more advanced mode of production.

Between these two "poles" of analysis, the favorable and the unfavorable views of capitalism, lies Marx's original theory of cyclical development. In Marx's work, the dynamics of business cycles are based on fluctuations of the industrial reserve army (which strictly speaking encompasses not only the unemployed but also the underemployed ready to change employment, especially those working in agriculture or other backwards industries) and their impact on wages.

In the upward phase, incomes grow and the industrial reserve army shrinks. This gradually brings about a shift in bargaining power favorable to workers, who will demand higher wages. However, the growth of real wages produces a growth of labor costs, which induces firms to introduce more capital-intensive methods of production, substituting workers with machines. The reduction in the reserve army is thus stopped and then reversed, and with it wages begin to stagnate (in the recession stage) and even fall (in depression). This process marks the downward phase of the cycle, which is however reversed as increased mechanization brings about higher productivity, which implies a reduction in the costs of labor per unit of output and thus a growth in the profit rate (on Marx's views on mechanization, see Roth, 2010). Recovered profitability ignites the beginning of a new ascending phase, with firms beginning to hire again, and the reserve army stabilizing and then shrinking again.

Evidently, this new cycle starts from a higher level of productivity due to the accumulation of capital that has endogenously taken place in the previous cycle.

What we think should especially be highlighted here is that Marx's theory is at the same time a theory of technical change and a theory of the evolution over time of unemployment and of the distributive shares of income.

The latter aspect has been especially taken up by Richard Goodwin in his model of the business cycle, which then became an analytical reference point for several Marxian and non-Marxian scholars (for a history of the development of Goodwin's thought on aggregate dynamics, see Sordi and Vercelli, 2006).

Separately, the theory of technical change implied by the dynamic substitution of machines for workers, which may be traced back at least to the third edition of David Ricardo's *Principles* (Roncaglia, 2005), has been studied by various post-Keynesian authors (in particular Sylos Labini, 1984). In what follows, we attempt an experiment at investigating what impact the inclusion of the "machinery effect" has on Goodwin's model.

A representation of Goodwin's model

The mathematical formulation of Goodwin's model resembles the system of differential equations independently developed by Vito Volterra (1860–1940) and Alfred J. Lotka (1880–1949). As is well known, the pair of equations was aimed at studying the problem of "biological association" by formally representing the cohabitation of two species in a closed environment, one assumed to represent a predator, the other prey. Following Medio (1979), the model can be represented as follows:

$$\dot{l} = L(w,l) = (\alpha - \beta w)l \tag{1}$$

$$\dot{w} = W(w,l) = (-\gamma + \delta l)w \tag{2}$$

where the following relations hold:

$$\alpha = \beta - (x+n) \tag{3}$$

$$\gamma = v + x \tag{4}$$

and where β is the income (Y) to capital (K) ratio, l is the employment rate, w is the labor share of gross domestic product (GDP) (W/Y), x is an exogenous rate of technical progress, n is an exogenous rate of population growth, and v is the rate of change of the labor share when $\dot{l} = 0$.

As highlighted in Medio's Ph.D. thesis, this formulation implies a number of specific assumptions. Some such hypotheses are only implicit, e.g., there are only two inputs of production (labor and capital) and all variables are expressed in real terms (that is, there is no money in the model); while some of these assumptions concern the mathematical representation of the model's parameters, e.g., the exogeneity and constancy of the rates of change of population and of technical progress, or they more closely concern the economic interpretation of the model, e.g., β denoting a constant capital/income ratio or the implicit hypothesis that salaries are fully consumed and profits fully invested.

The model, as is well known, purports to study the aggregate fluctuations of a closed economy (compare, e.g., Goodwin, 1967). Business cycles are produced by the structural nonlinearity of the system implied by the multiplicative terms in (1) and (2). In a nutshell, the model predicts that in the "boom" phase high profits produce high investments that sustain economic growth; as the employment rate (l) grows, salaries grow too, raising the wage bill ratio to GDP (w). The increase in w, however, reduces investments, producing an increase in unemployment (i.e., a reduction of l); this in turn induces a reduction of the wage share, until profits start growing again.

In several aspects – e.g., the influence of the "reserve army" of the unemployed on wage growth, or the capitalists' drive to accumulate expressed by the implicit assumption that all profits are invested – this model recalls several interesting Marxian concepts, some of which were shortly recalled above. However, since both w and l are constrained to take on values between 0 and 1 (under plausible assumptions), the choice of the space (w, l) allows us to consider economic cycles – as it were – independently of the growth process (this is of course a consequence of the choice of the space in which to represent the model, not a feature of the model itself).

Goodwin was aware of the limitations of considering cycles and growth as independent phenomena, even just from the mathematical point of view. For example, in case of nonlinearity (as in the model presented here) it is not possible to formally separate a time trend from a cycle. As mentioned above, among the economic reasons for considering cycle and growth as manifestations of the same complex phenomenon, Goodwin (1955) highlights Schumpeter's theory of the business cycle. Specifically, Goodwin agrees with Schumpeter (1934) that the ultimate driver of the growth process must be technological innovations (he adds, coupled with population growth), and that perturbations in the growth process originate from such innovations taking place in "clusters." However, differently from Schumpeter, he formalizes such intuition in a framework that does not disregard Keynes' notion of effective demand. Differently from this road, we instead aim here to propose an alternative modification of Goodwin's original model, aimed at partly representing a crucial feature of Marx's own theory of the business cycle. This will be done in the next section by modifying the model's assumptions concerning investments and technological progress.

Introducing new assumptions

Given what was said on the integration of growth and cycle, it seems convenient to modify the model presented here specifically concerning the hypothesis of a constant rate of technical progress. As recognized by Ricardo and Marx, an increase of workers' real wages induces capitalists to invest and replace workers with machines, i.e., to increase what Marx called "constant capital" (c) at the expense of Marx's "variable capital" (v).

Accordingly, in our model we introduce the assumption $I = f(w)$, with $f_w > 0$. In turn, this process induces technical progress "embodied" in the new capital goods (i.e., the fact that new machinery is more productive than older ones). As a consequence, the rate of technical progress too becomes an endogenous variable in the model, positively correlated with the wage level:

$$x = g(w) \text{ with } g_w > 0.$$

This relation is analogous to what Sylos Labini (1984) called the "Ricardo effect" of a positive impact of wage growth (in his treatment, relative to the price of capital goods) on productivity. Assuming linearity of both f and g, we obtain

$$x = \xi w.$$

However, as mentioned, we are also interested in analyzing the suitability of the model to represent some aspects of Marx's theory at a larger level. For this reason, the specific way in which technical progress has been introduced in the model, i.e., through an increase in the "organic composition of capital" (c/v), seems to require also a modification of β. Indeed, the term βw in equation 1 is equal to $\beta w = \frac{Y}{K} \cdot \frac{W}{Y} = \frac{W}{K}$, which in this model is the inverse of the organic composition of capital.

In this framework, the tendency to the increase in the organic composition of capital, predicted by Marx, is linked to the parallel tendency of the rate of profit to fall (although this is not necessarily true in a multi-commodity world, as shown by Schefold, 1976). Indeed, since the profit rate is $\pi = \frac{Y-S}{K}$,

$$\pi = \frac{Y-S}{K} = \frac{Y}{K}\left(1 - \frac{W}{Y}\right) = \beta(1-w)$$

and since $1 \geq w \geq 0$ it immediately follows that β and π move in the same direction. Incidentally, recent literature finds an empirical tendency towards a "gradual rise of wealth–income ratios in recent decades" in developed economies (Piketty and Zucman, 2014).

In order to reduce the analytical complexity of the problem, we introduce Marx's law(s) of motion of capitalism as an exogenous trend. Therefore, β is a decreasing function of time:

$$\beta = g(t) = \varepsilon + e^{-t} \text{ with } \varepsilon > 0.$$

The additive term ε has no economic interpretation. Indeed, it constrains β to be larger than 1, which is highly unrealistic, since e^{-t} is a number between 0 and 1 for positive values of t. However, the assumption is instrumental in shifting the following graphical analysis in the desired quadrant.

Effects of the modifications to the model

In order to plug into the model our two new hypotheses, it is necessary to replace two parameters by two functions. Essentially, we make endogenous two exogenous variables. Thus, the new system is:

$$\dot{l} = L(w,l) = l(\beta - n - \beta w) - xl = l\left(\varepsilon + e^{-t} - n - \left(\varepsilon + e^{-t}\right)w\right) - \xi wl$$

$$\dot{w} = W(w,l) = w(-v + \delta l) - mw = w(-v + \delta l) - \xi w^2$$

By considering e^{-t} as a constant, the only stable point of interest, i.e., the stable point with positive coordinates, is $A = (a_1, a_2)$, where: $a_1 = \frac{1 + e^{-t} - n}{1 + e^{-t} + \xi}$ and $a_2 = \frac{\xi a_1 + v}{\delta}$. However, since e^{-t} depends on time, we have as a result an infinity of stable points, which tend toward $\left(\frac{1-n}{1+\xi}, \frac{\xi\frac{1-n}{1+\xi} + v}{\delta}\right)$ when $t \to 0$. This result is shown in Figure 5.1.

In Figure 5.1 the stable points are the intersections between the red lines and the blue line. To improve clarity, the vertical axis represents the l values while the horizontal axis represents the ratio of salaries to income.

At this point, by studying the dynamic behavior of the new system around each stable point A_t, we notice that they are all attractive fires, which means that the system geometrically draws a spiral moving toward lower values of l and w and, at the same time, coils toward its stable points.

To show this mathematically, we need to start by defining the Jacobian matrix of the system:

$$D = \begin{pmatrix} \varepsilon + e^{-t} - n - \left(\varepsilon + e^{-t}\right)w - \xi w & -\left(\varepsilon + e^{-t}\right)l - \xi l \\ \delta w & -v + \delta l - 2\xi w \end{pmatrix}$$

If each stable point A_t is plugged into D, by writing its characteristic polynomial, we obtain that the eigenvalues of D are all necessarily complex conjugates with negative real numbers. Algebraically:

$$P_\gamma\left(a_1^t, a_2^t\right) = \left(\varepsilon + e^{-t} - n - \left(\varepsilon + e^{-t}\right)a_1^t - \xi a_1^t - \gamma\right)\left(-v + \delta a_2^t - 2\xi a_1^t - \gamma\right) - \left(-\left(\varepsilon + e^{-t}\right)a_2^t - \xi a_2^t\right)\left(\delta a_1^t\right)$$

where $P_\gamma\left(a_1^t, a_2^t\right)$ is the characteristic polynomial computed in $\left(a_1^t, a_2^t\right)$.

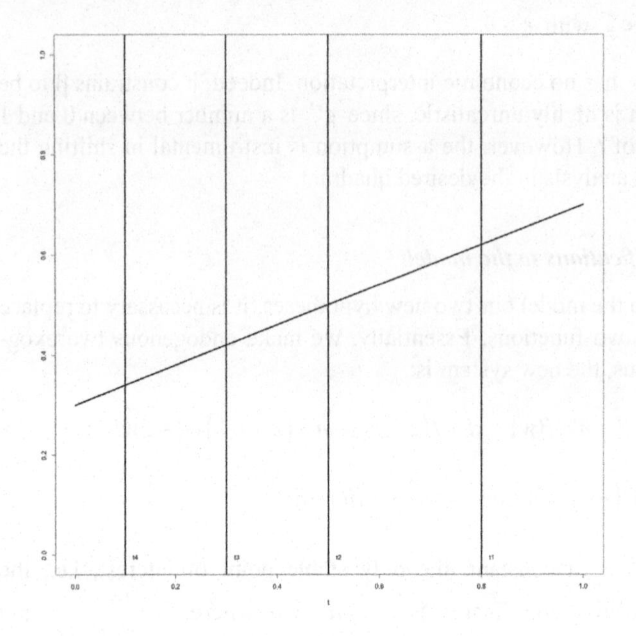

Figure 5.1 Stable points for different values of t

The roots of the polynomial give us information on the dynamic nature of the stable points. Its discriminant is as follows:

$$\begin{aligned}\varnothing =&\left(-\left(\varepsilon+e^{-t}-n-\left(\varepsilon+e^{-t}\right)a_1^t-\xi a_1^t\right)-\left(-v+\delta a_2^t-2\xi a_1^t\right)\right)^2\\&-4\left[\left(\varepsilon+e^{-t}-n-\left(\varepsilon+e^{-t}\right)a_1^t-\xi a_1^t\right)\left(-v+\delta a_2^t-2\xi a_1^t\right)\right.\\&\left.-\left(\delta a_1^t\right)\left(-\left(\varepsilon+e^{-t}\right)a_2^t-\xi a_2^t\right)\right]\end{aligned}$$

and by making the following realistic assumptions about the parameters:

$$a_1^t \in (0,1)\,\forall t$$
$$a_2^t \in (0,1)\,\forall t$$
$$n \cong 1$$
$$v \leq 1$$
$$\delta \geq 1$$
$$\xi \cong 1$$

we find that $\Delta < 0$. Furthermore, we notice that the sign of Δ will remain the same even by supposing less realistic hypotheses about the parameters (such as $n \neq 1$), which means the eigenvalues of the Jacobian matrix will always be complex numbers, therefore each stable point will be a fire.

At this stage of the analysis, it is necessary to check whether they are attractive, or rather repulsive fires. By considering the real number of the polynomial roots, we have:

$$Re(\gamma) = \left(\frac{\varepsilon + e^{-t} - n - \left(\varepsilon + e^{-t}\right)a_1^t - \xi a_1^t - v + \delta a_2^t - 2\xi a_1^t}{2} \right)$$

which due to our assumptions above is strictly negative ($Re(\gamma) < 0$). In addition, by simulating the quantities Δ and $Re(\gamma)$ respectively for different values of t and by using the previously given values for the parameters, we notice that each stable point related to the t-system is an attractive fire, as shown in Table 5.1.

Furthermore, to further increase the understanding of the qualitative behavior of the system, Figure 5.2 shows the phase diagrams related to a set of different stable points.

Some conclusions

The last period of Goodwin's life (the "Italian period") was characterized by the attempt to merge both cycle and growth issues in a single dynamic, mainly using the latest techniques adopted by many physicians of that time, i.e., chaos theory. Goodwin was fascinated by the Schumpeterian idea of formulating "economic evolution as technical progress in the shape of swarms," and he supported the

Table 5.1 Δ and $Re(\gamma)$ for different values of t

t	Δ	$Re(\lambda)$
0	–5.17222	–0.16667
1	–1.51411	–0.07768
2	–0.48353	–0.03169
3	–0.16643	–0.01214
4	–0.05959	–0.00454
5	–0.02169	–0.00168
6	–0.00795	–0.00062
7	–0.00292	–0.00023
8	–0.00107	–0.00008
9	–0.00039	–0.00003
10	–0.00015	–0.00001

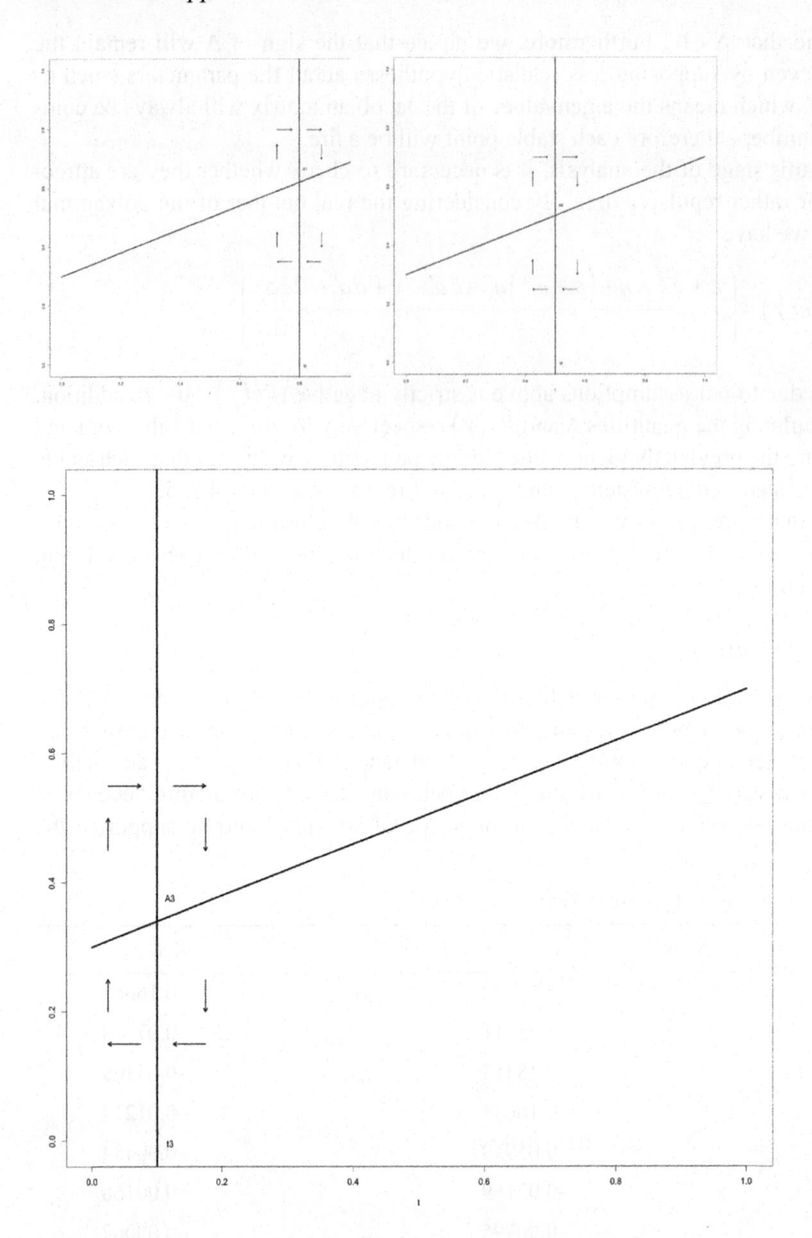

Figure 5.2 Phase diagrams for three different values of t

idea that a technological shift would not happen monotonically, but through a cyclical path.

To formulate this, a different version of the original model is adopted by the author, and an additional equation concerning innovative investments is introduced. These grow logistically, using our terminology, according to the quadratic function $mb\left(k-\frac{k^2}{c}\right)$. With the aim of formulating in one single system the whole problem of long and short waves "as a chaotic growth oscillator," he employed Rössler's model, through which the intrinsic nature of the system to vibrate within a wide range of different behaviors is envisaged. In addition, a bounded region of the phase space constrains the evolution of the system, consequently showing its lack of growth. Curiously, this too is a conclusion to which Schumpeter, in his later life, had arrived. In his *Capitalism, Socialism and Democracy*, Schumpeter (1942) characterizes innovation as an increasingly routine effort, materialized in the R&D expenditure of large corporations, which both dampens and regulates the discovery of new technologies.

On the whole, Goodwin's later approach, strongly characterized by chaos theory, does not allow clearly distinguishable patterns to be identified for its main variables of interest. He characterizes this result as implying "that this system exhibits the kind of irregularity characteristic of economic statistics" (Goodwin, 1990).

Differently from Goodwin's later ideas, the main objective of our work is to endogenize the technical progress as a linear function of the wage share of income, with the principal aim of keeping the dynamic as clear as possible from the economic point of view, and to avoid losing its symmetrical structure. However, our model too exhibits a tendency to a decrease in its fluctuations.

Indeed, the spiral drawn by the system tends towards the stable point $\left(a_1^{\infty},a_2^{\infty}\right)=\left(\frac{1-n}{1+\xi},\frac{\xi\frac{1-n}{1+\xi}+v}{\delta}\right)$. Hence, for $t\to+\infty$, $\dot{l}\to 0$ and $\dot{w}\to 0$.

Moreover, the system constantly moves towards the southwestern region of the plan, i.e., each new cycle begins with a lower level of the two variables. This implies that, in its cyclical growth, the economy becomes ever more capital-intensive, and that – among its oscillations –the industrial reserve army – to put it in Marxian terms – tends to grow over time.

These two results, broadly in line with some of Marx's laws of motion of capitalism, and possibly with recent empirical evidence, show that, while it is probably impossible to summarize all of Marx's several insights (even assuming agreement on their interpretation) into a single model, Goodwin's model can, to some extent, be used to try and translate in formal terms some of them.

References

Fine B., Saad-Filho A. and Boffo M. (2012), *The Elgar companion to Marxist economics*, Cheltenham: Edward Elgar.

Goodwin R.M. (1955), "A model of cyclical growth", in Lundberg E. (ed.), *The business cycle in the post-war world*, London: Macmillan.

Goodwin R.M. (1967), "A growth cycle", in Feinstein C.H. (ed.), *Socialism, capitalism and economic growth*, Cambridge: Cambridge University Press, pp. 54–58.

Goodwin R.M. (1985), "A personal perspective on mathematical economics", *Banca Nazionale del Lavoro Quarterly Review*, vol. 38 n. 152, pp. 3–11.

Goodwin R.M. (1990), *Chaotic economic dynamics*, Oxford: Clarendon Press.

Hanappi H. (2014), "Schumpeter and Goodwin", *MPRA Paper*, n. 59932, University Library of Munich.

Marx K. (1867–1894), *Das Kapital*, Hamburg: O. Meissner.

Marx K. and Engels F. (1848), *Manifest der Kommunistischen Partei*, London: J.E. Burghard.

Medio A. (1979), *Teoria non lineare del ciclo economico*, Bologna: Il Mulino.

Piketty T. and Zucman G. (2014), "Capital is back: wealth-income ratios in rich countries, 1700–2010", *The Quarterly Journal of Economics*, vol. 129 n. 3, pp. 1255–1310.

Roncaglia A. (2005), *The wealth of ideas*, Cambridge: Cambridge University Press.

Roth R. (2010), "Marx on technical change in the critical edition", *The European Journal of the History of Economic Thought*, vol. 17 n. 5, pp. 1223–1251.

Schefold B. (1976), "Different forms of technical progress", *The Economic Journal*, vol. 86, pp. 806–19.

Schumpeter J.A. (1934), *The theory of economic development: an inquiry into profits, capital, credit, interest and the business cycle*, New Brunswick: Transaction Publishers.

Schumpeter J.A. (1942), *Capitalism, socialism and democracy*, New York: Harper & Brothers.

Sordi S. and Vercelli A. (2006), "Discretely proceeding from cycle to chaos on Goodwin's path", *Structural Change and Economic Dynamics*, vol. 17, pp. 415–436.

Sylos Labini P. (1984), *The forces of economic growth and decline*, Cambridge, MA: MIT Press.

Tavani D. and Zamparelli L. (2015), "Endogenous technical change, employment and distribution in the Goodwin model of growth cycle", *Studies in Nonlinear Dynamics & Econometrics*, vol. 19 n. 2, pp. 209–216.

von Arnim R. and Barrales J. (2015), "Demand-driven Goodwin cycles with Kaldorian and Kaleckian features", *Review of Keynesian Economics*, vol. 3 n. 3, pp. 351–373.

6 The role of unions as working class representation

Gloria Kutscher and Edeltraud Hanappi-Egger

Increasing structural inequality in distribution

Inequality develops by segregation of social groups. Groups can appear in different constitutions and often have an official and institutionalized form. An important link between social segregation and inequality is capital (Bowles et al., 2009). According to Bowles (2012), the only way of emancipating disadvantaged people is to install regulatory mechanisms which redistribute capital. Thus to pave the way for equality, group consciousness and redistribution processes need to be set in motion. But, the trend in Europe shows an opposite dynamic. There has been an increase in a skewed distribution of income and wealth, which has led to added inequality (Atkinson et al., 2012; Piketty, 2014; Piketty & Zucman, 2013; Therborn, 2012). The distribution of disposable household income since the 1980s has continuously become more unequal in OECD countries. In 1980 the top 10% earned seven times as much as the bottom 10% while in 2014 the top 10% earned 10 times as much. This is because the disposable household income of the top 10% rose further than that of others, and the bottom-income households had higher income losses during and after the economic crisis of 2008. Clearly income inequality has increased (OECD, 2015). This can be seen in the Gini coefficient. The Gini-coefficient shows how national income (or wealth) is distributed. A Gini-coefficient of 1 shows a maximal unequal income distribution in a country whereas a Gini-coefficient of 0 depicts that national incomes are equally distributed within society. Most often values lie between 0.3 and 0.5 (Wilkinson & Pickett, 2010). In the mid-1980s the Gini coefficient of the OECD countries stood at 0.29. By 2013 it had risen to an average of 0.32. Germany, for example, had an increase from 0.25 to 0.30, Sweden from approximately 0.18 to 0.27 and the USA approximately from 0.34 to 0.41 (OECD, 2015).

The distribution of wealth has progressed even more unequally than that of income (Alvaredo et al., 2013, Atkinson et al., 2012; Davies et al., 2011; Piketty, 2014). Wealth has regained the significance it had 100 years ago, leaving a few heirs and rentiers and a wealth-less majority. The concentration of wealth is stronger than the concentration of income; it is held by a much smaller group of people. Regarding wealth the Gini coefficient lies in the range of about 0.6–0.8, which is considerably higher compared to the Gini coefficient for income inequality. Wealth, although much more unequally distributed, has a high correlation with income distribution, which means that people who own much mostly earn more too (Davies et al., 2011; OECD, 2013; Piketty, 2014). The rising inequality in both income and wealth is contrasted with the living standard which in some countries is so high that it does not significantly contribute to a better quality of life any more. But, at the same time, resources that provide a high quality of life are unequally distributed.

The relationship between income (or economic prosperity) and life expectancy or self-perception of happiness is strong but has a peak and reaches a plateau where more income does not provide more positive effects. The plateau was reached for life expectancy in 2010 approximately at 15 thousand US dollar per capita annual income and for well-being approximately 25 thousand US dollar per capita annual income in Western countries.

Further, the more unequal a society is, the more social problems occur. Different research approaches concerning social inequality show that the more unequal a society, is the more it suffers from an erosion of rules, pathologies, such as health issues, morality attitudes and the like. Thus highly unequal distribution results in ill societies where people at the bottom of the class hierarchy have not only a higher risk of suffering from various kinds of illnesses but also in a social sense have a greater risk of school drop-out, no trust in institutions or society as a whole, a higher risk of becoming a criminal and less chance of social mobility (Wilkinson & Pickett, 2010).

Viewed from an age perspective, while in the mid-1980s the age group most at risk of poverty were people older than 66 years, today that group is young people under the age of 26. Practically the course of risk of poverty was turned around regarding age groups. On average anchored poverty (the real low-income benchmark fixed to pre-crisis level) rose in that period by 1%. In contrast it has doubled in countries such as Greece or Spain as they were far more severely hit by the economic crisis of 2008. Socio-economic discrimination is empirically evident in a far greater percentage of households then the bottom 10%. Roughly half of households suffer from rising inequality in terms of educational attainment, skills and employment (OECD, 2015, pp. 26–27). They have poorer opportunities and their achievements give them less social mobility then the other parts of society.

A major part of life is the sphere of work. In terms of employment the last few decades have led to a precarization of employment contracts and security and benefit packages. Since the mid-1990s more than half of newly created jobs have been non-standard.[1] This has hit lower-skilled workers and employees more than the higher-skilled population. Job polarization is a result of changes in the labour market resulting in two clusters of low-skilled jobs and high-skilled jobs at the ends of the labour market spectrum. Obviously what vanishes are middle-class routine jobs. This leaves even more people in precarious work positions (OECD, 2015). The process of precarization of labour, especially for low- to middle-skilled employees or workers, has been a subject of scholarly discussion (Arnold & Bongiovi, 2012; Emmenegger, 2012; Standing, 2011). These people are subject to exploitation and a disadvantaging working environment whose repercussions reach beyond the sphere of work into social and political life.

People working and living precariously are a heterogeneous group deriving from different socio-economic and occupational backgrounds and are also heterogeneous regarding their diversity categories. They share a common characteristic though: working and living in precarity. The commonality thus is a fearful and insecure live. The precariat is also not the working class in the traditional sense of the definition. The traditional working class has established security of apprenticeship, work conditions, wage stability and institutionalized representation. The precarious group lacks all those characteristics. The traditional working class though is shrinking while the new precarious and heterogeneous class is on the rise. Standing (2011), along with others, accuses neo-liberal labour and market practices of the increasing precarization of society. Neo-liberal tendencies facilitate competitiveness and believe in meritocracy and individualism as well as flexibility. In the liberal and free market precarity has different forms of impact which individually but also interacting simultaneously influence people's living and working situation. Precarity may affect citizenship, residency, labour and work and wages, and social protection (Standing, 2011).

The emerging mechanisms of inequality are thought to lie in societal relations of power and hierarchy which are transformed into employment relations, wealth and income distribution and social exclusion (Wright, 2015). In order to change these processes the discussion needs to focus on the involved actors from a social class identity (as a prerequisite for class consciousness) and representation perspective.

The role of the working class in equality processes

Traditionally the working class was the group which engaged in social movement for redistribution and equality (Donado & Wälde, 2012; Hanappi & Hanappi-Egger, 2012, 2013; Hanappi-Egger & Hanappi, 2011; Lukács, 1983; Mann, 1973; Ollman, 1972; Therborn, 2012). But, despite the increase in structural inequality, there are no social class processes detectable in Western Europe, which could lead to a new overall working class mobilization (Hanappi & Hanappi-Egger, 2013; Michaels, 2006; Therborn, 2012). Two processes have been identified as explanations for this trend: the tendency of generalization and individualization (Bennett, 2012; Bottero, 2004; Hanappi & Hanappi-Egger, 2012; Hanappi-Egger & Hanappi, 2011; Holvino, 2010; Jones, 2011; Lott, 2002; Michaels, 2006; Piketty & Zucman, 2013; Weber, 2010).

The first process deals with generalization of society in the sense of generalizing all into the middle class. This thinking denies the existence of the working class in the present society structure. This tendency makes the socio-economic position an individual and private matter (Jones, 2011; Michaels, 2006). The individualization tendency evokes a shift into the individual and private sphere, which makes collective justice issues and distribution difficult (Bennett, 2012; Holvino, 2010; Lott, 2002). These practices add to the decline of the positive working-class identification as wealth and social mobility in this regard are associated with individual effort (Bennett, 2012; Hanappi & Hanappi-Egger, 2012; Jones, 2011; Lott, 2002; Wallace & Junisbai, 2003) The consequence is that structurally belonging people do not identify with the working class easily. And for that reason they do not perceive themselves as members of the respective political, economic and social institutions (Hanappi & Hanappi-Egger, 2012; Holvino, 2002; Michaels, 2006; Weber, 2010). Identity is a construct which creates a sense of sameness within groups, providing meaning and a social anchor (Brubaker & Cooper, 2000; Gleason, 1983; Reese-Schäfer, 1999). Working class identity concerns primarily the understanding of one`s interests as class interests and class-based hierarchy and disadvantage (Greenwood & Christian, 2008; Mann, 1973).

In this regard Fraser (1995, 2000, 2005) formulated this challenge as the "recognition/redistribution dilemma". Following that theory disadvantaged people suffer from two inequalities. The first inequality is rooted in economic injustice, which becomes manifest in the political-economic structure of society and its institutions, in the form of exploitation, economic marginalization and deprivation. The second inequality is cultural and symbolic injustice. Its consequences can be found in social patterns of representation, interpretation and communication. This can lead to cultural domination though socio-economically stronger groups, non-recognition of a socio-economically weak group, disrespect and lack of representation of group interests. Thus, on the one hand inequality means maldistribution and on the other hand it means misrecognition (Fraser, 1995, 2000). Relating to the working class, considered as a socio-economically weak group, this dilemma is twofold: firstly, they lack class identity, which is the first and foremost step to class consciousness and action (Mann, 1973). In order to foster redistribution processes, they need recognition on individual, group and representational levels (Fraser, 1995, 2000; Hanappi-Egger & Hanappi, 2011). Secondly, they need redistribution of different forms of capital, particularly economic resources.

In this contribution social class and especially the working class are defined and perceived from the exploitation-centred perspective and a multi-dimensional capital perspective. The exploitation-centred perspective is political because primarily it is concerned with issues of social justice and inequality and it is socio-economically relevant because it is based on the Marxian idea of hierarchy and dominance within the production process, thus labour relations (Wright, 2000a, 2000b, 2005). Further, two multi-capital approaches are interesting in this context. The first approach stems from Hanappi and Hanappi-Egger (2012), who propose an "exploitation-index" based on five characteristics: power, wealth and income, consumption pattern, education and leisure time (Hanappi & Hanappi-Egger, 2012, 2013).

In Bourdieu`s theory power and hierarchy are also generated by the incorporation of different types of capital (Bourdieu, 1985; Wright, 2005). In this regard society is constructed by means of the individual and group position in the multi-dimensional social space given capital acquisition and incorporation. The social space is plotted on three capitals: economic capital (income, wealth), cultural capital (incorporated cultural capital, e.g., education and material cultural goods) and social capital (family background, social relationships, networks). The position of a person is based on the incorporation and possession of these capitals. Their amount provides a specific position, and with that prestige, power, habitus and symbolic power. Inequalities result from the possession, the incorporation and the institution of these capitals. The working class therefore is dependent on labour and for that reason is in an antagonistic relationship with employers in work relations which are characterized by a hierarchical relationship (Rehm & Zuckerstätter, 2013; Wright, 2005). In additiona to economic capital (income, wealth, depth), the working class is defined by their amount of cultural and social capital and implications for leisure time and consumption (Hanappi & Hanappi-Egger, 2012; Savage et al., 2013).

Social class relations are a continuous process which is shaped by specific socio-historical developments and the achievements of people who are engaged in class movement (Sylos Labini, 1988). In the last decades changes caused by globalization, tertiarization, and migration have led to a work environment in Western Europe which is characterized by partialization and dualization of work (Berry & Bell, 2012; Emmenegger, 2012; Standing, 2011). Especially the tertiarization process results in a rapid decline of peasants and industrial workers and an increase of people working in the private and public sectors. These processes lead to a change in class structure and the identifying class characteristics. Distinct class division from pure occupation is not as clearly separated as it was up to the 1980s. Thus the working class has changed its inner structure as regards working conditions and occupation field but also in diversity characteristics (Hanappi & Hanappi-Egger, 2012; Sylos Labini, 1988). From a diversity perspective social class means that working people, no matter whether blue- or white-collar workers or employees in non-traditional working class occupations, are all working people despite their differences. These differences can be viewed on four different dimensions of diversity. The internal dimension subsumes individual diversity categories. The big six are age, gender, sexual orientation, physical ability, ethnicity and race. The external dimension includes categories of social factors and life experiences to which an individual is attached. Such categories are the place where a person lives, personal habits, religion, parental and marital status, work experience and income. The organizational dimensions provide information about the individual's occupation, seniority, work and content field, status in the organization and affiliation with employee representative organizations (Gardenswartz & Rowe, 2008; Hyman & Gumbrell-McCormick, 2013). Considering all the heterogeneity in the workplace there are considerable unifying characteristics. Such characteristics are needs and interests regarding security, work conditions, wage and vulnerability and dependence in employment relations. The sense of belonging to the working class is strongly associated with the workplace and functions as a supra-categorical dimension (multiple categories determine social class attachment).

The union is required to account for all this heterogeneity while keeping people under a supra-categorical umbrella of union organization.

The role of the union as third party in working class identification

Identification with social class is the first and foremost step of the working class consciousness framework. Collective identity is a specifically important function of people's personal needs because it comprises a sense of "belongingness, distinctiveness, respect, understanding (or meaning), and agency" (Simon & Klandermans, 2001, p. 321). The subsequent steps in the class consciousness and class action framework are opposition, the perception of hierarchy and readiness for class action. Class identity is the recognition of shared grievances and aspirations. People who identify with their social class understand their interests and the need for class collectivity (Duncan, 1999; Greenwood & Christian, 2008; Mann, 1973).

The social context and additional groups are important to class opposition. Class opposition can be understood as the continual negotiation (with the aid of different resources) between the disadvantaged and disadvantaging class. These two parties are not the sole groups in class relations; third parties are traditionally involved in class struggle (Simon & Klandermans, 2001; Wright, 2000b). Thus, class relations have a tripartite group structure. The third party has a mediating and representing function. This position can be filled by different groups such as the general public, political parties, interest and representation organizations (Simon & Klandermans, 2001). In class opposition the most important third party is traditionally the trade union (Donado & Wälde, 2012; Phelan, 2007a). When the working class as the disadvantaged group involves the trade union and the general public as the third party in their struggle against the opposed party, their power struggle becomes a politicized issue because making it so becomes a matter of public interest (Klandermans, 2014, p. 4). The Marxist framework certainly includes that working class people constrained in the production and exploitation system need intellectuals as a third party who would represent their demands and lead the working class (Hanappi & Hanappi-Egger, 2013).

Gramsci ([1930] 2005) states that every social group which evolves generates one or more types of intellectuals. To Gramsci all persons are intellectuals but "organic" intellectuals have a core function in the preservation of hegemony and the awareness of their own position within the economic, social and political field (Gramsci, [1930] 2005, p. 49). The intellectuals are not different because of the nature of their level within society; they are all educated and specialized in some field. They are different in how they place their activities within social relations and how they decide to have their place in the complex of social relations. These "organic" intellectuals put their intellectual knowledge into the service of society and as a result they are different from pure "specialists" (Gramsci, [1930] 2005).

To Gramsci the most important characteristic of any group, when it moves towards a dominant position, is that it becomes involved in struggle for the conquest of the ideology, which is archived faster when the respective group has its own "organic" intellectuals. "Organic" intellectuals are the connecting element between the complex of superstructures (civil and political society) and mediate between the social groups involved in employment relations. Based on the connection with the fundamental social groups and the position within the superstructure the intellectuals have different "organic quality", meaning a different position in the hierarchy of positions (Gramsci, [1930] 2005). For class organization and representation, and because parts of the working class do not have these capabilities, representation by "organic" intellectuals is indispensable. Hanappi and Hanappi-Egger (2013) illustrate the importance of "organic" intellectuals. For example, the union can be understood as an institutionalized form of representation and union leaders as "organic" intellectuals.

The different sorts of capital are essential for group formation. The less capital the actors have, the less they are able to form into a working class and gain the power to be politically salient. But, actors with more capital have the possibility of sharing their accumulated capital with less powerful actors, which helps them to understand the rules of the social space and create or maintain institutionalized representation such as unions, social parties or mobilization (Bourdieu, 1985). In Bourdieu`s perception a class exists and is real (not only in the theoretical or formal sense) as long as there is an institutionalized representative who is granted the representation power (Bourdieu, 1985).

The Power Resource Theory assigns a central role to the collective organization of workers (Pontusson, 2013). Following this theory working class power is mobilized by resources transferred by the unions and social and leftist political parties to the workers. Without class organization the power concentrates further in the hands of a few, even in democracies. Power in this regard is defined as capital. According to the Power Resource Theory the more effective the working class organization is, the more equally distributed the capital (Bradley et al., 2003).

Following these concepts, a social class can be established, legitimized and noticed in the public and political sphere through representation. Representatives are an important part of the recognition and redistribution process. Union representatives are functionaries who are acting in order to represent their clientele's interests in a clear and publicly apparent way. Substantial to representation are the publicly shared common beliefs of the class regarding perception and interpretation of social processes and further proposed causes of action or solutions. Thus, important activities of the union are the representation of the working class at a symbolic level, the representation of their relations to different actors and of the relationship within the class (Klages, 2009).

People who have a strong normative opinion about social justice and equality are more likely to be associated with union membership and union engagement (Checchi et al., 2010). As Gramsci states ([1930] 2005), representatives do not have to experience the grievances themselves. It is more a form of ideological deprivation, which is a deprivation felt on behalf of the exploited by unexploited individuals or groups. This can cause consciousness and participation in social change, although these individuals or groups do not directly benefit from this action (Duncan, 1999).

Institutions and institutional representation – the position of the union

Institutionals are a result of a constantly ongoing social, political and economic-driven process, where institutions are formed and maintained or challenged. Their emergence is based on the existing structural and subjective group process (Bourdieu, 1985). Hodgson defines institutions as durable "systems of established and embedded social rules that structure social interactions" (Hodgson, 2007, p. 1). Social structures include in this regard "all sets of social relations, including the episodic and those without rules, as well as social institutions" (Hodgson, 2007, p. 1). Institutions guide and affect individual and group behaviour and interaction as well as distribution processes of different resources (Kaufman, 2012). Organizations then are special forms of institutions which involve "(a) criteria to establish their boundaries and to distinguish their members from non-members, (b) principles of sovereignty concerning who is in charge and (c) chains of command delineating responsibilities within the organization" (Hodgson, 2007, p. 2). According to this definition organizations can be viewed as a special case of institutions, and institutions as a special case of social structures (Hodgson, 2007). By this definition the union is an organization with high cohesiveness, rules, norms and membership and a hierarchical structure. Individual attitudes and behaviour are not isolated but are developed and maintained in the social context influenced by social structures such as institutions. The advancement of institutions is in turn dependent on individual and group attitudes and behaviour and previous social structures. Thus, to explain social phenomena, all levels (micro/individual, meso/group, macro/institution) as well as their interaction and interdependence should be taken into consideration (Hodgson, 2007). Individuals can however change their attitudes and preferences and this has an impact on the structure of an institution. But, simultaneously, the institution can change people's attitudes or even life realities, such as their socio-economic position. Further, institutions develop and maintain routines and habits, within the institution and regarding their members (Hodgson, 2007; Kaufman, 2012).

According to Stölting (1999) an institution is a result of habitualized and normative attitudes, practices and rules constituting its structure. Successful habitualization needs, besides those attitudes and practices, the general public. The general public needs to internalize the existence of the institution through its public legitimization. The party shares ideas which are objectified. The institutional structure is essentially associated with a main idea which has a legitimizing and idealizing function but also allows for criticism. The main idea is associated with the object and thus is not arbitrary but is a stable core of the institution and shows its primary purpose. The main idea can be understood as the ideal which is the reason for the public legitimization. The main idea is stable throughout reforms and changes. For this reason it can be stabilizing as well as activating to the evolution of the institution. All institutional attitudes and actions are interpreted through this main idea. But the interpretation of the core idea of an institution can differ (Stölting, 1999).

Institutions can be organizations if they incorporate a main idea, which is accepted and legitimized by the public. The public in this context is a group with a normative characterization (Stölting, 1999).

The main function of an institution is the representation of their members or who they perceive to belong. A group grants legitimacy to the institution, which then installs representatives who incorporate the legitimized social identity of the group (Bourdieu, 1985, p. 36ff). The group grants power to the representatives.

The representatives thus act on behalf of the belonging group. In the communication process they provide norms, values and identifying characteristics to their members and society at large. They do so by using a meaningful und symbolic way of describing the circumstances or matters. Central is the depiction of their perception in the form of political interpretation and evaluation of social, political and economic circumstances, their development and possible measures. One major task is to put the represented group and its interests into the public sphere and show the relationship to other groups (Klages, 2009). But, if the representative institution becomes estranged from the belonging group, they lose symbolical representation power and actual political power (Bourdieu, 1985). If the institution cannot sufficiently realize the main idea, or the opinion about the idea is negative, the institution becomes instable. Communication about the issues associated with the main idea is an essential part of the identifying connection to the perceived belonging group of an institution (Stölting, 1999).

In regard to the working class and the union, the institutionalized representatives approach the identified group working class people who belong to the union and represent their interests, shaping them through communication. In turn the working class people feel and show their commitment to their group and thus to the union and for that reason shape its structure. When there is a loss of membership density and people do not feel as working class any more, although structurally belonging, there may be a conflict in the identification processes, communication and interaction between the perceived members and the union. For that reason the union's position needs to be identified based on its strengths and weaknesses so that it can best fulfil its representational task.

Current union challenges – strengths and weaknesses

The redistribution of capital in order to foster equality is best accomplished through official regulatory mechanisms. The union is an example of just such a mechanism (Bowles, 2012). Yet representation research has shown that unions have in recent years found it difficult to sustain sufficient legitimacy to ensure powerful representation (Godard & Frege, 2014). This difficulty can be attributed to fundamental changes within tertiarization, organizational structures, a heterogeneous workforce, individual work contracts and flexible work hours (Phelan, 2007a; Pontusson, 2013; Standing, 2011; Wallace & Junisbai, 2003). These changes have undermined effective representation of the working class because the union is being forced to abandon instruments traditionally used to protect this group, such as collective agreements and statutory job protection (Checchi et al., 2010; Keller, 2013). In line with the challenges of a transformed job market, union membership has drastically declined in many European countries. At a certain point the low membership density can have a negative effect on the legitimacy of union representation (Blaschke, 2007; Godard & Frege, 2014; Phelan, 2007b; Pontusson, 2013). Reasons offered for this decline have been globalization and the associated international assimilation of industrial relations, as well as deindustrialization and a shift from an industrial economy to a service-based economy.

Another challenging factor is an increasingly heterogeneous workforce, which places unions in a challenging position between inclusive and exclusive solidarity (Ebbinghaus et al., 2009). Inclusive solidarity will only attract those working class individuals who have attained a median position in terms of wages and employment status. Yet an exclusive solidarity runs the risk of undermining identification between the union and the group if nobody feels addressed. Union power is fundamentally rooted in an inclusive understanding of the workforce, so that all workers can be represented and have a sense of belonging (Checchi et al., 2010; Keller, 2013). Thus, while the union has expended a great deal of effort in ensuring inclusive representation, it seems that it is reaching fewer and fewer working class people (Godard & Frege, 2014; Keller, 2013). This loss of identification weakens the position of the working class as well as the legitimation of the union as a third party.

Despite the weaknesses the union still has considerable strengths which sustains its important role in working class representation (Lucas, 2011; Turner & D'Art, 2012). Despite falling union density the majority (72%) of European citizens asked thought that the union is necessary in order to protect working class wages and working conditions (Turner & D'Art, 2012, p. 32). This positive attitude towards the union is strongly associated with lower education and occupation of manual or white-collar occupations, and a left political orientation. Also, satisfaction with income level and perceived necessity for the union are related (Turner & D'Art, 2012). The union is mainly responsible for establishing, and where possible maintaining and furthering, standards of work, such as work conditions, work pay or health issues (Donado & Wälde, 2012). Besides the traditional form of union representation newer forms of employee organization emerge, encouraging more one-on-one formal or informal communication, generally organized at a local rather than global level. For example, there are emerging forms of local employee organization which are set up within the organization where employees can turn, or which can take more traditional structured forms such as shop stewardships or work councils.

While novel forms of employee organization and expression are increasing, traditional union organization remains the most effective way of representing workers' interests (Budd et al., 2010; Charlwood & Terry, 2007). Research has shown that individuals who are affiliated with unions voice their interests much more effectively than those who reject or lack such representation. It also has been shown that non-union forms of representation are less effective, are less likely to be accepted by organizations and hence are generally less accessible to employees (Charlwood & Terry, 2007). The optimal situation seems to be that the traditional union should incorporate newer ways of employee communication and representation into its standard procedure.

Future directions for the union

Social inequality is rising and shows severe consequences for the working class. They experience greater social mobility barriers and have a greater risk of suffering from a variety of consequences arising from social disadvantage (OECD, 2015; Wilkinson & Pickett, 2010). In this period characterized by high inequality, the union's role in working-class representation becomes especially relevant.

Some research has shown that the union has difficulty representing the interests of groups which fall outside standard contracts and working conditions and also groups of people with diversity characteristics outside of heteronormativity (Arnold & Bongiovi, 2012; Emmenegger, 2012; OECD, 2015; Standing, 2011). The union needs to make these its prime issues. This is especially necessary as work precarity has risen and tertiarization has shaken up the job market, leaving the working class with few secure working-class jobs. The growing collectivity of precariously working persons is the new working class which can be compared to working class conditions before it gained bargaining power. Further the heterogeneous groups within the working class collectivity may not be perceived as a part of the working class and for that matter need special attention to be able to identify with the working class (Hanappi & Hanappi-Egger, 2012; Michaels, 2006). These groups share different diversity characteristics, such as age, gender or migration background (Gardenswartz & Rowe, 2008). For example, a young generation comes into a highly precarious labour market which has little to offer regarding training or security (OECD, 2015; Standing, 2011). A shared working class identity is a prerequisite for working class people in finding a unifying sense of their interests and shared grievances. The legitimation and representational power of the union is dependent on a strong group identity. As organic intellectuals, union representatives possess characteristics such as high cultural and social capital which can be applied in working class representation (Bourdieu, 1985; Gramsci, [1930] 2005). Thus the union has an important role in working class leadership and representation. They have the ability and resources to provide information and create a feeling of belongingness within the working class despite their heterogeneity. For this reason the union needs to re-establish the working class position in society and represent their interests before the policy makers and employers.

In the past the union has played an important role in achieving standards and better life conditions for the working class and had an immense impact on shaping values of social justice which are still intact today (Donado & Wälde, 2012). As the social context is changing and the working class changes its inner structure, the union needs to move in synchronicity with its needs and interests so it can again become a powerful and legitimized organization.

Based on this discussion, some suggestions for future union foci can be derived. The union should incorporate alternative approaches in its representational techniques. This could have better resonance for some groups within the diverse workforce. To account for the increasing work and life precarity of the new working class, the union needs to make precarity and atypical work a visible topic in a way that the new working class as a whole profits from these changes. Further, it needs to make the private, service and care field more visible in terms of representation and link them to the working class. Finally, as an inclusive representation the union needs a clear unifying anchor to form class identity and consciousness.

Note

1 Following Vosko et al. (2003), non-standard jobs are part-time, temporary self-employment or holding multiple jobs not obtained voluntarily and which do not provide sufficient security.

References

Alvaredo, F., Atkinson, A. B., Piketty, T., & Saez, E. (2013). The top 1 percent in international and historical perspective. *The Journal of Economic Perspectives, 2*(3), 3–20. doi:10.3386/w19075.

Arnold, D., & Bongiovi, J. R. (2012). Precarious, informalizing, and flexible work: Transforming concepts and understandings. *American Behavioral Scientist.* doi:10.1177/0002764212466239.

Atkinson, A. B., Piketty, T., & Saez, E. (2012). *Top Incomes in the Long Run of History.* Berkeley: UC Berkeley, Institute for Research on Labor and Employment. Retrieved from http://escholarship.org/uc/item/8fd8654h (accessed 25 September 2014).

Bennett, J. (2012). Chav-spotting in Britain: The representation of social class as private choice. *Social Semiotics*, 1–17. doi:10.1080/10350330.2012.708158.

Berry, D., & Bell, M. P. (2012). Inequality in organizations: Stereotyping, discrimination, and labor law exclusions. *Equality, Diversity and Inclusion: An International Journal, 31*(3), 236–248.

Blaschke, S. (2007). Austria: Corporatist unionism in crisis. In C. Phelan (Ed.), *Trade Union Revitalisation Trends and Prospects in 34 Countries* (pp. 245–257). Bern: Peter Lang.

Bottero, W. (2004). Class identities and the identity of class. *Sociology, 38*(5), 985–1003. doi:10.1177/0038038504047182.

Bourdieu, P. (1985). *Sozialer Raum und "Klassen": Leçon sur la leçon [Social Space and "Classes": Lesson About the Lesson].* Frankfurt am Main: Suhrkamp.

Bowles, S. (2012). *The New Economics of Inequality and Redistribution.* Cambridge: Cambridge University Press.

Bowles, S., Loury, G. C., & Sethi, R. (2009). Group inequality. Unpublished paper. Santa Fe: Santa Fe Institute.

Bradley, D., Huber, E., Moller, S., Nielsen, F., & Stephens, J. D. (2003). Distribution and redistribution in postindustrial democracies. *World Politics, 55*(02), 193–228. doi:10.1353/wp.2003.0009.

Brubaker, R., & Cooper, F. (2000). Beyond "identity". *Theory and Society, 29*(1), 1–47. doi:10.1023/A:1007068714468.

Budd, J. W., Gollan, P. J., & Wilkinson, A. (2010). New approaches to employee voice and participation in organizations. *Human Relations, 63*(3), 303–310. doi:10.1177/0018726709348938.

Charlwood, A., & Terry, M. (2007). 21st-century models of employee representation: Structures, processes and outcomes. *Industrial Relations Journal, 38*(4), 320–337. doi:10.1111/j.1468-2338.2007.00451.x.

Checchi, D., Visser, J., & Van De Werfhorst, H. G. (2010). Inequality and union membership: The influence of relative earnings and inequality attitudes. *British Journal of Industrial Relations, 48*(1), 84–108. doi:10.1111/j.1467-8543.2009.00757.x.

Davies, J. B., Sandström, S., Shorrocks, A., & Wolff, E. N. (2011). The level and distribution of global household wealth. *Economic Journal, 121*(551), 223–254. doi:10.1111/j.1468-0297.2010.02391.x.

Donado, A., & Wälde, K. (2012). How trade unions increase welfare. *The Economic Journal, 122*(563), 990–1009. doi:10.1111/j.1468-0297.2012.02513.x.

Duncan, L. E. (1999). Motivation for collective action: Group consciousness as mediator of personality, life experiences, and women's rights activism. *Political Psychology, 20*(3), 611–635. doi:10.1111/0162-895X.00159.

Ebbinghaus, B., Göbe, C., & Koos, C. (2009). Inklusions- und Exklusionsmechanismen gewerkschaftlicher Mitgliedschaft: Ein europaischer Vergleich [Inclusion and exclusion mechanisms in union membership: A European comparison]. In R. W. P. Stichweh (Ed.), *Inklusion und Exklusion: Analysen zur Sozialstruktur und sozialen Ungleichheit [Inclusion and Exclusion: Analyses of the Social Structure and Social Inequality]* (pp. 341–359). Wiesbaden: VS Verlag.

Emmenegger, P. (2012). *The Age of Dualization: The Changing Face of Inequality in Deindustrializing Societies*. Oxford: Oxford University Press.

Fraser, N. (1995). From redistribution to recognition? Dilemmas of justice in a 'Post-Socialist' age. *New Left Review*, 68.

Fraser, N. (2000). Rethinking recognition. *New Left Review*, 107–120.

Fraser, N. (2005). Reframing justice in a globalizing world. *New Left Review*, 69–88.

Gardenswartz, L., & Rowe, A. (2008). *Diverse Teams at Work: Capitalizing on the Power of Diversity*. Alexandria, VA: Society for Human Resource Management.

Gleason, P. (1983). Identifying identity: A semantic history. *The Journal of American History, 69*(4), 910–931. doi:10.2307/1901196.

Godard, J., & Frege, C. (2014). Worker perceptions of representation and rights in Germany and the USA. *European Journal of Industrial Relations, 20*(1), 73–89. doi:10.1177/0959680113516846.

Gramsci, A. ([1930] 2005). The intellectuals. In S. P. Hier (Ed.), *Contemporary Sociological Thought* (pp. 49–57). Toronto, ON: Canadian Scholars' Press.

Greenwood, R. M., & Christian, A. (2008). What happens when we unpack the invisible knapsack? Intersectional political consciousness and inter-group appraisals. *Sex Roles, 59*(5–6), 404–417. doi:10.1007/s11199-008-9439-x.

Hanappi, H., & Hanappi-Egger, E. (2012). *Middle class or in the middle of a class?* Paper presented at the AHE-Conference "Political Economy and the Outlook for Capitalism, Paris, France.

Hanappi, H., & Hanappi-Egger, E. (2013). Gramsci meets Veblen: On the search for a new revolutionary class. *Journal of Economic Issues, 47*(2), 375–381. doi:10.2753/JEI0021-3624470210.

Hanappi-Egger, E., & Hanappi, H. (2011). *Exploitation re-visited: New forms, same ideologies?* Paper presented at the AHE-Conference, Nottingham, UK.

Hodgson, G. M. (2007). Institutions and individuals: Interaction and evolution. *Organization Studies, 28*(1), 95–116. doi:10.1177/0170840607067832.

Holvino, E. (2002). Class: "A difference that makes a difference" in organizations. *Diversity Factor, 10*(2), 28. doi:213050451.

Holvino, E. (2010). Intersections: The simultaneity of race, gender and class in organization studies. *Gender, Work & Organization, 17*(3), 248–277. doi:10.1111/j.1468-0432.2008.00400.x.

Hyman, R., & Gumbrell-McCormick. (2013). Collective representation at work: Institutions and dynamics. In C. Frege & J. Kelly (Eds.), *Comparative Employment Relations in the Global Economy* (pp. 49–70). Abingdon: Routledge.

Jones, O. (2011). *Chavs: The Demonization of the Working Class*. London: Verso.

Kaufman, B. E. (2012). An institutional economic analysis of labor unions. *Industrial Relations: A Journal of Economy and Society, 51*, 438–471. doi:10.1111/j.1468-232X.2012.00686.x.

Keller, B. (2013). Interessensvertretung bei atypischen Beschäftigungsverhältnissen [Interest representation in case of atypical employment relations]. In H. Hoßfeld & W. Nienhüser (Eds.), *Macht und Employment Relations Festschrift für Werner Nienhüser [Power and Employment Relations Festschrift for Werner Nienhüser]* (pp. 57–61). Munich: Reiner Hampp Verlag.

Klages, J. (2009). *Meinung, Macht, Gegenmacht: Die Akteure im politischen Feld [Opinion, Power, Counterpower: Actors in the Political Field]*. Hamburg: VSA-Verlag.

Klandermans, P. G. (2014). Identity politics and politicized identities: Identity processes and the dynamics of protest. *Political Psychology, 35*(1), 1–22. doi:10.1111/pops.12167.

Lott, B. (2002). Cognitive and behavioral distancing from the poor. *American Psychologist, 57*(2), 100–110. doi:10.1037/0003-066X.57.2.100.

Lucas, K. (2011). Blue-collar discourses of workplace dignity: Using outgroup comparisons to construct positive identities. *Management Communication Quarterly, 25*(2), 353–374. doi:10.1177/0893318910386445.

Lukács, G. (1983). *Geschichte und Klassenbewusstsein: Studien über marxistische Dialektik [History and Class Consciousness]*. Darmstadt: Luchterhand.

Mann, M. (1973). *Consciousness and Action Among the Western Working Class*. London: Macmillan.

Michaels, W. B. (2006). *The Trouble with Diversity: How we Learned to Love Identity and Ignore Inequality*. New York: Metropolitan Books.

OECD. (2013). *OECD Guidelines for Micro Statistics on Household Wealth*. Paris: OECD Publishing.

OECD. (2015). *In it Together: Why Less Inequality Benefits All*. Paris: OECD Publishing.

Ollman, B. (1972). Toward class consciousness next time: Marx and the working class. *Politics and Society, 3*(1), 24. doi:10.1177/003232927200300101.

Phelan, C. (2007a). *Trade Union Revitalisation Trends and Prospects in 34 Countries*. Bern: Peter Lang.

Phelan, C. (2007b). Worldwide trends and prospects for trade union revitalisation. In C. Phelan (Ed.), *Trade Union Revitalisation Trends and Prospects in 34 Countries* (pp. 11–38). Bern: Peter Lang.

Piketty, T. (2014). *Capital in the Twenty-first Century*. Cambridge, MA: Belknap Press of Harvard University Press.

Piketty, T., & Zucman, G. (2013). *Capital is Back: Wealth–Income Ratios in Rich Countries, 1700–2010*. London: Centre for Economic Policy Research.

Pontusson, J. (2013). Unionization, inequality and redistribution. *British Journal of Industrial Relations, 51*(4), 797–825. doi:10.1111/bjir.12045.

Reese-Schäfer, W. (1999). *Identität und Interesse: Der Diskurs der Identitätsforschung [Identity and Interest: Discourse in Identity Research]*. Opladen: Leske + Budrich.

Rehm, M., & Zuckerstätter, S. (2013). *Austria: A Classless Society?* Vienna: Kammer für Arbeiter und Angestellte für Wien.

Savage, M., Devine, F., Cunningham, N., Taylor, M., Li, Y., Hjellbrekke, J., . . . Miles, A. (2013). A new model of social class? Findings from the BBC's great British class survey experiment. *Sociology, 47*(2), 219–250. doi:10.1177/0038038513481128.

Simon, B., & Klandermans, B. (2001). Politicized collective identity. A social psychological analysis. *American Psychologist, 56*(4), 319–331. doi:10.1037/0003-066X.56.4.319.

Standing, G. (2011). *The precariat the new dangerous class*. London: Bloomsbury Academic.

Stölting, E. (1999). Informelle Machtbildung und Leitideen im institutionellen Wandel [Informal power emergence and main ideas in institutional change]. In T. Edeling, W. Jann, & D. Wagner (Eds.), *Institutionenökonomie und Neuer Institutionalismus. Überlegungen zur Organisationstheorie [Institutional Economics and New Institutionalism. Reflections of Organisational Theory]* (pp. 111–131). Opladen: Leske + Budrich.

Sylos Labini, P. (1988). *Die neuen Klassenverhältnisse [original title: Le classi sociali negli anni `80]*. Frankfurt am Main: Campus Verlag.

Therborn, G. (2012). Class in the 21st century. *New Left Review*, 78, 5–29.

Turner, T., & D'Art, D. (2012). Public perceptions of trade unions in countries of the European Union: A causal analysis. *Labor Studies Journal, 37*(1), 33–55. doi:10.1177/0160449x11429266.

Vosko, L. F., Zukewich, N., & Cranford, C. (2003). Precarious jobs: A new typology of employment. *Perspectives on Labour and Income, 4*(10), 16–26.

Wallace, M., & Junisbai, A. (2003). Finding class consciousness in the new economy. *Research in Social Stratification and Mobility, 20*, 385–421. doi:10.1016/S0276-5624(03)20010-X.

Weber, L. (2010). *Understanding Race, Class, Gender, and Sexuality: A Conceptual Framework*. New York: Oxford University Press.

Wilkinson, R., & Pickett, K. (2010). *The Spirit Level: Why Equality is Better for Everyone*. London: Penguin Books.

Wright, E. O. (2000a). *Class Counts*. Cambridge: Cambridge University Press.

Wright, E. O. (2000b). Class, exploitation, and economic rents: Reflections on Sorenson's "Sounder Basis" Erik Olin Wright. *The American Journal of Sociology, 105*(6), 1559–1571. doi:10.1086/210464.

Wright, E. O. (2005). *Approaches to Class Analysis*. Cambridge: Cambridge University Press.

Wright, E. O. (2015). Class and inequality in Piketty. *Contexts, 14*(1), 58–61. doi:10.1177/1536504214567853.

7 The emergence of evolutionary-institutional thought in Russia[1]

Svetlana Kirdina

The evolutionary-institutional school of thought did not emerge in Russia, but in the United States and Western Europe during the 1920s and 1930s. In this inquiry we investigated how selected Russian and Soviet scholars perceived, and also dealt with, the emergence of this challenging field of study, and also how some key ideas were thwarted while others were selected for absorption into the social and economic sciences over the last century.

Our inquiry consists of four sections followed by a conclusion. The first section introduces and seeks to define the notion of "inversion cycles" that are thought to characterize and also limit Russian social development. Our second section deals with some of the critics of the evolutionary-institutional tradition in economic thought as advanced by Soviet thinkers in the 1930s through to the 1980s. The third section presents institutional thinking derived from selected contributions of Soviet political economists and sociologists. The fourth section considers the spread of this tradition in social science and economic thought in Russia, starting with the early post-Soviet era and continuing to the present. Finally, the main conclusions are presented in summarized form.

Inversion cycles and discontinuities in Russian social development

At the beginning of the 1990s, Alexandr Akhiezer introduced the idea that Russia's society can be understood as "split." In the view advanced by Akhiezer (1991, p. 195), what are termed "inversion cycles" contribute to discontinuous patterns for Russia, and can be visualized as oscillating vibrations moving between two contrasting poles. These cycles are noted to relate to an outright rejection of a full set of societal values and practices that should be, but are not, preserved and relied upon as previously accumulated knowledge.

Adding to this line of thinking Susanna Matveeva (1997, p. 20) stresses that inversion cycles tend to prove disruptive and thereby contribute to disorganization, reducing prospects for societal progress. Disruptions can occur when previously held values conflict with values and a related societal disorganization in a subsequent historical era. Akhiezer relates such inversion cycles to the weakness of what is defined as a "median utilitarian culture" in Russia, investigated in works authored by Nikolai Berdyaev (1915), and that refer to the creation of new elements of culture that cannot be integrated with the previous polar extremes.

One way that inversion cycles manifest themselves and work themselves out is that, over a period of Russian history, each new turn in social development denies the hard-earned cultural practices and traditions that could be garnered from the previous era. In this sense, inversion cycles can indeed violate the unity and continuity of Russian society, rendering social development if not impossible, then extremely costly, as mistakes that are made tend to be irreversible. The long Soviet era, and even the shorter era known by the term *Perestroika* which arose and fell in the second half of the 1980s, offer vivid examples of inversion cycles, demonstrating that, as a previous era is cast out, members of Russian society are faced with starting a new era that is plagued by opposing and even conflicting values, rendering those seeking to offer leadership in the current era largely unable to synthesize values drawn from the previous era.

For this inquiry we think that Akhiezer's notion of inversion cycles offers a fruitful framework for our efforts to understand how evolutionary-institutional thought has been perceived and dealt with in Russia. While Akhiezer's notion and application of inversion cycles serve to frame our inquiry, his thinking is also supported by our findings, which we introduce below.

Soviet political economy and institutional thought

When formed into a well-developed and comprehensive approach, as well as being a deserving field in Economic Science, Institutional Economics spread internationally during the Decade of the 1920s.[2] For some decades prior, and in the United States, Thorstein Veblen (1857–1929) generated a selection of seminal articles and books that established and advanced this field of inquiry. In the United Kingdom and France, notable authors such as John Hobson (1858–1940) and François Simiand (1873–1935) offered somewhat similar contributions. In Russia during the 1920s and 1930s there emerged what may be described as a "socio-institutionalist" approach. In considering this approach author L. M. Ippolitov (2008, p. 46) noted the importance of Peter Struve, as well as some other economists, who departed from Russia after the Bolshevik Revolution of 1917 and contributed towards advancing Russian institutional thought from abroad. With the rise and later domination of bolshevism as a political ideology, which was put in to practice in the newly established Soviet Union, evolutionary-institutional thinking entered into what we define as a *thwarted phase*, as this field of inquiry, generated overseas, met pointed and harsh criticisms from those in the nascent Soviet Union seeking ideological and scientific purity along the Marxist–Leninist line. This line played such a central role in the development of economic thinking in that formative and also turbulent era of early, Soviet economic history.

One could view the first part of the 20th century as composed of decades during which those advancing ideas in Economic Science were engaged in competing not only for influence, but also dominance. Before the 1917 revolution, Karl Marx's writings were better known in Russia than anywhere else in the world, except in

Germany and Great Britain. The first translation of Marx's famous tome *Das Kapital, Band I* (1867) was undertaken from the original German to the Russian language and published in Russia in 1872. The first Russian edition with a print run of 3,000 copies outran the 1,000 copies that were printed as the first edition in neighboring Germany. Ten years later the *Communist Manifesto,* that Marx and Friedrich Engels had coauthored in 1848, was translated by Georgi Plekhanov and published in Russia.

Up to the start of the 20th century Marx's thinking increased in popularity among Russian intellectuals and in this manner came to exert effects on public opinion and later on the course of Russian history. After the successes of the Bolshevik Revolution of 1917, Marx's ideas were drawn upon to form the basis of the official ideology for the nascent Soviet Union. What contributed to widespread acceptance of his thinking within the Soviet context is that Marx not only advanced a critique of capitalism, but he also offered a vision, according to Kirdina (2006), of an improved society that resolved some of the key contradictions of capitalism in a manner that also proved congruent with a centralized society forged in Russia long before the start of the 20th century.

The ascendency of the Bolsheviks to dominance with the October Revolution of 1917 and, the post civil war founding of the Soviet Union in 1921, led to a full endorsement of Marx's orientation, while simultaneously limiting the prospects for alternative economic approaches, including evolutionary-institutional thinking.

For the duration of the 70-year-long Soviet era the institutional tradition in economics advanced by Veblen and some others was regarded coolly, for this school of thought was held suspect and deemed a competitor to the dominant Marxian interpretation based upon dialectics. In his book, *Foundations of Leninism* (published in Russian in 1924), Josef Stalin offered and delineated "Marxism–Leninism" as the Soviet Union's official ideology and approach to economic governance. Stalin (1939, p. 3) emphasized its importance as "the theory and practice of the dictatorship of the proletariat" that would also be "serving the interests of the working class." And this particular requirement became the main criterion for evaluation of other social and economic concepts. Therefore, if an economic theory was judged to serve "the interests of the bourgeoisie," perceived as a reactionary class during those times, such an economic doctrine or concept was marked as "vulgar" and for limiting inquiry to surface phenomena without penetrating into the deeper structures of social relations of production that clearly included class relations.

In addition, an officially termed "political economy of socialism" was spelled out by the Soviet leadership for investigating and explaining developments taking place in the recently formed Soviet economic and social order. And curiously, within this environment of officially sanctioned Marxism–Leninism, critiques emerged and took the form of competing schools. However, these competing schools were relegated to the periphery and were designated as forms of "bourgeois (vulgar) political economy," and, in this manner, were safely categorized and then presented as contributions to the "history of economic thought." These are the conditions under which evolutionary-institutional (including Veblen's) thinking got started in the Soviet Union during the early years of the Grand Experiment.

One of the first references to American institutionalism, in general, and to Veblen's contribution, in particular, can be found in *The Subjective School in Political Economy* (1928), authored by Israel Blyumin. As a Soviet economist and historian of economic thought, Blyumin's writings suggest that institutionalism offers a theoretical alternative to marginalism, in the tradition established by Alfred Marshall which came to dominate in Great Britain and across the vast colonial and post-colonial empire. Towards the end of his book, entitled *Sketches of Modern Bourgeois Theoretical Economics (On the Characterization of the Social School)*, Blyumin (1930) registered as the first to present Veblen's seminal ideas in explicit detail to the economists of the Soviet Union. However, we find it important to stress that with his book Blyumin also sought to characterize trends and tendencies in bourgeois economic theory. And in doing so, Blyumin (1961, p. 172) explicitly denounced Veblen as a "bourgeois economist" and for his "justification of private property and . . . apology for capitalism." In Blyumin's view (1961, p. 173), American institutionalism can be defined as being close to a school of "social orientation," and this school of thought is noted as reactionary "as other areas of vulgar bourgeois political economy."

In the second volume of his three-volume set, *Criticism of Bourgeois Political Economy,* Blyumin (1962) further criticized selected contributions of Veblen and also John R. Commons. In the view of Blyumin, these American institutionalists failed in using appropriate Marxian analytical categories and in emphasizing the importance of historical materialism, class struggle, and revolution – as their writings relied upon "non-scientific" (evolutionist and idealistic) categories. Blyumin labeled institutionalists as apologists operating under the flag of reformism with ideas defending monopoly capitalism. In addition, Blyumin (1962, p. 342) directly criticized these American institutionalists for accepting and asserting that there is indeed a "possibility of resolving peacefully the antagonistic contradictions of capitalism" and for attempting to modify American capitalism by introducing and integrating what John R. Commons refers to as the notion of "reasonable." In the Preface to his book *Legal Foundations of Capitalism* (1924), Commons applies this term "reasonable" as an adjective describing "value," "safety," "the wage," and even "conduct." Though Commons notes difficulties in offering a clear definition of what is meant by *reasonable*, he connects its meaning with court rulings that interpret this term as what can be sustained over time.

Though some of Blyumin's critical points regarding institutionalism were clearly polemical in character, still many of his points proved accurate and have retained their importance and relevance until the present. Among these enduring contributions, Blyumin (1962, p. 337) lamented the vagueness of the concept of "institution," that also tends to be defined differently by selected contributors. These varying definitions render theoretical classification difficult, as well as the processing of empirical data – what might also be argued later created room for the emergence of New Institutionalism in the traditions established by Ronald Coase, Oliver Williamson, and Douglass North, in particular. In addition, Blyumin wrote of some of the historical relationships between the changing conditions and the need for new theoretical understandings. He indicated that

American and European institutionalism could be viewed as an outgrowth of new tendencies in the development of capitalist economies; such as the increasing concentration of capital and, relatedly, the dominant roles assumed by monopolies, as well as the changing roles of the banking sector, the growth of the trade union movement, and the relative strengthening of the role of collective (social) over individual interests.

At the time that Blyumin leveled his critiques, seminal contributions of established institutionalists had not been translated into the Russian language. In our interpretations, the pointed criticisms posed by Blyumin offered the service of spelling out the comprehensive views advanced by the institutionalist thinkers that he considers. Because his critiques were not intended to enrich the new Soviet political economy of socialism with the importation of institutionalist ideas, this suggests to us a fairly clear example of what we interpret as a sign of the proclivity for inversion cycles, noted by Alexandr Akhiezer and introduced above, that are evidenced by an absence of a "median utilitarian culture." This tendency suggests that, instead of spreading and benefiting from novel and possibly useful ideas, such ideas were held at the long end of a broom.

Likely influenced by Blyumin's critiques, negative perceptions of institutional thought endured over the next decades. Appearing in the 1950s as an entry into *The Great Soviet Encyclopedia,* "Institutionalists" were characterized as "the most vicious enemies of the working class among all of the representatives of vulgar political economy" (Bolshaya Sovetskaya Entsiklopediya, 1953, p. 239). Russian scholars were prone to stress that institutionalists offered a theoretical justification for capitalism and in this manner contributed towards its further development. More pointedly, institutionalists were thought to be "in the service of imperialist reaction" (see, for example, Alter, 1948, 1961, 1971). Relatedly, in the subsequent edition of the *The Great Soviet Encyclopedia,* V. S. Afanasyev (1972, p. 296) stressed that institutionalism should be understood as a "vulgar trend in American bourgeois political economy."

As pointed and as harsh as these critiques appear nevertheless, some Soviet researchers followed the development of institutionalism from within the confines of the Soviet Union's academic and scientific discipline labeled as "critique of bourgeois political economy." Included along with Blyumin, Alter, and Afanasyev are thinkers and authors such as K. B. Kozlova (1987), V. D. Sikora (1983), and Sofia Sorokina (1981).

In fact, Sorokina (1981) is known for authoring the first monograph appearing in the Russian language and that was exclusively devoted towards offering a clear analysis of institutionalism and its advances over time. Our research suggests that her book delivers the most complete statement of institutional concepts and their critiques, and we can note that this book, first published in 1981, was reprinted twice during the year 2011. Of special interest is that Sorokina emphasizes that starting with the 1960s, institutionalist ideas spread among economists throughout the world, but not back home in the USSR. She is of the expressed opinion that the widespread renaissance in institutionalist thinking was further goaded by the economic recession of 1974–1975, and efforts related to mitigating the downturn suggested a lack of effectiveness of Keynesian concepts and especially of a state's ability to regulate an economy and implement policies that could reverse such a downturn. In her opinion, the popularity of the ideas advanced by Keynes and his followers, along with exponents of the neoclassical school as a whole, fell into disfavor and institutional ideas attracted new supporters. Sorokina (1981, p. 3) stressed that: "institutionalism emerged as one of the main trends in contemporary bourgeois economics." In addition, she stressed that institutional thinking went far beyond the United States and included widely acclaimed thinkers such as Swedish economist Gunnar Myrdal, the French economist François Perry, among others.

In spite of these acknowledgments by Sorokina, and in accordance with the platform of the XXVI Congress of the Communist Party of the Soviet Union held in 1981, efforts in the social science disciplines remained focused on "criticisms of anti-communism, the bourgeois, and revisionist concepts of social development, and for exposing the falsifiers of Marxism-Leninism" (Proceedings of the XXVI Congress of the Communist Party of the Soviet Union, 1981). Such positions hampered the possibilities for fruitful exchanges of ideas between Soviet social scientists and those advancing institutional thought from outside of the Soviet Union.

While efforts on the part of officials indeed hampered advances in institutional thinking in the Soviet Union, the battles fought to thwart its arrival and spreading influences lessened in intensity. One outcome worth noting is the emergence of a better-balanced analysis of the views of institutionalists, and that some of the most important contributions coming in from abroad were actually translated, published, and distributed.

Thorstein Veblen's *The Theory of the Leisure Class: An Economic Study in Institutions* registers as one of the first contributions to appear in this manner. Initially published in the United States in 1899, Veblen's first book was finally translated more than 80 years later and then disseminated in Russian in book form in 1984. It is important to note that the Russian translation of Veblen's first book registers as especially significant, and one measure of its significance is that this book's long and complete "Introduction" stretched to 54 pages, offering a biography of Veblen, as well as a comprehensive summary of the main ideas that he had contributed over the course of his productive career. Sorokina authored this comprehensive "Introduction" to the Russian edition and she also undertook the task of translation. Important to note is that the subtitle of *An Economic Study in Institutions* did not appear in the Russian edition, as the word "institution" was still banned in the 1980s.

The abstract for this book indicates that the views of Veblen were judged as still inappropriate in the Soviet Union. However, Sorokina (1981) emphasized that "[Veblen] . . . acted with sharp criticisms of capitalism, the financial oligarchy, and the leisure class." This statement justified the translation of his work into Russian with a recommendation to read it, not only the "specialists in the field of bourgeois economic theories," but also other Soviet "scientists and teachers of social sciences."

Institutionalist approaches of Soviet thinkers

In the USSR, Economic Science was divided into selected research areas, and these divisions were also affected by the importance of the respective areas relative to the larger world. Our research suggests that what we label as a "window to the outside world" was opened for specialists who studied tendencies in bourgeois political economy. Important to consider is that the bulk of Soviet theorists remained focused on the field of the political economy of socialism, and because of their specializations, members of this large community tended to remain unaware of tendencies in economic thought taking place outside of the Soviet Union's borders.

Notwithstanding this and commencing during the 1980s, some Soviet research scientists began to quietly and gently introduce new concepts that did not fit into the *procrustean bed* of the official ideology, with its Marxian emphasis upon the productive forces, production relations, and class. A category of organizational and economic relations proposed by prominent Russian economist-academician Leonid Abalkin, in his books *The Dialectic of the Socialistic Economy* (1981), serves as one of the attempts to introduce institutionalist categories into official thinking and is clearly found in the title *Institutionalism in Russian Economic Thought*, a book coauthored by Oleg Inshakov and Daniil Frolov (2002, vol. 2, p. 206). It was Abalkin who suggested that the Russians differentiate their social and economic relationships from organizations. Years later, and with the benefit of hindsight, we can note that this proposed division paralleled ideas also advanced in the writings of Douglass North, and so was seen as an important advance in the orientation of the institutionalist framework emerging in post-Soviet Russia. However, Abalkin failed in offering a clearly defined institutionalist approach in his writings, although he actively supported the development of institutionalist research as Russia emerged out of the post-Soviet era.[3]

While topics dealing with the political economy of socialism remained largely closed to those researchers interested in advancing institutionalist thinking, the discipline of sociology benefited from greater degrees of methodological freedom. As early as 1971 the journal *Kommunist*, which served as the official organ of the Central Committee of the Communist Party, published an article jointly authored by G.E. Glezerman, V.Z. Kelly and N.V. Pilipenko entitled: "Historical Materialism: The Theory and Methodology of Scientific Knowledge and Revolutionary Action." The appearance of this article assisted in creating an area of autonomy in sociological research through introducing an approach with three tiers that, with time, came to be officially recognized. In accordance with this approach, the upper level of sociological knowledge should be recognized as "sociological theory," in general, and as Marxian philosophy (*historical materialism*), in particular. The second tier includes specific sociological theories definable as sections of so-called "*scientific communism.*" The third tier was defined as "empirical" and could be based upon focused surveys and case studies.

As a prominent and respected Soviet sociologist, Vladimir Yadov (1990, p. 3), later stressed that this article by Glezerman *et al.* emphasized that the discipline of Sociology does not stand in contradiction to either Marxist philosophy or Marxist ideology and, in this manner, Yadov managed to create some room for sociological inquiry that included the use of approaches that had previously been suppressed by official sanctions.

Our interpretation is that this article's publication helped to facilitate a compromise that offered Soviet scholars an opportunity to carry out research at the level of the third tier, while freeing these scholars from having to peg their research to official doctrine. What got labeled as "Empirical Sociology" could then focus, not only on the theoretical discussions, but also on field studies, statistical analysis, and sociological surveys that assisted in bringing this discipline further and further away from official doctrine and closer and closer to social science reality. This newly created space for sociology allowed for developing ways for summarizing collected empirical data of studies undertaken.

With this newly created room for scientific inquiry, the Novosibirsk School of Economic Sociology (NSES) was formed, and as Kirdina (2013) emphasizes, was also distinguished by its orientation towards a systemic analysis of social phenomena through insightful empirical research and interpretation. This school initially emerged as a department focused on societal problems within the Institute of Economy and Industrial Engineering of the Siberian Branch of the Academy of Sciences of the USSR (now the Russian Academy of Sciences). As the NSES defined itself and its research orientations, its members decided to focus on developments taking place at home in the USSR, and later in transitioning Russia. Emphasis was then placed upon finding out and establishing the stable and enduring institutions that have proved integral to Russian economic development over the long run. This school rejects the idea that the framework associated with a market economy is to be considered as the universal organizational model. Furthermore, the Novosibirsk school stresses that economic relations are not to be investigated in an atomistic fashion, but as integral to the entire social structure. Furthermore, this orientation can be related to the meaning of an "embedded" economy in the sense advanced by Karl Polanyi in his 1944 classic, *The Great Transformation.*

Members of the team of sociologists from Novosibirsk are often referred to as the "social economists," and this is noted and emphasized in the writings of Irina Davydova (1997) and Vilen Ivanov (2003). As leader of the NSES in the mid-1980s, Tatyana Zaslavskaya (1985) introduced the term and related concepts of a *social mechanism of economic development.* In a subsequent and coauthored work, Zaslavskaya and R.V. Ryvkina (1991) further developed the meaning of this expression. We judge this as the key development that placed *institutions* at the core of social science inquiry in Russia in the late Soviet era, as this registers as the first attempt to employ elements of institutional analysis in the USSR.[4] Key elements of Zaslavskaya's thinking were officially presented for the Western audience in 1990, although before then his ideas were known through a publication titled *Novosibirsk Report*, which we assess reads something like a manifesto (its text was published in a book by Tatyana Zaslavskaya (2007, pp. 11–32). In addition, the appearance of these ideas helped to initiate sharp criticisms of social conditions in the Soviet Union. It is rumored that someone leaked a copy of this *Report* from the closed conference in Novosibirsk in April 1983, and then the *Washington Post* published this information in August of that year (https://en.wikipedia.org/wiki/Novosibirsk_Report). A journalist then referred to this document through the *Washington Post* (1983) as the *first bird* of General Secretary Michael Gorbachev's reform program that would later be popularized as *Perestroika.*

While Soviet economists were coerced to adhere to the official line, these noted advances by the Novosibirsk School promoted an understanding that *institutions* proved integral and helped to constitute the subject matter for sociology inquiry.

Russian institutional thought more recently

While it could be argued that institutional thought experienced a long incubation period stretching over many decades, the situation changed after 1991 and with the start of Russia's transition to market economy. It should be recognized that the sudden and unexpected collapse of the Soviet experiment brought with it an abrupt end to Marxism–Leninism as an official ideology underpinning the social and economic sciences. Indeed, these were dramatic times and so dramatic that established – even famous – economists decided to toss out their libraries accumulated over the years, as they were suddenly faced with reinitiating their education. In short order former Soviet economists were faced with joining the world's larger economic *conversation,* borrowing this term and metaphor from Arjo Klamer (2007). Initially, in the vacuum created from the outright rejection of the tradition of the political economy of socialism, the neoclassical approach was quickly introduced into university curricula in Economic Science. However, this approach proved inadequate for explaining many of the challenges facing a post-Soviet Russia. There were a host of reasons cited, including that markets had not been thoroughly introduced for allocating the factors of production of land, labor, and capital. Because of the rapid pace of transition away from planned and towards market economy, the neoclassical approach failed to win over the lion's share of economists at the start of the post-Soviet era. In addition, the neoclassical discourse tended to scare away many potential members from joining, for this school poses barriers for understanding by relying upon reduction and an abstract-deductive approach that also includes highly specific tools and computing for advancing research. Problems integral to adopting the neoclassical paradigm thereby created and provided fertile ground for institutionalist approaches. For a thorough description of these developments, please see, for example, contributions from Daniil Frolov (2007; Inshakov and Frolov, 2002), L. Moscowskiy (2005), Rustem Nureyev and Vladimir Dementiev (2005), and Nataliya Makasheva (2006).

In sum, we could now list and detail three of the main causes promoting the spread of institutional thought in post-Soviet Russia. First, is the sudden and unexpected collapse of the Soviet experiment in "real, existing socialism," accompanied by a disbelief in what had been the supporting doctrines. Consequently, institutionalists who had been studying capitalist economies and societies shifted to a new position and were no longer seen as ideological opponents, but rather as wanted members of the new generation of potential theoretical contributors. Second, newly found openness of post-Soviet Russia to global markets, including the markets for ideas, provided new channels through which the achievements of foreign economists, institutional theorists among them, were received in the new Russia. Third, the popularity of institutionalist thought was conditioned by a pressing need for an active construction of new institutions necessary for a quickly transforming Russia. So the privatization of Russian industry and the accompanying emergence of visible oligarchs that were also seen as integral to the transition to market economy rendered Veblen's penetrating critiques of the power of big business increasingly relevant to the Russian context. In 2007, Veblen's *The Theory of Business Enterprise* [1904] was introduced. The Russian translation of this book was published by Delo (and means "Business" in Russian). Delo should be recognized as a publishing house that became specialized in translations of evolutionary-institutional works drawn from foreign sources, and that could be effectively disseminated across a broad Russian readership. About ten titles in the evolutionary-institutional tradition were translated and published between 1997 and 2012, and through this one publishing house.

If we now return to the ideas advanced by Alexandr Akhiezer related to inversion cycles, then Russia in the post-Soviet era could be described as entering into the opposite phase of what during the Soviet era was dominated by emphasis on an official version of the political economy of socialism. In short, the post-Soviet era marks the transition from institutional thought in a *thwarted phase* to a *flourishing phase*. This can be expressed as – over time – the "minus sign" dramatically shifts to "plus" in the perception of institutionalism (Figure 7.1).

Our interpretation of what is represented in Figure 7.1 is that in the 1990s there took place a sharp transition away from criticizing and rejecting institutional thought in the economic arena, to the dissemination of ideas across a large domestic community of economists, including ideas that also penetrated and altered university curricula. Author Daniil Frolov (2007, 2009) defined the 1990s and this first decade of transition as an active "transplanting" of foreign institutional thinking into Russian economic and social thought. This decade could also be considered in a sense as a *golden age*, defined by the largely uncontrolled and uninterrupted flow of economic ideas into Russia. During this first decade of transition, numerous writings of Western authors were translated and published, and, characteristically, were presented with comprehensive introductions. In most cases, these introductions also provided platforms for Russian scholars to offer their professional judgments of ideas coming in from Western economists. Substantial financial support from abroad, especially from the United States and European Union countries, assisted with rapid translations into Russian and then the publication and dissemination of notable works authored by foreign institutionalists, as well as preparations for the first generation of university textbooks on institutional economics that were widely distributed throughout the geographic territory of the Russian Federation. Foreign foundations and organizations – such as the Soros Foundation, USAID, the World Bank, plus some European Science

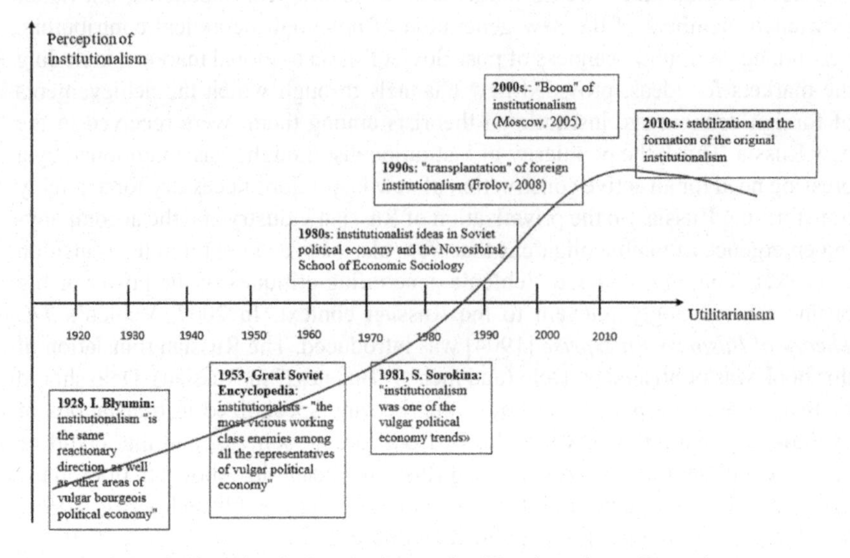

Figure 7.1 Institutionalism in Russia: in search of Berdyaev's median culture

Foundations – proved instrumental. We can also note the financing and supporting of contacts between Russian economists with their foreign counterparts. Numerous educational, as well as research and publishing, projects that involved hundreds of experts from Russia and some of the former Soviet republics were included. This first decade of transition could be judged as a period for quickly bringing Russian institutionalists up to a world standard.

Discussion and conclusion

At the start of this inquiry we distinguished two distinct phases in the Russian perception of institutional thought. We defined the *thwarted phase* by its tendency of outright rejection of institutional thought during the long Soviet era, and this rejection seems related to the Soviet leadership's interest in ensuring the dominance of their Marxist–Leninist lines. Then, with the ending of the Soviet era, we can notice dramatic increases in levels of interest in institutional thought that might also be defined as the *flourishing phase*. In these respects, our research tends to conform with Akhiezer's understanding and uses of inversion cycles for shedding some needed light on Russian historical experiences that also include intellectual history.

From this angle, we could then consider some of the contributions of Russian institutionalists as efforts to reduce the swings of such cycles, and through, in a sense, offering a median utilitarian culture that attempts to create new middle ground for ameliorating Russia's historic tendencies to rapidly move towards polar extremes without drawing bearings from the past. For institutionalists, this means the creation of original Russian concepts that serve to integrate native advancements into the original institutional thought selected from abroad, and then integrated into Soviet and now Russian economic thought.

It was emphasized that, for the duration of almost all of the Soviet era, economists, especially, were affected by restrictions stemming from an official political economy of socialism based upon Marxian ideas in Soviet interpretation. And consequently, economists faced limited opportunities for absorbing, much less originating, ideas in the evolutionary-institutional tradition. The exception was to critique institutional contributions for their spurious bourgeois tendencies.

Our understanding is that, with the ending of the Soviet era, and starting with the 1992 founding of the Russian Federation, the transition era of the last two decades has indeed offered Russian thinkers greater opportunities for exposure to and adoption of foreign ideas in social and economic sciences.

In the current era the group dominating institutional studies in Russia largely relies upon ideas advanced by foreign institutionalists. At the same time a discernible group of Russian-based institutionalists has already emerged and is on its way towards becoming well established. Some of their contributions are already reflected in dictionaries and encyclopedias, with terms and meanings such as "institutional trap" (Polterovich, 2008) and "institutional matrix theory" (Kirdina, 2010), to start the list. Then there are contributions from Makasheva (2006), Moscowskiy (2005), Inshakov and Frolov (2002) as well as Frolov (2007, 2008, 2013): advancing writings that investigate and measure the significance of the rise of a home-grown Russian institutionalism. With these advances in mind, recent advances in Russian institutional thought now require domestic biographers and historians focused on social and economic thought.

To complete this inquiry, we would like to note that meaningful collaboration among Russian institutionalists and their foreign counterparts serves as a particularly useful way to form a dialogic utilitarian culture, and thereby assist in overcoming the swings of inversion cycles and the tendency for the splitting of Russian society, of which Akhiezer ([1991] 1997) warns. The prominent Russian economist Leonid Abalkin (2001, p. 73) emphasizes that:

> [t]he task of the revival of the Russian school of economic thought as an organic part of the world of science has to be undertaken. And it is not a return to the old, but the ability to understand the realities of the coming century. There is reason to believe that tomorrow belongs to those who are actively involved in creating a new paradigm of social science; who will determine the country's place in the system of alternatives for its future development; and who are able to creatively combine an analysis of global changes in our world while also preserving the uniqueness of Russian civilization.

And in this new era, certainly when compared to the Soviet era, we have established that institutional thought has advanced rapidly and also spread broadly, taking firm root. And certainly to the extent that further advances in the method and approach to institutional thinking are now identifiably growing out of Russian soil.

Notes

1 Funding for this study was supported by the Russian Foundation for Humanities, research project number 14-02-00422.
2 In our inquiry we rely upon the terms *evolutionary-institutional economics, institutionalism, institutional thinking, and institutional thought* more or less interchangeably. Our understanding of the use of these terms draws from and reflects back upon what is termed Original Institutional Economics, a field in Economic Science that finds its origins in the seminal writings of Thorstein Veblen.
3 Out of respect for Albakin's promotion of evolutionary-institutional thinking in Russia, in 2015, the Center for Evolutionary Economics, located in Moscow, introduced the Leonid Abalkin Award recognizing achievements in institutional and evolutionary research advanced by members of the younger generation of Russian scholars.
4 As one of the authors of this inquiry, Svetlana Kirdina also served as a member of NSES and worked directly together with Tatyana Zaslavskaya in the 1980s and 1990s in Novosibirsk.

References

Abalkin, Leonid. 1981. *The Dialectic of the Socialistic Economy* (in Russian). Moscow: Mysl.

Abalkin, Leonid. 2001. *The Russian School of Economic Thought: The Search of Self-Determination* (in Russian). Moscow: Institut Economiki.

Afanasyev, V. S. 1972. Institutionalism. In: *The Great Soviet Encyclopedia*. 3rd ed., Vol. 10 (in Russian). Moscow: Sovetskaya Entsiklopediya.

Akhiezer, Alexandr. 1991. *Russia: Criticism of Historical Experience. Volume 2. (Sociocultural Dictionary)* (in Russian). Novosibirsk: Sibirskiy Chronograph.

Akhiezer, Alexandr. [1991] 1997. *Russia: Criticism of Historical Experience. Volume 1. From the Past to Future* (in Russian). Novosibirsk: Sibirskiy Chronograph.

Alter, L. B. 1948. *Bourgeois Economists of the U.S. in the Service of Imperialist Reaction* (in Russian). Moscow: Gosplanizdat.

Alter, L. B. 1961. *The Bourgeois Political Economy of the United States* (in Russian). Moscow: Izdatel'stvo socio-economicheskoy literatury.

Alter, L. B. 1971. *Selected Works. Bourgeois Political Economy of the United States* (in Russian). Moscow: Nauka.

Berdyaev, Nicolai. 1915. *The Soul of Russia* (in Russian). Moscow: I.D. Sytin.

Blyumin, Izrail. 1928. *The Subjective School in Political Economy* (in Russian). Moscow: Izdatel'stvo Komakademii.

Blyumin, Izrail. 1930. *Sketches of Modern Bourgeois Theoretical Economics (On the Characterization of Social School)* (in Russian). Moscow: Kommunisticheskaya Akademiya, Institut Ekonomiki.

Blyumin, I. G. 1961. *History of Economic Thought (Essays on the Theory)*. in FY Polyansky, ed. (in Russian). Moscow: Gosudarstvennoe izdatel'stvo "Vyschaya shkola".

Blyumin, I. G. 1962. Institutionalism. In: *Criticism of Bourgeois Political Economy. In 3 volumes*, Vol. II. *Criticism of Modern English and American Political Economy* (in Russian). Moscow: Izdatel'stvo akademii nauk SSSR, pp. 336–352.

Bolshaya Sovetskaya Entsiklopediya. 1953. *Great Soviet Encyclopedia, Second Edition*. Vol. 18. Moscow: Sovetskaya Entsiklopediya.

Commons, J. R. 1924. *Legal Foundations of Capitalism*. New York: Macmillan.

Davydova, I. 1997. Die Nowosibirsker Soziologische Schule: Aufstieg und Niedergang eines regionalen sozialwissenschaftlichen Zentrums in Oswald Ingrid, Possekel Ralf,

Stykow Petra, Wielgolis Jan (Ed.) *Socialwissenschaft in Rusland*. Vol. 2. *Analysen russischer Forschungen zu Sozialstruktur, Wählerverhalten, Regionalentwicklung, ethnischen Konflikten, Geopolitik, nationalen Interessen und Sowjetgeschichte*. Berlin: Berliner Debatte, pp. 151–172.

Frolov, Daniil. 2007. How we taught institutionalism in Russia (in Russian). *Economic Herald of the Rostov State University*, 5(3): 155–164.

Frolov, Daniil. 2008. Institutional evolution of post-soviet institutionalism (in Russian). *Voprosy Economiki*, 4: 130–140.

Frolov, Daniil. 2009. *Prospects for the Russian Institutional Economics*. Paper for the First Economic Congress on 10 December 2009 (in Russian). http://www.econorus.org/consp/d21.html (accessed 12 May 2015).

Frolov, Daniil. 2013. Metaphorism of institutionalism: Physicalism vs biologism (in Russian), *Terra Economicus*, 11(3): 34–51.

Glezerman, G. E., Kelly, V. Z., & Pilipenko, N. V. 1971. Historical materialism: The theory and methodology of scientific knowledge and revolutionary action (in Russian), *Kommunist*, 4: 60–70.

Inshakov, O., & Frolov, Daniil. 2002. *Institutionalism in Russian Economic Thought* (in Russian), Vol. 1 and 2. Volgograd: Izdatel'snvo Volgogradskogo gosudarstvennogo universiteta.

Ippolitov, L. M. 2008. Birth of institutionalist economics in Russia (about a methodological discussion of the 1920s) (in Russian), *Vestnik isntututa ekonomiki Rossiyskoy akademii nauk*, 4: 43–57.

Ivanov, V. N. 2003. The Novosibirsk sociological school. In: *Sociological Encyclopedia* (in Russian), Vol. 2. Moscow: Mysl.

Kirdina, Svetlana. 2006. Glance and poverty of the political economy of socialism (in Russian), *Jurnal Ekonomitcheskoi Theorii*, 2: 19–39.

Kirdina, Svetlana. 2010. Institutional matrix theory. In: Osipov, G.V., & Miskvichev, L.N. (Eds), *Sociological Dictionary* (in Russian). Moscow: INFRA-M.

Kirdina, Svetlana. 2013. New systemic institutional approach for comparative political and economic analysis, *Review of Radical Political Economy*, 45(3): 341–348.

Klamer, Arjo. 2007. *Speaking of Economic: How to Get in the Conversation*. London: Routledge.

Kozlova, K. B. 1987. *Institutionalism in American Political Economy* (in Russian). Moscow: Nauka.

Makasheva, Nataliya. 2006. Economics in Russia in the transformation period (end of the 1980s until the 1990s): Revolution and scientific knowledge increasing (in Russian). In: *Beginnings: Studying the Economy of Both the Structure and Process*. Moscow: GU-WSHE, pp. 400–426.

Marx, Karl. [1867] 1990. *Das Kapital, Band I*. London: Penguin.

Marx, Karl, & Engels, Frederick. 1848. *The Communist Manifesto*. New York: International Publishers.

Matveeva, Susanna. 1997. Split society: The path and the fate of Russia in socio-cultural theory by Alexandr Akhiezer (in Russian). In: Akhiezer, Alexandr (Ed.), *Russia: Criticism of Historical Experience. Volume 1. From the Past to Future*. Novosibirsk: Sibirskiy Chronograph, pp. 3–41.

Moscowskiy, L. 2005. Limits of institutionalism (in Russian). *The Economist*, 6: 74–81.

Nureyev, R. M., & Dementiev, V. V. 2005. Formation of the post-soviet institutionalism (in Russian). In: Nureyev, R.M., & Dementiev, V.V. (Eds), *Post-Soviet Institutionalism*. Donetsk: Kashtan, pp. 446–479.

Polanyi, Karl. 1944. *The Great Transformation.* New York: Farrar and Rinehart.

Polterovich, Victor "Institutional Trap". 2008. *New Palgrave Dictionary of Economics and Law, Second Edition.* Available at SSRN: http://ssrn.com/abstract=1751839.

Proceedings of the XXVI Congress of the Communist Party of the Soviet Union. 1981 (in Russian). Moscow: Politizdat. http://publ.lib.ru/ARCHIVES/K/KPSS/_KPSS.html#026 (accessed 20 March 2015).

Sikora, V. D. 1983. *Anti-Orthodox Economic Theory (Critical Analysis)* (in Russian). Kiev: Vishcha Shkola.

Sorokina, Sofia. 1981. *Scenarios for the Future, or Illusions of the Past?: On Institutionalism as the Trend n of Bourgeois Economic Thought* (in Russian). Moscow: Izdatel'stvo Mysl'.

Stalin, Josef. 1939 (1924). *Foundations of Leninism.* Moscow: Foreign Language Press.

Veblen, Thorstein. 1904. *The Theory of Business Enterprise.* New York: Charles Scribner's Sons.

Veblen, Thorstein. 1899. *The Theory of the Leisure Class: An Economic Study in Institutions*. New York: Macmillan.

Yadov, V. A. 1990. "Reflections on the subject of sociology" (in Russian). *Sociological Studies*, 2:3–16.

Zaslavskaya, Tatyana. 1985. On the social mechanism of economic development (in Russian). In: *Ways of Improving the Social Mechanism of the Soviet Economy.* Novosibirsk: IEiOPP SB RAS.

Zaslavskaya, Tatyana. 1990. *The Second Socialist Revolution: An Alternative Soviet Strategy*. Bloomington, IN: Indiana University Press, p. 241.

Zaslavskaya, T. I. 2007. *Selected Works. Transformation Process in Russia: Searching for New Methodology*, Volume Two (in Russian). Moscow: Publishing House "Economika".

Zaslavskaya, Tatyana., & Ryvkina, Rozalina. 1991. *Sociology of Economic Life: Essays on the Theory* (in Russian). Moscow: Nauka.

8 Market performance – liquidity or knowledge?

Evidence from the market for corporate control

Killian McCarthy and Wilfred Dolfsma

Introduction

The definition of the market remains hotly debated (cf. Rosenbaum, 2000). Economists argue that markets are places where supply and demand meet to determine prices. The more 'liquid' the markets, they argue – that is, the more that the market facilitates the purchase or sale of an asset without causing drastic change in the asset's price – the better, because in liquid markets buyers find sellers, and deals get done. Management scholars, however, argue that markets are also locations in which relevant knowledge coalesces. They argue that the more relevant information the better, because in markets with high levels of relevant information, buyers understand sellers, and the deals, and ensure the better deals are concluded.

In both cases, geography, of course, plays an interesting role. Most transactions are done by partners in the same geographic location, but in an increasingly globalised world, geographic proximity is no longer required to do business. Geography, however, limits the flow of information; tacit information – regarding, for example, what constitutes a fair price and with whom one should and should not do business – degrades with distance. The result, therefore, is the segmentation of 'the' market into multiple, separate, but overlapping markets, possibly compounded by the 'liability of foreignness' (Hymer, 1976); that is, the creation costs 'based on a particular company's unfamiliarity with and lack of roots in the [market]' (Zaheer, 1995, p. 342). We know that geographic borders and the liability of foreignness predict deal performance. The question that remains is: how do differences in the way in which markets function impact deal performance? What happens, for example, if a firm enters an efficient, well-functioning market, and another firm doesn't?

In this chapter, we define the markets as an 'institutionalised exchange, where a consensus over prices and other information may be established' (Hodgson, 1999, p. 269). We study a market in which complex goods are traded: firms themselves. We build a sample of sample of 35,709 mergers and acquisitions, completed in the period from January 1, 1990 to December 31, 2012. In each case, and for each acquiring firm's city, we estimate the levels of 'market liquidity' and 'market knowledge' using different network analysis tools. We estimate 'market liquidity' by estimating each city's 'degree centrality' (Freeman, 1979), and we estimate 'market knowledge' by estimating each city's 'betweenness centrality' (Freeman, 1979). We then estimate deal performance, using the a market-adjusted event study, and determine how these factors impact performance, and indeed determine which of these effects is biggest (cf. Fuller et al., 2002).

Literature

Markets are physical or virtual places in which parties voluntarily exchange specific goods. Market transactions are voluntary exchanges, between two or more partners, both of whom aim to create and to capture value. Market transactions are often completed with a medium of exchange, such as money, and often involve a degree of uncertainty about what is exchanged, and how it will be valued in the future.

Classical economics suggests that markets function well in one of two circumstances. Firstly, markets function well when they are liquid – meaning that the market can facilitate the purchase or sale of an asset without causing drastic change in the asset's price – because in a liquid market supply and demand can be more readily reconciled (Zuidhof, 2014). In a liquid market, buyers are more likely to find what they are looking for, without having to settle for a less attractive good, meaning that better deals are done. Secondly, markets function well when there is information. Markets with more relevant knowledge, Austrian economists, such as Friedrich Hayek (1945) suggest, mean that fewer mistakes are made, and so again better deals are done.

Geography, of course, plays an interesting role in this equation. Most transactions are done by partners in the same geographic location, but in an increasingly globalised world, geographic proximity is no longer required to do business. Geography, however, limits the flow of information; tacit information – regarding, for example, what constitutes a fair price and with whom one should and should not do business – degrades with distance. The result, therefore, is the segmentation of 'the' market into multiple, separate, but overlapping markets, possibly compounded by the 'liability of foreignness' (Hymer, 1976); that is, the creation costs 'based on a particular company's unfamiliarity with and lack of roots in the [market]' (Zaheer, 1995, p. 342). We know that geographic borders and the liability of foreignness predict deal performance. The question that remains is: how do differences in the way in which markets function impact deal performance? What happens, for example, if a firm enters an efficient, well-functioning market, and another firm doesn't?

The current literature leads us to suggest that entering a well-functioning market will improve performance, while entering a less well-functioning market will reduce performance. The suggestion is that 'foreign' firms – by which we mean firms from outside the market – will be at a disadvantage, according to the liability of foreignness, but *ceteris paribus* it is better to enter into a better-functioning market. Thus:

Hypothesis 1: Deals done in more liquid markets perform better.
Hypothesis 2: Deals done in markets with more relevant knowledge will perform better.

Methods

Empirical setting

We tested our hypotheses using the market for corporate control. The market for corporate control is the market in which ownership in companies is traded. This market is an interesting empirical setting for a number of reasons: firstly, because the market is an active one; about 30,000 deals are done a year, or one deal every 18 minutes (McCarthy & Dolfsma, 2012), and some $682bn worth of deals were concluded in the first quarter of 2016 alone.[1] The second reason is that trades done in this market are complex, highly dependent on regulation in place, keenly future-oriented, and concluded by exceptionally highly knowledgeable players. In this knowledge-intensive market, the types of deals concluded, if not the type of deals considered by players, are diverse. Knowledge thus appears to be an important ingredient for performance of deals done, but also the likelihood that supply-and-demand preferences and conditions are met with. The latter indicates that deals done in a more liquid market should be expected to do well.

Data

We used Thomson SDC to build our acquisition sample. We refined this to include all deals between January 1, 1990 and December 31, 2012, which did not involve recapitalisation, repurchase of own shares or a spin-off to existing shareholders. We only included deals for more than 10 million US$, announced by publicly listed acquirers, in which the location of both the target and the acquiring firms were reported. We excluded deals involving the public authorities, such as the US government, and all deals in which the acquirer and the target were part of the same group. Doing so, we created an initial sample of 35,709 mergers and acquisitions. Figure 8.1 illustrates the geographic spread of the 35,709 acquiring firms in our sample.

Market function

We measured market function in terms of centrality, arguing that more central locations are more liquid, and more exposed to more information. We used social network analysis (SNA) to describe centrality. SNA allows for an analysis about how knowledge spreads through a network of interconnected locations in which players are active (Freeman, 1979; Aalbers & Dolfsma, 2015). From the perspective of SNA, partners doing deals from a particular location can be viewed in the aggregate as a node in a network connecting to partners in another location that in turn can be viewed in the aggregate as a node. Nodes for our purposes are markets where market players are based. Relations or ties between nodes are formed by the deals done between partners in a location (market). We measured each location's centrality in the network using two different centrality measures (see Opsahl et al., 2010, for an overview). The first and the simplest measure of centrality – degree centrality – considers the number of ties that each node in the network possesses,

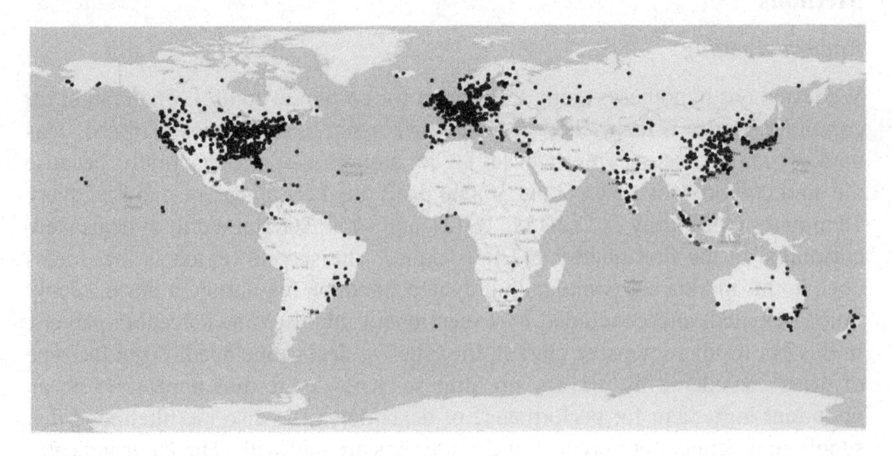

Figure 8.1 The geographic spread of the sample

compared to the total size of the network. The second, betweenness centrality, is a measure of the number of times a node is included on the shortest path between other nodes in the network. Betweenness centrality, therefore, considers the degree to which a node bridges between any two other nodes (e.g. Gilsing et al., 2008). We calculated both measures, given that both measures capture different elements of network centrality. Specifically, we proxied 'market liquidity' as each city's 'degree centrality' (Freeman, 1979), and we proxied 'market knowledge' by estimating each city's 'betweenness centrality' (Freeman, 1979).

Performance

We measured deal performance using a market-adjusted event study (Brown & Warner, 1980, 1985; Fuller et al., 2002; Schoenberg, 2006; Papadakis & Thanos, 2010; Gregory et al., 2013). This technique is, today, the most commonly employed measure of acquisition performance in the strategic literature on acquisition performance (King et al., 2004; McNamara et al., 2008; Zollo & Meier, 2008).

An event study is a tool used for assessing the way in which an event – such as an acquisition – causes a change in the value of a firm (Brown & Warner, 1980, 1985). In an event study, historical data are used to forecast 'normal' performance at a future date. Comparing this 'forecast' of how the firm should have performed – in the absence of an event – with 'actual' data on how the firm performed – in the presence of the event – provides an indicator of the firm's 'abnormal' return; this is the change in value, above or below the firm's expected value, attributable to the event. The sum of the acquirer's abnormal returns (ARs) in a predefined period of time (the 'event window') is referred to as the cumulative abnormal returns (CARs).

More specifically, we calculated the firm's abnormal return of firm *i*:

$$AR_{i,t} = R_{i,t} - E\left[R_{i,t}\right] \tag{1}$$

where $R_{i,t}$ is the actual return and $E[R_{i,t}]$ is the estimated or normal return (Brown & Warner, 1980, 1985; MacKinlay, 1997; McNamara et al., 2008; Duso et al., 2010). Normal returns are then calculated as:

$$E\left[R_{i,t}\right] = \alpha_i + \beta_i R_{m,t} + \varepsilon_{i,t} \tag{2}$$

where α_i is the intercept coefficient, β_i is the slope, $R_{m,t}$ the formation of the benchmarks used and $\varepsilon_{i,t}$ is expected to be equal to 0 (Brown & Warner, 1980, 1985; MacKinlay, 1997). The abnormal returns in the event window are added, to create the CAR to the firm as:

$$CAR_i\left[t_1, t_2\right] = \sum_{t=t_1}^{t_2} AR_{i,t} \tag{3}$$

Strategic management studies often use accounting-based measures of acquisition performance, such as return on assets (e.g., Ramaswamy, 1997). CARs are thought to be the more appropriate measure because: (1) the event study methodology is the most frequently used analytical approach for measuring acquisition performance (e.g. Capron & Pistre, 2002; King et al., 2004; McNamara et al., 2008; Zollo & Meier, 2008); (2) acquisition effects are not immediately reflected in the financial statements of an acquirer, because it often takes 6 months to 3 years before the acquirer realises the effects (Rhoades, 1983), and during this period, many confounding factors, such as changes in product mix, investment strategy and management, as well as execution of additional acquisitions, may affect firm performance; (3) accounting-based performance measures can be misleading because accounting procedures are not uniform across firms and industries (Benston, 1985); and (4) research has shown that *ex ante* measures of acquirer abnormal returns are highly correlated with *ex post* measures of acquisition performance, demonstrating that event study methodology has predictive validity (Healy et al., 1992).

Following the practice in the literature, we compute abnormal returns to the shareholder of the acquiring firm using a number of different event windows (see Martynova & Renneboog, 2008 for a review). We calculate: a (+1,–1) CAR to the acquiring firm, from 1 trading day before the announcement to 1 day after (CAR1); a (+1,–2) CAR, from 2 trading days before the announcement to 1 day after (CAR2); a (+1,–5) CAR, from 5 trading days, or 1 week before the announcement to 1 day after (CAR5); and a (+1,–20) CAR, from 20 trading days, or 4 weeks, or 1 month, before the announcement to 1 day after (CAR1). It is standard practice to include the period prior to the announcement in the estimation to capture the effect of rumours and information leakages, which drive up the firm's share price, in anticipation of future performance gains (Schwert, 1996). In order to remove the effect of outliers, we winsorised all CARs between 1 and

99%. Data limitations, at this point, reduced the sample of acquisitions for which we could calculate performance from 35,709 to 19,273. We dropped the remaining deals from our analysis.

Controls

A number of acquirer-, target-, and deal-specific characteristics are known to impact the way in which the market responds to the announcement of a deal (see, e.g. King et al., 2004). We controlled for: (1) the *per cent acquired,* in terms of how much of the target the acquirer purchases, because deals for less than 100% often run into more difficulties in the integration phase; (2) acquirer's *financial slack* – which we define as the acquirer's operating cash flow, normalised by total assets over the last four quarters before the announcement – because Jensen (1986) suggests that financial slack predicts sub-par acquisition performance; (3) the acquirer's *prior performance* – which we estimate as the acquirer's return on assets the year before the acquisition – because research shows that prior performance predicts future performance (Morck et al., 1990); (4) *acquirer market-to-book ratio* – which is a ratio of the acquirer's market value to its book value – because Rau and Vermaelen (1998) show that market-to-book ratios predict acquisition behaviour and performance; (5) *relatedness* – which we identified using an indicator variable set equal to 1 if the target and acquirer share the same primary two-digit standard industrial classification (SIC) code – because research-related acquisitions outperform unrelated acquisitions (Chatterjee, 1986); and (6) *cross-border deals* – which we identified with a dummy set equal to 1 if the target and the acquirer are from different countries – because the international business literature is premised upon the suggestion that international borders imply costs. The data to construct these variables were collected from Datastream.

Table 8.1 reports the correlation and descriptive statistics for our key variables. We winsorised each of the control variables, between 0.05 and 99.5%, to remove outliers. We tested each of the controls for the normality assumption, using a Shapiro–Wilk test, and employed the logs of any variables (*acquirer's financial slack, acquirer's prior performance*) which failed this test when entering these in our model.

Estimation

We estimated the impact of centrality on performance using standard ordinary least squares (OLS) regression techniques. We controlled, in all estimates, for unobserved effects by including: (1) year dummies; and (2) industry dummies for the acquirers and target industry, using each firm's two-digit SIC codes

Results

We estimated eight OLS regression models. Tables 8.2 and 8.3 report the results. Table 8.2 reports four OLS models in which the independent measure is betweenness

Table 8.1 Descriptive statistics

	Mean	*SD*	*Min.*	*Max.*	*1*	*2*	*–3*	*4*	*5*	*6*	*7*	*8*	*9*	*10*	*11*	*12*
1 CAR1	0.01	0.06	–0.16	0.24	1.00											
2 CAR2	0.01	0.14	–0.40	0.51	0.43	1.00										
					0.00											
3 CAR5	0.01	0.08	–0.22	0.31	0.68	0.60	1.00									
					0.00	0.00										
4 CAR20	0.01	0.14	–0.40	0.51	0.43	1.00	0.60	1.00								
					0.00	–1.00	0.00									
5 Degree centrality	151.28	104.12	1.00	379.00	–0.03	–0.01	–0.03	–0.01	1.00							
					0.00	–0.09	0.00	–0.09								
6 Betweeness centrality	0.01	0.01	0.00	0.04	–0.02	–0.01	–0.02	–0.01	0.86	1.00						
					0.00	–0.21	–0.01	–0.21	0.00							
7 Per cent acquired	97.20	9.44	51.00	100.00	0.00	0.01	0.01	0.01	0.05	–0.06	1.00					
					–0.65	–0.07	–0.06	–0.07	0.00	0.00						
8 Acquirer's financial slack (log)	–2.90	0.99	–11.01	3.44	0.00	–0.01	0.00	–0.01	0.00	–0.09	0.08	1.00				
					–0.62	–0.47	–0.77	–0.47	–0.90	0.00	0.00					
9 Acquirer's prior performance (log)	1.82	0.84	–4.61	6.06	–0.01	–0.02	–0.01	–0.02	–0.02	–0.09	0.08	0.81	1.00			
					–0.15	–0.03	–0.25	–0.03	–0.05	0.00	0.00	0.00				
10 Acquirer's market-to-book ratio	0.00	0.15	–3.33	19.15	0.00	–0.01	–0.01	–0.01	0.00	0.00	0.00	0.01	0.01	1.00		
					–0.54	–0.32	–0.45	–0.32	–0.54	–0.56	–0.69	–0.24	–0.32			
11 Related acquisition	0.35	0.48	0.00	1.00	0.00	–0.01	–0.01	–0.01	–0.01	–0.02	0.01	–0.03	–0.03	0.00	1.00	
					–0.62	–0.25	–0.11	–0.25	–0.20	0.00	–0.07	0.00	0.00	–0.95		
12 Cross-border acquisition	0.26	0.44	0.00	1.00	0.01	0.00	0.00	0.00	–0.09	0.01	–0.09	0.00	0.02	–0.01	–0.01	1.00
					–0.35	–0.82	–0.85	–0.82	0.00	–0.26	0.00	–0.84	–0.06	–0.46	–0.10	

centrality. The models differ in the dependents that they use: model 1 uses the winsorised CAR of the firm in the (+1,–1) window (CAR1), model 2 use the winsorised CAR of the firm in the (+1,–2) window (CAR2), and so on. All four models are consistent, and suggest that the betweenness centrality of the acquiring firms location has a negative impact on deal performance.

Table 8.3 reports this exercise, this time using degree centrality as the independent centrality measure. Again, the four models present a consistent story: models 5–8 report that the degree centrality of the acquiring firm's location has a negative and significant impact on the performance of the acquisition.

The relatively low r-squared in each case – between 3% and 9% – is typical of event studies. For example: Moeller et al. (2005) used an event study, and OLS

Table 8.2 Betweenness centrality and performance

Variables	*(1)* *wCAR1*	*(2)* *wCAR20*	*(3)* *wCAR5*	*(4)* *wCAR20*
Betweeness centrality	–0.10***	–0.17***	–0.11***	–0.17**
	(–2.668)	(–1.869)	(–2.143)	(–1.869)
Per cent acquired	0.00	0.00	0.00	0.00
	(0.275)	(1.067)	(1.260)	(1.067)
Acquirer's financial slack (log)	0.00	0.00	0.00	0.00
	(1.385)	(0.281)	(0.325)	(0.281)
Acquirer's prior performance (log)	–0.00	–0.00	–0.00	–0.00
	(–1.559)	(–1.053)	(–0.417)	(–1.053)
Acquirer's market-to-book ratio	–0.00	–0.01	–0.00	–0.01
	(–0.667)	(–1.406)	(–1.001)	(–1.406)
Related acquisition	0.00	0.00	–0.00	0.00
	(0.133)	(0.774)	(–0.204)	(0.774)
Cross-border acquisition	0.00*	0.00	0.00	0.00
	(1.664)	(0.395)	(0.653)	(0.395)
Year dummies	Yes	Yes	Yes	Yes
Acquirer industry dummy	Yes	Yes	Yes	Yes
Target industry dummy	Yes	Yes	Yes	Yes
Constant	–0.01	0.04	–0.00	0.04
	(–0.695)	(0.927)	(–0.026)	(0.927)
Observations	13,661	13,661	13,661	13,661
Adjusted r-squared	0.09	0.05	0.03	0.05
F	2.145	1.640	1.438	1.640

t-statistics in parentheses

***$p < 0.01$, **$p < 0.05$, *$p < 0.1$

Table 8.3 Degree centrality and performance

Variables	*(5)* *wCAR1*	*(6)* *wCAR20*	*(7)* *wCAR5*	*(8)* *wCAR20*
Degree centrality	–0.00***	–0.00***	–0.00***	–0.00**
	(–4.307)	(–1.487)	(–3.199)	(–1.487)
Per cent acquired	0.00	0.00	0.00	0.00
	(0.567)	(1.227)	(1.489)	(1.227)
Acquirer's financial slack (log)	0.00	0.00	0.00	0.00
	(1.451)	(0.320)	(0.376)	(0.320)
Acquirer's prior performance (log)	–0.00	–0.00	–0.00	–0.00
	(–1.531)	(–0.997)	(–0.386)	(–0.997)
Acquirer's market-to-book ratio	–0.00	–0.01	–0.00	–0.01
	(–0.679)	(–1.404)	(–1.008)	(–1.404)
Related acquisition	0.00	0.00	–0.00	0.00
	(0.187)	(0.818)	(–0.159)	(0.818)
Cross-border acquisition	0.00	0.00	0.00	0.00
	(1.332)	(0.303)	(0.413)	(0.303)
Year dummies	Yes	Yes	Yes	Yes
Acquirer industry dummy	Yes	Yes	Yes	Yes
Target industry dummy	Yes	Yes	Yes	Yes
Constant	–0.01	0.04	–0.00	0.04
	(–0.742)	(0.886)	(–0.065)	(0.886)
Observations	13,661	13,661	13,661	13,661
Adjusted *r*-squared	0.09	0.05	0.04	0.05
F	2.257	1.628	1.493	1.628

t-statistics in parentheses

***$p < 0.01$, **$p < 0.05$, *$p < 0.1$

estimation, to investigate the performance of 6,596 mergers and acquisitions, and reported adjusted *r*-squares of 2.4–5.6%; Morck and Yeung (1992) used an event study, and OLS estimation to investigate the announcement of 322 internationalisations, and reported *r*-squares of 0–4.3%; Muller and Kräussl (2011) used an event study, and OLS estimation, to study the announcement of 354 corporate disaster donations, and reported adjusted *r*-squares of 4–6%; and McNamara and Baden-Fuller (2007) used an event study, and OLS estimation, to investigate the returns to research and development announcement by biotechnology firms, and reported *r*-squares of 1–7%, using a sample of 180 firms. As our results fit within this range, we can be confident as to the goodness of fit of our model.

Conclusions

Markets are suggested to work well in economics if they are either liquid in the sense of relatively many suppliers and buyers seeking to do deals, or well stocked with knowledge. The first view is related to textbook economics, while the second is connected with the Austrian view of economics and in particular with Friedrich Hayek. Empirically, these views can be captured using social network analysis of deals done in the market for corporate control (mergers and acquisitions). As we explained at length in the methods section, deals connecting locations where target and acquirer are based constitute networks; locations with a high degree of centrality are liquid, and locations with a high betweenness centrality are locations where much knowledge is accumulated. If our assumption of the market for corporate control is a proper indicator of how markets function is a correct one, the results we are able to present are a cause for further consideration of how exactly markets actually work. We find that neither does well, contrary to expectations. Much more seems to be involved than liquidity in a market and players generally being knowledgeable (cf. Rosenbaum, 2000; Hodgson, 2015).

Our results are highly suggestive in this sense. What some qualitative research and suggestions by practitioners suggest is that it matters which players take on what position in the market, and also how they internally organise and are externally connected (Podolny, 2001; Owen-Smith & Powell, 2004). How specific markets are institutionally organised and which players exactly have knowledge is likely to affect average deal performance more than high-level or aggregate characterisations about markets. Who has access, directly or indirectly, to what information can also be expected to make a difference. If and to what extent this is the case is currently not a feasible topic for research because of a lack of quantitative data. In the short to medium term, qualitative case study research can offer first-off insights to further substantiate and specify this suggestion. The role of consultancies advising and brokering deals is likely to be an important one, and one which we invite further researchers to expand upon.

Note

1 *Financial Times*, April 1, 2016.

References

Aalbers, H. L. & Dolfsma, W. 2015. *Innovation Networks*. London: Routledge.

Benston, G. 1985. The self-serving management hypothesis: Some evidence. *Journal of Accounting & Economics* 7: 67–83.

Brown, S. J., & Warner J. B. 1980. Measuring security price performance. *Journal of Financial Economics* 8: 205–258.

Brown, S. J., & Warner, J. B. 1985. Using daily stock returns: The case of event studies. *Journal of Financial Economics* 14: 3–31.

Capron, L., & Pistre, N. 2002. When do acquirers earn abnormal returns? *Strategic Management Journal* 23: 781–794.

Chatterjee, S. 1986. Types of synergy and economic value: The impact of acquisitions on merging and rival firms. *Strategic Management Journal* 7: 119–139.

Duso, T., Gugler, K., & Yurtoglu, B. B. 2010. Is the event study methodology useful for merger analysis? A comparison of stock market and accounting data. *International Review of Law and Economics* 30(2): 186–192.

Freeman, L. C. 1979. Centrality in social networks: Conceptual clarification. *Social Networks* 1(3): 215–239.

Fuller, K., Netter, J., & Stegemoller, M. 2002. What do returns to acquiring firms tell us? Evidence from firms that make many acquisitions. *Journal of Finance* 57: 1763–1793.

Gilsing, V., Nooteboom, B., Vanhaverbeke, W., Duysters, G., & van den Oord, A. 2008. Network embeddedness and the exploration of novel technologies: Technological distance, betweenness centrality and density. *Research Policy* 37(10): 1717–1731.

Gregory, A., Jeanes, E., Tharyan, R., &Tonks, I. 2013. Does the stock market gender stereotype corporate boards? Evidence from the market's reaction to directors' trades. *British Journal of Management* 24(2): 174–190.

Hayek, F. A. 1945. The use of knowledge in society. *American Economic Review* 35(4): 519–530.

Healy, P. M., Palepu, K. G., & Ruback, R. S. 1992. Does corporate performance improve after mergers? *Journal of Financial Economics* 31: 135–175.

Hodgson, G. M. 1999. *Economics and Utopia.* London: Routledge.

Hodgson, G. M. 2015. Markets. in J. B. Davis & W. Dolfsma (eds), *The Elgar Companion to Social Economics*, 2nd Ed. Cheltenham, UK: Edward Elgar.

Hymer, S. H. 1976. *The International Operations of National Firms: A Study of Direct Foreign Investment.* Cambridge, MA: MIT Press.

Jensen, M. 1986. Agency costs of free cash flow, corporate finance, and takeovers. *American Economic Review* 76(2): 323–329.

King, D. R., Dalton, D. R., Daily, C. M., & Covin, J. G. 2004. Meta-analyses of post-acquisition performance: Indications of unidentified moderators. *Strategic Management Journal* 25: 187–200.

MacKinlay, A. C. 1997. Event studies in economics and finance. *Journal of Economic Literature* 35: 13–39.

Martynova, M., & Renneboog, L. 2008. A century of corporate takeovers: What have we learned and where do we stand? *Journal of Banking and Finance* 32: 2148–2177.

McCarthy, K. J., & Dolfsma, W. A. 2012. *Merger and Acquisitions in the 21st Century.* London: Routledge.

McNamara, P., & Baden-Fuller, C. 2007. Shareholder returns and the exploration–exploitation dilemma: R&D announcements by biotechnology firms. *Research Policy* 36(4): 548–565.

McNamara, G., Haleblain, J., & Dykes, B. 2008. The performance implications of participating in an acquisition wave: Early mover advantages, bandwagon effects, and the moderating influence of industry characteristics and acquirer tactics. *Academy of Management Journal* 51: 113–130.

Moeller, S. B., Schlingemann, F. P., & Stulz, R. M. 2005. Wealth destruction on a massive scale? A study of acquiring-firm returns in the recent merger wave. *Journal of Finance* 60: 757–782.

Morck, R., & Yeung, B. 1992. Internalization: An event study test. *Journal of International Economics* 33(1–2): 41–56.

Morck, R., Shleifer, A., & Vishny, R. W. 1990. Do managerial objectives drive bad acquisitions? *Journal of Finance* 45: 31–48.

Muller, A., & Kräussl, R. 2011. Doing good deeds in times of need: A strategic perspective on corporate disaster donations. *Strategic Management Journal* 32(9): 911–929.

Opsahl, T., Agneessenns, F., & Skvoretz, J. 2010. Node centrality in weighted networks: Generalizing degree and shortest paths. *Social Networks* 32(2): 245–251.

Owen-Smith, J., & Powell, W. W. 2004. Knowledge networks as channels and conduits: The effects of spillovers in the Boston biotechnology community. *Organization Science* 15(1): 5–21.

Papadakis, V. M., & Thanos, I. C. 2010. Measuring the performance of acquisitions: An empirical investigation using multiple criteria. *British Journal of Management* 21(4): 859–873.

Podolny, J. M. 2001. Networks as the pipes and prisms of the market1. *American Journal of Sociology* 107(1): 33–60.

Ramaswamy, K. 1997. The performance impact of strategic similarity in horizontal mergers: Evidence from the U.S. banking industry. *Academy of Management Journal* 40: 697–715.

Rau, P. R., & Vermaelen, T. 1998. Glamour, value and the post-acquisition performance of acquiring firms. *Journal of Financial Economics* 49: 223–253.

Rhoades, S. A. 1983. *Power, Empire Building and Mergers.* Lexington, MA: D.C. Heath.

Rosenbaum, E. F. 2000. What is a market? On the methodology of a contested concept. *Review of Social Economy* 58(4): 455–482.

Schoenberg, R. 2006. Measuring the performance of corporate acquisitions: An empirical comparison of alternative metrics. *British Management Journal* 17(s1): 361–370.

Schwert, G. W. 1996. Markup pricing in mergers and acquisitions. *Journal of Financial Economics* 41: 153–162.

Zaheer, S. 1995. Overcoming the liability of foreignness. *Academy of Management Journal* 38(2): 341–363.

Zollo, M., & Meier, D. 2008. What is M&A performance? *Academy of Management Perspectives* 22(3): 55–77.

Zuidhof, P-W. 2014. Thinking like an economist: The neoliberal politics of the economics textbook. *Review of Social Economy* 72(2): 157–185.

Part II

Methods of evolutionary political economy

9 Macroeconomic policy in DSGE

Methodological pitfalls, patches or new clothes?[1]

Andrea Roventini and Giorgio Fagiolo

Introduction

At the dawn of 2008, a large number of contributions claimed that monetary – and, more generally, economic – policy was finally becoming more of a science (Gal′ı and Gertler, 2007; Goodfriend, 2007; Mishkin, 2007; Taylor, 2007). Macroeconomic policies could resort to the application of a core set of "scientific principles" (Mishkin, 2007, p. 1), stemming from the so-called New Neoclassical Synthesis (NNS: Goodfriend, 2007; Woodford, 2009), grounded in dynamic stochastic general equilibrium (DSGE) models.[2]

What is more, the available toolbox of economic policy rules was deemed to work exceptionally well not only for normative purposes, but also for descriptive ones. For example, Taylor (2007) argued that "while monetary policy rules cannot, of course, explain all of economics, they can explain a great deal" (p. 1) and also that "although the theory was originally designed for normative reasons, it has turned out to have positive implications which validate it scientifically" (abstract). Given these Panglossian premises, scientific discussions on economic policy seemed therefore to be ultimately confined to either fine-tuning the "consensus" model, or assessing the extent to which elements of art (appropriable by the policy maker) still existed in the conduct of policies (Mishkin, 2007).[3]

Unfortunately, as happened with two famous statements made, respectively, by Francis Fukuyama (1992) about an alleged "end of history," and by many physicists in the recent debate on a purported "end of physics" (see, e.g., Lindley, 1994), these positions have been proven to be substantially wrong by subsequent events. Indeed, the "perfect storm" which followed the bankruptcy of Lehman Brothers on September 15, 2008 brought financial markets to the edge of collapse, causing in turn the worst recession developed economies have ever seen since the Great Depression, and is still threatening the stability of many countries. What is worse, mainstream DSGE-based macroeconomics appears to be badly equipped to deal with the turmoil we have been facing. As Krugman (2011) points out, not only did orthodox macroeconomists not forecast the crisis, but they did not even admit the possibility of such an event and, even worse, they did not provide any useful advice to policy makers to put the economy back on a steady growth path (see also Stiglitz, 2011, 2015). On the same line, DeLong (2011) reported that when the former US Secretary of the Treasury Lawrence Summers was asked what economics could offer to understand the crisis, he quoted the works of Bagehot, Minsky, and Kindleberger, which appeared more than 30 years ago. This is so because the DSGE approach "has become so mesmerized with its own internal logic that it has begun to confuse the precision it has achieved about its own world with the precision that it has about the real one" (Caballero, 2010, p. 85).

In that respect, the Great Recessions turned out to be a natural experiment for economic analysis, showing the inadequacy of the predominant theoretical frameworks. DSGE scholars have reacted to such a failure, trying to amend their models with, e.g., financial friction, homeopathic doses of agent heterogeneity, and exogenous fat-tailed shocks. At the same time, an increasing number of leading economists have claimed that the 2008 "economic crisis is a crisis for economic theory" (Colander et al., 2009; Farmer and Foley, 2009; Krugman, 2009, 2011; Caballero, 2010; Kirman, 2010, 2016; DeLong, 2011; Kay, 2011; Stiglitz, 2011, 2015; Dosi, 2012). Their view, which we fully share here, is that the basic assumptions of mainstream DSGE models, e.g., rational expectations, representative agents (RAs), perfect markets, prevent the understanding of basic phenomena underlying the current economic crisis and, more generally, macroeconomic dynamics.[4]

In order to better articulate these points, this the following chapter (Chapter 10) extend and update the discussion presented in Fagiolo and Roventini (2012). In this chapter, we firstly argue that new developments and extensions of DSGE models are certainly welcome, but instead of performing such a Ptolemaic exercise (Caballero, 2010; Stiglitz, 2011, 2015; Dosi, 2012) – adding a plethora of new "epicycles" to fix flawed models – economists should consider the *economy as a complex evolving system*, i.e., as an ecology populated by heterogeneous agents whose far-from-equilibrium interactions continuously change the structure of the system (more on that in Farmer and Foley, 2009; Kirman, 2010, 2016; Rosser, 2011; Dosi, 2012; Battiston et al. 2016). This is indeed the methodological core of agent-based computational economics (ACE: Tesfatsion, 2006; LeBaron and Tesfatsion, 2008), a stream of research whose keywords are heterogeneity, bounded rationality, endogenous out-of-equilibrium dynamics, and direct interactions among economic agents, which is extensively covered in Chapter 10. There, we discuss how such an alternative approach allows models to be built that, from a descriptive perspective, are able to reproduce many features of the 2008 economic crisis, such as asset bubbles, resilience of interbank networks, self-organized criticality, and financial accelerator dynamics. We also explore the extent to which ACE models can configure themselves as effective laboratories to design economic policies and to test their effects on macroeconomic dynamics.

The structure of this paper essentially mimics the first part of its predecessor (Fagiolo and Roventini, 2012), whilst extending and updating all sections with new material from recent methodological improvements and new applications. In particular, the second section surveys the approach to policy of NNS. Then, we discuss the main theoretical and empirical difficulties of DSGE models, followed by a review of recent developments in DSGE macroeconomics. The final section takes stock of the foregoing discussion and concludes.

DSGE models and economic policy

Let us begin by presenting how policy analysis is usually carried out in DSGE models, which are at the center of NNS (Goodfriend and King, 1997). The canonical DSGE model has a real-business-cycle (RBC) core supplemented with monopolistic competition, nominal imperfections, and a monetary policy rule (for a more detailed exposition of the DSGE model, cf. Clarida et al., 1999; Woodford, 2003; Galì and Gertler, 2007).

In line with RBC tradition, the backbone of DSGE models is the standard stochastic neoclassical growth model with variable labor supply: the economy is populated by an infinitely lived representative household, and by a representative firm, whose homogeneous production technology is hit by exogenous shocks. All agents form their expectations rationally (Muth, 1961). The New Keynesian flavor of the model is provided by money, monopolistic competition, and sticky prices. Money has usually only the function of unit of account and the nominal rigidities incarnated in sticky prices allow monetary policy to affect real variables in the short run. The RBC scaffold of the model allows the computation of the "natural" level of output and real interest rate, that is, the equilibrium values of the two variables under perfectly flexible prices. In line with Wickselian tradition, the "natural" output and interest rate constitute a benchmark for monetary policy: the central bank cannot persistently push output and the interest rate away from their "natural" values without creating inflation or deflation. Finally, imperfect competition and possibly other real rigidity imply that the "natural" level of output is not socially efficient.

The plain-vanilla version of the DSGE model is represented by three equations: the expectation-augmented investment-saving (IS) equation, the New Keynesian Phillips (NKP) curve, and a monetary policy rule. The expectation-augmented IS equation constitutes the aggregate-demand building block of the NNS model and it stems from the goods market-clearing condition and the Euler equation of the representative household (under the assumption of perfect capital markets):

$$\tilde{y}_t = E_t \tilde{y}_{t+1} - \sigma(i_t - E_t \pi_{\{t+1\}} - r^{n_t}), \tag{1}$$

where $\tilde{y}$ is the output gap (i.e., the percentage gap between real output and its "natural" level), σ is the intertemporal elasticity of substitution of consumption, i is the nominal interest rate, π is inflation, r^n is the "natural" interest rate and E^t stands for the (rational) expectation operator. Note that, in line with the traditional IS-liquidity preference–monetary supply (LM) model, the IS equation postulates a negative relation between the output gap and the interest rate gap.

The aggregate-supply building block of the NNS model boils down to an NKP curve. By combining the Dixit and Stiglitz (1977) model of monopolistic competition and the Calvo (1983) model of staggered prices, one obtains that in any given period firms allowed to adjust prices fix them as a weighted average of the current and expected future nominal marginal cost. The NKP curve can be obtained by combining the log-linear approximation of the optimal price-setting choice, the price index, and the labor-market equilibrium:

$$\pi_t = \kappa\tilde{y}_t + \beta E_t \backslash \pi_{\{t+1\}} + u_t, \tag{2}$$

where β is the subjective discount factor of the representative household and κ depends both on the elasticity of marginal cost with respect to output and on the sensitivity of price adjustment to marginal cost fluctuations (i.e., frequency of price adjustment and real rigidities induced by price complementarities). The term u is usually considered a "cost-push shock": it captures the fact that the natural level of output may not coincide with the socially efficient one for the presence of real imperfections such as monopolistic competition, labor market rigidities, etc.[5]

The model is closed with the monetary policy rule. The derivation of the optimal monetary policy rule is carried out adopting a welfare criterion: taking a second-order Taylor series approximation of the utility of the representative household, one can derive a welfare loss function for the central bank that is quadratic in inflation and in deviations of output from its socially efficient level (see Woodford, 2010). Alternatively, one can plug a "simple" rule such as the Taylor (1993) rule (see Howitt, 1992, and Taylor and Williams, 2010, for a survey; more on that below):

$$t = r_t + \varphi_\pi \pi_t + \varphi_y \tilde{y}_t, \tag{3}$$

where i^τ is the interest rate target of the central bank, $\varphi_y > 0$ and $\varphi_\pi > 1$.

Before performing policy exercises with DSGE models, one ought to assess their empirical performance and calibrate their parameters. At this stage, in a medium-scale DSGE model (see e.g., Smets and Wouters, 2003, 2007; Christiano et al., 2005) different types of shock (e.g., government spending and private consumption disturbances) are usually added to improve the estimation. Moreover, as the assumption of forward-looking agents prevents DSGE models matching the econometric evidence on the co-movements of nominal and real variables (e.g., the response of output and inflation as to a monetary policy shock is too fast to match the gradual adjustment showed by the corresponding empirical impulse-response functions), one has to introduce a legion of "frictions" – often not justified on theoretical grounds – such as predetermined price and spending decisions, indexation of prices and wages to past inflation, sticky wages, habit formation in preferences for consumption, adjustment costs in investment, variable capital utilization, etc. However, in almost all DSGE models the labor market is not explicitly modeled and unemployment is not contemplated (a notable exception is Blanchard and Galì (2010), who introduce a search and matching model of labor market).

From an econometric perspective, DSGE models are naturally represented as a vector auto-regression (VAR) model. The estimation of the resulting econometric model is usually carried out either with a limited information approach or by full-information likelihood-based methods (see Fernandez-Villaverde et al., 2016, for a detailed description of solution and estimation methods for DSGE models).

Limited information approach

The strategy of the limited information approach to estimate and evaluate DSGE models is usually the following (e.g., Rotemberg and Woodford, 1999; Christiano et al., 2005):

1 Specify the monetary policy rule and the laws of motion for the shocks.
2 Split the parameters in two sets and calibrate the parameters in the first set, providing theoretical or empirical justifications for the chosen values.
3 After having fixed the timing of the endogenous variables, estimate via ordinary least squares the coefficients of the monetary policy rule and obtain the impulse-response functions as to a monetary policy shock.
4 Recover the second set of parameters by minimizing the distance between the model-generated and empirical impulse-response functions.
5 Finally, given the structural parameter values and the VAR, identify the other structural shocks by imposing, if necessary, additional restrictions.

The empirical performance of the model is then measured by comparing the impulse-response functions generated by the model with the empirical ones.

Full information approach

The full information approach was initially discarded to estimate DSGE models because maximum-likelihood (ML) methods deliver implausible estimates. However, with the introduction of Bayesian techniques, the full information approach regained popularity and it is now commonly employed (see, e.g., Smets and Wouters, 2003, 2007). Bayesian estimation is carried out according to the following steps:

1 If necessary place restrictions on the shocks in order to allow later identification. For instance, Smets and Wouters (2003) assume that technology and preference shocks follow an independent first-order autoregressive process with independent and identically distributed (i.i.d.) Gaussian error terms, whereas "cost-push" and monetary policy shocks are i.i.d. normal white-noise processes.
2 Employ the Kalman filter to compute the likelihood function of the observed time series.
3 Form the prior distribution of the parameters, choose their initial values through calibration, preliminary exploratory exercises, and/or to get some desired statistical properties.
4 Combine the likelihood function with the prior distribution of the parameters to obtain the posterior density, which is then used to compute parameter estimates.

One can then assess the empirical performance of the estimated DSGE model comparing its marginal likelihood with that of standard VAR models (i.e., the Bayes factor) and the model-generated cross-covariances *vis-à-vis* the empirical ones.

Policy analysis

Once one has recovered the parameters of the model by estimation or calibration and has identified the structural shocks, policy-analysis exercises can finally be carried out. More specifically, after having derived the welfare loss function, one can assess the performance of the subset of "simple" policy rules that guarantee the existence of a determinate equilibrium or the more appropriate parametrization within the class of optimal monetary policy rules. This can be done via simulation, by buffeting the DSGE model with different structural shocks and computing the resulting variance of inflation and output gap and the associated welfare losses of the different monetary policy rules and parameterizations employed (see, e.g., Rotemberg and Woodford, 1999; Galì and Gertler, 2007). In practice, assuming that the DSGE model is the "true" data-generating process (DGP) of the available time series, one is evaluating how the economy portrayed by the model would react to the same structural shocks observed in the past if the monetary policy followed by the central bank were different. Adding the public sector to the plain-vanilla DSGE model, one can also study the effects of fiscal policies. More specifically, one can compute the impulse response functions to analyze the impact on gross domestic product (GDP) dynamics of government spending and tax shocks (see, e.g., Cogan et al., 2009).

Policy with DSGE models: a safe exercise?

There are three types of problems which undermine the usefulness of DSGE models for policy analyses. Such problems are theoretical, empirical and related to the political economy of DSGE models. Let us discuss each in turn.

Theoretical issues

As DSGE models are general equilibrium (GE) models rooted in the Arrow–Debreu tradition with some minor non-Walrasian features (e.g., sticky prices), they are plagued by the same well-known problems of GE models (see Kirman, 1989, for a classical reference).

First, the well-known Sonnenschein (1972), Mantel (1974), Debreu (1974) theorems prove that the uniqueness and stability of the GE cannot be attained even if one places stringent and unrealistic assumptions about agents. Moreover, Saari and Simon (1978) show that an infinite amount of information is required to reach the equilibrium for any initial price vector.

Given such nihilist conclusions, neoclassical economists took the short cut of the RA to obtain stable and unique equilibrium. Indeed, if the choices of heterogeneous agents collapse to the RA ones, one can circumvent all the aggregation problems and develop GE macroeconomic models with rigorous Walrasian micro-foundations grounded on rationality and constrained optimization.

However, the RA assumption is far from being innocent: there are (at least) four reasons why it cannot be defended (Kirman, 1992).[6] First, individual rationality does not imply aggregate rationality: one cannot provide any formal justification to support the assumption that at the macro level agents behave as a maximizing individual. Second, even if one forgets the previous point, one cannot safely perform policy analyses with RA macro models, because the reactions of the RA to shocks or parameter changes may not coincide with the aggregate reactions of the represented agents. Third, even if the first two problems are solved, there may be cases where, given two situations, *a* and *b*, the RA prefers *a*, whereas all the represented individuals prefer *b*. Finally, the RA assumption introduces additional difficulties at the empirical level, because whenever one tests a proposition delivered by an RA model, one is also jointly testing the very RA hypothesis. Hence, the rejection of the latter hypothesis may show up in the rejection of the model proposition that is being tested.

Forni and Lippi (1997, 1999) show that basic properties of linear dynamic microeconomic models are not preserved by aggregation if agents are heterogeneous (see also Pesaran and Chudik, 2011). For instance, microeconomic co-integration does not lead to macroeconomic co-integration, Granger causality may not appear at the micro level, but it may emerge at the macro level, aggregation of static micro-equations may produce dynamic macro-equations. As a consequence, one can safely test the macroeconomic implications of microeconomic theories only if agents' heterogeneity is explicitly and carefully modeled.

More generally, the RA assumption implies that there is a one-to-one correspondence between the micro and macro levels. In particular, macroeconomic dynamics is compressed into microeconomics. In the section on political economy issues, below, we will see that this simplification prevents DSGE models accounting for complex phenomena.

The last theoretical issue concerns the existence and determinacy of the system of rational-expectation equilibrium conditions of DSGE models. If the exogenous shocks and fluctuations generated by the monetary policy rule are "small," and the "Taylor principle" holds (i.e., $\varphi_\pi > 1$; see eqn. 3, above), the rational-expectation equilibrium of the DSGE model presented above (Woodford, 2003)[7] exists and is *locally* determinate. This result allows one to compute impulse-response functions in the presence of "small" shocks or parameter changes and to safely employ log-linear approximations around the steady state. Unfortunately, the existence of a *local* determinate equilibrium does not rule out the possibility of multiple equilibria at the *global* level (see, e.g., Schmitt-Grohé and Uribe, 2000; Benhabib et al. 2001; Ascari and Ropele, 2009). This is a serious issue because there is always the possibility, e.g., if the laws of motion of the shocks are not properly tuned, that the DSGE model enters into an explosive path, thus preventing the computation of impulse-response functions and the adoption of the model for policy analysis exercises.

Empirical issues

The second stream of problems concerns the empirical validation of DSGE models. The estimation and testing of DSGE models are usually performed assuming that they represent the true DGP of the observed data (Canova, 2008). This implies that the ensuing inference and policy experiments are valid only if the DSGE model mimics the unknown DGP of the data.[8]

As mentioned above, DSGE models can be represented as a VAR of the form:

$$A_0(\varphi)x_t = H_1(\varphi)x_{\{t-1\}} + H_2(\varphi)E_t, \tag{4}$$

where x are both endogenous and exogenous variables, φ is the vector of the parameters of the model, and E contains the errors. If the matrix A_0 is invertible, one can obtain a reduced-form VAR representation of the DSGE model.

Following Fukac and Pagan (2006), the econometric performance of DSGE models can be assessed along with the identification, estimation, and evaluation dimensions. Before going into depth on this type of analysis, two preliminary potential sources of problems must be discussed. First, the number of endogenous variables contemplated by DSGE models is usually larger than the number of structural shocks. This problem may lead to stochastic singularity and is typically solved by adding measurement errors or increasing the number of structural shocks (see Fernandez-Villaverde et al., 2016). Second, H_1 and H_2 are reduced-rank matrixes. This problem is circumvented by integrating variables out of the VAR (eqn. 4) as long as H_1 and H_2 become invertible. This process leads to a vector autoregressive moving average representation of the DSGE model.

This is not an innocent transformation for two reasons: (i) if the moving average component is not invertible, the DSGE model cannot have a VAR representation; and (ii) even if the VAR representation of the DSGE model exists, it may require an infinite number of lags (more on that in Fernandez-Villaverde et al., 2005, 2016; Alessi et al. 2007; Ravenna, 2007).

Identification

Given the large number of non-linearities present in the structural parameters (θ), DSGE models are hard to identify (Canova, 2008). This leads to a large number of identification problems, which can affect the parameter space either at the local or at the global level. A taxonomy of the most relevant identification problems can be found in Canova and Sala (2009).[9]

To sum them up: (i) different DSGE models with different economic and policy implications could be observationally equivalent (i.e., they produce indistinguishable aggregate decision rules); (ii) some DSGE models may be plagued by under- or partial identification of their parameters (i.e., some parameters are not present in the aggregate decision rules or are present with a peculiar functional form); and (iii) some DSGEs may be exposed to weak identification problems (i.e., the mapping between the coefficients of the aggregate decision rules and the structural parameters may be characterized by little curvature or by asymmetries), which could not even be solved by increasing the sample size.

Identification problems lead to biased and fragile estimates of some structural parameters and do not allow correct evaluation of the significance of the estimated parameters applying standard asymptotic theories. This opens a ridge between the real and DSGE DGPs, depriving parameter estimates of any economic meaning and making policy analysis exercises useless (Canova, 2008). For instance, Schorfheide (2008) found that the parameters of the NKP curve estimated in 42 DSGE models published in academic journals ranged from zero to 4. In most cases, identification problems can only be mitigated by appropriately re-parameterizing the model.[10]

Estimation

The identification problems discussed above partly affect the estimation of DGSE models. DSGE models are very hard to estimate by standard ML methods, because ML estimator delivers biased and inconsistent results if the system is not a satisfying representation of the data. This turns out to be the case for DSGE models (see the evaluation section, below) and it helps to explain why ML estimates usually attain absurd values with no economic meaning and/or they are incompatible with a unique stable solution of the underlying DSGE model.

A strategy commonly employed when the DSGE model is estimated following the limited-information approach (cf. above) consists in calibrating the parameters that are hard to identify and then estimating the others. Given the identification problems listed above, Canova (2008) argues that this strategy works only if the calibrated parameters are set to their "true" values. If this is not the case, estimation does not deliver correct results that can be used to address economic and policy questions (see also Canova and Sala, 2009).

Bayesian methods apparently solve the estimation (and identification) problems by adding a prior function to the (log) likelihood function in order to increase the curvature of the latter and obtain a smoother function. However, this choice is not harmless: if the likelihood function is flat – and thus conveys little information about the structural parameters – the shape of the posterior distribution resembles the one of the prior, reducing estimation to a more sophisticated calibration procedure carried out on an interval instead of a point (see Fukac and Pagan, 2006; Canova, 2008). Unfortunately, the likelihood functions produced by most DSGE models are quite flat (see, e.g., the exercises performed by Fukac and Pagan, 2006). In this case, informal calibration is a more honest and internally consistent strategy to set up a model for policy analysis experiments (Canova, 2008).

Evaluation

DSGE models should be capable of reproducing as many empirical stylized facts as possible. For instance, following Fukac and Pagan (2006), one can check: (i) whether variables with deterministic trend cotrend; (ii) whether I(1) variables co-integrate and the resulting co-integrating vectors are those predicted by the model; (iii) the consistency (with respect to data) of the dynamic responses (e.g., autocorrelation, bivariate correlations); (iv) the consistency of the covariance matrix of the reduced form errors with the one found in the data; and (v) the discrepancies between the time series generated by the model and real-world ones. In light of the Great Recession, the last point is particularly important: can DSGE models jointly account for the occurrence of mild and deep downturns (Stiglitz, 2015)?

Fukac and Pagan (2006) performed such exercises on a popular DSGE model. First, they found that cotrending behaviors cannot be assessed because data are demeaned (a practice commonly followed by DSGE modelers). However, the computation of the technology growth rates compatible with the observed output growth rates shows that the possibility of technical regress is very high. Second, there are no co-integrating vectors, because output is the only I(1) variable. Third, the model is not able to successfully reproduce the mean, standard deviations, autocorrelations, and bivariate correlations observed in real data. In addition, the DSGE model predicts the constancy of some "great" ratios (in line with the presence of a steady state of the economy), but this is not confirmed by real data. For instance, Fernandez-Villaverde et al. (2016) found a discrepancy between US and DSGE-generated data, as DSGE models are not able to catch the increasing upward trend in the consumption–output ratio and the falling labor share. Fourth, many off-diagonal correlations implied by the covariance matrix of the errors are significantly different from zero, contradicting the DSGE model assumption of uncorrelated shocks. Fifth, the tracking performance of the model depends heavily on the assumed high serial correlation of the shocks.

Recent empirical evidence has found that non-linearities in the economic system can lead to different impacts of macroeconomic policies according to the state of the economy (see, e.g., Auerbach and Gorodnichenko, 2012) and financial markets (Mittnik and Semmler, 2013; Ferraresi et al., 2014). In DSGE models, the effects of monetary and fiscal policies are time-invariant, even if the economy is trapped in a depression. More generally, DSGE models can do well in "normal" time, but they cannot account for crises and deep downturns (Stiglitz, 2015). This is not surprising, since macroeconomic time-series distributions are well approximated by fat-tail densities (Fagiolo et al., 2008) and DSGE models typically assume Gaussian distributed shocks.[11] Moreover, Ascari et al. (2015) found that, even if fat-tailed Laplace shocks are assumed, the distributions of the time series generated by DSGE models have much thinner tails than those observed in real data. The propagation mechanism of DSGE models appears to work in the wrong direction, smoothing instead of magnifying shocks.

The results just described seem to support Favero (2007) in claiming that modern DSGE models are exposed to the same criticisms advanced against the old-fashioned macroeconometric models belonging to the Cowles Commission tradition: they pay too much attention to the identification of the structural model (with all the problems described above) without testing the potential misspecification of the underlying statistical model (see also Johansen, 2006; Juselius and Franchi, 2007).[12] In DSGE models,

> restrictions are made fuzzy by imposing a distribution on them and then the relevant question becomes what is the amount of uncertainty that we have to add to model based restrictions in order to make them compatible not with the data but with a model-derived unrestricted VAR representation of the data.
>
> (Favero, 2007, p. 29)

If the statistical model is misspecified, policy analysis exercises lose significance, because they are carried out in a "virtual" world whose DGP is different from the one underlying observed time-series data.

Political-economy issues

Given the theoretical problems and the puny empirical performance of DSGE models, one cannot accept the principles of the positive economics approach summarized by the "as if" argument of Milton Friedman (1953). The assumptions of DSGE models can no longer be defended, invoking arguments such as parsimonious modeling or data matching. This opens a Pandora's box, as one should study how the legion of assumptions of DSGE models affect their policy conclusions.

DSGE models presume a very peculiar framework, where RAs endowed with rational expectations take rational decisions by solving dynamic programming problems. This implies that: (i) agents perfectly know the model of the economy; (ii) agents are able to understand and solve every problem they face without making any mistakes; and (iii) agents know that all other agents behave according to the first two points. In practice, agents are endowed with a sort of "Olympic" rationality and have free access to the whole information set.[13]

Rational expectation is the short-cut employed by DSGE model to deal with uncertainty. Such strong assumption rises many issues.[14] First, rational expectations are a property of the economic system as a whole, individual rationality is not a sufficient condition for letting the system converge to the rational expectations fixed-point equilibrium (Howitt, 2011). Moreover, it is unreasonable to assume that agents possess all the information required to attain the equilibrium of the whole economy (Caballero, 2010), especially in periods of strong structural transformation, like the Great Recession, that require policies never tried before (e.g., quantitative easing, see Stiglitz, 2011, 2015). Agents can also have the "wrong" model of the economy and available data are not sufficient to refute it (see the seminal contribution of Woodford, 1990, among the rich literature on sunspots.). Hendry and Minzon (2010) point out that when "structural breaks" affect the underlying stochastic process that governs the evolution of the economy, the learning process of agents introduce further non-stationarity into the system, preventing the economy to reach an equilibrium state. In such a framework, predictors grounded on robust devices performs better. More generally, in presence of Knightian uncertainty (Knight, 1921; Keynes, 1936, 1937), "rational" agents should follow heuristics as they always outperform more complex expectation formation rules (Gigerenzer, 2007; Gigerenzer and Brighton, 2009). Assuming that agents behaving according to what suggested by the psychological and sociological evidence allow then to build models which better account for macroeconomic phenomena (Akerlof, 2002) including the current crisis (Akerlof and Shiller, 2009). Finally, given such premises, no wonder that empirical tests usually reject the full-information, rational expectation hypothesis (see e.g., Guzman, 2009; Coibion and Gorodnichenko, 2011; Gennaioli et al., 2015).

The representative-agent (RA) assumption prevent DSGE models to address distributional issues, which are one of the major cause of the Great Recession and they are fundamental for studying the effects of policies. Indeed, increasing income (Atkinson et al., 2011) and wealth (Piketty and Zucman, 2014) inequalities induced households to indebt more and more over time paving the way to the subprime mortgage crisis (Fitoussi and Saraceno, 2010; Stiglitz, 2011). In this framework, redistribution matters and different policies have a different impact on the economy according to the groups of people they are designed for (e.g., unemployed benefits have large multipliers than tax cuts for high-income individuals, see Stiglitz, 2011). The study of redistributive policies require then models with heterogenous not RAs.

The RA assumption coupled with the implicit presence of a Walrasian auctioneer, which sets prices before exchanges take place, rule out almost by definition the possibility of interactions carried out by heterogeneous individuals. This prevents DSGE model to accurately study the dynamics of credit and financial markets. Indeed, the assumption that the RA always satisfies the transversality condition, removes the default risk from DSGE models (Goodhart, 2009). As a consequence, agents face the same interest rate (no risk premia) and all transactions can be undertaken in capital markets without the need of banks.[15] The abstraction from default risks does not allow DSGE models to contemplate the conflict between price and financial stability that Central Banks always face (Howitt, 2011): they just care about the *n*th-order distortions caused by price misalignments which can eventually result in inflation without considering the huge costs of financial crisis (Stiglitz, 2011, 2015). No surprise that DSGE models work fine in normal time but they are unequipped not only to forecast but also to explain the current crisis (Goodhart, 2009; Krugman, 2011).

In the same vein, DSGE models are not able to account for involuntary unemployment. Indeed, even if they are developed to study the welfare effects of macroeconomic policies, unemployment is not present or it only stems from frictions in the labor market or wage rigidities. Such explanations are especially hard to believe during deep downturns like the Great Recession. In DSGE models, the lack of heterogeneous, interacting firms and workers/consumers prevents a study of the emergence of coordination failures (Cooper and John, 1988), which could lead to an insufficient level of aggregate demand and to involuntary unemployment.

As a consequence of the "as if" methodology, the macroeconomics of DSGE models does not appear to be truly grounded on microeconomics (Stiglitz, 2011, 2015). For instance, DSGE models do not take into account the micro and macro implications of imperfect information. Moreover, the behavior of agents is often described with arbitrary specification of the functional forms. The commonly employed (Dixit and Stiglitz, 1977) utility function provides a bad description of agents' behavior toward risk. Similarly, the Cobb–Douglas production function is not suited for studying income distribution issues.

More generally, within the Neoclassical-DSGE paradigm there is a sort of internal contradiction. On the one hand, strong assumptions such as rational expectations, perfect information, and complete financial markets are introduced *ex ante* to provide a rigorous and formal mathematical treatment of the problems and to allow for policy recommendations. On the other hand, many imperfections (e.g., sticky prices, rule-of-thumb consumers) are introduced *ex post* without any theoretical justification only to allow the DSGE model to match the data. This process is far from being innocuous: Chari et al. (2009) point out that the high level of arbitrariness of DSGE models in the specifications of structural shocks may leave them exposed to the Lucas critiques, preventing them from being usefully employed for policy analysis. Adopting less stringent – but in tune with the microeconomic statistical evidence – assumptions may contribute to jointly solving many empirical puzzles without introducing an army of *ad hoc* imperfections.

Another possible issue concerns how business cycles arise in the DSGE framework. More specifically, the theory of business cycles embedded in DSGE models is exogenous: the economy rests in the steady state unless it is hit by a stream of exogenous stochastic shocks. As a consequence, DSGE models do not explain business cycles, preferring instead to generate them with a sort of *deus ex machina* mechanism. This could explain why even in normal times DSGE models are not able to match many business cycle stylized facts or have to assume serially correlated shocks to produce fluctuations resembling the ones observed in reality (cf. Zarnowitz, 1985, 1997; Cogley and Nason, 1993; Fukac and Pagan, 2006). Even worse, the subprime mortgage crisis clearly shows how bubbles and, more generally, endogenously generated shocks are far more important for understanding economic fluctuations (Stiglitz, 2011, 2015). How policymakers can assess the impact of policies in models not explaining business cycles is an open issue. For instance, the Great Recession revealed that the Federal Reserve doctrine about cleaning up after asset bubbles burst was patently wrong.

Moving to the normative side, one supposed advantage of the DSGE approach is the possibility of deriving optimal policy rules. However, policymakers adopting optimal policy rules face certain costs – the strict assumptions at the root of DSGE models – but uncertain benefits. As argued by Gal'ı (2008), optimal monetary policy rules cannot be used in practice, because they require knowledge of the "true" model of the economy, the exact value of every parameter, and the real-time value of every shock. Moreover, when the "true" model of the economy and the appropriate loss function are not known, rule-of-thumb policy rules can perform better than optimal policy rules (Brock et al., 2007; Orphanides and Williams, 2008). Indeed, in complex worlds with pervasive uncertainty (e.g., financial markets), regulation should be simple (Haldane, 2012).

Recent developments in DSGE modeling: patches or new cloth?

The failure of DSGE models to account for the Great Recession sparked new research avenues, which were also partly trying to address the critiques reported above. More specifically, researchers in the DSGE camp have tried to include a financial sector to the barebone model, consider agents' heterogeneity and bounded rationality, and explore the impact of rare shocks on the performance of DSGE models. In this section, we provide a bird's-eye view of such recent developments.

The new generation of DSGE model with *financial frictions* is mostly grounded on the financial accelerator framework (Bernanke et al., 1999), which provides a straightforward explanation why credit and financial markets can affect real economic activity. The presence of imperfect information between borrowers and lenders introduces a wedge between the cost of credit and those of internal finance. In turn, the balance sheets of lenders and borrowers can affect credit and the real sector via the supply of credit and the spread on loan interest rates (see Gertler and Kiyotaki, 2010, for a survey). In Curdia and Woodford (2010), the presence of both patient and impatient consumers justifies the existence of a stylized financial intermediary, which copes with default risk, charging a spread on its loan subject to exogenous, stochastic disturbances. They found that optimal monetary policy does not change and the Central Bank should keep on controlling the short-term interest rate (see also Curdia and Woodford, 2015). In the model of Gertler and Karadi (2011), households can be (randomly) workers or bankers. In the latter case, they provide credit to firms, but as they are constrained by deposits and the resources they can raise in the interbank market, a spread emerges between loan and deposit interest rates (see Christiano et al., 2011, 2013, for a similar framework where interest rate spread arises from exogenous firms' failure risk). They found that during crises, unconventional monetary policy (i.e., Central Bank providing credit intermediation) is welfare enhancing (see also Curdia and Woodoford, 2011; and Gertler and Kiyotaki, 2010 for an extended analysis of credit policies).[16]

The foregoing papers allow for some form of *mild heterogeneity* among agents. The introduction of two types of agent allow DSGE models to explore new issues such as debt deflations or inequality (most DSGE models with heterogeneous agents are grounded on Krusel and Smith, 1998). For instance, Eggertsson and Krugman (2012) introduced patient and impatient agents and exposed the latter to exogenous debt limit shocks, which forced them to deleverage. They found that the model can account for Fisher debt deflations and liquidity traps, and support expansionary fiscal policies, as multipliers can be higher than one. Kumhof et al. (2015) studied the link between rising inequality, household leverage, and financial crises employing a DSGE model where top-earner households (5% of the income distribution) lend to the bottom ones (95% of the income distribution). They showed that an exogenous inequality shock induces low-income households to increase their indebtedness, raising their rational willingness to default and, in turn, the probability of a financial crisis.

An increasing number of DSGE models allow for various forms of *bounded rationality* (see Dilaver et al., 2016, for a survey). In one stream of literature, agents know the equilibrium of the economy and form their expectations as if they were econometricians, by using the available observation to compute their parameter estimates via ordinary least square (the seminal contribution is Evans and

Honkapohja, 2001; see also Deak et al., 2015, for a DSGE model with individual rationality). Building on Brock and Hommes (1997), in an increasing number of DSGE models (see e.g., Branch and McGough, 2011; De Grauwe, 2012; Anufriev et al., 2013; Massaro, 2013), agents can form their expectations using an ecology of different learning rules (usually fundamentalist vs. extrapolative rules). As the fraction of agents following different expectations rules changes over time, "small" shocks can give raise to persistent and asymmetric fluctuations and endogenous business cycles may arise.[17]

Finally, a new generation of DSGE models tries to account for *deep downturns* and *disasters*.

Curdia et al. (2014) estimated the Smets and Wouters (2007) model assuming that Student's-*t* distributed shocks. They found that the fit of the model improved and rare deep downturns are relevant (see also Fernandez-Villaverde and Levintal, 2016, for a DSGE model with exogenous time-varying rare disaster risk). A similar strategy is employed by Canzoneri et al. (2016) to allow the effects of fiscal policies to change over time. By adding countercyclical exogenous bank intermediation costs to the Curdia and Woodford (2011) model, they obtained state-dependent fiscal multipliers, which can be abundantly higher than in recessions.

Discussion and conclusions

The recent advances in DSGE models are impressive and seem to solve many of the problems mentioned above. But can they be truly considered real improvements in the DSGE research paradigm? We think that the answer is *negative*.

Let us consider first DSGE models with financial frictions. They certainly perform better than standard DSGE models, but the way they introduce finance is completely *ad hoc,* resorting to exogenous shocks and predetermined categories of agents (patient vs. impatient or random probability of becoming "banker"). In that, they just scratch the surface of the impact of credit and finance on real economic dynamics without explicitly modeling the behavior of banks (e.g., endogenous risk taking), accounting for the role of network interactions, and studying the implications of endogenous money. Moreover, also DSGE models with financial frictions avoid explicitly considering the interactions occurring among heterogeneous agents, which is a pervasive feature of credit (and real) markets.

The same critiques can be applied to other streams of research. Whenever heterogeneity is taken into account, there are two types of agents exogenously determined (e.g., rich and poor), facing exogenous shocks and no possibilities of interaction. DSGE models can now encompass both mild and deep downturns, but they only assume them, increasing the degrees of freedom of the models. Indeed, business cycles are still triggered by exogenous shocks, which come from a fat-tailed distribution, or they have massive negative effects.[18] When bounded rationality is present, agents can be either rational or non-rational or, alternatively, they estimate the parameters of the shared model of the economy. In the latter case, interactions are not relevant, while in the first case, they affect the dynamics of the economy only indirectly via the evolving proportion of agents adopting different expectation rules.

In light of the foregoing discussion, we believe that the new developments in the DSGE camp are certainly welcome, but they are just patches added to a torn cloth. The relevant question then becomes, how many patches can one add before trashing it? We believe that the emperor has no clothes, and macroeconomics should be grounded on recent developments in complexity science. In that, ACE (Tesfatsion and Judd, 2006; LeBaron and Tesfatsion, 2008; Farmer and Foley, 2009) may certainly represent a valuable tool. Chapter 10 tries exactly to explore whether this guess is grounded on solid methodological bases. In particular, we perform an anatomy of agent-based models in economics and address the question of whether they can be considered as valuable tools as far as policy-oriented macroeconomic analysis is concerned.

Notes

1 Thanks to Mattia Guerini, Francesco Lamperti, Manuel Scholz-W¨ackerle, and Tania Treibich. All usual disclaimers apply. This paper has been supported by two European Union Horizon 2020 grants: no. 649186 – Project ISIGrowth and no. 640772 – Project Dolfins.
2 For an introduction, see Clarida et al. (1999), Woodford (2003) and Gal´ı and Gertler (2007). Cf. also Colander (2006b) for a historical perspective.
3 In contrast, according to Howitt (2011), “macroeconomic theory has fallen behind the practice of central banking” (p. 2). From the same camp, Mankiw (2006) thinks that macroeconomists should not behave as scientists but as engineers trying to solve practical problems. See also Summers (1991) for an extremely pessimistic view of the possibility of taking *any* economic model seriously econometrically. On these points see also Mehrling (2006).
4 More precisely, in the section on policy with DSGE models, we argue that the DSGE policy apparatus is plagued by a long list of serious problems concerning theoretical issues (i.e., having to do with formal inconsistencies of the model – given its assumptions), empirical difficulties (i.e., related to empirical validation of DSGE models), and political-economy issues (i.e., concerning the absence of any justification for the often unrealistic and over-simplifying assumptions used to derive policy implications). See also Colander (2006a).
5 Robert Solow commented that, although the NKP curve might be new, it is neither Keynesian, nor a Phillips curve. Indeed, the NKP curve implies that: (i) inflation jumps instantaneously whenever there is a variation in the output gap; (ii) positive output gaps lead to a fall in the inflation rate; and (iii) disinflation is not costly (see Carlin and Soskice, 2014, for a detailed discussion).
6 A discussion of the limits of the representative assumption in light of the current crisis is contained in Kirman (2010).
7 Of course, also other monetary policy rules different from the Taylor rule (cf. eqn. 3) can lead to a local determinate rational-expectation equilibrium.
8 On this and related points addressing the statistical vs. substantive adequacy of DSGE models, see Poudyal and Spanos (2013).
9 See also Beyer and Farmer (2004).
10 Fukac and Pagan (2006) also argue that identification problems are usually partly mitigated by arbitrarily assuming serially correlated shocks.
11 An exception is Curdia et al. (2014), where shocks are drawn from a Student-*t* distribution. More on that below.

12 On the contrary, the LSE–Copenhagen school follows a macroeconometric modeling philosophy orthogonal to the one followed by DSGE modelers. Scholars of the LSE–Copenhagen approach have concentrated their efforts on improving the statistical model in order to structure data with an identified co-integrated VAR that could then be used to produce stylized facts for theoretical models (Johansen and Juselius, 2006; Juselius and Franchi, 2007).

13 This is what mainstream macroeconomics consider "sound microfoundations." However, as Kirman (2016) put it: "the rationality attributed to individuals is based on the introspection of economists rather than on careful empirical observation of how individuals actually behave."

14 As Kirman (2016) put it, Muth (1961) was very aware that rational expectation is a convenient short cut, but little evidence suggests that it provides a satisfactory explanation of economic reality.

15 Moreover, since agents can swap IOUs without facing any credit risk, money has only the function of unit of account and it can be ruled out from DSGE models. Indeed, when money is present in the utility function of consumers, the transactions requiring money are assumed to be sufficiently unimportant, so for "reasonable" calibrations, money-augmented DSGE models deliver almost the same results as the standard ones (Woodford, 2003, chapter 2)

16 Large-scale DSGE models with financial frictions have been recently developed at he International Monetary Fund (Benes et al., 2014) and at the Federal Reserve (Del Negro et al., 2013).

17 Lengnick and Wohltman (2016) develop a hybrid DSGE model where the financial market is represented by an agent-based model. See also Guerini et al. (2016) for an agent-based model which can be directly compared to a plain-vanilla DSGE model.

18 Fagiolo et al. (2008) found that GDP growth rate distributions are well proxied by double exponential densities, which dominate both Student's-*t* and Levy-stable distributions. In light of such results, the choice of Curdia et al. (2014) to draw shocks from a Student's-*t* distribution is not only *ad hoc*, but not supported by empirical evidence.

References

Akerlof, G. A. (2002), "Behavioral Macroeconomics and Macroeconomic Behavior", *American Economic Review*, 92: 411–433.

Akerlof, G. A. and R. J. Shiller (2009), *Animal Spirits: How Human Psychology Drives the Economy, and Why it Matters for Global Capitalism*, Princeton, NJ, Princeton University Press.

Alessi, L., M. Barigozzi and M. Capasso (2007), "A Review of Nonfundamentalness and Identification in Structural VAR models", Working Paper 2007/22, Laboratory of Economics and Management (LEM), Pisa, Italy, Scuola Superiore Sant'Anna.

Anufriev, M., T. Assenza, C. Hommes and D. Massaro (December 2013), "Interest Rate Rules and Macroeconomic Stability Under Heterogeneous Expectations", *Macroeconomic Dynamics*, 17: 1574–1604.

Ascari, G. and T. Ropele (2009), "Trend Inflation, Taylor Principle, and Indeterminacy", *Journal of Money, Credit and Banking*, 41: 1557–1584.

Ascari, G., G. Fagiolo and A. Roventini (2015), "Fat-Tails Distributions and Business-Cycle Models", *Macroeconomic Dynamics*, 19: 465–476.

Atkinson, A. B., T. Piketty and E. Saez (2011), "Top Incomes in the Long Run of History", *Journal of Economic Litarature*, 49: 3–71.

Auerbach, A. J. and Y. Gorodnichenko (2012), "Fiscal Multipliers in Recession and Expansion", in *Fiscal Policy after the Financial Crisis*, National Bureau of Economic Research.

Battiston, S., D. J. Farmer, A. Flache, D. Garlaschelli, A. Haldane, H. Heesterbeeck, C. Hommes, C. Jaeger, R. May and M. Scheffer (2016), "Complexity Theory and Financial Regulation", *Science*, 351: 818–819.

Benes, J., M. Kumhof and D. Laxton (2014), "Financial Crises in DSGE Models: A Prototype Model", IMF Working Paper 14/57, Washington, DC, International Monetary Fund.

Benhabib, J., S. Schmitt-Grohé and M. Uribe (2001), "The Perils of Taylor Rules", *Journal of Economic Theory*, 96: 40–69.

Bernanke, B., M. Gertler and S. Gilchrist (1999), "The Financial Accelerator in a Quantitative Business Cycle Framework", in J. Taylor and M. Woodford (eds.), *Handbook of Macroeconomics*, Amsterdam: Elsevier Science.

Beyer, A. and R. E. A. Farmer (2004), "On the Indeterminacy of New-Keynesian Economics", Working Paper Series No. 323, Frankfurt, Germany: European Central Bank.

Blanchard, O. and J. Galì (2010), "Labor Markets and Monetary Policy: A New Keynesian Model with Unemployment", *American Economic Journal: Macroeconomics*, 2: 1–30.

Branch, W. A. and B. McGough (2011), "Monetary Policy and Heterogeneous Agents", *Economic Theory*, 47: 365–393.

Brock, W. A. and C. Hommes (1997), "A Rational Route to Randomness", *Econometrica*, 65: 1059–1095.

Brock, W. A., S. Durlauf, J. M. Nason and G. Rondina (2007), "Simple Versus Optimal Rules as Guides to Policy", *Journal of Monetary Economics*, 54: 1372–1396.

Caballero, R. J. (2010), "Macroeconomics after the Crisis: Time to Deal with the Pretense-of-Knowledge Syndrome", *Journal of Economic Perspectives*, 24: 85–102.

Calvo, G. A. (1983), "Staggered Prices in a Utility-Maximizing Framework", *Journal of Monetary Economics*, 12: 383–398.

Canova, F. (2008), "How Much Structure in Empirical Models?", in T. Mills and K. Patterson, (eds.), *Palgrave Handbook of Econometrics.* Volume 2, Applied Econometrics, London, Palgrave Macmillan.

Canova, F. and L. Sala (2009), "Back to Square One: Identification Issues in DSGE Models", *Journal of Monetary Economics*, 56: 431–449.

Canzoneri, M., F. Collard, H. Dellas and B. Diba (2016), "Fiscal Multipliers in Recessions", *The Economic Journal*, 126: 75–108.

Carlin, W. and D. Soskice (2014), *Macroeconomics: Institutions, Instability, and the Financial System*, Oxford: Oxford University Press.

Chari, V. V., P. J. Kehoe and E. R. McGrattan (2009), "New Keynesian Models Are Not Yet Useful for Policy Analysis", *American Economic Journal: Macroeconomics*, 1: 242–266.

Christiano, L. G., M. Eichenbaum and C. L. Evans (2005), "Nominal Rigidities and the Dynamic Effects of a Shock to Monetary Policy", *Journal of Political Economy*, 113: 1–45.

Christiano, L. G., R. Motto and M. Rostagno (2011), "Financial Factors in Economic Fluctuations", Working Paper Series 1192, Frankfurt, European Central Bank.

Christiano, L. G., R. Motto and M. Rostagno (2013), "Risk Shocks", *American Economic Review*, 104: 27–65.

Clarida, R., J. Galí and M. Gertler (1999, December), "The Science of Monetary Policy: A New Keynesian Perspective", *Journal of Economic Literature*, 37: 1661–1707.

Cogan, J. F., T. Cwik, J. B. Taylor and V. Wieland (2009), "New Keynesian versus old Keynesian Government Spending Multipliers", *Journal of Economic Dynamics & Control*, 34: 281–295.

Cogley, T. and J. M. Nason (1993), "Impulse Dynamics and Propagation Mechanisms in a Real Business Cycle Model", *Economic Letters*, 43: 77–81.

Coibion, O. and Y. Gorodnichenko (2011), "Information Rigidity and the Expectations Formation Process: A Simple Framework and New Facts", Working Paper Series 16537, Cambridge, MA, NBER.

Colander, D. (ed.) (2006a), *Post Walrasian Macroeconomics*, Cambridge: Cambridge University Press.

Colander, D. (2006b), "Post Walrasian Macroeconomics: Some Historic Links", in D. Colander, (ed.), *Post Walrasian Macroeconomics*, Cambridge: Cambridge University Press.

Colander, D., H. Folmer, A. Haas, M. D. Goldberg, K. Juselius, A. P. Kirman, T. Lux and B. Sloth (2009), "The Financial Crisis and the Systemic Failure of Academic Economics", Technical Report, 98th Dahlem Workshop, Cambridge, MA, MIT Press.

Cooper, R. W. and A. John (1988), "Coordinating Coordination Failures in Keynesian Models", *Quarterly Journal of Economics*, 103: 441–463.

Curdia, V. and M. Woodford (2010), "Credit Spreads and Monetary Policy", *Journal of Money, Credit and Banking*, 42: 3–35.

Curdia, V. and M. Woodford (2011), "The Central-Bank Balance Sheet as an Instrument of Monetary Policy", *Journal of Monetary Economics*, 58: 54–79.

Curdia, V. and M. Woodford (2015), "Credit Frictions and Optimal Monetary Policy", NBER Working Paper 21820, Cambridge, MA, National Bureau of Economic Research.

Curdia, V., M. Del Negro and D. Greenwald (2014), "Rare Shocks, Great Recessions", *Journal of Applied Econometrics*, 29: 1031–1052.

Deak, S., P. Levine and B. Yang (2015), "A New Keynesian Behavioural Model with Individual Rationality and Heterogeneous Agents", Working Paper, Guildford, University of Surrey.

Debreu, G. (1974), "Excess Demand Function", *Journal of Mathematical Economics*, 1: 15–23.

De Grauwe, P. (2012), "Booms and Busts in Economic Activity: A Behavioral Explanation", *Journal of Economic Behavior & Organization*, 83: 484–501.

Del Negro, M., M. Eusepi, M. P. Giannoni, A. Sbordone, A. Tambalotti, M. Cocci, R. Hasegawa and M. H. Linder (2013), "The FRBNY DSGE Model", Technical Report 647, New York, Federal Reserve Bank of New York Staff Reports.

DeLong, J. B. (2011, May), "Economics in Crisis", *The Economists' Voice*, 8, May.

Dilaver, O., R. Jump and P. Levine (2016), "Agent-based Macroeconomics and Dynamic Stochastic General Equilibrium Models: Where Do We Go from Here?", Discussion Papers in Economics 01/16, Guildford, University of Surrey.

Dixit, A. and J. Stiglitz (1977), "Monopolistic Competition and Optimum Product Diversity", *American Economic Review*, 67: 297–308.

Dosi, G. (2012), *Economic Organization, Industrial Dynamics and Development*, Chapter Introduction, Cheltenham: Edward Elgar.

Eggertsson, G. B. and P. Krugman (2012), "Debt, Deleveraging, and the Liquidity Trap: A Fisher–Minsky–Koo Approach", *Quarterly Journal of Economics*, 127: 1469–1513.

Evans, G. W. and S. Honkapohja (2001), *Learning and Expectations in Macroeconomics*. Princeton, NJ, Princeton University Press.

Fagiolo, G. and A. Roventini (2012), "Macroeconomic Policy in DSGE and Agent-based Models", *Revue de l'OFCE*, 124: 67–116.

Fagiolo, G., M. Napoletano and A. Roventini (2008), "Are Output Growth-Rate Distributions Fat-Tailed? Some Evidence from OECD Countries", *Journal of Applied Econometrics*, 23: 639–669.

Farmer, D. J. and D. Foley (2009), "The Economy Needs Agent-Based Modeling", *Nature*, 460: 685–686.
Favero, C. (2007), "Model Evaluation in Macroeconometrics: From Early Empirical Macroeconomic Models to DSGE Models", Working Paper 327, Milan, Italy: IGIER, Bocconi University.
Fernandez-Villaverde, J. and O. Levintal (2016), "Solution Methods for Models with Rare Disasters", Working Paper 21997, Cambridge, MA, National Bureau of Economic Research.
Fernandez-Villaverde, J., J. F. Rubio-Ramirez and T. J. Sargent (2005), "A, B, C's, (and D's) for Understanding VARs", Technical Working Paper 308, Cambridge, MA, NBER.
Fernandez-Villaverde, J., J. F. Rubio-Ramirez and F. Schorfheide (2016), "Solution and Estimation Methods for DSGE Models", Working Paper 21862, Cambridge, MA, NBER.
Ferraresi, T., A. Roventini and G. Fagiolo (2014), "Fiscal Policies and Credit Regimes: A TVAR Approach", *Journal of Applied Econometrics*, 30: 1047–1072.
Fitoussi, J. and F. Saraceno (2010), "Inequality and Macroeconomi Performance", Document de Travail 2010–13, Paris, OFCE, Science Po.
Forni, M. and M. Lippi (1997), *Aggregation and the Microfoundations of Dynamic Macroeconomics*, Oxford: Oxford University Press.
Forni, M. and M. Lippi (February 1999), "Aggregation of Linear Dynamic Microeconomic Models", *Journal of Mathematical Economics*, 31: 131–158.
Friedman, M. (1953), "The Methodology of Positive Economics", in M. Friedman (ed.), *Essays in Positive Economics*, Chicago: University of Chicago Press.
Fukac, M. and A. Pagan (2006), "Issues in Adopting DSGE Models for Use in the Policy Process", Working Paper 10/2006, Crawford, Australia, Centre for Applied Macroeconomic Analysis.
Fukuyama, F. (1992), *The End of History and the Last Man*, London: Penguin.
Galì, J. (2008), *Monetary Policy, Inflation, and the Business Cycle: An Introduction to the New Keynesian Framework*, Princeton, NJ: Princeton University Press.
Galì, J. and M. Gertler (2007), "Macroeconomic Modelling for Monetary Policy Evaluation", *Journal of Economic Perspectives*, 21: 25–46.
Gennaioli, N., Y. Ma and A. Shleifer (2015), "Expectations and Investment", NBER Working Paper 21260, Cambridge, MA, National Bureau of Economic Research.
Gertler, M. and P. Karadi (2011), "A Model of Unconventional Monetary Policy", *Journal of Monetary Economics*, 58: 17–34.
Gertler, M. and N. Kiyotaki (2010), "Financial Intermediation and Credit Policy in Business Cycle Analysis", in B. M. Friedman and M. Woodford, (eds.), *Handbook of Monetary Economics*, Amsterdam: North Holland.
Gigerenzer, G. (2007), *Gut Feelings. The Intelligence of the Unconscious*, New York: Viking.
Gigerenzer, G. and H. Brighton (2009), "Homo Heuristicus: Why Biased Minds Make Better Inferences", *Topics in Cognitive Science*, 1: 107–143.
Goodfriend, M. (2007), "How the World Achieved Consensus on Monetary Policy", *Journal of Economic Perspectives*, 21: 47–68.
Goodfriend, M. and R. King (1997), "The New Neoclassical Synthesis and the Role of Monetary Policy", *NBER Macroeconomics Annual*, 12: 231–282.
Goodhart, C. A. E. (2009), "The Continuing Muddles of Monetary Theory: A Steadfast Refusal to Face Facts", *Economica*, 76: 821–830.

Guerini, M., M. Napoletano and A. Roventini (2016), "No Man Is an Island: The Impact of Heterogeneity and Local Interactions on Macroeconomic Dynamics", Working Paper Series 2016/24, Laboratory of Economics and Management (LEM), Pisa, Italy Scuola Superiore Sant'Anna.

Guzman, G. (2009), "Using Sentiment Surveys to Predict GDP Growth and Stock Returns", in L. R. Klein, (ed.), *The Making of National Economic Forecasts*, Edward Elgar: Cheltenham, 319–351.

Haldane, A. (2012), "The Dog and the Frisbee", Central bankers' speeches, Basel, BIS.

Hendry, D. and G. Minzon (2010), "On the Mathematical Basis of Inter-temporal Optimization", Economics Series Working Papers 497, Oxford, University of Oxford.

Howitt, P. (1992), "Interest Rate Control and Nonconvergence to Rational Expectations", *Journal of Political Economy*, 100: 776–800.

Howitt, P. (2011), "What Have Central Bankers Learned from Modern Macroeconomic Theory?", *Journal of Macroeconomics* 34, 11–22.

Johansen, S. (2006), "Confronting the Economic Model with the Data", in D. Colander, (ed.), *Post Walrasian Macroeconomics*, Cambridge, Cambridge University Press.

Johansen, S. and K. Juselius (2006), "Extracting Information from the Data: A European View on Empirical Macro", in D. Colander (ed.), *Post Walrasian Macroeconomics*, Cambridge: Cambridge University Press.

Juselius, K. and M. Franchi (2007), "Taking a DSGE Model to the Data Meaningfully", *Economics: The Open-Access, Open-Assessment E-Journal*, 1: 4.

Kay, J. (2011), "The Map is Not the Territory: An Essay on the State of Economics", New York, Technical Report, Institute for New Economic Thinking.

Keynes, J. M. (1936), *The General Theory of Employment, Interest, and Money*, New York: Prometheus Books.

Keynes, J. M. (1937), "The General Theory of Employment", *Quarterly Journal of Economics*, 51: 209–223.

Kirman, A. P. (1989), "The Intrinsic Limits of Modern Economic Theory: The Emperor Has no Clothes", *Economic Journal*, 99: 126–139.

Kirman, A. P. (1992), "Whom or What Does the Representative Individual Represent?", *Journal of Economic Perspectives*, 6: 117–136.

Kirman, A. P. (2010), "The Economic Crisis is a Crisis for Economic Theory", *CESifo Economic Studies*, 56: 498–535.

Kirman, A. P. (2016), "Ants and Nonoptimal Self-Organization: Lessons for Macroeconomics", *Macroeconomic Dynamics*, doi:10.1017/S1365100514000339.

Knight, F. (1921), *Risk, Uncertainty, and Profits*, Chicago: Chicago University Press.

Krugman, P. (2009), "How did Economics Get it So Wrong?", *New York Times Magazine*, 36–44.

Krugman, P. (2011), "The Profession and the Crisis", *Eastern Economic Journal*, 37: 307–312.

Krusel, P. and A. A. Smith (1998), "Income and Wealth Heterogeneity in the Macroeconomy", *Journal of Political Economy*, 106: 867–896.

Kumhof, M., R. Ranciere and P. Winant (2015), "Inequality, Leverage, and Crises", *American Economic Review*, 105: 1217–1245.

LeBaron, B. and L. Tesfatsion (2008), "Modeling Macroeconomies as Open-Ended Dynamic Systems of Interacting Agents", *American Economic Review*, 98: 246–250.

Lengnick, M. and H.-W. Wohltman (2016), "Optimal Monetary Policy in a New Keynesian Model with Animal Spirits and Financial Markets", *Journal of Economic Dynamics & Control*, 64: 148–165.

Lindley, D. (1994), *The End of Physics*. New York, Basic Books.
Mankiw, G. N. (2006), "The Macroeconomist as Scientist and Engineer", *Journal of Economic Perspectives*, 20: 29–46.
Mantel, R. (1974), "On the Characterization of Aggregate Excess Demand", *Journal of Economic Theory*, 7: 348–353.
Massaro, D. (2013), "Heterogeneous Expectations in Monetary DSGE Models", *Journal of Economic Dynamics & Control*, 37: 680–692.
Mehrling, P. (2006), "The Problem of Time in the DSGE Model and the Post Walrasian Alternative", in D. Colander, (ed.), *Post Walrasian Macroeconomics*, Cambridge: Cambridge University Press.
Mishkin, F. S. (2007), "Will Monetary Policy Become More of a Science", Working Paper 13566, Cambridge, MA, NBER.
Mittnik, S. and W. Semmler (2013), "The Real Consequences of Financial Stress", *Journal of Economic Dynamics & Control*, 37: 1479–1499.
Muth, J. F. (1961), "Rational Expectations and the Theory of Price Movements", *Econometrica*, 29, 315–335.
Orphanides, A. and J. C. Williams (2008), "Robust Monetary Policy with Imperfect Knowledge", *Journal of Monetary Economics*, 54: 1406–1435.
Pesaran, H. M. and A. Chudik (2011), "Aggregation in Large Dynamic Panels", Working Paper Series 3346, Munich, CESifo.
Piketty, T. and G. Zucman (2014), "Capital is Back: Wealth-Income Ratios in Rich Countries, 1700–2010", *Quarterly Journal of Economics*, 129: 1155–1210.
Poudyal, N. and A. Spanos (2013), "Confronting Theory with Data: Model Validation and DSGE Modeling", Working Paper, Blacksburg, VA, Department of Economics, Virginia Tech, USA.
Ravenna, F. (2007), "Vector Autoregressions and Reduced Form Representations of DSGE Models", *Journal of Monetary Economics*, 54: 2048–2064.
Rosser, B. J. (2011), *Complex Evolutionary Dynamics in Urban-Regional and Ecologic-Economic Systems: From Catastrophe to Chaos and Beyond*, New York: Springer.
Rotemberg, J. and M. Woodford (1999), "Interest Rate Rules in an Estimated Sticky Price Model", in J. Taylor, (ed.), *Monetary Policy Rules*. Chicago: University of Chicago Press.
Saari, D. and C. P. Simon (1978), "Effective Price Mechanisms", *Econometrica*, 46: 1097–1125.
Schmitt-Grohé, S. and M. Uribe (2000), "Price Level Determinacy and Monetary Policy under a Balanced-Budget Requirement", *Journal of Monetary Economics*, 45: 211–246.
Schorfheide, F. (2008), "DSGE Model-Based Estimation of the New Keynesian Phillips Curve", *FRB Richmond Economic Quarterly*, 94, Fall Issue: 397–433.
Smets, F. and R. Wouters (2003), "An Estimated Dynamic Stochastic General Equilibrium Model of the Euro Area", *Journal of the European Economic Association*, 1: 1123–1175.
Smets, F. and R. Wouters (2007), "Shocks and Frictions in US Business Cycles: A Bayesian DSGE Approach", *American Economic Review*, 97: 586–606.
Sonnenschein, H. (1972), "Market Excess Demand Functions", *Econometrica*, 40: 549–556.
Stiglitz, J. (2011), "Rethinking Macroeconomics: What Failed, and How to Repair It", *Journal of the European Economic Association*, 9: 591–645.
Stiglitz, J. (2015), "Towards a General Theory of Deep Downturns", Working Paper 21444, Cambridge, MA, NBER.
Summers, L. (1991), "The Scientific Illusion in Empirical Macroeconomics", *Scandinavian Journal of Economics*, 93: 129–148.

Taylor, J. (1993), "Discretion Versus Policy Rules in Practice", *Carnegie-Rochester Series on Public Policy*, 39: 195–214.

Taylor, J. (2007), "The Explanatory Power of Monetary Policy Rules", Working Paper 13685, Cambridge, MA, NBER.

Taylor, J. B. and J. C. Williams (2010), "Simple and Robust Rules for Monetary Policy", in B. M. Friedman and M. Woodford (eds.), *Handbook of Monetary Economics* Volume 3, Amsterdam, Elsevier.

Tesfatsion, L. (2006), "ACE: A Constructive Approach to Economic Theory", in L. Tesfatsion and K. Judd, (eds.), *Handbook of Computational Economics II: Agent-Based Computational Economics*, Amsterdam, North Holland.

Tesfatsion, L. and K. Judd (eds.) (2006), *Handbook of Computational Economics II: Agent-Based Computational Economics*, Amsterdam, North Holland.

Woodford, M. (1990), "Learning to Believe in Sunspots", *Econometrica*, 58: 277–307.

Woodford, M. (2003), *Interest and Prices: Foundations of a Theory of Monetary Policy*, Princeton, NJ, Princeton University Press.

Woodford, M. (2009), "Convergence in Macroeconomics: Elements of the New Synthesis", *American Economic Journal: Macroeconomics*, 1: 267–279.

Woodford, M. (2010), "Optimal Monetary Stabilization Policy", in B. M. Friedman and M. Woodford (eds.), *Handbook of Monetary Economics,* Volume 3, Amsterdam, Elsevier.

Zarnowitz, V. (1985), "Recent Works on Business Cycles in Historical Perspectives: A Review of Theories and Evidence", *Journal of Economic Literature*, 23: 523–580.

Zarnowitz, V. (1997), "Business Cycles Observed and Assessed: Why and How They Matter", Working Paper 6230, Cambridge, MA, NBER.

10 Macroeconomic policy in agent-based models

New developments and challenges ahead[1]

Giorgio Fagiolo and Andrea Roventini

Introduction

It is now widely acknowledged that the "perfect storm" which followed the bankruptcy of Lehman Brothers on September 15, 2008 not only caused the worst recession developed economies have ever seen since the Great Depression, but it also brought about a deep crisis for economic theory (Colander et al., 2009; Farmer and Foley, 2009; Krugman, 2009, 2011; Caballero, 2010; Kirman, 2010, 2016; DeLong, 2011; Kay, 2011; Stiglitz, 2011, 2015; Dosi, 2012). Indeed, as we have argued at length in Chapter 9, the basic assumptions of mainstream dynamic stochastic general equilibrium (DSGE) models, the predominant theoretical frameworks in macroeconomics nowadays, prevent the understanding of basic phenomena underlying the current economic crisis and, more generally, macroeconomic dynamics. There, we have suggested that a more fruitful research avenue should escape the strong theoretical requirements of DSGE models (e.g., equilibrium, rationality, representative agent) and consider economies as *complex evolving systems* (more on that in Farmer and Foley, 2009; Kirman, 2010, 2016; Rosser, 2011; Dosi, 2012; Battiston et al., 2016). This implies thinking of economies as ecologies populated by heterogeneous agents, whose far-from-equilibrium interactions continuously change the structure of the system.

Here, we build on such preliminary discussion and explore whether that approach, known as agent-based computational economics (ACE), might allow models to be built that, from a descriptive perspective, are able to reproduce many features of the 2008 economic crisis, such as, e.g., asset bubbles, resilience of interbank networks, self-organized criticality, and financial accelerator dynamics (see below for more detail).

Furthermore, we ask whether, on the normative side, the extreme flexibility of the set of assumptions regarding agent behaviors and interactions typically featured in ACE models (often called agent-based models, ABMs) can allow effective laboratories to be built to design policies and test their effects on macroeconomic dynamics. Indeed, as this chapter shows, an increasing number of macroeconomic policy applications have been already devised and explored concerning fiscal and monetary policies, bank regulation, structural reforms in the labor market, and climate change policies. Certainly, given its relatively young age, in the ACE approach there are still open issues that should be addressed. The most important ones concern empirical validation, over-parametrization, estimation and calibration, and comparability between different models. Nevertheless, papers addressing such issues have blossomed in recent years (cf. section on model selection and empirical validation, below). The success of ACE models in delivering policy implications while simultaneously explaining the observed micro and macro stylized facts is encouraging for the development of a new way of doing macroeconomic theory.

This chapter essentially extends the second part of its predecessor (Fagiolo and Roventini, 2012). In particular, the ACE paradigm is introducted and policy macroeconomic ABM applications reviewed. Finally, the chapter concludes by telegraphically accounting for some methodological issues related to policy in ACE models and the ensuing research avenues that these problems open up.

Agent-based models and economic policy

From DSGE to agent-based models

In Chapter 9, we extensively discussed the theoretical, empirical, and political-economy problems plaguing DSGE models. Given such a negative scenario, the positive economics approach advocated by Milton Friedman would suggest removing or changing the plethora of underlying assumptions in order to improve the performance of the model.

This recommendation is reinforced by two related observations. First, the assumptions underlying DSGE models become a sort of straitjacket that precludes the model from being flexible enough to allow for generalizations and extensions. Second, the unrealism of these assumptions prevents policy makers fully trusting the policy prescriptions developed with DSGE models.

It is far from clear why within the mainstream DSGE paradigm there is a widespread conservative attitude with no significant attempts to substitute the "Holy Trinity" assumptions of rationality, greed, and equilibrium (Colander, 2005) with more realistic ones. For instance, Akerlof (2007) argues that a broader definition of agents' preferences which takes into account the presence of realistic norms can violate many neutrality results of neoclassical economics without resorting to imperfections. Moreover, introducing heterogeneous agents or substituting the rationality assumption with insights from behavioral economics could substantially change the working of DSGE models. This position is also advocated in a recent work by Sinitskaya and Tesfatsion (2015), who explored models where economic agents are "locally constructive," that is, they are constrained by their interaction networks, information, beliefs, and physical states when making decisions.

In any case, if neoclassical economists truly align themselves with those advocating an instrumentalist approach to scientific research, they should agree that when models display estimation and validation (descriptive) problems such as those exhibited by DSGE ones, the only way out would be to modify the models' assumptions. As Wren-Lewis (2016) argues, the neoclassical revolution, which ultimately paved the way for the development of DSGE models, was mainly based on ideas and not events. In other words, he argues that models based on mainstream economics "focus on explaining only partial properties of the data" and share "an obsession with internal consistency," which "comes straight from the methodology." Given this lack of attention to explaining the events, experimenting with alternative sets of assumptions, supported by empirical data and experimental evidence, would be the recommendation that an instrumentalist researcher would provide. *A fortiori*, this should become an urgent research project to pursue if, in addition, the model, as happens in the DSGE case, also displays problems on the normative side.

This is exactly the research avenue that a growing number of scholars have been pursuing in the last two decades. Dissatisfied with standard macroeconomic, micro-founded, general-equilibrium-based neoclassical models like those discussed above, they have begun to devise an entirely new paradigm labeled as agent-based computational economics, or ACE). The philosophical underpinnings of ACE largely overlap with those of similar, complementary approaches known in the literature as "post Walrasian macroeconomics" (Colander, 2006b) and "evolutionary economics" (Nelson and Winter, 1982; Dosi and Nelson, 1994). The overlap is often so strong that one might safely speak of an emerging "heterodox synthesis." Such a large supply of heterodox models is exactly the basin which Setterfield (2016) argues central bankers and policy makers should draw from, in order to "entertain more eclectic views of how the economy functions."

The basic exercise ACE tries to perform is building models based on more realistic assumptions as far as agent behaviors and interactions are concerned, where *more realistic* here means rooted in empirical and experimental microeconomic evidence (Kirman, 2016). For example, following the body of evidence provided by cognitive psychologists (see, for example, among a vast literature, Kahneman and Tversky, 2000; Gigerenzer, 2007; Gigerenzer and Brighton, 2009), the assumptions of perfect rationality and foresight are replaced with those of bounded rationality and adaptive behavior. More generally, ACE scholars share the view that agents in the model should have "the same information as do the economists modeling the economy" (Colander, 2006a, p. 11). Similarly, insights from network theory (e.g., Albert and Barabasi, 2002) and social interactions (e.g., Brock and Durlauf, 2001) suggest moving away from the unrealistic and oversimplifying assumptions concerning agents' interactions typically employed in neoclassical models and allowing for direct, non-trivial interaction patterns. Finally, the widespread evidence on persistent heterogeneity and turbulence characterizing markets and economies indicatesthat crazy simplifications such as the representative agent assumption should be abandoned, as well as the presumption that economic systems are (and must be observed) in equilibrium, and to focus instead on out-of-equilibrium dynamics endogenously fueled by interactions among heterogeneous agents.

In other words, ACE can be defined as the computational study of economies thought as complex evolving systems (Tesfatsion, 2006a). Notice that neoclassical economics, on the contrary, typically deals with economies conceived as simple, linear, homogeneous, and stationary worlds. It should not come as a surprise that the class of models used by ACE to explore the properties of markets, industries, and economies (ABMs) are far more complicated – and harder to analyze – objects than their neoclassical counterparts. In the following section we will therefore begin by outlying the basic building blocks of ABMs. Next, we will address the question of how ABMs can be employed to deliver normative implications. Then, we will briefly review some examples of policy exercises in ABMs. Some final remarks about the pros and cons of using ABMs for policy analysis will be left for the concluding section.

Building blocks of ABMs

The last two decades have seen a rapid growth of agent-based modeling in economics. An exhaustive survey of this vast literature is of course beyond the scope of this work.[2] However, before proceeding, it is useful to introduce the ten main ingredients that tend to characterize economic ABMs.

1 *A bottom-up perspective.* A satisfactory account of a decentralized economy is to be addressed using a bottom-up perspective. In other words, aggregate properties must be obtained as the macro outcome of a possibly unconstrained microdynamics going on at the level of basic entities (agents). This contrasts with the top-down nature of traditional neoclassical models, where the bottom level typically comprises a representative individual and is constrained by strong consistency requirements associated with equilibrium and hyper-rationality.
2 *Heterogeneity.* Agents are (or may be) heterogeneous in almost all their characteristics.
3 *The evolving complex system approach.* Agents live in complex systems that evolve through time. Therefore, aggregate properties are thought to emerge out of repeated interactions among simple entities, rather than from the consistency requirements of rationality and equilibrium imposed by the modeler.
4 *Non-linearity.* The interactions that occur in ABMs are inherently non-linear. Additionally, non-linear feedback loops exist between micro and macro levels.
5 *Direct (endogenous) interactions.* Agents interact directly. The decisions undertaken today by an agent directly depend, through adaptive expectations, on the past choices made by other agents in the population.
6 *Bounded rationality.* The environment in which real-world economic agents live is too complex for hyper-rationality to be a viable simplifying assumption. It is suggested that one can, at most, impute to agents some local and partial (both in time and space) principles of rationality (e.g., myopic optimization rules). More generally, agents are assumed to behave as boundedly rational entities with adaptive expectations.
7 *The nature of learning.* Agents in ABMs engage in the open-ended search for dynamically changing environments. This is due to both the ongoing

introduction of novelty and the generation of new patterns of behavior; but also on the complexity of the interactions between heterogeneous agents (see point 5 above).

8 *"True" dynamics*. Partly as a consequence of adaptive expectations (i.e., agents observe the past and form expectations about the future on the basis of the past), ABMs are characterized by true, non-reversible, dynamics: the state of the system evolves in a path-dependent manner.[3]
9 *Endogenous and persistent novelty*. Socio-economic systems are inherently non-stationary. There is the ongoing introduction of novelty in economic systems and the generation of new patterns of behavior, which are themselves a force for learning and adaptation. Hence, agents face "true (Knightian) uncertainty" (Knight, 1921) and are only able to partially form expectations on, for instance, technological outcomes.
10 *Selection-based market mechanisms*. Agents typically undergo a selection mechanism. For example, the goods and services produced by competing firms are selected by consumers. The selection criteria that are used may themselves be complex and span a number of dimensions.

The basic structure of ABMs

Models based on (all or a subset of) the ten main ingredients discussed above typically possess the following structure. There is a population – or a set of populations – of agents (e.g., consumers, firms), possibly hierarchically organized, whose size may or may not change in time. The evolution of the system is observed in discrete time steps, $t = 1, 2, \ldots$ Time steps may be days, quarters, years, etc. At each t, every agent i is characterized by a finite number of microeconomic variables $x_{i,t}$ (which may change across time) and by a vector of microeconomic parameters θ_i (that are fixed in the time horizon under study). In turn, the economy may be characterized by some macroeconomic (fixed) parameters Θ.

Given some initial conditions $x_{i,0}$ and a choice for micro and macro parameters, at each time step $t > 0$, one or more agents are chosen to update their microeconomic variables. This may happen randomly or can be triggered by the state of the system itself. Agents selected to perform the updating stage collect their available information about the current and past state (i.e., microeconomic variables) of a subset of other agents, typically those they directly interact with. They plug their knowledge about their local environment, as well as the (limited) information they can gather about the state of the whole economy, into heuristics, routines, and other algorithmic, not necessarily optimizing, behavioral rules. These rules, as well as interaction patterns, are designed so as to mimic empirical and experimental knowledge that the researcher may have collected from his/her preliminary studies.

After the updating round has taken place, a new set of microeconomic variables is fed into the economy for the next-step iteration: aggregate variables X_t are computed by simply summing up or averaging individual characteristics. Once again, the definitions of aggregate variables closely follow those of statistical aggregates (i.e., gross domestic product (GDP), unemployment, etc.).

The stochastic components possibly present in decision rules, expectations, and interactions will in turn imply that the dynamics of micro and macro variables can be described by some (Markovian) stochastic processes parameterized by micro and macro parameters. However, non-linearities which are typically present in decision rules and interactions make it hard to analytically derive laws of motion, kernel distributions, time-t probability distributions for the stochastic processes governing the evolution of micro and macro variables.

This suggests that the researcher must often resort to computer simulations in order to analyze the behavior of the ABM at hand. Notice that in some simple cases such systems allow for analytical solutions of some kind. Needless to say, the more one injects into the model assumptions sharing the philosophy of the building blocks discussed above, the less tractable turns out to be the model, and the more one needs to resort to computer simulations. Simulations must be intended here in a truly constructive way, e.g., to build and "grow" a society "from the bottom up," in the spirit of object-oriented programming.

Descriptive analysis of ABMs

When studying the outcomes of ABMs, the researcher often faces the problem that the economy he/she is modeling is by definition out of equilibrium. The focus is seldom on static equilibria or steady-state paths. Rather, the researcher must more often look for long-run statistical equilibria and/or emergent properties of aggregate dynamics (that is, transient statistical features that last suffficiently long to be observed and considered stable as compared to the time horizon of the model; see Lane, 1993, for an introduction). Such an exploration is by definition very complicated and it is made even more difficult by the fact that the researcher does not even know in advance whether the stochastic process described by its ABM is ergodic or not and, if it somehow converges, how much time will take for the behavior to become sufficiently stable.

Suppose for a moment that the modeler knows, e.g., from a preliminary simulation study or from some *ex ante* knowledge coming from the particular structure of the ABM under study, that the dynamic behavior of the system becomes sufficiently stable after some time horizon T^* for (almost all) points of the parameter space. Then a possible procedure that can be implemented to study the output of the ABM runs like the one synthetically depicted in Figure 10.1.

Given some choice for initial conditions, micro and macro parameters, assume to run our system until it relaxes to some stable behavior (i.e., for at least $T > T^*$ time steps). Suppose we are interested in a set $S = \{s_1, s_2, \ldots\}$ of statistics to be computed on micro and macro simulated variables. For any given run the program will output a value for each statistic. Given the stochastic nature of the process, each run will output a different value for the statistics. Therefore, after having produced M independent runs, one has a distribution for each statistic containing M observations, which can be summarized by computing its moments.

Recall, however, that moments will depend on the choice made for initial conditions and parameters. By exploring a sufficiently large number of points in the

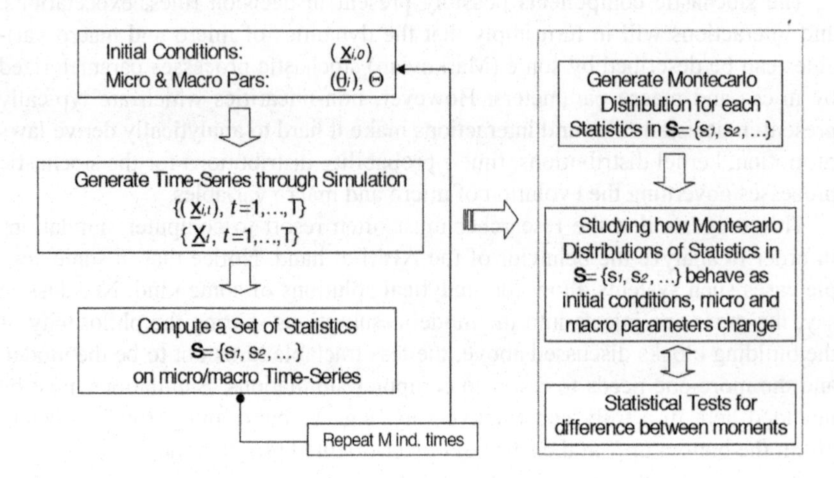

Figure 10.1 A schematic procedure for studying the output of an agent-based model

space where initial conditions and parameters are allowed to vary, computing the moments of the statistics of interest at each point, and assessing how moments depend on parameters, one might get quite a deep *descriptive* knowledge of the behavior of the system (Figure 10.1).

So far, we have naively assumed that the data generation process (DGP) described by the ABM under study is ergodic and stationary. But is it possible to quantitatively check this assumption? Recent research indeed provides alternatives to the researcher interested in statistically assessing such an issue, and therefore better understand the behavior of the model, and draw inferences about the real system it is intended to represent (Richiardi et al., 2006). As an example, Grazzini (2012) discusses the use of Wald–Wolfowitz tests applied to ABMs and shows that, under appropriate settings, these procedures can detect non-stationarity and non-ergodicity.

Model selection and empirical validation

From the foregoing discussion it clearly emerges that in agent-based modeling (as in many other modeling endeavors) one often faces a trade-off between descriptive accuracy and explanatory power of the model. The more one tries to inject into the model "realist" assumptions, the more the system becomes complicated to study and the less clear the causal relations going from assumptions to implications are. ABM researchers are well aware of this problem and have been trying to develop strategies to guide the process of assumption selection. For example, one can try to solve the trade-off between descriptive capability and explanatory power either by beginning with the most simple model and complicating it step-by-step (i.e., the so-called KISS strategy, an acronym standing for "keep it simple, stupid!") or by starting with the most descriptive model and simplifying it as much as possible (i.e., the so-called KIDS strategy, "keep it descriptive, stupid!"). A third, alternative strategy prescribes instead starting with an existing model and successively complicating it with incremental additions (this strategy might be labeled TAPAS, which stands for "take a previous model and add something").

In all these procedures, the extent to which the ABM is able to empirically replicate existing reality should play a crucial role in discriminating the point at which any procedure should stop.[4]

Notice that the very structure of ABMs naturally allows one to take the model to the data and validate it against observed real-world observations. Indeed, an ABM can be thought to provide a DGP, which we think real-world observations are a realization of. More precisely, let us suppose that we believe that observed data are generated by an unknown (to us) colossal DGP, with an almost infinite number of parameters, which we can label as real-world DGP (rwDGP). Suppose further that such rwDGP can be broken into reasonable smaller weakly exogenous components, each one with a reasonable number of parameters, and each one describing a small set of variables that we are interested in, on the basis of a small set of other variables. Building an ABM means attempting to approximate one of those small rwDGPs. Due to its stochastic structure, an ABM actually mimics the small rwDGP we are studying by a theoretical DGP that generates the same variables each time we run the model. Of course, we only have one observation generated by the rwDGP, and this makes any inference very difficult (but this has to do with another story, which philosophers call the problem of induction).

Many approaches to empirical validation (and selection) of ABMs can be in principle taken, and the debate is very open here.[5]

For example, one might select among ABMs (and within different parameter setups of the same ABM) with respect to the number of stylized facts each is able to jointly replicate. A typical procedure to be followed starts with asking whether a particular model can simultaneously reproduce some set of stylized facts for a given parametrization (a sort of "exercise in plausibility"); then exploring what happens when the parameter setup changes; finally, investigating if some meaningful causal explanation can be derived out of that step-by-step analysis. This approach has been recently criticized, in that it is not able to identify the correct causal structures that may have generated the observed evidence. Indeed, as argued by Guerini and Moneta (2016), many alternative causal structures can underlie the set of statistical dependencies observed in the data. To attempt to overcome this issue, Guerini and Moneta (2016) propose, firstly, estimating the causal structure incorporated in the model using its simulated outputs, and then comparing it with the causal structure detected in the real-world data that the model aspires to replicate. Both causal structures are derived from fitting vector autoregression models, estimated using both artificial and real-world data by means of causal search algorithms.

Alternatively, one can first select among parameters by calibrating the model (e.g., by directly estimating parameters, when possible, with micro or macro data) and then judging to what extent the calibrated model is able to reproduce the stylized facts of interest. A recent stream of literature tries to pursue this idea and recover the parameters of ABMs using some form of parameter estimation (or calibration). For example, Gilli and Winker (2003), Alfarano et al. (2005), Winker et al. (2007), and Grazzini et al. (2013) employ different blends of indirect estimation methods, whereas Grazzini and Richiardi (2015) propose estimating parameters of ergodic ABMs using simulated minimum distance. Note that this latter technique has the merit of being potentially applicable to both the long-run equilibria of the model and during adjustment phases. Conversely, Recchioni et al. (2015) approach the problem of calibrating the free parameters of ABMs as a non-linear constrained optimization, which can be solved numerically via gradient-based methods, whereas Fabretti (2012) employs search technologies coming from genetic algorithms to explore the space of all possible parameter combinations in simple ABMs of financial markets. More recently, Grazzini et al. (2015) have suggested a Bayesian inference approach, as opposed to simulated minimum distance, to estimate ABM parameters, whereas Lamperti (2015, 2016) resorts to information-criteria techniques to quantify the distance between the true probabilistic dynamics of the output of the model and the data (to be minimized in order to achieve estimation), without needing to impose any stationarity requirements (see also Barde, 2015).

Notice that, unlike economists supporting the New Neoclassical Synthesis NS approach – who hold strong theoretical priors rooted in the DSGE model – ACE scholars are more interested in developing plausible theories, which however are not dogmatically deemed to be the "correct" ones (on this point, see also Colander, 2006a). Therefore, estimation and calibration of ABM parameters must not be intended as a way of identifying their true, real-world values, but rather singling out ranges wherein true parameters could lie. In this respect, we note also that parameter estimation of ABMs may easily become not computationally viable, especially when the number of parameters to be estimated is large and data availability is scarce.

One of the problems related to all these validation exercises is rooted in their computational requirements. As discussed in Grazzini et al. (2015), the curse of dimensionality makes the practical application of the tools discussed nearly impossible for medium- and large-scale ABMs. To address this problem, Lamperti et al. (2016b) have proposed to use machine learning surrogates to conveniently filter the parameter space of simulation models, dramatically reducing the computational effort needed to explore the behavior of the model when many parameters are at stake.

No matter the empirical validation procedure actually employed, its basic goal is often to restrict the size of the set of free parameters. In fact, over-parameterized models are difficult to interpret and analyze, because no one knows whether the same conclusions could have been obtained in a simpler, less parameterized model. Even if empirical validation allows one to restrict the set of free parameters to a reasonably sized one, many methodological problems still remain when the model is used to perform policy experiments. If any parametrization represents an alternative world, which one should be employed to assess policy performance? What is the role of initial conditions? What kind of sensitivity analysis should be performed? Recent developments try to mitigate over-parameterization issues by resorting to phase diagrams (Gualdi et al., 2015), Kriging meta-modeling (Salle and Yıldızoğlu, 2014; Bargigli et al., 2016; Dosi et al., 2016d), and machine-learning surrogates (Lamperti et al., 2016b). We shall briefly come back to these issues in the concluding remarks.

For the moment it is important to notice that the methodological debate within the agent-based community is very lively. Among many interesting lines of methodological research, one of the most crucial ones concerns the issue of realism of the assumptions in economic models (for a more general appraisal, see Schlefer, 2012). Indeed, whereas many ABM scholars argue that their approach allows for more realism in the way individual behaviors and interactions are accounted for in theoretical models (as opposed to neoclassical ones), others have maintained that ABM must also have a trade-off between successful model building and empirical accuracy of assumptions (Deichsel and Pyka, 2009). Therefore, in order to provide ABMs that deliver meaningful statistical implications, agent-based researchers must often employ assumptions that are not the most descriptively accurate ones.

Policy experiments in ABMs: some considerations

ABMs configure themselves as a very powerful device to address policy questions in more realistic, flexible, and modular frameworks. Indeed, as far as economic policy is concerned, ABMs have many advantages as compared to neoclassical tools like the DSGE model, which we organize below into two classes: theory and empirics.

Theory

ABMs, contrary to neoclassical ones, do not impose any strong theoretical consistency requirements (e.g., equilibrium, representative individual assumptions, rational expectations). This is because they are not required *ex ante* to be analytically solvable. Such no-straitjacket condition allows for an extremely higher flexibility in model building. If this is coupled with a serious empirical-validation requirement (see below), we are in the presence of a semi-instrumentalist approach, where bad (but empirically plausible) assumptions can be replaced with better (and empirically plausible) ones if the model does not perform as expected. Notice also that, in the absence of strong consistency conditions, assumptions can be replaced in a modular way, without impairing the analysis of the model. Indeed, in standard neoclassical models one cannot simply replace the optimization assumption with another one just because the model does not behave well, as that would possibly destroy its analytical solvability. This is not so in ABMs: assumptions – or simply small elements of them – can be taken off the shelf and easily implemented in the model thanks to the flexibility of computer programming languages.

Empirics

As discussed above, ABMs can be thought of as generators of alternative worlds, i.e., theoretical DGPs that approximate the unknown one. In contrast to neoclassical models, the structure of ABMs allows them to take them to the data more easily. This can be done in two ways. First, one can validate the inputs of ABMs, i.e., fine-tune modeling assumptions about individual behaviors and interactions to make them more similar to the observed ones. Second, one can validate the model on the output side, by, e.g., restricting the space of parameters, individual behaviors and interactions, and initial conditions to those that allow the model to replicate the stylized facts of interest. This allows for a degree of realism that is much higher than that exhibited by DSGE models (Farmer and Foley, 2009). Furthermore, thanks to the theoretical flexibility discussed above, ABMs can target a rich ensemble of stylized facts at different levels of aggregation (i.e., micro vs. macro regularities). This is a major advantage of ABMs *vis-à-vis* DSGE ones, which are typically built – in order to retain analytical solvability – to explain one or two single macro stylized facts (see the discussion in Aoki, 2006, for more details), and cannot replicate any micro empirical regularities given the representative-agent assumption.

But how can one actually conduct policy experiments in ABMs? In a very natural way, indeed. Take again the procedure for ABM descriptive analysis outlined in Figure 10.1. Recall that micro and macro parameters can be designed in such a way to mimic real-world key policy variables like tax rates, subsidies, interest rates, and money and other key behavioral measures affecting individual incentives in growth, innovation, or technologically related policies. Moreover, initial conditions might play the role of initial endowments and therefore describe different distributional setups. In addition, interaction and behavioral rules employed by economic agents can be easily devised so as to represent alternative institutional, market, or industry setups. Since all these elements can be freely interchanged, one can investigate a huge number of alternative policy experiments and rules, the consequences of which can be assessed either qualitatively or quantitatively (e.g., by running standard statistical tests on the distributions of the statistics in *S*). For example, one might statistically test whether the effect on the moments of the individual consumption distribution (average, etc.) will be changed (and if so, by how much) by a percentage change in any given consumption tax rate. Most importantly, all this might be done while preserving the ability of the model to replicate existing macroeconomic stylized facts (e.g., some time-series properties of observed aggregate variables such as persistence of output growth-rate fluctuations, relative standard deviations, cross-correlations), as well as microeconomic empirical regularities (e.g., firm size distributions, firm productivity dynamics, firm investment patterns).

Macroeconomic policy in ABMs: a survey

The number of ABMs dealing with policy issues has been increasing fast over time[6] and such a trend has received new inputs after the Great Recession uncovered many weakness of DSGE models. This success is partly due to the fact that policy makers appear to be more and more willing to believe in results stemming from detailed simulation models (such as ABMs), where the underlying economic structure can be observed,[7] rather than in general insights produced by quite abstract mathematical models such as DSGE ones.

The number of ABMs addressing policy issues is becoming so large that a survey of the whole literature would probably deserve a whole book rather than a paper. ABMs have indeed been employed in many different policy arenas such as industrial dynamics, market design, environmental regulation, and traffic management. We focus our attention on the subset of ABMs evaluating the impact of macroeconomic policies, which can be straightforwardly compared to DSGE models and respond to the new theoretical and empirical challenges raised by the Great Recession. More specifically, in what follows we classify ABMs in five areas, namely fiscal policy, monetary policy, macroprudential policy, labor market policy, and climate change policy.

Fiscal policy

The Great Recession has reawakened interest in employing fiscal policies to tackle economic downturns. An advantage of ABMs *vis-à-vis* mainstream ones is the possibility to jointly study the short- and long-run impact of fiscal policies.

Dosi et al. (2010) try to do so developing an ABM, bridging Keynesian theories of demand generation and Schumpeterian theories of technology-fueled economic growth (the K + S model; see Dosi et al. 2014, for a survey). In the full-fledged version, the K + S model is populated by heterogeneous capital-good firms, consumption good-firms, consumers/workers, banks, Central Bank, and a public sector. Capital-good firms perform research and development (R&D) and sell heterogeneous machine tools to consumption-good firms. Consumers supply labor to firms and fully consume the income they receive. Banks provide credit to consumption-good firms to finance their production and investment decisions. The Central Bank fixes the short-run interest rate and the government levies taxes and provides unemployment benefits. The model is able to endogenously generate growth and jointly account for mild recessions and deep downturns. Moreover, it is able to replicate an ensemble of stylized facts concerning both macroeconomic dynamics (e.g., cross-correlations, relative volatilities, output distributions) and microeconomic ones (firm size distributions, firm productivity dynamics, firm investment patterns). After having been empirically validated according to the output generated, the K + S model is employed to study the impact of fiscal policies (i.e., tax rate and unemployment benefits) on average GDP growth rate, output volatility, and unemployment rate. The authors find that Keynesian fiscal policies are a necessary condition for economic growth and they can be successfully employed to dampen economic fluctuations.[8] Moreover, Dosi et al. (2013) find a strong interaction between income distribution and fiscal policies: the more income distribution is skewed toward profits, the greater the case for fiscal policies to dampen macroeconomic fragility.[9]

Different fiscal austerity policies are studied in Dosi et al. (2015). They find that fiscal consolidation rules are "self-defeating," as they depress the economy without improving public finances. Similar conclusions are reached by Teglio et al. (2015), employing the EURACE model (Cincotti et al., 2012b). Moreover, the negative effects of fiscal policies are magnified by higher levels of income inequality (Dosi et al., 2015). Finally, austerity policies can also reduce long-run productivity and GDP growth, by harming innovation rate and the diffusion of new technologies (Dosi et al., 2016b) and firms' investment rates (Bassi and Lang, 2016). In fact, stabilization policies can affect both short- and long-run dynamics, as found also by Russo et al. (2007) and Harting (2015).

A series of ABMs explore the interactions between financial instability and fiscal policies. Napoletano et al. (2015) built an ABM populated by heterogeneous households facing time-varying credit constraints. They found that deficit-spending fiscal policy dampens the magnitude and persistence of bankruptcy shocks. Moreover, the size of the multipliers changes over time and it is related to the evolution of credit rationing. Chiarella and Di Guilmi (2012) explored the consequences of financial fragility from the firms' perspective, developing an ABM with Minskyan flavor, where the investment of heterogeneous firms is conditioned by market expectations, money can either be exogenous or endogenous, and the government can levy taxes on profits or private wealth. The model shows that, with endogenous money and credit, a wealth tax is a more effective stabilization policy than a tax on profit. Relatedly, in an ABM with heterogeneous workers, firms, and banks interacting in markets through a decentralized matching protocol, Riccetti et al. (2014) found that during extended crises triggered by bank defaults and financial instability, the government sector can stabilize the economy.

Finally, the impacts of different expectation-formation mechanisms are studied in the K + S model by Dosi et al. (2016a). Starting from the Brock and Hommes (1997) framework, they found that austerity policies are self-defeating even when agents can switch among different expectation rules (e.g., adaptive, trend-follower expectations), as in Anufriev et al. (2013). Moreover, in line with Gigerenzer (2007) and Gigerenzer and Brighton (2009), they found that the performance of the economy does not improve when agents are more rational. On the contrary, when agents employ ordinary least squares to form their forecasts, individual and collective performance worsen as structural breaks and Knightian uncertainty cannot be taken into account. Relatedly, Haber (2008) studied the interactions between different expectation-formation mechanisms and fiscal and monetary policies in an ABM. He found that the introduction of more sophisticated expectations reduced the effects of fiscal policy, whereas it increased the impact of monetary policy.

Monetary policy

DSGE models have mostly dealt with monetary policy, searching for the best monetary rule. At the same time, the current Great Recession has revealed the importance of credit and financial markets and shown that monetary policy alone is not sufficient to put economies back on their steady growth path. This has triggered novel research efforts in the DSGE camp, as discussed in Chapter 9. At the same time, the emphasis of ABMs on heterogeneity and interactions makes them natural candidates to study the effects of monetary policies (and bank regulation; cf. section on financial instability, bank regulation and macroprudential policies, below) in a framework characterized by financial fragility (e.g., Delli Gatti et al., 2005a; Dosi et al., 2013, 2015; Caiani et al., 2015), bankruptcy cascades (e.g., Delli Gatti et al., 2010; Battiston et al., 2012), and deleveraging dynamics (e.g., Raberto et al., 2012; Seppecher and Salle, 2015).

A growing set of ABMs employ Taylor rules to explore the effects of monetary policy on the economy. In this respect, such policy analysis exercises are similar to the ones conducted with DSGE models, but the complexity-rooted approach of ABM can bring fresh new insights.

The K + S model is employed by Dosi et al. (2015) to study the impact of a "conservative" Taylor rule focused only on inflation *vis-à-vis* a dual-mandate one, which aim also at stabilizing the unemployment rate. They found that the dual-mandate Taylor rule is more efficient in stabilizing the economy (a similar result is found in Raberto et al., 2008; Delli Gatti and Desiderio, 2015) without substantially increasing the inflation rate. However, the transmission channel is different from the traditional one employed by DSGE models grounded on the interest rate. Indeed, the presence of a credit channel implies that a dual-mandate monetary rule reduces the destabilizing effects of credit pro-cyclicality, providing both banks and firms with a stronger financial record on the eve of recessions. More generally, there appear to be strong interactions not only between fiscal and monetary policies but also between macroprudential and monetary ones (more on that in Popoyan et al., 2015, and the papers presented in the following section). Finally, the effects of monetary policies become sharper as the level of income inequality increases (see also Dosi et al., 2013).

Alternative commitment *vis-`a-vis* discretionary monetary strategies is studied in Delli Gatti et al. (2005b) in an economy populated by heterogeneous, interacting firms and workers. In the commitment strategy, the Central Bank employs a fixed-parameter Taylor rule, whereas in the discretionary one, the parameters of the Taylor rule change according to a genetic algorithm, mimicking a learning process. The authors found that pervasive capital market imperfections imply that monetary policy affects the economy through the credit channel and that money is not neutral in the long run. Moreover, the Taylor principle does not hold and the adaptive rule outperforms the commitment one according to the standard loss function criterion.

Relatedly, Arifovic et al. (2010) studied the time-inconsistency problem faced by Central Banks in an ABM where the interaction between a boundedly rational, evolutionary learning policy maker and a population of heterogeneous agents determines the actual inflation rate. The agents can either believe the inflation rate announced by the Central Bank or employ an adaptive learning scheme to forecast future inflation. Simulations show that the Central Bank learns to sustain an equilibrium with a positive, but fluctuating, fraction of "believers," and that this outcome is Pareto-superior to the equilibrium determined by standard models.

Finally, Salle et al. (2013) studied the performance of inflation targeting monetary policy in a model where heterogeneous agents (firms and consumers) adopt heuristics, but they continuously learn employing a genetic algorithm. They found that the credibility of the inflation target plays a major role in achieving the objectives of monetary policies, and the transparent communication of such a target by the Central Bank is instrumental to increasing its credibility and in turn its ability to stabilize the economy. The foregoing conclusions are generalized in Salle (2015) with a model in which agents form their expectations according to artificial neural networks.

The effects of unconventional monetary policy are explored in Cincotti et al. (2010), who developed an ABM based on the EURACE platform to assess the effects of quantitative-easing monetary policy, in which the Central Bank finances government deficit by buying treasury bonds. Simulation results show that the performance of the economy improves when expansionary fiscal policy and quantitative-easing monetary policy are implemented. However, such expansionary policies raise inflation and lead to higher output volatility in the long run.

Arifovic and Maschek (2012) consider an open economy framework (see also Rengs and Wackerle, 2014), where a Central Bank fixes the interest rate in order to try to avoid the emergence of a currency crisis, which is triggered by the (heterogeneous) devaluation expectations of investors, changing via a social evolutionary learning process. They found that decreasing the interest rates under the menace of a possible currency attack is more effective than defending the currency, as the latter policy increases the outflow of funds.

Financial instability, bank regulation, and macroprudential policies

The Great Recession has not only revealed the importance of credit and financial markets for the real dynamics, but it has also uncovered the lack of research on the effects of macroprudential regulation and on its interactions with monetary policy (see, e.g., Blanchard et al., 2013). Given their emphasis on heterogeneity and interactions, ABMs are a natural tool to address such issues.

The role of loan-to-value ratios and static capital-adequacy regulation akin to the Basel II framework are studied in Ashraf et al. (2011), with an ABM where heterogeneous firms interact with banks, providing them credit. Simulations of the model, calibrated to US data, show that during deep downturns bank credit can stabilize the economy, easing the entry of new firms and avoiding the bankruptcy of the incumbents. As a consequence, less strict microprudential bank regulation (i.e., higher loan-to-value ratios and lower capital-adequacy ratios) allows the economy to recover faster from a crisis.

Somewhat similarly, Dosi et al. (2013) found that, in the bank-augmented K + S model, higher loan-to-value ratios positively affect macroeconomic growth when firms can rely less on internal funds. Employing the EURACE model, Raberto et al. (2012) found that lower capital-adequacy ratios can spur growth in the short run, but the higher stock of private debt can lead to higher firm bankruptcies, credit rationing, and more serious economic downturns in the long run.

The impact of capital and reserve requirements is studied in van der Hoog and Dawid (2015) with the Eurace@Unibi model (Dawid et al., 2012). Simulation results show that stricter liquidity regulations are better suited to reduce output volatility and prevent deep downturns, whereas more stringent capital requirements obtain opposite results as they increase credit pro-cyclicality (see also van der Hoog, 2015).

Alternative resolution mechanisms of banking crises – i.e., liquidation of distressed institution, bank bail-out or bail-in – are studied in Klimek et al. (2015). They found that, during expansions, closing the distressed bank is the best policy to achieve financial and economic stability, whereas bail-in is the desired one during recessions.

Finally, the impact of Basel II regulation on financial market dynamics is studied in Poledna et al. (2014), with an ABM populated by fund managers and representative noisy trader, bank, and fund investor (see also Aymanns and Farmer, 2015). The simulation of the ABM shows that Basel II has a destabilizing impact on the market by increasing the amount of synchronized buying and selling needed to achieve deleveraging. As a consequence, Basel II reduces default risk when leverage is low, but it magnifies it when leverage is high.

A new generation of ABMs has been recently employed to study the effects of the introduction of Basel III macroprudential regulation and its possible interactions with monetary policy to achieve both price and financial stability.[10] Popoyan et al. (2015) extended the ABM developed in Ashraf et al. (2011) to address such issues, exploring the joint and stand-alone impact of the different levers of Basel III for alternative monetary policies, e.g., conservative, dual-mandate Taylor rule, or "leaning-against-the-wind" monetary rule focused on inflation, output gap, and credit growth. Simulation results show that a triple-mandate Taylor rule and the fully fledged Basel III prudential regulation is the best policy mix to improve the stability of the banking sector and smooth output fluctuations. However, results close to the Basel III first-best can be achieved in a much more simplified regulatory framework by adopting just minimum capital requirements and counter-cyclical capital buffers (see also Cincotti et al., 2012a, for similar conclusions concerning the stabilizing role of counter-cyclical capital buffers). Moreover, the components of Basel III are non-additive: the inclusion of an additional lever does not always improve the performance of the macroprudential regulation and their joint impact is more effective than the sum of their individual contributions.

In line with the previous results, also Krug et al. (2015) found that Basel III improves the resilience of the banking system and the effects of microprudential instruments are non-additive. Moreover, surcharges on systemic important banks increase financial regulation complexity without increasing the stability of the banking sector. A strong complementarity between macroprudential and monetary policy is also found in Krug (2015): in line with the Tinbergen principle, a "leaning-against-the-wind" monetary rule is not sufficient alone to prevent financial instability. The ABM developed by Da Silva and Tadeu Lima (2015) provided somewhat different results: countercyclical capital buffer can lose its efficacy in stabilizing the financial system when combined with some monetary rules, and interest rate smoothing is the most successful monetary policy strategy.

The modeling of the *network* structure of an economy is difficult in DSGE models. This lack of consideration has prevented such models from explaining the emergence, depth, and diffusion of the current crisis, where the topological properties of the credit market network have a fundamental role. Taking a complexity theory perspective and combining network theory and ABM can improve financial regulation and provide early signals, which could help to avoid the occurrence of financial crises (Battiston et al., 2016). For instance, Battiston et al. (2012) have shown that the financial network is more resilient for intermediate levels of risk diversification than for the highest one.

The resilience of the banking network to liquidity shocks was studied by Gai et al. (2011) developing an ABM of the interbank lending network where heterogeneous banks are randomly connected together though unsecured claims and repo activities. The impact of idiosyncratic liquidity shocks is then analyzed for different network configurations, degrees of connectivity between banks, haircut assumptions, and balance sheet characteristics of financial institutions. The model shows that greater degree of complexity and concentration in the bank network augment the fragility of the system, increasing the probability of contagion phenomena and liquidity crises similar to the ones experienced in the Great Recession. Policy experiments show possible ways (e.g., tougher microprudential liquidity regulation, counter-cyclical liquidity requirements) of reducing the network externalities responsible for the emergence of systemic crisis.

The effects of solvency shocks are considered in Krause and Giansante (2012), who found that the topological properties of the interbank lending network affect the diffusion of crises originated by the failure of a failing bank. Gaffeo and Molinari (2016) studied the resilience of the banking network as regards a sequence of merging and acquisitions episodes which affected its topology. They found that the consolidation of the banking network has different impact on systemic risk according to the size of interbank market and bank capitalization. As a consequence, policy makers should monitor the time evolution of the interbank network before authorizing bank consolidation.[11]

An increasing number of ABMs analyze the connections between bank and firm networks and macroeconomic performance. Gabbi et al. (2015) added a stylized real sector to an ABM of the banking network and studied the impact of some macroprudential regulations (e.g., counter-cyclical capital buffers). They found that the impact of the regulatory framework on bank performance varied in a complex way with the state of the economy, the degree of connectivity of the interbank network, and the amount of available information on bank risks.

The emergence of a network-based financial accelerator is analyzed in Delli Gatti et al. (2010), who developed an ABM populated by heterogeneous banks, financially constrained downstream and upstream firms interacting on a continuously evolving credit network. Simulation results show that the emergence and evolution of the network-based financial accelerator lead to financial crises and business cycles. Hence, policy makers can try to design a structure for the credit network in order to reduce the magnifying effects of the financial accelerator (e.g., Grilli et al., 2014, found that macroeconomic performance increases with network connectivity up to a certain threshold). In particular, in an extended version of the model, Riccetti et al. (2013a) found that leverage has a destabilizing effect, increasing the risk in the economy and dampening the effects of monetary policy (relatedly, Lengnick et al., 2013, found that interbank market stabilizes the economy during normal times but it acts as a destabilizer during crises). Moreover, if the banking system is not sufficiently capitalized, a surge in Central Bank interest rate may increase its fragility, whereas an increase of the reserve coefficient improves the resilience of bank network to shocks. Starting from previous works, Catullo et al. (2015) developed an early-warning indicator for crises grounded on the evolution of the firm–bank credit network.

The housing market as a source of financial instability and contagion possibly leading to crises has started to be addressed by ABMs. Geanakoplos et al. (2012) built an ABM of the housing market for the greater Washington, DC, area. The model matches the house price and housing market indices from 1997–2010 and it suggests that the housing boom and bust has been mainly driven by leverage rather than interest rates. Gangel et al. (2013) studied the contagion effects of foreclosure in a real-estate market and found that the time a foreclosed property stays in the market has a much stronger effect on market stability than any contagion effect. Such results suggest that policy makers should simplify and speed up the process of dissolving foreclosed houses.

Labor market policy

In DSGE models, labor market is not usually modeled and unemployment is not contemplated (see Chapter 9). This prevents the study of problems related to involuntary unemployment, structural reforms, and human capital policies.

The K + S model is extended in Dosi et al. (2016c) to account for different microfounded labor-market regimes characterized by different levels of wage flexibility, labor mobility, and institutions (e.g., minimum wage, unemployment benefits). The model generates persistent involuntary unemployment and it accounts for several stylized facts of the labor market (e.g., wage, Beveridge and Okun curves, productivity, unemployment and vacancy rate volatility). Simulation results also show that more rigid labor markets and labor relations lead to higher productivity and GDP growth, as well as to lower inequality, unemployment, and output volatility. In line with the intuitions of Stiglitz (2011, 2015), the negative effects of wage flexibility on macroeconomic dynamics are found also in Napoletano et al. (2012) and Seppecher (2012), while Riccetti et al. (2013b) found that unemployment benefits stabilize output fluctuations.

In a series of papers, Dawid et al. (2014a, b) employed the Eurace@Unibi model to analyze the convergence of regions characterized by local labor markets where workers have heterogeneous skills. In particular, they studied the impact of policies aimed at improving workers skills' and firms' technological adoption on innovation, commuting flows, inequality dynamics, and economic convergence. Simulation results show that both policies are complementary and that human capital policies foster regional cohesion only if labor markets are separated (Dawid et al., 2014b). Moreover, the effects of policies depend on the flexibility of the labor markets (Dawid et al., 2014a).

Climate policy

General equilibrium models are not well suited to analyze the effects of climate policies as their strong (hyper-rational representative agent) and often *ad hoc* assumptions (Pindyck, 2013) conflict with the strong non-linearities, tipping points, and irreversible dynamics associated with climate change. On the contrary, ABMs can naturally account for out-of-equilibrium dynamics in a framework characterized by strong uncertainties. Not surprisingly, a new generation of ABMs studying the intricate links between economic growth and climate at regional, national, and global level has blossomed in the last years.

The interactions between complex economic dynamics and climate change are explored in the LAGOM model family (Mandel et al., 2010; Wolf et al., 2013b), where economic growth is endogenously generated by a spatially explicit production network. As in each region carbon emissions are a by-product of energy production, the model can be employed to assess the effect of different mitigation policies.

Gerst et al. (2013) expanded the K + S model (Dosi et al., 2010) to account for energy inputs as well as for a simplified energy system. They employed the model to compare a business-as-usual framework *vis-`a-vis* policy scenarios where a carbon tax is introduced and its revenues are employed to provide rebates to households, to support industrial R&D, or to invest in carbon-free R&D. The model is calibrated on US data and simulated to the end of the 21st century. They found that all the policy schemes reduce greenhouse gas emissions, but only the carbon-free R&D policy allows a swift transition away from "dirty"-energy technologies, and, in turn, to higher economic growth.

The latter policy scheme allows carbon emissions to be minimized also in the ABM developed by Rengs et al. (2015). However, the best performance in terms of unemployment is achieved when the government levies taxes on carbon emissions rather than on labor. Starting from an ABM of technology diffusion, Robalino and Lempert (2000) found that a combined strategy of carbon taxes and technology subsidies is the best policy to reduce greenhouse gas emissions.

Building on the K + S model, Isley et al. (2013) explored how firms can both innovate to reduce their carbon intensity and lobby the government to alter carbon taxes. Simulation results show that carbon-reducing technological opportunities have a strong impact on the decarbonization rate of the economy as well as on the carbon price lobby. Different types of green fiscal (carbon tax, tax relief, and breaks on investment in renewable energy) and targeted monetary policies (green bonds and quantitative easing) are simulated in the Eirin model (Monasterolo and Raberto, 2016), which combines system dynamics and agent-based features. They found that green policy measures permit improvement in economic performance, and reduction of financial instability *vis- `a-vis* a business-as-usual scenario.

Finally, Lamperti et al. (2016a) expanded the K + S model to provide a detailed representation of climate-economic non-linear feedbacks in order to test the short- and long-run effects of different ensembles of innovation, fiscal and monetary policies in scenarios where climate disasters can considerably harm the economic dynamics.

Concluding remarks

The Great Recession has prompted a debate about the state of macroeconomic theory. Certainly, we stand in the camp of those arguing that macroeconomics has entered in a Dark Age (Krugman, 2011). Indeed, as discussed in Chapter 9, DSGE models suffer from a series of dramatic problems and difficulties concerning their inner logic consistency, the way they are taken to the data, the extent to which they are able to replicate existing reality, and the realism of their assumptions. These problems are so deep that they prevent DSGE models even from conceiving the possibility of the current crisis and proposing viable solutions to policy makers. The acknowledgment of such limitations has stimulated new research, which has led to the introduction in DSGE models of financial frictions, a mild form of agent heterogeneity and bounded rationality, as well as fat-tailed exogenous shocks. We think that these new developments are welcome but they patch a cloth, which it is not possible to mend. Indeed, the intrinsic difficulties of DSGE models are so hard to solve within the straitjacket of the neoclassical paradigm (rationality, equilibrium, etc.) that a different research avenue, grounded on complexity science, is more fruitful.

This alternative paradigm does actually exist and it is called ACE. The section on ABMs and economic policy, above, has been devoted to a (necessarily) brief discussion of its philosophical underpinnings, building blocks, and policy applications. As our survey shows, the number of areas where ACE policy experiments have been already applied with success is rather vast and rapidly increasing, especially after the policy challenges posed by the Great Recession. To have a better feel of this, it suffices to compare the number and breadth of the ABM applications surveyed in Fagiolo and Roventini (2012) with those covered here.

The discussion of the section on ABMs and economic policy has also outlined the most prominent values added deriving from performing policy experiments within an ACE approach. These include behavioral assumptions grounded on empirical and experimental evidence; ACE's extreme modeling flexibility; the friendly relation of ABMs with empirical data; the ease of carrying out empirical-validation exercises; the almost infinite possibility of experimentation; and, last but not least, the positive impact that a more realistic and algorithmically structured model can have on political decision makers, as compared to obscure and un-intuitive mathematical neoclassical models.

Of course, as happens for the New Neoclassical Synthesis, many issues are still far from being settled and the debate is very open. Here, by way of conclusion, we recall some of them.

The first issue – which we can label as the problem of over-parametrization – has to do with the role played by micro and macro parameters in ABMs. As mentioned, ABMs are often over-parameterized, for one typically injects in the specification of agents' behavioral rules and interaction patterns many ingredients in order to meet as far as possible what he/she observes in reality. Suppose for simplicity that initial conditions do not matter. Even if empirical validation can provide a way to reduce free parameters, the researchers are almost always left with an ABM whose behavior depends on many free parameters. Many questions naturally arise. How can one interpret these different parameterizations? Which one should be used if one employs the model to deliver policy implications? Should one perfectly calibrate (if possible) the model using the data so that no free parameters are left? Should policy implications be robust to alternative parameterizations instead? Notice that this issue is closely related to a common critique that ABMs usually face: if an ABM contains many free parameters and it is able to reproduce a given set of stylized facts, how can one be sure that it represents the minimal mechanisms capable of reproducing the same set of stylized facts? This point reminds the "unconditional objects" critique in Brock (1999) and it is certainly true for "oversized" ABMs. Despite the fact that such an issue is still not completely settled, much progress has been made in recent years on this side, as our discussion on estimation and calibration of ABM parameters indicates.

The second issue concerns the role played by initial conditions. Recall that (if random ingredients are present in the model) any ABM can be considered as an artificial (stochastic) data generation process (mDGP) with which we try to approximate the one that generated the data that we observe (i.e., the rwDGP). The question is: is the rwDGP ergodic or not? If the underlying rwDGP is thought to be non-ergodic (as well as the theoretical mDGP described in the ABM), then initial conditions matter. This raises a whole host of problems for the modeler. The modeler needs to identify the "true" set of initial conditions in the empirical data, generated by the rwDGP, in order to correctly set the initial parameters of the model. Even if the "perfect database" exists, this is a very difficult task. How far in the past does one need to go in order to identify the correct set of initial values for the relevant micro and macro variables? There is a possibility of infinite regress. If this is the case, then one may need data stretching back a very long time, possibly before data started to be collected. Again, as compared to the situation discussed in Fagiolo and Roventini (2012), there has been some progress also in this respect, especially in the efforts devoted to identifying ergodicity tests for ABMs (see above).

This issue is closely related to a third one, regarding the relation between simulated and real-world data. While in principle we could generate as many theoretical observations as we like, in practice we may only have a few such empirical realizations (possibly only one!). If we believe that the empirical observations come from an underlying DGP that could have been "played twice" (i.e., could have generated alternative observations, other than the one we have), the problem of comparing simulated with empirical data becomes very complicated.

All the three issues above affect any stochastic, dynamic (economic) model, DSGE-based ones included. Indeed, they are the subject of never-ending debates among philosophers of science, since they raise fundamental questions related to probability, modeling, and inference (see, e.g., Fagiolo et al., 2007b). Nevertheless, the large majority of those advocating the New Neoclassical Synthesis approach seem not to care about them. In our view, the fact that they instead occupy center stage in the current ACE debate is another signal of the vitality of this young but promising paradigm.

The last issue worth mentioning is specific to ACE and it concerns the comparability of different ABMs. DSGE models are all built using a commonly shared set of behavioral rules (e.g., representative agents solving stochastic dynamic optimization problems) and their empirical performance is assessed with common techniques (i.e., vector autoregression models). This allows us to develop a common protocol about "how to do macroeconomics with DSGE models" and it eases the comparison of the results produced by competing models. Given the relatively infancy of the ACE paradigm, the lack of such a widespread agreement among the ACE community hinders the dialogue among different ABMs, reducing the comparability of their results, and possibly slowing down new developments. In that respect, the development of common documentation guidelines (Wolf et al., 2013a), dedicated languages and platforms[12] can surely improve the situation, increase the exchanges among ACE scholars, and reduce the entry cost to agent-based modeling.

Notes

1 Thanks to Mattia Guerini, Francesco Lamperti, Manuel Scholz-W¨ackerle, and Tania Treibich. All usual disclaimers apply. This paper has been supported by two European Union Horizon 2020 grants: no. 649186 – Project ISIGrowth and no. 640772 – Project Dolfins.
2 This subsection and the following ones draw heavily from Pyka and Fagiolo (2007) and Fagiolo et al. (2007b). For further details see, among others, Dosi and Egidi (1991), Lane (1993), Dosi et al. (2005), Colander (2006a), Tesfatsion (2006b), and Tesfatsion and Judd (2006).
3 This has to be contrasted with the neoclassical approach, where agents hold rational expectations and, as Mehrling (2006, p. 76) put it, "the future, or rather our ideas about the future, determines the present."
4 For a more in-depth discussion of empirical validation in ABMs, we refer the reader to Fagiolo et al. (2007a), Pyka and Werker (2009), and papers therein.
5 See the special issues edited by Fagiolo et al. (2007a) in *Computational Economics* and by Pyka and Werker (2009) in the *Journal of Artificial Societies and Social Simulations*, and the paper by Scott Moss (2008).
6 See, for example. the papers contained in the special issues on ABMs and economic policies edited by Dawid and Fagiolo (2008) and Gaffard and Napoletano (2012).
7 Moss (2002) discusses the importance of involving the actual decision makers in the process of the generation of ABMs for policy evaluation.
8 More generally, the model of Dosi et al. (2010) highlights a strong complementarity between Keynesian policies affecting demand and Schumpeterian policies affecting innovation.
9 The impact of inequality on macroeconomic performance is also explored in Ciarli et al. (2012), Isaac (2014), Cardaci and Saraceno (2015), and Russo and Gallegati (2016).
10 Alternative macroprudential and regulation policies are explored in van der Hoog (2015) employing the Eurace@Unibi model.
11 See Galbiati and Soramaki (2011) for an ABM studying the efficiency of the interbank payment system under alternative system configurations.
12 Among an increasing number of languages and platforms for ABM one can consider NetLogo (https://ccl.northwestern.edu/netlogo/), LSD (http://www.labsimdev.org/Joomla_1-3/), JAS-mine (http://www.jas-mine.net), and JMAB (https://github.com/S120/jmab/tree/master).

References

Akerlof, G. A. (2007), "The Missing Motivation in Macroeconomics", *American Economic Review*, 97: 5–36.

Albert, R. and A. L. Barabasi (2002), "Statistical Mechanics of Complex Networks", *Reviews of Modern Physics,* 4: 47–97.

Alfarano, S., T. Lux and F. Wagner (2005), "Estimation of Agent-Based Models: The Case of an Asymmetric Herding Model", *Computational Economics*, 26: 19–49.

Anufriev, M., T. Assenza, C. Hommes and D. Massaro (2013), "Interest Rate Rules and Macroeconomic Stability Under Heterogeneous Expectations", *Macroeconomic Dynamics*, 17: 1574–1604.

Aoki, M. (2006), "Not More So: Some Concepts Outside the DSGE Framework", in D. Colander (ed.), *Post Walrasian Macroeconomics*, Cambridge: Cambridge University Press.

Arifovic, J. and M. K. Maschek (2012), "Currency Crisis: Evolution of Beliefs and Policy Experiments", *Journal of Economic Behavior & Organization,* 82: 131–150.

Arifovic, J., H. Dawid, C. Deissenberg and O. Kostyshyna (2010), "Learning Benevolent Leadership in a Heterogenous Agents Economy", *Journal of Economic Dynamics & Control*, 34: 1768–1790.

Ashraf, Q., B. Gershman and P. Howitt (2011), "Banks, Market Organization, and Macroeconomic Performance: An Agent-Based Computational Analysis", Cambridge, MA: Working Paper 17102, NBER.

Aymanns, C. and D. J. Farmer (2015), "The Dynamics of the Leverage Cycle", *Journal of Economic Dynamics & Control*, 50: 155–179.

Barde, S. (2015), "A Practical, Universal, Information Criterion over Nth Order Markov Processes", Discussion Paper 15/04, Kent: University of Kent School of Economics.

Bargigli, L., L. Riccetti, A. Russo and M. Gallegati (2016), "Network Calibration and Metamodeling of a Financial Accelerator Agent Based Model", Working Papers: Economics 2016/01, Florence: Universita' degli Studi di Firenze, Dipartimento di Scienze per l'Economia e l'Impresa.

Bassi, F. and D. Lang (2016), "Investment Hysteresis and Potential Output: A Post-Keynesian–Kaleckian Agent-Based Approach", *Economic Modelling*, 52: 35–49.

Battiston, S., D. Delli Gatti, M. Gallegati, B. Greenwald and J. Stiglitz (2012), "Liaisons dangereuses: Increasing Connectivity, Risk Sharing, and Systemic Risk", *Journal of Economic Dynamics & Control*, 36: 1121–1141.

Battiston, S., D. J. Farmer, A. Flache, D. Garlaschelli, A. Haldane, H. Heesterbeeck, C. Hommes, C. Jaeger, R. May and M. Scheffer (2016), "Complexity Theory and Financial Regulation", *Science*, 351: 818–819.

Blanchard, O., M. G. Dell'Ariccia and M. P. Mauro (2013), "Rethinking Macro Policy II: Getting Granular Granular", Technical Report 13/03, Washington, DC: IMF Staff Discussion Paper.

Brock, W. A. (1999), "Scaling in Economics: A Reader's Guide", *Industrial and Corporate Change*, 8: 409–446.

Brock, W. A. and S. N. Durlauf (2001), "Interactions-Based Models", in J. Heckman and E. Leamer (eds), *Handbook of Econometrics,* Volume 5, Amsterdam: North Holland.

Brock, W. A. and C. Hommes (1997), "A Rational Route to Randomness", *Econometrica*, 65: 1059–1095.

Caballero, R. J. (2010), "Macroeconomics After the Crisis: Time to Deal with the Pretense-of-Knowledge Syndrome", *Journal of Economic Perspectives*, 24: 85–102.

Caiani, A., A. Godin, E. Caverzasi, M. Gallegati, S. Kinsella and J. Stiglitz (2015), "Agent Based-Stock Flow Consistent Macroeconomics: Towards a Benchmark Model", Research Paper 15–87, New York: Columbia Business School.

Cardaci, A. and F. Saraceno (2015), "Inequality, Financialisation and Economic Crises: an Agent-Based Macro Model", Working Paper 2015–27, Paris: OFCE.

Catullo, E., M. Gallegati and A. Palestrini (2015), "Towards a Credit Network Based early Warning Indicator for Crises", *Journal of Economic Dynamics & Control*, 50: 78–97.

Chiarella, C. and C. Di Guilmi (2012), "The Fiscal Cost of Financial Instability", *Studies in Nonlinear Dynamics & Econometrics*, 16: 1–27.

Ciarli, T., A. Lorentz, M. Savona and M. Valente (2012), "The Role of Technology, Organisation, and Demand in Growth and Income Distribution", Working Paper Series 2012/06, Laboratory of Economics and Management (LEM), Pisa, Italy: Scuola Superiore Sant'Anna.

Cincotti, S., M. Raberto and A. Teglio (2010), "Credit Money and Macroeconomic Instability in the Agent-based Model and Simulator Eurace", *Economics: The Open-Access, Open-Assessment E-Journal*, 4: 1–32.

Cincotti, S., M. Raberto and A. Teglio (2012a), "Macroprudential Policies in an Agent-Based Artificial Economy", *Revue de l'OFCE*, 124: 205–234.

Cincotti, S., A. Teglio and M. Raberto (2012b), "The Eurace Macroeconomic Model and Simulator", in *Agent-based Dynamics, Norms, and Corporate Governance. The Proceedings of the 16th World Congress of the International Economic Association*, New York: Palgrave.

Colander, D. (2005), "The Future of Economics: The Appropriately Educated in Pursuit of the Knowable", *Cambridge Journal of Economics*, 29: 927–941.

Colander, D. (2006a), "Introduction", in D. Colander (ed.), *Post Walrasian Macroeconomics*, Cambridge: Cambridge University Press.

Colander, D. (ed.) (2006b), *Post Walrasian Macroeconomics*, Cambridge: Cambridge University Press.

Colander, D., H. Folmer, A. Haas, M. D. Goldberg, K. Juselius, A. P. Kirman, T. Lux and B. Sloth (2009), "The Financial Crisis and the Systemic Failure of Academic Economics", Technical Report, 98th Dahlem Workshop, Cambridge, MA: MIT Press.

Da Silva, M. A. and G. Tadeu Lima (2015), "Combining Monetary Policy and Prudential Regulation: An Agent-Based Modeling Approach", Working Paper 394, Brasilia: Banco Central do Brasil.

Dawid, H. and G. Fagiolo (eds) (2008), Special Issue on "Agent-Based Models for Economic Policy Design", *Journal of Economic Behavior and Organization*, 67.

Dawid, H., S. Gemkow, P. Harting, S. van der Hoog and M. Neugart (2012), "The Eurace@ Unibi Model: An Agent-Based Macroeconomic Model for Economic Policy Analysis", Technical Report 05-2012, Bielefeld: Bielefeld Working Papers in Economics and Management.

Dawid, H., P. Harting and M. Neugart (2014a), "Cohesion Policy and Inequality Dynamics: Insights from a Heterogeneous Agents Macroeconomic Model", Working Paper Series 34, SFB 882.

Dawid, H., P. Harting and M. Neugart (2014b), "Economic Convergence: Policy Implications from a Heterogeneous Agent Model", *Journal of Economic Dynamics & Control*, 44: 54–80.

Deichsel, S. and A. Pyka (2009), "A Pragmatic Reading of Friedman's Methodological Essay and What it Tells Us for the Discussion on ABMs", *Journal of Artificial Societies and Social Simulation (JASSS)*, 12: 6.

Delli Gatti, D. and S. Desiderio (2015), "Monetary Policy Experiments in an Agent-Based Model with Financial Frictions", *Journal of Economic Interaction and Coordination*, 10: 265–286.

Delli Gatti, D., C. Di Guilmi, E. Gaffeo, G. Giulioni, M. Gallegati and A. Palestrini (2005a), "A New Approach to Business Fluctuations: Heterogeneous Interacting Agents, Scaling Laws and Financial Fragility", *Journal of Economic Behavior & Organization*, 56: 489–512.

Delli Gatti, D., E. Gaffeo, M. Gallegati and A. Palestrini (2005b), "The Apprentice Wizard: Monetary Policy, Complexity and Learning", *New Mathematics and Natural Computation*, 1: 109–128.

Delli Gatti, D., M. Gallegati, B. Greenwald, A. Russo and J. Stiglitz (2010), "The Financial Accelerator in an Evolving Credit Network", *Journal of Economic Dynamics & Control*, 34: 1627–1650.

DeLong, J. B. (2011, May), "Economics in Crisis", *The Economists' Voice*.

Dosi, G. (2012), *Economic Organization, Industrial Dynamics and Development, Chapter Introduction*, Cheltenham: Edward Elgar.

Dosi, G. and M. Egidi (1991), "Substantive and Procedural Uncertainty: An Exploration of Economic Behaviours in Changing Environments", *Journal of Evolutionary Economics*, 1: 145–168.

Dosi, G. and R. R. Nelson (1994), "An Introduction to Evolutionary Theories in Economics", *Journal of Evolutionary Economics*, 4: 153–172.

Dosi, G., L. Marengo and G. Fagiolo (2005), "Learning in Evolutionary Environment", in K. Dopfer (ed.), *Evolutionary Principles of Economics*, Cambridge: Cambridge University Press.

Dosi, G., G. Fagiolo and A. Roventini (2010), "Schumpeter Meeting Keynes: A Policy-Friendly Model of Endogenous Growth and Business Cycles", *Journal of Economic Dynamics & Control*, 34: 1748–1767.

Dosi, G., G. Fagiolo, M. Napoletano and A. Roventini (2013), "Income Distribution, Credit and Fiscal Policies in an Agent-Based Keynesian Model", *Journal of Economic Dynamics & Control*, 37: 1598–1625.

Dosi, G., M. Napoletano, A. Roventini and T. Treibich (2014), "Micro and Macro Policies in Keynes+Schumpeter Evolutionary Models", Working Paper Series 2014/21, Laboratory of Economics and Management (LEM), Pisa, Italy: Scuola Superiore Sant'Anna.

Dosi, G., G. Fagiolo, M. Napoletano, A. Roventini and T. Treibich (2015), "Fiscal and Monetary Policies in Complex Evolving Economies", *Journal of Economic Dynamics & Control*, 52: 166–189.

Dosi, G., M. Napoletano, A. Roventini, J. Stiglitz and T. Treibich (2016a), "Expectation Formation, Fiscal Policies and Macroeconomic Performance when Agents are Heterogeneous and the World is Changing", Working Paper Series, Pisa, Italy: Laboratory of Economics and Management (LEM), Scuola Superiore Sant'Anna.

Dosi, G., M. Napoletano, A. Roventini and T. Treibich (2016b), "The Short- and Long-Run Damages of Fiscal Austerity: Keynes beyond Schumpeter", in J. Stiglitz and M. Guzman (eds), *Contemporary Issues in Macroeconomics*, London: Palgrave Macmillan.

Dosi, G., M. Pereira, A. Roventini and M. E. Virgilito (2016c), "When More Flexibility Yields More Fragility: The Microfoundations of Keynesian Aggregate Unemployment", Working Paper Series 2016/06, Pisa, Italy: Laboratory of Economics and Management (LEM), Scuola Superiore Sant'Anna.

Dosi, G., M. Pereira and M. E. Virgillito (2016d), "On the Robustness of the Fat-Tailed Distribution of Firm Growth Rates: A Global Sensitivity Analysis", Working Paper Series 2016/12, Pisa, Italy: Laboratory of Economics and Management (LEM), Scuola Superiore Sant'Anna.

Fabretti, A. (2012), "On the Problem of Calibrating an Agent Based Model for Financial Markets", *Journal of Economic Interaction and Coordination*, 8: 277–293.

Fagiolo, G. and A. Roventini (2012), "Macroeconomic Policy in DSGE and Agent-based Models", *Revue de l'OFCE*, 124: 67–116.

Fagiolo, G., C. Birchenhall and P. Windrum (eds) (2007a), Special Issue on "Empirical Validation in Agent-Based Models", *Computational Economics*, 30.

Fagiolo, G., A. Moneta and P. Windrum (2007b), "A Critical Guide to Empirical Validation of Agent-Based Models in Economics: Methodologies, Procedures, and Open Problems", *Computational Economics*, 30: 195–226.

Farmer, D. J. and D. Foley (2009), "The Economy Needs Agent-Based Modeling", *Nature*, 460: 685–686.

Gabbi, G., G. Iori, S. Jafarey and J. Porter (2015), "Financial Regulations and Bank Credit to the Real Economy", *Journal of Economic Dynamics & Control*, 50: 117–143.

Gaffard, J.-L. and M. Napoletano (eds) (2012), *Agent-Based Models and Economic Policy*, Volume 124, Paris: Revue de l'OFCE.

Gaffeo, E. and M. Molinari (2016), "Macroprudential Consolidation Policy in Interbank Networks", *Journal of Evolutionary Economics*, 26: 77–99.

Gai, P., A. Haldane and S. Kapadia (2011), "Complexity, Concentration and Contagion", *Journal of Monetary Economics*, 58: 453–470.

Galbiati, M. and K. Soramaki (2011), "An Agent-Based Model of Payment Systems", *Journal of Economic Dynamics & Control*, 35: 859–875.

Gangel, M., M. J. Seiler and A. Collins (2013), "Exploring the Foreclosure Contagion Effect Using Agent-Based Modeling", *Journal Real Estate Finance and Economics*, 46: 339–354.

Geanakoplos, J., R. Axtell, D. J. Farmer, P. Howitt, B. Conlee, J. Goldstein, M. Hendrey, M. Palmer and C.- Y. Yang (2012), "Getting at Systemic Risk Via an Agent-Based Model of the Housing Market", *American Economic Review*, 102: 53–58.

Gerst, M. D., P. Wang, A. Roventini, G. Fagiolo, G. Dosi, R. B. Howard and M. E. Borsuk (2013), "Agent-Based Modeling of Climate Policy: An Introduction to the ENGAGE Multi-level Model Framework", *Environmental Modelling & Software*, 44: 62–75.

Gigerenzer, G. (2007), *Gut Feelings. The Intelligence of the Unconscious*, New York: Viking.

Gigerenzer, G. and H. Brighton (2009), "Homo Heuristicus: Why Biased Minds Make Better Inferences", *Topics in Cognitive Science*, 1: 107–143.

Gilli, M. and P. Winker (2003), "A Global Optimization Heuristic for Estimating Agent Based Models", *Computational Statistics & Data Analysis*, 42: 299–312.

Grazzini, J. (2012), "Analysis of the Emergent Properties: Stationarity and Ergodicity", *Journal of Artificial Societies and Social Simulation*, 15.

Grazzini, J. and M. Richiardi (2015), "Estimation of Ergodic Agent-Based Models by Simulated Minimum Distance", *Journal of Economic Dynamics & Control*, 51: 148–165.

Grazzini, J., M. Richiardi and L. Sellad (2013), "Indirect Estimation of Agent-Based Models. An Application to a Simple Diffusion Model", *Complexity Economics*, 2: 25–40.

Grazzini, J., M. Richiardi and M. Tsionas (2015), "Bayesian Estimation of Agent-Based Models", Working Paper Series 145, Turin: LABORatorio R. Revelli, Centre for Employment Studies.

Grilli, R., G. Tedeschi and M. Gallegati (2014), "Bank Interlinkages and Macroeconomic Stability", *International Review of Economics and Finance*, 34: 72–88.

Gualdi, S., M. Tarzia, F. Zamponi and J. Bouchaud (2015), "Tipping Points in Macroeconomic Agent-Based Models", *Journal of Economic Dynamics & Control*, 50: 29–61.

Guerini, M. and A. Moneta (2016), "A Method for Agent-Based Models Validation", Working Paper Series 2016/16, Pisa, Italy: Laboratory of Economics and Management (LEM), Scuola Superiore Sant'Anna.

Haber, G. (2008), "Monetary and Fiscal Policies Analysis with an Agent-Based Macroeconomic Model", *Journal of Economics and Statistics*, 228: 276–295.

Harting, P. (2015), "Stabilization Policies and Long Term Growth: Policy Implications from an Agent-Based Macroeconomic Model", Technical Report 06-2015, Bielefeld: Bielefeld Working Papers in Economics and Management.

Isaac, A. G. (2014), "The Intergenerational Propagation of Wealth Inequality", *Metroeconomica*, 65: 571–584.

Isley, S., R. Lempert, S. Popper and R. Vardavas (2013), "An Evolutionary Model of Industry Transformation and the Political Sustainability of Emission Control Policies", Technical Report, Santa Monica, CA: RAND Corporation.

Kahneman, D. and A. Tversky (eds) (2000), *Choices, Values, and Frames*. Cambridge, MA: Cambridge University Press.

Kay, J. (2011), "The Map is Not the Territory: An Essay on the State of Economics", Technical Report, New York: Institute for New Economic Thinking.

Kirman, A. P. (2010), "The Economic Crisis is a Crisis for Economic Theory", *CESifo Economic Studies*, 56: 498–535.

Kirman, A. P. (2016), "Ants and Nonoptimal Self-Organization: Lessons for Macroeconomics", *Macroeconomic Dynamics*, doi:10.1017/S1365100514000339.

Klimek, P., S. Poledna, D. J. Farmer and S. Thurner (2015), "To Bail-Out or to Bail-In? Answers from an Agent-Based Model", *Journal of Economic Dynamics & Control*, 50: 144–154.

Knight, F. (1921), *Risk, Uncertainty, and Profits*, Chicago: Chicago University Press.

Krause, A. and S. Giansante (2012), "Interbank Lending and the Spread of Bank Failures: A Network Model of Systemic Risk", *Journal of Economic Behavior & Organization*, 83: 583–608.

Krug, S. (2015), "The Interaction Between Monetary and Macroprudential Policy: Should Central Banks "Lean Against the Wind" to Foster Macro-Financial Stability?", Economics Working Paper 2015–08, Kiel: Christian-Albrechts-University of Kiel.

Krug, S., M. Lengnick and H.-W. Wohltman (2015), "The Impact of Basel III on Financial (In)stability: An Agent-Based Credit Network Approach", *Quantitative Finance*, 15: 1917–1932.

Krugman, P. (2009), "How did Economics Get it So Wrong?", *New York Times Magazine*, 36–44.

Krugman, P. (2011), "The Profession and the Crisis", *Eastern Economic Journal*, 37: 307–312.

Lamperti, F. (2015), "An Information Theoretic Criterion for Empirical Validation of Time Series Models", Lem papers series, Pisa, Italy: Laboratory of Economics and Management (LEM), Scuola Superiore Sant'Anna.

Lamperti, F. (2016), "Empirical Validation of Simulated Models through the GSL-div: an Illustrative Application", LEM Papers Series 2016/18, Pisa, Italy: Laboratory of Economics and Management (LEM), Scuola Superiore Sant'Anna.

Lamperti, F., G. Dosi, M. Napoletano, A. Roventini and S. Sapio (2016a), "Faraway, so Close: An Agent-Based Model for Climate, Energy and Macroeconomic Policies", Working paper series, Pisa, Italy: Laboratory of Economics and Management (LEM), Scuola Superiore Sant'Anna.

Lamperti, F., A. Sani, A. Mandel and A. Roventini (2016b), "Agent Based Model Exploration and Calibration Using Machine Learning Surrogates", Working Paper Series, Pisa, Italy: Laboratory of Economics and Management (LEM), Scuola Superiore Sant'Anna.

Lane, D. A. (1993), "Artificial Worlds and Economics, Part I and II", *Journal of Evolutionary Economics*, 3: 89–107 and 177–197.

Lengnick, M., S. Krug and H.-W. Wohltman (2013), "Money Creation and Financial Instability: An Agent-Based Credit Network Approach", *Economics: The Open-Access, Open-Assessment E-Journal*, 7: 2013–2032.

Mandel, A., C. Jaeger, S. Fuerst, W. Lass, D. Lincke, F. Meissner, F. Pablo-Marti and S. Wolf (2010), "Agent-Based Dynamics in Disaggregated Growth Models", Working Paper 2010.77, Paris: CES.

Mehrling, P. (2006), "The Problem of Time in the DSGE Model and the Post Walrasian Alternative", in D. Colander, (ed), *Post Walrasian Macroeconomics*, Cambridge: Cambridge University Press.

Monasterolo, I. and M. Raberto (2016), "A Hybrid System Dynamics – Agent Based Model to Assess the Role of Green Fiscal and Monetary Policies", Technical Report, SSRN. Available online at: http://papers.ssrn.com/sol3/papers.cfm?abstract_id=2748266 (accessed October 4, 2016).

Moss, S. (2002), "Policy Analysis from First Principles", *Proceedings of the US National Academy of Sciences*, 99: 7267–7274.

Moss, S. (2008), "Alternative Approaches to the Empirical Validation of Agent-Based Models", *Journal of Artificial Societies and Social Simulation*, 11 (http://jasss.soc.surrey.ac.uk/11/1/5.html).

Napoletano, M., G. Dosi, G. Fagiolo and A. Roventini (2012), "Wage Formation, Investment Behavior and Growth Regimes: An Agent-Based Analysis", *Revue de l'OFCE*, 124: 235–261.

Napoletano, M., J.-L. Gaffard and A. Roventini (2015), "Time-Varying Fiscal Multipliers in an Agent-Based Model with Credit Rationing", Working Paper Series 2015/19, Pisa, Italy: Laboratory of Economics and Management (LEM), Scuola Superiore Sant'Anna.

Nelson, R. R. and S. G. Winter (1982), *An Evolutionary Theory of Economic Change*, Cambridge: The Belknap Press of Harvard University Press.

Pindyck, R. (2013), "Climate Change Policy: What Do the Models Tell Us?", *Journal of Economic Literature*, 51: 860–872.

Poledna, S., S. Thurner, D. J. Farmer and J. Geanakoplos (2014), "Leverage-Induced Systemic Risk under Basle II and other Credit Risk Policies", *Journal of Banking & Finance*, 42: 199–2012.

Popoyan, L., M. Napoletano and A. Roventini (2015), "Taming Macroeconomic Instability: Monetary and Macro Prudential Policy Interactions in an Agent-Based Model", Working Paper Series 2015/33, Pisa, Italy: Laboratory of Economics and Management (LEM), Scuola Superiore Sant'Anna.

Pyka, A. and G. Fagiolo (2007), "Agent-Based Modelling: A Methodology for Neo-Schumpeterian Economics", in H. Hanusch and A. Pyka (eds), *The Elgar Companion to Neo-Schumpeterian Economics*, Cheltenham: Edward Elgar Publishers.

Pyka, A. and C. Werker (2009), "The Methodology of Simulation Models: Chances and Risks", *Journal of Artificial Societies and Social Simulation (JASSS)*, 12: 1.

Raberto, M., A. Teglio and S. Cincotti (2008), "Integrating Real and Financial Markets in an Agent-Based Economic Model: An Application to Monetary Policy Design", *Computational Economics*, 32: 147–162. doi: 10.1007/s10614-008-9138-2.

Raberto, M., A. Teglio and S. Cincotti (2012), "Debt Deleveraging and Business Cycles. An Agent-Based Perspective", *Economics: The Open-Access, Open-Assessment E-Journal*, 6 (http://www.economics-ejournal.org/economics/discussionpapers/2011-31).

Recchioni, M. C., G. Tedeschi and M. Gallegati (2015), "A Calibration Procedure for Analyzing Stock Price Dynamics in an Agent-Based Framework", *Journal of Economic Dynamics & Control*, 60: 1–25.

Rengs, B. and M. Wackerle, "A Computational Agent-Based Simulation of an Artificial Monetary Union for Dynamic Comparative Institutional Analysis", in *Proceedings of the 2014 IEEE Conference on Computational Intelligence for Financial Engineering & Economics*, pp.427–434.

Rengs, B., M. Wackerle, A. Gazheli, M. Antal and J. van den Bergh (2015), "Testing Innovation, Employment and Distributional Impacts of Climate Policy Packages in a Macro-Evolutionary systems Setting", Vienna: Working Paper 83, WWWforEurope.

Riccetti, L., A. Russo and M. Gallegati (2013a), "Leveraged Network-Based Financial Accelerator", *Journal of Economic Dynamics & Control*, 37: 1626–1640.

Riccetti, L., A. Russo and M. Gallegati (2013b), "Unemployment Benefits and Financial Leverage in an Agent Based Macroeconomic Model", *Economics: The Open-Access, Open-Assessment E-Journal*, 7: 2013–2042.

Riccetti, L., A. Russo and M. Gallegati (2014), "An Agent Based Decentralized Matching Macroeconomic Model", *Journal of Economic Interaction and Coordination*, 10: 305–332.

Richiardi, M., R. Leombruni, N. J. Saam and M. Sonnessa (2006), "A Common Protocol for Agent-Based Social Simulation", *Journal of Artificial Societies and Social Simulation*, 9 (http://jasss.soc.surrey.ac.uk/9/1/15.html).

Robalino, D. and R. Lempert (2000), "Carrots and Sticks for New Technology: Abating Greenhouse Gas Emissions in a Heterogeneous and Uncertain World", *Integrated Assessment*, 1: 1–19.

Rosser, B. J. (2011), *Complex Evolutionary Dynamics in Urban-Regional and Ecologic-Economic Systems: From Catastrophe to Chaos and Beyond*. New York: Springer.

Russo, A., M. Catalano, M. Gallegati, E. Gaffeo and M. Napoletano (2007), "Industrial Dynamics, Fiscal Policy and R&D: Evidence from a Computational Experiment", *Journal of Economic Behavior & Organization*, 64: 426–447.

Russo, R. L., A. Gallegati and M. Gallegati (2016), "Increasing Inequality, Consumer Credit and Financial Fragility in an Agent Based Macroeconomic Model", *Journal of Evolutionary Economics*, 26: 25–47.

Salle, I. (2015), "Modeling Expectations in Agent-Based Models: An Application to Central Bank's Communication and Monetary Policy", *Economic Modelling*, 46: 130–141.

Salle, I. and M. Yıldızo˘glu (2014), "Efficient Sampling and Meta-Modeling for Computational Economic Models", *Computational Economics*, 44: 507–536.

Salle, I., M. Yıldızo˘glu and M.-A. Senegas (2013), "Inflation Targeting in a Learning Economy: An ABM Perspective", *Economic Modelling*, 34: 114–128.

Schlefer, J. (2012), *The Assumptions Economists Make*. Harvard: Harvard University Press.

Seppecher, P. (2012), "Flexibility of Wages and Macroeconomic Instability in an Agent-Based Computational Model with Endogenous Money", *Macroeconomic Dynamics*, 16: 284–297.

Seppecher, P. and I. Salle (2015), "Deleveraging Crises and Deep Recessions: A Behavioural Approach", *Applied Economics*, 47: 3771–3790.

Setterfield, M. (2016), "Won't Get Fooled Again: Or Will We? Monetary Policy, Model Uncertainty, and 'Policy Model Complacency'", Working Papers 1516, New York: New School for Social Research, Department of Economics.

Sinitskaya, E. and L. Tesfatsion (2015), "Macroeconomies as Constructively Rational Games", *Journal of Economic Dynamics & Control*, 61: 152–182.

Stiglitz, J. (2011), "Rethinking Macroeconomics: What Failed, and How to Repair It", *Journal of the European Economic Association*, 9: 591–645.

Stiglitz, J. (2015), "Towards a General Theory of Deep Downturns", Working Paper 21444, Cambridge, MA: NBER.

Teglio, A., A. Mazzocchetti, L. Ponta, M. Raberto and S. Cincotti (2015), "Budgetary Rigour with Stimulus in Lean Times: Policy Advices from an Agent-Based Model", Working Papers 2015/07, Castellón, Spain: Economics Department, Universitat Jaume I.

Tesfatsion, L. (2006a), "ACE: A Constructive Approach to Economic Theory", in L. Tesfatsion and K. Judd (eds), *Handbook of Computational Economics II: Agent-Based Computational Economics*, Amsterdam: North Holland.

Tesfatsion, L. (2006b), "Agent-Based Computational Modeling and Macroeconomics", in D. Colander (ed.), *Post Walrasian Macroeconomics*, Cambridge: Cambridge University Press.

Tesfatsion, L. and K. Judd (eds) (2006), *Handbook of Computational Economics II: Agent-Based Computational Economics*, Amsterdam: North Holland.

van der Hoog, S. (2015), "The Limits to Credit Growth: Mitigation Policies and Macroprudential Regulations to Foster Macrofinancial Stability and Sustainable Debt", Working Papers in Economics and Management 08-15, Bielefeld: University of Bielefeld.

van der Hoog, S. and H. Dawid (2015), "Bubbles, Crashes and the Financial Cycle: Insights from a Stock-Flow Consistent Agent-Based Macroeconomic Model", Working Papers in Economics and Management 01-2015, Bielefeld: University of Bielefeld.

Winker, P., M. Gilli and V. Jeleskovic (2007), "An Objective Function for Simulation Based Inference on Exchange Rate Data", *Journal of Economic Interaction and Coordination*, 2: 125–145.

Wolf, S., J.-P. Bouchaud, F. Cecconi, S. Cincotti, H. Dawid, H. Gintis, S. van der Hoog, C. C. Jaeger, D. V. Kovalevsky, A. Mandel and L. Paroussos (2013a), "Describing Economic Agent-Based Models. Dahlem ABM Documentation Guidelines", *Complexity Economics*, 2: 63–74.

Wolf, S., S. Furst, A. Mandel, W. Lass, D. Lincke, F. Pablo-Marti and C. Jaeger (2013b), "A Multi-Agent Model of Several Economic Regions", *Environmental Modelling & Software*, 44: 25–43.

Wren-Lewis, S. (2016, January), "Unravelling the New Classical Counter Revolution", *Review of Keynesian Economics*, 4: 20–35.

11 Credit-driven business cycles in an agent-based macro model

Marco Raberto, Reynold Christian Nathanael, Bulent Ozel, Andrea Teglio, and Silvano Cincotti

Introduction

This chapter addresses the crucial issue of the interplay between credit and business cycles in an economy by means of an enriched version of the agent-based model and simulator Eurace. Eurace is a fully specified agent-based economic model, which includes different types of agents and integrates different types of markets (Cincotti et al., 2010, 2012; Raberto et al., 2012; Teglio et al., 2012, 2015). Agents include households, which act as consumers, workers, and financial investors; consumption goods producers as well as a capital goods producers; banks; a government; and a central bank. Agents interact in different types of market, namely, markets for consumption goods and capital goods; a labor markets; a credit market and a financial market for stocks and government bonds. Except for the financial market, all markets are characterized by decentralized exchange with price-setting behavior on the supply side. Agents' decision processes are characterized by bounded rationality and limited information gathering and computational capabilities (Tesfatsion, 2003; Tesfatsion and Judd, 2006); thus, agents' behavior follows adaptive rules derived from the management literature about firms and banks, and from experimental and behavioral economics of consumers and financial investors. Furthermore, the Eurace model presented in this chapter has been enriched by a housing market where households are allowed to buy and sell homogeneous housing units as well as borrow mortgages from the banking system.

The Eurace model is particularly suited to investigate the interplay between credit and business cycles as it fully addresses the endogenous nature of credit in modern economies (McLeay et al., 2014; Werner, 2014). The dynamics of credit in the model depends on the supply side, ON the banking system, which is constrained by Basel capital adequacy regulatory provisions (Blum and Hellwig, 1995; Santos, 2001), whereas, on the demand side, credit depends on firms' liquidity needs to finance production activity and, in the enriched version of the model presented here, also on households' mortgage demand for house purchases.

Previous results pointed out a dependence of real economic variables, such as gross domestic product (GDP), unemployment rate, and aggregate capital stock, on the amount of credit in the economy that was exogenously controlled by the value of banks' capital adequacy ratios (Raberto et al., 2012; Teglio et al., 2012).

This dependence varied significantly according to the chosen evaluation horizon. In general, regulations allowing for a high leverage of the banking system, i.e., banks' low capital ratios, tended to boost the economy in the short run, while resulting in chains of bankruptcies and economic depression in the medium and long run. On the contrary, a tighter regulatory framework of capital ratios was shown to provide a slower growth rate in the short run but a higher and less volatile medium- and long-term growth. In this study, we further investigate the role of credit in the economy by considering the additional source of endogenous credit-money creation given by households' mortgage demand for house purchase. To this purpose, considering also their recognized relevance for the economy (Muellbauer and Murphy, 2008), we have designed a housing market and a mortgaging mechanism in the Eurace agent-based macroeconomic model.

Despite its acknowledged importance for financial stability, the literature provides only a few agent-based models of the housing market. Furthermore, in most of these models, the main focus is the market mechanism and price formation, while the housing market is standalone and does not interact with the rest of the economy. In particular, the model by Gilbert et al. (2009) consists only of sellers, buyers, and real-estate agents, while households' income as well as other variables are provided exogenously. The study by Ge (2014) shows that a loose debt-to-income constraint for households leads to a high volatility of housing prices; however shocks to the model are again exogenously given. The model by Axtell et al. (2014) is specifically tailored for the housing market in the city of Washington, DC. The model has a micro-level focus on households' real-estate purchasing behaviors and is able to generate a housing bubble of approximately the same size as occurred earlier in Washington. Finally, Erlingsson et al. (2014) developed a housing market model integrated within a real economy and pointed out the relevance for both housing bubble formation and economic stability of the maximum amount of debt service-to-income ratio allowed to households.

The remainder or the paper is organized as follows. The next section gives an overview of the Eurace housing market model, followed by a presentation and analysis of the computational experiment results, and lastly we outline the conclusions and the future directions of research.

The Eurace model

In this study, we have enriched the original Eurace model by introducing homogeneous housing assets, mortgage lending, and a housing market into the artificial economy. The new modeling features introduced in this study are described in the following section.

The original Eurace model has been extensively described in the Appendix of Teglio et al. (2015). It is worth remembering here that every agent in Eurace is described by a double-entry balance sheet that reports agents' assets and liabilities. Table 11.1 presents the balance sheet entries of the different agent types populating the model, including the new entries introduced in this study, i.e., housing units and mortgages. Balance sheet entries can be regarded as the state variables of any agent and the state of the Eurace economy can be described as the whole set of the balance sheet variables of any agent along with the prices formed in the different markets. The dynamics of balance sheet variables is determined by agents' plan and the resulting interaction among different agents in the relevant markets (see Teglio et al., 2015, for further details). The balance sheet approach to agents' modeling allows us to check the consistency at any time step between stocks and flows in the model, both at the level of the single agent and at the aggregate one. We believe that this is a critical feature in particular in a model where the creation/destruction of the endogenous money stock plays a crucial role in determining economic activity.

A simulation time step can be considered as a business day and is characterized by financial market operations, i.e., the trading of stock shares and government bonds; however, agents' economic planning and actions occur with a periodicity set at multiples of the elementary time step, i.e., 5 business days (say a week), 20 business days (say a month), or even 240 steps (say a year). For instance, the housing market is active once a month, households set their consumption budget on a monthly basis but make purchases with a weekly periodicity, firms' decision about production, hiring, pricing, investments, and financing are made on a monthly basis but are asynchronous, i.e., each firm is characterized by a particular day of the month when it is supposed to take its decisions. Finally, at the beginning of every month, the Central Bank sets the policy rate whereas government issues an amount of government bonds to cover its liquidity needs; tax rates instead are adjusted on a yearly basis according to the predefined fiscal policy.

Table 11.1 Balance sheets of agents populating the Eurace economy

Agent	*Assets*	*Liabilities*
Household	Liquidity Stock shares portfolio Government bonds Housing units	Mortgages Equity
Consumption goods producers	Liquidity Capital goods Inventories	Debt Equity
Capital goods producers	Liquidity	Equity
Bank	Liquidity Loans Mortgages	Deposits Standing facility with the Central Bank Equity
Government	Liquidity	Outstanding government bonds
Central Bank	Liquidity Loans to banks Goverment bonds	Outstanding fiat money Deposits Equity

The Eurace housing market

This extended version of the Eurace model integrates a housing market into the Eurace artificial economy and enables us to explore the role of housing market and mortgage lending within the economy and their impact on business cycles. Households and banks are the players in the housing market; households are endowed with homogeneous housing units that they can trade among themselves; banks grant mortgages to households on request to allow the purchasing of housing units.

The main features characterizing the housing market that have been introduced in this study concern: (i) households' seller and buyer behaviors in the housing market; (ii) house-pricing mechanism; (iii) mortgage requests and banks' mortgage lending behavior; and (iv) households' mortgage fire sale and default conditions. Figure 11.1 presents a scheme of Eurace components, including the new one related to the housing market.

Households' decision making in the housing market is mainly subject to random behavior, as we wanted to focus our attention more on the credit aspects of the housing market, and their impact on the economy as a whole, than on the behavioral ones. In particular, the parameter Φ sets the probability for each household to be active in the housing market on the first day of each month. Furthermore, any household, if randomly selected to be active, can assume the role of buyer or seller with equal likelihood. However, we also consider the case where a household is financially distressed, i.e., facing mortgage payments (interests + principal) higher than a given fraction θ_{fs} of income[1] (labor + capital), where both mortgage payments and income refer to the last quarter. In this case, say fire sale case, we stipulate that the household enters the housing market to

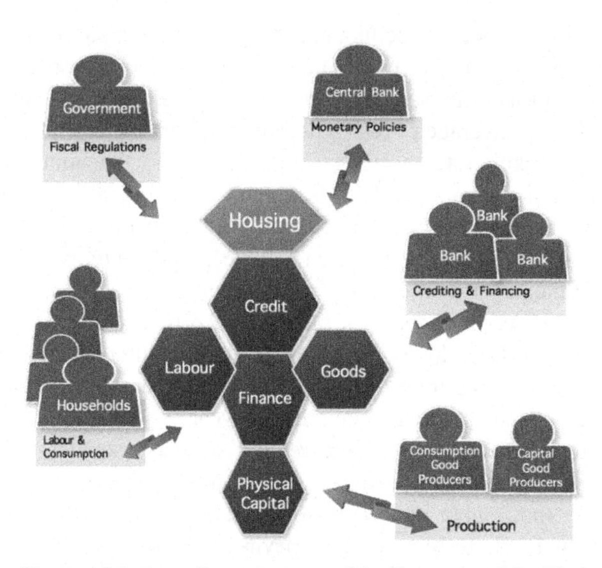

Figure 11.1 Overall components of the Eurace model with the housing market.

sell one housing unit at a discounted price with respect to the last average market price, in order to increase the likelihood of a transaction and then reduce the mortgage burden as well as the debt service.

The housing market is a posted-price market, where prices are set by suppliers and exchange is decentralized. Households can sell or buy one housing unit at a time. If a household is randomly selected to enter the housing market with a seller role, then that household posts one housing unit for sale at a price higher than the previous average market price by a percentage value which is a random draw uniformly distributed between 0 and φ_{up}. The rationale behind this modeling feature is that households which are randomly selected for the seller role do not have any particular necessity to liquidate their housing units and therefore are willing to sell only if they can realize a small random gain with respect to the latest average housing market price. Conversely, as anticipated in the previous paragraph, if a household enters the market with a seller role because financially distressed (fire sale case), then in order to facilitate liquidation, we assume this household posts one housing unit for sale at a price lower than the previous average market price by a percentage value which is a random draw uniformly distributed between 0 and φ_{down}.

Households that have been randomly selected as buyers are randomly queued and in turn purchase the cheapest available housing unit. A transaction takes place at the posted sale price if the household is able to get a mortgage from a bank to cover the entire value of the house. For the sake of simplicity, we assume that all granted mortgages are characterized by a loan-to-value ratio equal to 1; therefore households do not use their liquidity when buying a housing unit but just money borrowed from a bank. This modeling feature has been chosen in order to avoid direct and simultaneous interactions of the housing market purchasing behavior with saving and investing decisions in the financial market.

When a transaction takes place, the selling agent repays to the bank the mortgage associated with the sold housing unit. The housing market session closes when all buyers had their turn or there are no more houses for sale. A new housing price is then computed as the average of realized transaction prices.

Banks can provide variable-rate mortgages to households; the annualized mortgage rate is determined on a monthly basis as a mark-up on the rate set by the Central Bank. Households are due to reimburse the mortgage over a period of 30 years through monthly mortgage payments which include both the interest and the principal instalment. Principal instalments for each mortgage are constant over the repayment period and are computed as a ratio between the initial mortgage amount and 360, i.e., the mortgage duration in months. Monthly interest payments are determined by the outstanding mortgage principal and the annualized mortgage rate divided by 12, i.e., the number of months in a year.

Banks, whenever they receive a mortgage request by a household, assess the household capability to afford mortgage repayments by comparing the household's net income (both labor and capital) earned in the last quarter with the household's expected[2] quarterly mortgage payments, including both old outstanding mortgages and the new requested mortgage. Banks grant the requested mortgage only if the ratio between expected quarterly mortgage payments of the household and latest net quarterly income is lower than or equal to a pre-determined threshold, which is called debt service-to-income ratio.

Computational results

A number of preliminary simulations have been performed with the Eurace artificial economy populated by 3,000 households, 50 consumption goods producers, one capital good producer, one government, three banks, and one Central Bank. The economy has been simulated for 30 years and 20 different seeds of the pseudo-random number generator have been considered. Due to the necessity for high computational power, the experiments are performed on a 64-node Linux cluster. The values of the main parameters related to the housing market are reported in Table 11.2. Concerning the values of the parameters used in the whole model, we refer to the same value used and reported in Teglio et al. (2015).

We show in this section some preliminary results which give insight into the role of mortgage loans in the Eurace artificial economy. In order to consolidate our findings, further and deeper investigation is needed.

Empirical evidence points out that growth in loans to non-financial corporations tends to lag behind real GDP fluctuations, while loans to households tend to lead GDP growth (ECB Bulletin, 2013). Occasionally they are observed to follow a coincident pattern relative to GDP growth. We observed similar patterns in our experiments. Figure 11.2 displays a sample growth pattern over time. GDP vs. loan growth rates are shown in the upper panel and GDP vs. mortgage growth rates are plotted on the lower panel. The time series plots suggest that growth in mortgages in the economy leads to a growth in GDP which is followed by a growth in loans to firms.

Table 11.2 Values and description of parameters used in the housing market model

Symbol/acronym	*Description*	*Value*
Φ	Probability for each household of being active in the housing market	0%, 50%
φ_{up}	Sale price offers: maximum price percentage increase	2.5%
φ_{down}	Fire sale price offers: maximum price percentage decrease	5%
θ_{fs}	Fire sale threshold	0.6
θ_d	Mortgage default/write-off threshold	0.7
DSTI	Debt service-to-income ratio	0.5

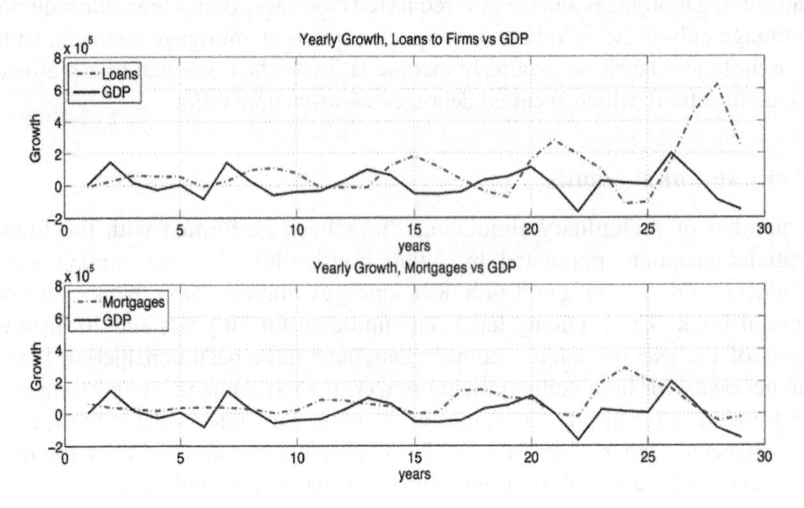

Figure 11.2 Growth in gross domestic product (GDP), loans, and mortgages within the Eurace artificial economy

In the current simulations, as discussed in previous sections, loan-to-value ratio is 1, which means that any housing transaction causes an injection of money in the economy whose size is equivalent to the nominal value of the housing unit. However, it should also be noted that households' financial credibility is checked according to different eligibility criteria prior to the release of the mortgage loan. In a way, the amount of mortgage in the current model follows empirical patterns of money supply in an economy. The lagging pattern of loans to firms over the business cycle may suggest that during recoveries, firms first finance investment expenditure using their internal funds, as cash flows improve during a recovery, and only later they seek external financing. On the other hand, it may also suggest that during recessions the reduction of their equity capital prevents banks from granting credit to firms. The lead of mortgages suggests that mortgages function as injection of liquidity to households' consumption budget, and hence an increase in demand, production, and GDP growth in the system. This, in turn, increases demand for investment by producers, which leads them to request more loans from the banking sector. Overall, what we observe is a pattern of systematic responses, where money creation via mortgages is answered by a growth in GDP and later an increase in loan requests for further investment in productions.

The impact of money injection into the system via mortgages is further depicted in Figures 11.3 to 11.5, where we compare the different paths observed for the main monetary and real economic variables in the cases of both absence and presence of a housing market and mortgage lending. The two cases are controlled by the value of the parameter Φ which sets the probability for households to be active in the housing market; when $\Phi = 0.0$, we have no transactions in the market and therefore no mortgage requests and then lending to households by banks, while in the case of Φ = 0.5, where on average half of households are active as buyers or sellers in the market, we have a relevant transaction and mortgage-lending activity. Furthermore, in Table 11.3 we present our results averaged over 20 seeds of the pseudo-random number generator.

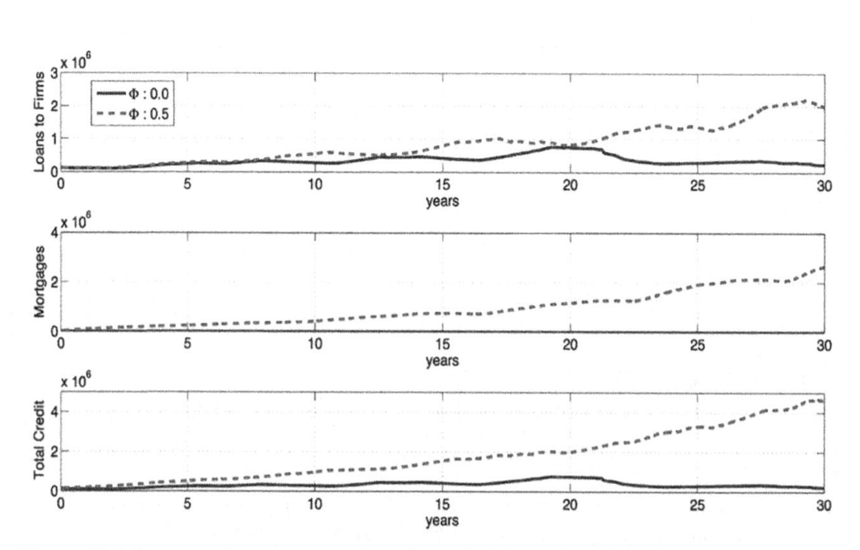

Figure 11.3 Loans to firms, mortgages to households, and total credit in Eurace artificial economy without mortgages (solid line —) and with mortgages (dashed line - -).

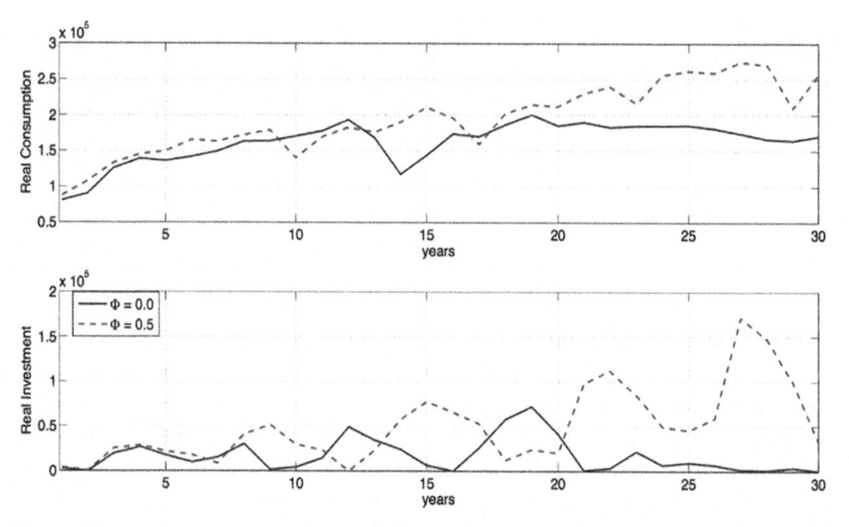

Figure 11.4 Real consumption and real investment in Eurace artificial economy without mortgages (solid line —) and with mortgages (dashed line - -)

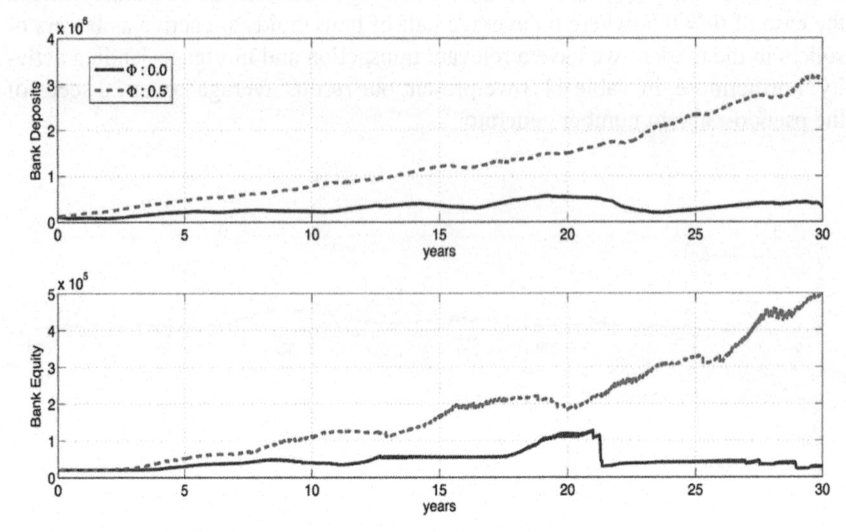

Figure 11.5 Bank deposits and bank equity of Eurace artificial economy without mortgages (solid line —) and with mortgages (dashed line - -).

Table 11.3 Simulation results for the Eurace artificial economy with and without the housing market. The values are reported as a percentage (%) and are computed as ensemble averages over 20 different seeds (simulations) of time averages over any single seed (simulation). Standard errors are shown in parentheses

	Without mortgages ($\Phi = 0.0$)	*With mortgages* ($\Phi = 0.5$)
Real GDP growth	3.38 (0.08)	3.85 (0.10)
Real consumption growth	2.93 (0.19)	3.07 (0.08)
Real investment growth	6.09 (1.29)	9.74 (0.29)
Total credit stock growth	6.95 (1.22)	9.93 (0.08)
Unemployment rate	7.07 (1.00)	6.52 (0.01)
Money wage growth	6.51 (0.44)	7.28 (0.06)
Bank equity growth	7.13 (0.67)	9.87 (0.17)

In the simulation scenario where mortgaging is active ($\Phi = 0.5$), it is shown that the additional mortgages create new money, raising households' consumption and firms' investments (Figure 11.4). The impact of money creation via mortgages can be observed by higher growth rates of wages and bank deposits as well as at banks' equity. Each one of these indicators has grown faster after having extended the artificial economy with a real-estate market. Comparative trends in consumption and investment are further shown in Figure 11.4. A clear increase in consumption as well as in investment is observed.

These results should be attributed to the higher endogenous money creation via households' mortgages (Figure 11.3). Furthermore, when the mortgaging mechanism is activated, the model produces a lower unemployment rate and higher wage, as presented in Table 11.3.

The presence of mortgage lending gives advantages to the banks through an increase of bank equity and bank deposits, as shown in Figure 11.5, which in turn eases the access to credit for firms' investment, as shown in Figure 11.4. Overall, results suggest that introduction of mortgages contributes to the macroeconomic system by increasing real consumption, real investment, wages, bank equity, bank deposits, and reducing the unemployment rate. This result is coherent with empirical facts on the global economy where real-estate markets play a significant role in driving an economic booms (Catte et al., 2004).

Concluding remarks

We have presented a preliminary study on the effects of the addition of a housing market along with mortgage lending in the Eurace model. Mortgages are intended to finance households' purchase of housing units, and represent a new endogenous money creation device, along with loans to firms. We have shown that the model is able to reproduce the basic stylized facts that describe the relation between loans, mortgages, and GDP. We have also shown that the introduction of mortgages into the economic system tends to amplify the business cycle and to improve the performance of the economy. However, these generic results should be tested using more varied economic scenarios and, in particular, they should be tested under different regulation schemes. Our intuition is that there is a trade-off between higher growth and economic stability, depending on the amount of mortgages that are allowed to be channeled into the economic system. Further studies will focus on these aspects.

Acknowledgments

The authors acknowledge EU-FP7 collaborative project SYMPHONY under grant no. 611875.

Notes

1 When the ratio between quarterly mortgage payments and income is higher than the threshold θ_d, then the household undergoes a mortgage-restructuring process with a consequent loss on the equity of the crediting bank.
2 In estimating expected mortgage payments, banks make the parsimonious assumption to consider constant interest rates in the future.

References

Axtell, R., Farmer, D., Geanakoplos, J., Carella, E., Conlee, B., Goldstein, J., Hendrey, M., Kalikman, P., Masad, D., Palmer, N., and Yang, C. (2014). An agent-based model of the housing market bubble in metropolitan Washington, D.C. Tech. rep., Deutsche Bundesbank Spring Conferences on Housing Markets and the Macroeconomy. https://www.bundesbank.de/Redaktion/EN/Downloads/Bundesbank/Research_Centre/Conferences/2014/2014_06_05_eltville_10_axtell.pdf (accessed September 30, 2016).

Blum, J., and Hellwig, M. (1995). The macroeconomic implications of capital adequacy requirements for banks. *European Economic Review*, 39(3): 739–749.

Catte, P., Girouard, N., Price, R., and Andre, C. (2004). The contribution of housing markets to cyclical resilience. *OECD Economic Studies*, 1: 125–156.

Cincotti, S., Raberto, M., and Teglio, A. (2010). Credit money and macroeconomic instability in the agent-based model and simulator eurace. *The Open-Access, Open-Assessment E-Journal*, 4(26).

Cincotti, S., Raberto, M., and Teglio, A. (2012). The Eurace macroeconomic model and simulator. In: Aoki, M., Binmore, K., Deakin, S., and Gintis, H. (Eds), *Complexity and Institutions: Markets, Norms and Corporations*. Basingstoke: Palgrave Macmillan, pp. 81–106.

ECB Bulletin, E. B. (2013). European central bank bulletin. Technical Report 10, ECB. Frankfurt am Mein: ECB Bulletin.

Erlingsson, E., Teglio, A., Cincotti, S., Stefansson, H., Sturluson, J., and Raberto, M. (2014). Housing market bubbles and business cycles in an agent-based credit economy. *Economics: The Open-Access, Open-Assessment E-Journal*, 8(8).

Ge, J. (2014). Who creates housing bubbles? An agent-based study. In: Alam, S. J., and Parunak, H. V. D. (eds), *Multi-Agent-Based Simulation XIV, Lecture Notes in Computer Science* (Vol. 8235). Berlin: Springer, pp. 143–150.

Gilbert, N., Howksworth, J. C., and Swinney, P. A. (2009). An agent-based model of the English housing market. *Association for the Advancement of Artificial Intelligence*. https://www.aaai.org/Papers/Symposia/Spring/2009/SS-09-09/SS09-09-007.pdf (accessed September 30, 2016).

McLeay, M., Radia, A., and Thomas, R. (2014). Money creation in the modern economy. *Bank of England Quarterly Bulletin*, 54(1): 14–27.

Muellbauer, J., and Murphy, A. (2008). Housing markets and the economy: The assessment. *Oxford Review of Economic Policy*, 24(1): 1–33.

Raberto, M., Teglio, A., and Cincotti, S. (2012). Debt, deleveraging and business cycles: An agent-based perspective. *Economics: The Open-Access, Open-Assessment E-Journal*, 6(27): 1–49.

Santos, J. A. (2001). Bank capital regulation in contemporary banking theory: A review of the literature. *Financial Markets, Institutions & Instruments*, 10(2): 41–84.

Teglio, A., Raberto, M., and Cincotti, S. (2012). The impact of banks' capital adequacy regulation on the economic system: An agent-based approach. *Advances in Complex Systems*, 15(suppl 2): 1250040.

Teglio, A., Mazzocchetti A., Ponta L., Raberto, M., and Cincotti, S. (2015). Budgetary rigour with stimulus in lean times: Policy advices from an agent-based model. *Universitat Jaume I Working Papers 2015/7*. https://ideas.repec.org/p/jau/wpaper/2015-07.html (accessed September 30, 2016).

Tesfatsion, L. (2003). Agent-based computational economics: Modeling economies as complex adaptive systems. *Information Sciences*, 149(4): 262–268.

Tesfatsion, L., and Judd, K. (2006). *Agent-Based Computational Economics, Volume 2 of Handbook of Computational Economics*. Amsterdam: North Holland.

Werner, R. (2014). Can banks individually create money out of nothing?: The theories and the empirical evidence. *International Review of Financial Analysis*, 36: 1–19.

12 Fiscal policy and redistribution in an evolutionary macroeconomic model of an artificial monetary union

Bernhard Rengs and Manuel Scholz-Wäckerle

Introduction

In economics there are theories of value and distribution and theories of development and growth; mostly these two blocks are separated from each other. This was the case in the classical political economy of Adam Smith, David Ricardo and John Stuart Mill and it still is the case after the neoclassical synthesis of John Hicks and Paul Samuelson. The latter economic theory has enforced this divide with the construction of micro- and macroeconomic analysis. Galbraith (2007) highlights that the still present problems of income inequality relate to a great extent to this scientific project of neoclassical divide and conquer. Karl Marx was one of the only ones who has explicitly emphasized the interdependent relations between value, wage labour, the introduction of the commodity form in capitalist exchange societies and the principle of accumulation that is representing the core of economic development as well as growth (Marx, 1867). Thereby Marx has provided a synthesized theory of value, distribution, development and growth in his critique of political economy. The Marxian analytical apparatus is a dynamic one that is highlighting economic development as a process of (re)structuration and ongoing alienation. Heterodox economists have always stressed that historical and institutional circumstances influence this course of economic development.

Galbraith (2007: 606) takes the historical and institutional role of the Bretton Woods system as an example that has secured development on a large scale, financed by the International Monetary Fund (in the short run) and the World Bank (in the long run). Its demise shifted financialization to the commercial banks and global finance. Eventually global income inequality had risen from the late 1970s onwards through the strengthening of global credit relations. Galbraith (2007) revisits Kuznets' hypothesis about the inverted U-shape relation of income per capita and inequality; he stresses the notion that a mere empirical data analysis of the Kuznets curve would not lead to such institutional and historical insights. Galbraith (2007: 602) argues that:

> What Kuznets offered was a general method for coming to some state of expectation concerning the pattern of inequalities that one might reasonably expect. That method consists of assessing inequality primarily as a matter of an appropriate pattern of inter-sectoral transitions.

It is the aspect of inter-sectoral transitions making economic development such a crucial phenomenon.

Eventually, Kuznets' hypothesis suggests that a developmental transition from an agrarian to an industrial economy implies a parallel increase in income but also in income inequality. When a certain level of average income is reached (during industrialization), income inequality tends to decrease again. However, as highlighted by Galbraith (2007) as well as Piketty (2014), the global macroeconomic picture of the last decades demonstrates that industrialized economies do not remain in such a steady state; they are rather subject to reverse tendencies where income inequality has shifted upwards again. Global finance represents one source of this reverse effect and industrial (re)structuration through free trade and labour mobility the other one. The latter goes beyond inter-sectoral transitions today and implies issues of international political economy. The trend of the last decades in international political economy went definitely in the direction of building large trade blocks such as the North American Free Trade Agreement (NAFTA), the Trans-Pacific Partnership (TPP) or the currently debated Transatlantic Trade and Investment Partnership (TTIP). Special cases among such free-trade arrangements are monetary unions, among them the three largest (by population) are given by the Indian rupee, the US dollar and the Euro zone. Free trade and labour mobility across countries introduce additional constraints into the macroeconomic picture, making the analysis of value and distribution via development and growth even more complex.

Rezai (2014) has recently presented a neo-Kaleckian framework to analyse a simplified two-country case in an aggregate way, with emphasis on devaluation and redistribution. The main argument is given in the very beginning: "The functional distribution of income in an economy affects its levels of demand and output" (Rezai, 2014: 1399). Elsewhere Carvalho and Rezai (2016) have explained that the functional distribution of income refers basically to a class-based distribution of different income groups, such as land-owning rentiers, capitalists and workers. In this model even this merely functional distribution has effects on demand and output stemming from different saving and investment propensities, as taken up in the post-Keynesian literature. A quite simple conclusion from models in this line of research suggests that "redistribution between income groups can increase the level of income", but this aspect represents "a trade-off between wage-earners and profit-earners in a closed economy framework" (Rezai, 2014: 1399). It is further argued that the assumption of a closed or small-open economy represents just a special case that does not instruct us on conditions of free trade and/or labour mobility. If trade is opened it allows "the analytical study of how shifts in distribution affect demand directly through their effects on consumption, investment and imports, and indirectly through their effects on foreign output and foreign import demand (i.e. domestic export demand)" (Rezai, 2014: 1400). This analysis is unique since it highlights the important relations between interactions of growth and income distribution with an emphasis on aggregate demand as well as the international trade network. A similar model of integrated economies was conducted by Godley and Lavoie (2012) with numerical simulations but not with this degree of generality. We employ an evolutionary macroeconomic model that responds endogenously on the macro level to changes in the micro- or mesoeconomic structure and vice versa. The particular advantage of this methodology is given by the possibility of analysing the evolution of the whole system, accounting for value and distribution as well as development and growth. This notion closes some central research gaps mentioned by Galbraith (2007) previously. Moreover it highlights crucial shortcomings in the computable general equilibrium approach – as conducted by Rezai (2014) – with its blind spots in micro- and mesoeconomic components of economic development, as we will outline in the next section in more detail.

In this chapter we investigate the effects of free trade and labour mobility in two artificial integrated economies with different but exogenously fixed fiscal policies and redistribution schemes. The analysis is done stepwise; first, the countries remain isolated from each other and we highlight their distinct path-dependent evolution on a macroeconomic scale. Second, we discuss the same computational simulation experiment in the case of integrated economies, i.e. basically with free trade. Third, we highlight the macroeconomic implications of an additional integration of those two economies with a limited form of labour mobility, as a major institutional pillar of monetary unions. The agent-based methodology allows a closer look at the micro- as well as macroeconomic effects of redistribution in two countries, one favouring labour and the other capital with fixed fiscal settings. The simulation experiments show that firm specialization within and across countries leads to labour commuting that is decisive for capacity utilization, aggregate demand and employment at the end of the day. To this extent we shed light on the micro- and macroeconomic implications of functional as well as personal income inequality and redistribution in a two-country monetary union from an evolutionary political economy perspective.

An evolutionary macroeconomic model of an artificial monetary union

The model we have developed is part of a new family of agent-based macroeconomic models that has emerged as a direct response to substantial shortcomings in macroeconomics (compare also Stiglitz, 2015). In particular these models feature heterogeneous agent populations and conceive the economy as a complex adaptive system, as specifically demanded by scholarly commentators in different contexts (see especially LeBaron and Tesfatsion, 2008; Farmer and Foley, 2009; Delli Gatti et al., 2010; Kirman, 2011; Stiglitz and Gallegati, 2011; Dosi, 2012). Many have already followed this agenda and brought these claims to life in agent-based macroeconomic models; compare Ciarli et al. (2010), Cincotti et al. (2010), Dosi et al. (2010), Delli Gatti et al. (2011), Seppecher (2012), Lengnick (2013), Riccetti et al. (2013), Chen et al. (2014) or, most recently, Caiani et al. (2016) and Lorentz et al. (2016) for new benchmark models in this emerging field of what can be considered as "evolutionary macroeconomics".

The model we have developed (see Rengs and Wäckerle, 2014) offers some features in comparison to the previous ones that are crucial for the analysis of integrated economies in our point of view. First of all, it is a political economy model that differentiates between wage and profit earners in a Marxian tradition. As highlighted by Wright (2015), class struggle represents primarily a Marxian conflict of power over the means of production, secondly a Weberian conflict of power over institutional redistribution and thirdly a Veblenian or Bourdieusian conflict of power over individualized cultural self-attachment, implying the contemporary continuous spectrum of stratification – "how to best realize interests under fixed rules" Wright (2015: x). Our evolutionary macroeconomic model mirrors all three components of this social class analysis in rough terms. We distinguish between workers and capitalists; the latter are explicitly modelled as firm and bank owners and gain their income as a share of operating surpluses. The Marxian notion characterizes an essential feature for modelling the evolution of the functional income distribution and builds the ground for a distinct class-based demand. The Weberian institutional conflict over redistribution is exogenously given in our simulation experiments. One country favours labour with a fixed fiscal policy and redistributes more to less wealthy households, whereas the other country favours capital and redistributes more to the wealthy.

Eventually, we model different consumer effects dependent on class associations, thereby wealthy capitalist households consume conspicuously (Veblen, 1899) and prefer expensive (Veblen effect) and rare goods (snob effect). In contrast, working-class households prefer cheap goods (normal price effect) and aim to imitate and emulate upper classes (bandwagon effect). The four different dynamic effects of consumption behaviour are in line with Leibenstein's (1950) analysis. To this extent, wealthy households aim to distance themselves from each other via cultural self-attachment (Bourdieu, 1984). Additionally consumption behaviour influences personal income distribution within the artificial society since households do not consume just what they need but also what they want, leading to growth in demand in the long run (Witt, 2001). This feature models explicitly a central post-Keynesian assumption, as previously mentioned, "The functional distribution of income in an economy affects its levels of demand and output" (Rezai, 2014: 1399). However, our evolutionary macroeconomic model allows the application of this assumption not just on the functional income level, but across the full range of personal income distribution. Thereby we are able to investigate a broader spectrum of scenarios.

The different patterns of consumer dynamics influence the evolving patterns of firm specialization and lead to a non-uniform distribution of firm size over time, in stark contrast to the standard microeconomic outcomes under perfect competition. Small firms may specialize in rare snob consumption (in terms of firm reputation) and large firms may sell cheaply for the masses. Although in the model there is just one homogeneous good, there is a differentiation in consumption channels through production via an explicitly modelled firm reputation scheme that households are following. The good is produced with the same production inputs (physical capital and labour), but may differ with regard to branding and price from firm to firm.

The second crucial feature relates to the integrated economies design, where we are able to simulate multiple countries either in isolated parallel experiments or in two different modes of economic integration: free trade and/or free labour mobility. The latter two modes are very interesting to investigate since they coincide with agent-based demand-dependent firm specialization in the corresponding expanding or shrinking economy. Thereby microeconomic specialization and meso-level institutionalization of consumption contribute to personal income, its agent-based demand and heterogeneous capacity utilization eventually. To this extent we are employing institutional co-evolutionary dynamics on a meso level (Wäckerle, 2014).

In the following we give a rough description of the general structure of the model; for a more detailed description for agents as well as institutions and organizations, we refer to Rengs and Wäckerle (2014). The agents are heterogeneous, boundedly rational decision makers that are either worker or capitalist (firm and bank owner) households. Firms have physical capital (machines, equipment) and labour as their input factors, represented in a linear, transformative and firm-based production function. Physical capital can be expanded via investment in machines bought from a single capital goods firm per country and depreciates annually. We maintain stock-flow consistency since capital goods profits made on behalf of final goods producers' investments are redistributed equally among capitalists in the respective economy. We simply assume that investment goods are owned and thereby controlled collectively by the capitalist class. Consumer goods firms may hire households from the set of unemployed; otherwise they are able to fire workers if they aim to reduce/adapt production output. Each consumer goods firm has only one private owner, who is the sole receiver of the firm's profits. Furthermore, firms use a simple short-run adaption strategy to determine required production, which is based on the assumption that overall demand will not change by huge amounts abruptly, or rather that huge deviations from their past production schedule are too risky. Thus, they try to estimate the demand for their product by basing their decision on their individual sales performance in the previous period. Their target is to keep their inventory after sales at a reserve level which is proportional to previous production (Godley and Lavoie, 2012). If they have sold more than the expected amount, but still have some reserve left, they slightly increase production. If they were completely sold out, they choose to increase production even more. If on the other hand they have stock left, they decrease production.

Firms and banks interact on a simplified credit market, and banks interact with the Central Bank. Firms always finance investments and reinvestments into physical capital with a new loan from a bank. They get further credit until their expected short-term profitability becomes too low and their expected debt too high. More specifically, banks will not grant more credit to firms whose estimated profit rate is lower than the bank's interest rate on firm credit or to firms that would then have more credit than bankable collateral (i.e. physical capital).

Once firms have determined how much they will produce, they set their price for the next/this period, following the same basic logic as the production amount and react to changes in demand for their goods, by monitoring the reserves in the inventory after sales. They base their price on the last period's price and consider changing it by slightly increasing or decreasing it by a fraction (dependent on the degree of mismatch between actual and expected sales) of a simulation-specific maximum amount (which is based on the average initial price in $t = 0$). The production costs serve as the lower limit of the net price. At the end of a fiscal year (a given number of simulation periods), all firms calculate their profits, pay corporate taxes to the government/state and distribute a large part of profits (after taxes) to the firm's owner (if positive profits existed).

In general, we follow the Keynesian assumption that planned consumption expenditure increases with real liquidity. Thereby, in the model, wealthier households (class-specific) are inclined to consume relatively less of their disposable income (compare Lengnick, 2013, for a similar implementation). As a simplification we assume that workers intend to consume a large share of their income, wealthy workers intend to consume a slightly smaller share, while capitalists finally intend to consume again a slightly smaller share than wealthy workers. The disposable income for workers is their monthly wage, whereas for capitalists we assume a fictitious income equal to a 12th of last year's dividends. Furthermore we assume that households with positive savings of all classes set aside a very small share of their savings for additional consumption.

If a household's savings account is empty and its bank account overdrafted (the only form of household debt in the model), they are regarded as bankrupt. Households of all classes may in this case only satisfy their needs by buying minimal subsistence consumption (fixed amount of goods) from their preferred vendors on the respective vendor list. Households that are not bankrupt try to satisfy their wants by buying from their preferred vendors on the respective shortlist until the remainder of their consumption budget (what was left after satisfying their needs) is spent or until their preferred vendors are outsold. Income which was not set aside for consumption or could not be spent on consumption for whatever reason is transferred to the household's savings accounts.

The state (government) collects taxes and uses them to finance social transfers to pensioners and unemployed households. Government surpluses are redistributed differently in the two economies. As a very crude proxy to government bonds we assume that banks and households finance the sovereign debt that exceeds available funds. The Central Bank is lender of last resort for banks, and furthermore provides commercial bank services for states as a minor secondary/tertiary function. The Central Bank keeps current accounts for governments (including overdraft functionality) and banks, as well as deposit facilities for banks, involving the payment or charging of interest. Banks keep current accounts for firms, the capital goods firm (which has equally sized accounts with every bank so as not to distort the banking system) and households (allowing for deficits) as well as separate savings accounts for households. In addition, they grant firm loans, whereas households cannot apply for loans in a regular way. At the end of a fiscal period, banks calculate their profits, pay corporate taxes to the government/state and transfer a large part of their profits (after taxes) to the bank's owner. Compare Appendix 1 for a complete overview of the timing of all events, in monthly and yearly phases.

Computational simulation experiments and results

The following simulation experiments are computed in three different scenarios. In the first scenario the two economies are isolated from each other. In the second scenario, we are dealing with basic economic integration along free trade and in the third scenario, we investigate tighter integration with free trade and basic labour mobility (i.e. commuting between the two countries). In the latter two scenarios, a Central Bank sets the interest rate and grants loans to commercial banks under a common currency and the two economies are integrated in an artificial monetary union.

Scenario 1: Isolated closed economies

In this setting, the two countries are completely separated from and do not influence each other, as indicated in Figure 12.1. However, the countries are still modelled from bottom up and the individual connections between households, firms and banks evolve differently over time, on a country-specific level.

In the following simulation experiments we initialized the two countries identically but with different settings for labour and the capital gains tax, as explained in the simulation parameter section in Appendix 2. Furthermore, the countries have two different redistribution mechanisms. In "Country 1," government surpluses are transferred to a higher degree to households with less wealth and in "Country 2" they are transferred to a higher degree to households with more wealth. To this extent we are able to test the micro- and macroeconomics effects from two different fiscal policy and redistribution settings, the first one roughly favouring labour and the second one capital. In general, individual wealth is adjusted for personal debt, i.e. the poorest household is the one with the highest debt. As a consequence, in "Country 1," the wealthiest household does not get any transfer at all while the households with the highest debt get the largest share of the transfer. "Country 2" implements the complete inverse mechanism, namely that the poorest or most indebted household does not get any share at all and the wealthiest gets the highest share. These fiscal policy and redistribution settings are identical for each of the three investigated scenarios.

Scenario 2: Integrated economies, a monetary union with free trade

In the second scenario we conducted a simulation experiment with free trade between the two countries, as stylized in Figure 12.2. The value-added tax is still paid to the domestic country.

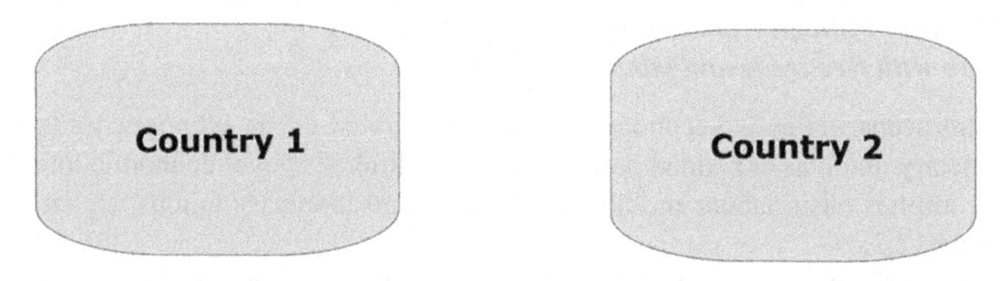

Figure 12.1 Isolated closed economies

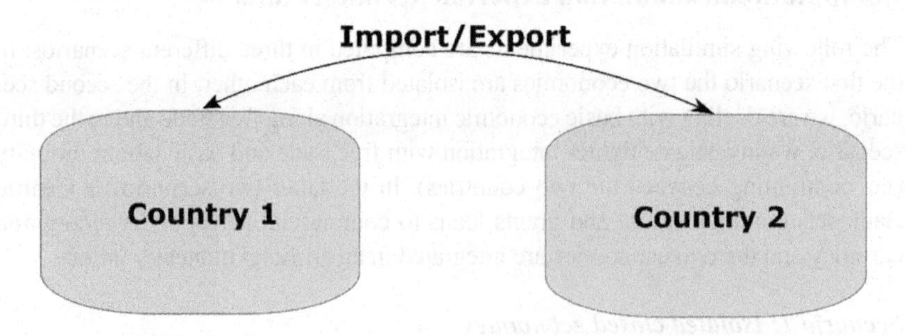

Figure 12.2 Integrated economies, a monetary union with free trade

During the setup phase the two economies are initialized separately, i.e. households start with preferring domestic firms only, while trade between the two countries immediately becomes possible at the start of the regular simulation run. Basically, households do not prioritize domestic firms any more from this point on. The two countries are in an economic trade and monetary union and households may buy their goods anywhere dependent on the social mediation of consumer preferences (bandwagon, Veblen and snob effects), as explained in the previous section. Additionally to these consumption dynamics, the capitalist households of the less successful country (in terms of gross domestic product (GDP)) imitate the capitalists of the more successful country. Thereby consumption has a significant impact on the interdependent structural development of the firm population in both countries. Capitalists from the country with a larger GDP may change their firm network and buy at a rather small and rarely followed firm on behalf of snob consumption, while capitalists from the other country will follow them. Obviously such small and rarely followed firms will expand production (if possible from the bank's perspective) to meet the increasing demand from the other country and will grow eventually. Such micro-behaviour turns into significant macroeconomic effects thereafter, because additional employment is needed in the one country and unemployment will necessarily rise due to decreasing demand in the other country. In this scenario the upper limit of firm growth is given by full employment in the country with the larger GDP, but this condition is not active any more in scenario 3.

Scenario 3: Integrated economies, a monetary union with free trade and labour mobility

In this scenario the two economies are still integrated via an economic trade and monetary union as explained previously. An additional step of economic integration implies basic labour mobility, as given in all monetary unions, stylized in Figure 12.3.

Basically there is no true migration between the two countries, but once full employment is reached in one country, firms can hire workers from the other

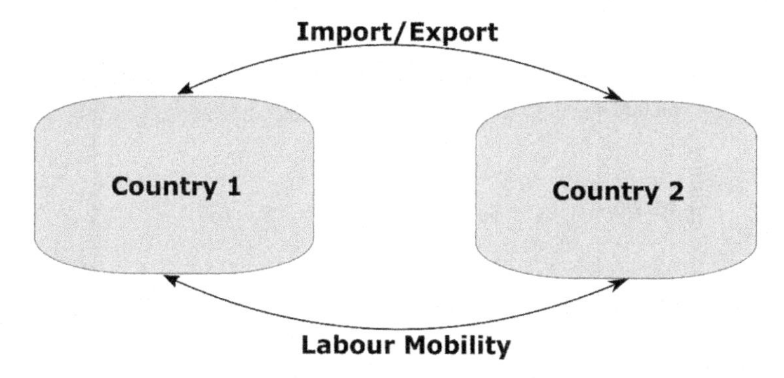

Figure 12.3 Integrated economies, a monetary union with free trade and labour mobility

country. This mechanism mimics – in a very stylized way – cross-country employment effects from structural differences in a monetary union. The workers hired from the foreign country commute in our simulation experiments; in fact they are not relocated to the foreign country.

Discussion of results

The generated data, computed from the simulation experiments, are characterized by a high degree of complexity that we aim to analyse with our following discussion of results. The following figures show annual numbers (although the basic time unit in the model is a month – compare Appendix 1), which are medians over annual aggregates of each scenario's 30 repetitions.

Figure 12.4 illustrates the development of sold quantities of final goods – i.e. aggregate demand – in the two economies over 30 years of simulation time. The time series denotes the aforementioned scenarios per country, highlighting "CENC.country.1" as the scenario for the isolated "closed economies" (CE) without labour mobility, i.e. no commuting (NC). "OENC.country.1" stands for the integrated open economies with trade (OE) but still without labour mobility, i.e. no commuting (NC). Finally "OEWC.country.1" represents the series with open economies as well as labour mobility, i.e. with commuting (WC). The two latter scenarios indicate different levels of economic integration within a monetary union. Figure 12.4 shows that demand (need and want consumption in total) remains quite steady in all cases on aggregate. This means in particular that the implemented model and its computational simulation are on the whole robust and stable over time even with such a high degree of complex interactions. Still the computational simulation is subject to sufficient fluctuations that it is endogenously creating a cyclical pattern in aggregate demand in all three scenarios.

This cyclical pattern in demand becomes even more visible in the median profit rates of the firms in the respective countries. Figure 12.5 demonstrates moreover

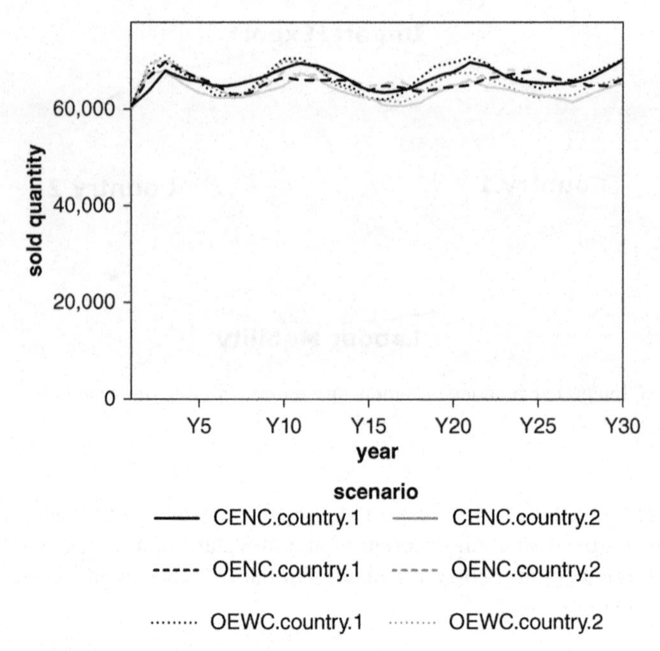

Figure 12.4 Sold quantities – aggregate demand (medians)

that "Country 1" outcompetes "Country 2" in all three scenarios for the median profit rate over 30 repetitions of this simulation experiment. In this regard we can highlight that the labour-favouring fiscal policy combined with the redistribution mechanism that is transferring government surpluses to a higher degree to households with less wealth induces higher profit rates in the median of all firms in both countries.

All the simulation experiments are computed with constant technological coefficients; there is no change in the labour productivity of both economies. Most interesting, as shown in Figure 12.6, is that capacity utilization decreases slightly but steadily in a cyclical pattern. This notion results from coordination effects in demand via self-organizing behaviour. In general, firms could produce more but the demand is never matched perfectly – there is no market clearing. Since the firms do not follow a production function with perfect substitution, but employ a linear transformative one, they cannot adjust that quickly and produce more and more below full capacity.

Otherwise, a redistribution to the top households in terms of wealth, as implemented in "Country 2", leads to a private debt crisis in all three scenarios after 15 years of simulation time, most severely in the open economy case with free trade but without labour mobility. This shows moreover that a labour-favouring fiscal policy plus a redistribution scheme that is transferring to a higher degree to the poor stabilizes the development of private debt even in a monetary union with endogenous restructuration.

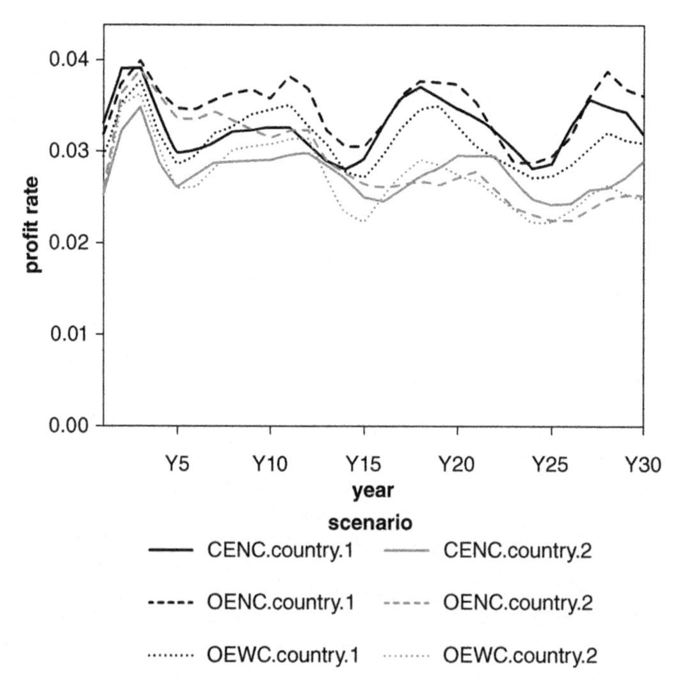

Figure 12.5 Profit rates (medians)

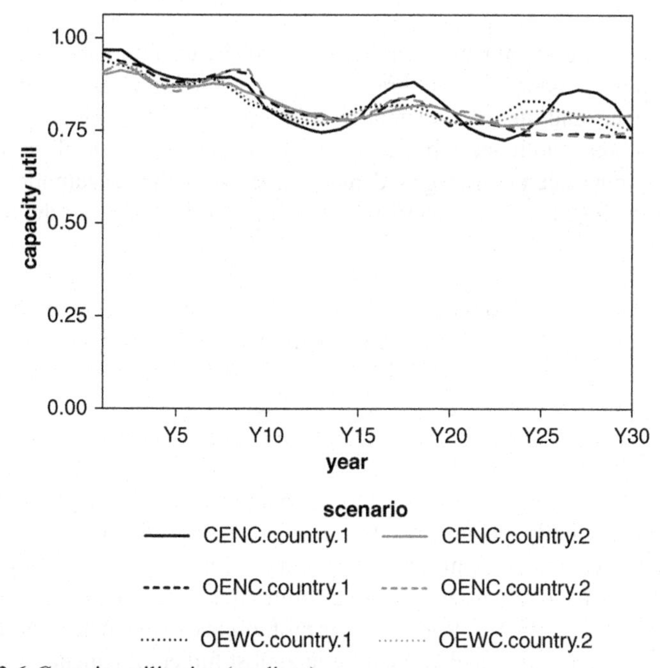

Figure 12.6 Capacity utilization (medians)

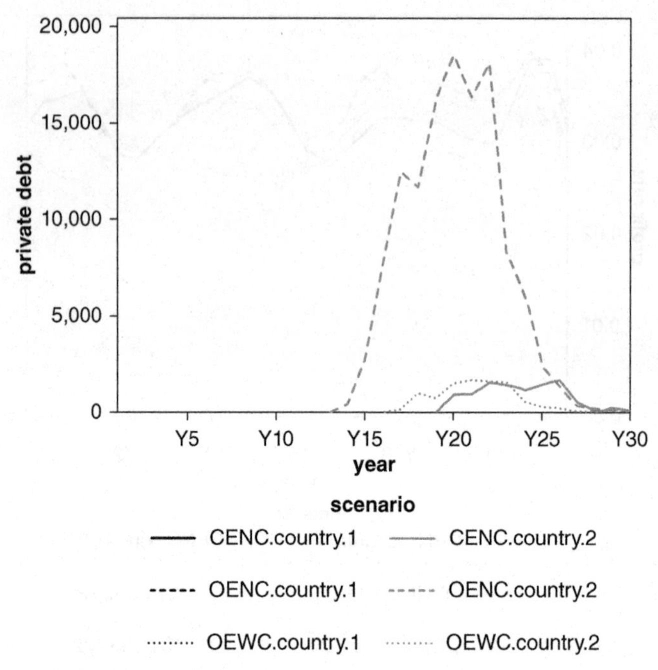

Figure 12.7 Private debt (medians)

In our model, government expenditure is given by unemployment benefits and pensions in both countries in all three scenarios. There is a clear relation between these payments and the development in GDP, as indicated in Figure 12.8, while the slope of both is influenced by the increase in the price level, as these are nominal values. In particular, aggregate demand depends on the consumption pursued by the unemployed and pensioners who receive their budget from the respective government.

Eventually, we refer to the unemployment rate for all three scenarios. In the median across 30 repetitions unemployment is in general rather low, at a maximum of 5%, as illustrated in Figure 12.9. Basically we can report that unemployment is dampened by labour mobility between countries, since full employment in one country decreases unemployment in the other one and vice versa. The cyclical pattern and periodicity in the unemployment rate are in line with the other measures; compare the development of sold quantity (Figure 12.4) and profit rate (Figure 12.5). Both latter measures face a boom phase between years 15 and 20 in all scenarios that is accompanied by a rise in capacity utilization (Figure 12.6). Right in advance of this boom we see an abrupt rise in unemployment in the years 12 to 17; firms have downsized due to a former decrease in demand. The resulting lower costs on firm side lead to higher profits since demand has stabilized and workers are hired again, finally resulting in almost full employment.

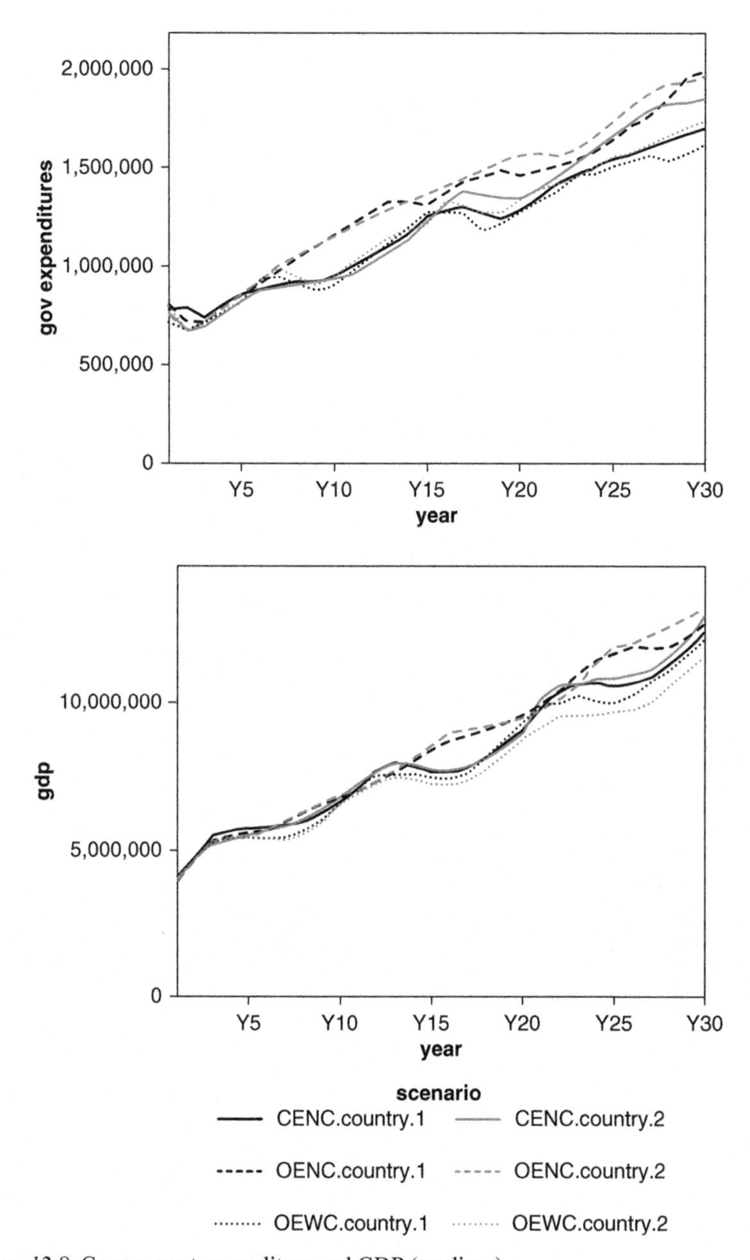

Figure 12.8 Government expenditure and GDP (medians)

Figure 12.10 shows the development of labour mobility over time and thus only the data of the monetary union scenarios with free trade as well as labour mobility (OEWC). The two time series represent medians again across the repetitions of the simulation experiment.

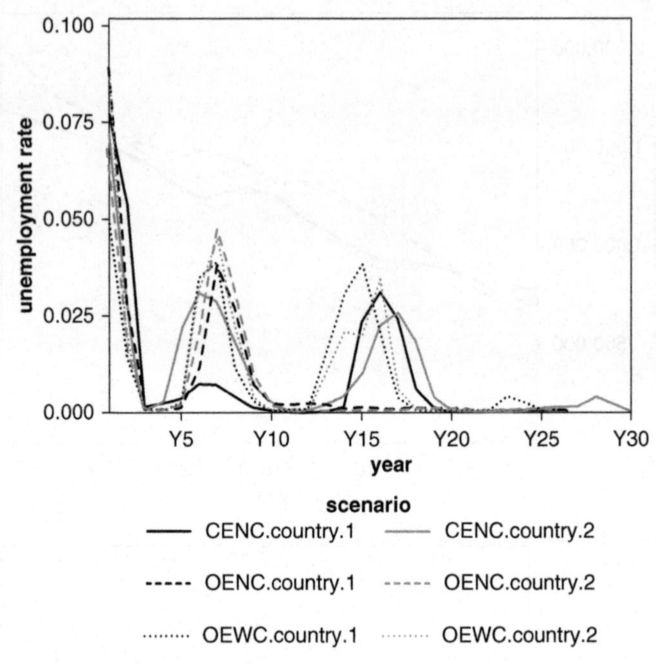

Figure 12.9 Unemployment rate (medians)

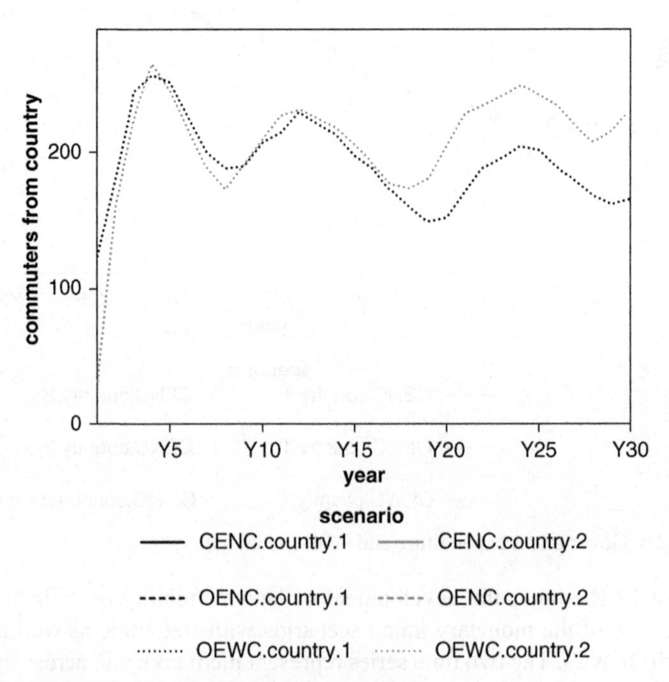

Figure 12.10 Labour mobility (commuting) – medians

Labour mobility is similar in both countries, with a share of around 8% of the labour force per country, signalling that the employment path is quite similar at the start. After 20 simulation years, the two series divide and there are more commuters living in "Country 2" while working in "Country 1." Simulation experiments indicate that in the long run the economy with a labour-favouring fiscal policy combined with a redistribution scheme transferring more to the poor ("Country 1") has fewer commuting workers leaving the country than the capital-favouring economy ("Country 2"). One could cautiously follow in this regard that "Country 1" has a slightly higher labour demand and thus a better employment situation than "Country 2" in the long run, when it comes to labour mobility in a monetary union. This aspect feeds back into government expenditure that is slightly lower than in "Country 2" and into a higher GDP that is slightly higher than in "Country 2" (compare Figure 12.8). The same is true for sold quantities (Figure 12.4) and profit rates (Figure 12.5). On the one hand the status-seeking imitation of the wealthiest capitalists in "Country 1" lures more demand into "Country 1" leading to firm growth and on the other hand the very same status-seeking consumption drives "Country 2" into a private debt crisis (compare Figure 12.7). In sum, there are significant advantages for "Country 1" in micro- as well as macroeconomic perspective in all three scenarios, but even more crucial in a monetary union. The simulation experiments have thereby shown that country-specific fiscal policy and redistribution can be effective game changers even in a monetary union.

Concluding remarks

The evolutionary macroeconomic model that we have briefly introduced aims to interlink value and distribution with development and growth again, thereby following the general appeal of Galbraith (2007). We employed the agent-based methodology to overcome this gap between micro, meso and macro. The investigated topic of fiscal policy and redistribution in an open economy context has recently been explored in depth from a post-Keynesian perspective (Rezai, 2014). The model presented in this paper – although with a focus on a monetary union – comes on the one hand to quite similar conclusions but with a finer granularity when it comes to micro–macro interlinkage. The agent-based methodology features a far less complicated analytical toolkit but brings a higher degree of complexity. This notion implies that arguments cannot be derived with such analytical rigour as done in the closed-form approach, but it also implies that arguments can be built on very concrete micro-meso-macro processes that are absent in the general equilibrium approach. This feature allows embeddedness in institutional and historical contexts and narratives of change, as highlighted by Galbraith (2007). One such process component is given by the political economy nature of our model that is able to represent endogenous social class dynamics via the functional as well as the personal income distribution. Eventually, simulation experiments have demonstrated that fiscal policy and redistribution do matter on a micro- and macroeconomic scale. We have shown that there are analytical arguments speaking for an implementation of a labour-favouring fiscal policy and a redistribution scheme transferring to a higher degree to the poor in contrast to a capital-favouring fiscal policy and a redistribution scheme transferring to the wealthy. This aspect is particularly significant in the case of a monetary union and highlights the necessity to discuss effective fiscal policies and redistribution schemes more prominently, even in a monetary union where country-specific fiscal potential is usually downplayed.

References

Bourdieu P (2010) [1984] *Distinction: A social critique of the judgement of taste.* Routledge, London.

Caiani A, Godin A, Caverzasi E, Gallegati M, Kinsella S, Stiglitz JE (2016) Agent based stock-flow consistent macroeconomics: Towards a benchmark model. *Journal of Economic Dynamics & Control* 69: 375–408.

Carvalho L, Rezai A (2016) Personal income inequality and aggregate demand. *Cambridge Journal of Economics* 40(2): 491–505.

Chen SH, Chang, CL, Wen MC (2014) Social networks and macroeconomic stability. *Economics: The Open-Access, Open-Assessment E-Journal* 8(16): 1–40.

Ciarli T, Lorentz A, Savona M, Valente M (2010) The effect of consumption and production structure on growth and distribution. A micro to macro model. *Metroeconomica* 61(1): 180–218.

Cincotti S, Raberto M, Teglio A (2010) Credit money and macroeconomic instability in the agent-based model and simulator Eurace. *Economics: The Open-Access, Open-Assessment E-Journal* 4: 2010–2026.

Delli Gatti D, Gaffeo E, Gallegati M (2010) Complex agent-based macroeconomics: A manife for a new paradigm. *Journal of Economic Interaction and Coordination* 5: 111–135.

Delli Gatti D, Desiderio S, Gaffeo E, Cirillo P, Gallegati M (2011) *Macroeconomics from the bottom-up.* Springer, Berlin.

Dosi G (2012) Economic coordination and dynamics: Some elements of an alternative "evolutionary" paradigm. LEM Working Paper Series 2012/08. Sant'Anna School of Advanced Studies, Pisa, Italy.

Dosi G, Fagiolo G, Roventini A (2010) Schumpeter meeting Keynes: A policy-friendly model of endogenous growth and business cycles. *Journal of Economic Dynamics and Control* 34(9): 1748–1967.

Farmer JD, Foley D (2009) The economy needs agent-based modelling. *Nature* 460: 685–686.

Galbraith JK (2007) Global inequality and global macroeconomics. *Journal of Policy Modelling* 29: 587–607.

Godley W, Lavoie M (2012) *Monetary economics. An integrated approach to credit, money, income, production and wealth*, 2nd edition. Palgrave MacMillan, London.

Kirman A (2011) *Complex economics: Individual and collective rationality*. Graz Schumpeter Lectures. Routledge, London.

LeBaron B, Tesfatsion L (2008) Modeling macroeconomies as open-ended dynamic systems of interacting agents. *American Economic Review* 98(2): 246–250.

Leibenstein H (1950) Bandwagon, snob, and Veblen effects in the theory of consumers' demand. *The Quarterly Journal of Economics* 64(2): 183–207.

Lengnick M (2013) Agent-based macroeconomics: A baseline model. *Journal of Economic Behavior & Organization* 86(C): 102–120.

Lorentz A, Ciarli T, Savona M, Valente M (2016) The effect of demand-driven structural transformations on growth and technological change. *Journal of Evolutionary Economics* 26(1): 219–246.

Marx K (2001) [1867] *Das Kapital. Kritik der politischen Ökonomie. Band 1: Der Produktionsprozeß des Kapitals.* 20. Auflage, Marx-Engels-Werke Band 23, Dietz Verlag, Berlin.

Piketty T (2014) *Capital in the twenty-first century.* Harvard University Press, Cambrdige, MA.

Rengs B, Wäckerle M (2014) A computational agent-based simulation of an artificial monetary union for dynamic comparative institutional analysis. In *2014 IEEE Conference on Computational Intelligence for Financial Engineering & Economics (CIFEr)* pp. 427–434. IEEE.

Rezai A (2014) Demand and distribution in integrated economies. *Cambridge Journal of Economics* 39(5): 1399–1414.

Riccetti L, Russo A, Gallegati M (2013) Unemployment benefits and financial leverage in an agent based macroeconomic model. *Economics: The Open-Access, Open-Assessment E-Journal* 7(42): 1–44.

Seppecher P (2012) Flexibility of wages and macroeconomic instability in an agent-based computational model with endogenous money. *Macroeconomic Dynamics* 16(s2): 284–297.

Stiglitz JE (2015) Reconstructing macroeconomic theory to manage economic policy. In: Laurent E, Cacheux JL, Le Cacheu J, Jasper D (eds) *Fruitful economics*. Papers in honor of and by Jean-Paul Fitoussi. Palgrave MacMillan, New York, pp. 20–56.

Stiglitz JE, Gallegati M (2011) Heterogeneous interacting agent models for understanding monetary economies. *Eastern Economic Journal* 37(1): 6–12.

Veblen T (2009) [1899] *The theory of the leisure class.* Oxford University Press, Oxford.

Wäckerle M (2014) *The foundations of evolutionary institutional economics: Generic institutionalism.* Routledge, Abingdon.

Wilensky U (1999) NetLogo. http://ccl.northwestern.edu/netlogo/. Center for Connected Learning and Computer-Based Modeling, Northwestern University. Evanston, IL.

Witt U (2001) Learning to consume: A theory of wants and the growth of demand. *Journal of Evolutionary Economics* 11(1): 23–36.

Wright EO (2015) *Understanding class.* Verso, London.

Appendix 1 – Timing of events

Monthly simulation phases

Founding phase

Households evaluate and initiate firm founding

Production phase

Firms demand estimation and pricing

Firms credit adjustment and production

Firms adapt prices

Sales and consumption phase

Government purchases products with low carbon intensity

Government calculates consumption subsidy base pre-consumption

Households check financial status

Households decide consumption budget

Households buy need goods

Households (capitalists) buy want goods

Households (workers) buy want goods

Households update need vendor lists

Households update want vendor lists

Households balance accounts with savings if indebted or declare bankruptcy

Wages payment phase

Firms pay wages

Government pays pensions

Government pays unemployment subsidies

Saving phase

Households transfer money to savings accounts

Interest and consolidation phase

Banks collect credit interest

Banks collect credit repayments

Banks calculate accounts interest

Banks calculate savings interest

Banks pay Central Bank loans interest

Banks pay Central Bank loans repayments

Firms' monthly accounting

Banks verify firms' solvency

Banks' monthly accounting

Banks calculate refinancing demands

Banks refinance at central bank

Banks transfer funds to facilities at central bank

Central banks pay reserve interest

Central banks pay deposit facilities interest

Government refinancing phase

Update macro indicators

Banks' monthly accounting

Central Bank's monthly accounting

Government monthly accounting

Country updates macro indicators

Annual simulation phases

Annual accounting phase

Banks collect and pay accounts interest

Banks pay savings interest

Firms calculate profits and pay taxes

Banks calculate profits and pay taxes

Firms distribute profits

Banks distribute profits

Capital goods firms distribute profits

Government updates annual statistics (annual taxes)

Country compiles annual report

Government checks minimum wage increase

Government increases unemployment subsidies if minimum wage increased

Government evaluates pension increase based on Consumer Price Index (CPI)

Firms evaluate wage increases based on CPI

Capital goods firm adapts prices based on CPI

Firms depreciate production capital

Appendix 2 – Technical details of the computational simulation

To implement the computational simulation of the presented model we chose the widely used Netlogo simulation environment (Wilensky, 1999), version 5.2, without any special Netlogo extensions.

The presented experiment was set up using Netlogo's built-in BehaviorSpace experiment management engine to repeat each scenario 30 times, each time using a different random seed to account for the random factors in the model. Aggregate time series data were generated directly by BehaviorSpace for each period, whereas micro-data were only saved for selected periods. Data analysis and visualization were realized using the R language (using the ggplot2 package).

The experiments were run with 6,000 households (3,000 per country), including workers, pensioners and capitalists, and started with an initial firm population of 300 firms (150 per country). Additionally the experiment included ten banks (five per country) and two rudimentary capital goods firms (one per country), two governments and a Central Bank. Other relevant simulation parameters are shown in Table 12.1.

Table 12.1 Main simulation parameters

Households	
Number of vendors on preferred lists	7
Number of regular replacement checks per month	1
Reserves of need consumption goods	1 period
Savings rate worker households	0.1
Savings rate wealthy worker households	0.15
Savings rate capitalist households	0.2
Initial savings endowment of worker households	$\gamma_1 * annualwage_{household}$ $\gamma_1 \sim U(1,2)$
Initial savings endowment of capitalist households	$10 * (initial\,minimumwage)$
Firms	
Initial ratio capital (individual firm level) to wages (annual)	2
Returns to scale (production function)	1
Production reserve stock rate	0.1
Unsold stock depreciation rate (per period)	0.5
Capital depreciation rate (annual)	0.1
Firm founding probability (monthly)	1/18
Banks	
Credit runtime	5 years
Credit interest rate (annual)	0.04
Account interest rate (annual)	0.01
Account overdraft rate (private credit, annual)	0.05
Savings interest rate (annual)	0.015
Central Bank deposit interest rate (annual)	0.01
Central Bank loans interest rate (annual)	0.02

Governments		
Initial minimum wage	1,000	
Initial unemployment subsidy	1,000	
Minimum wage increase minimal interval	5 years	
Employment protection duration	2 months	
Value-added tax rate	0.1	
Income tax rate (flat for all capitalist households)	0.15	
Corporate tax rate (banks, firms, capital goods firm)	0.15	
	Gov1	Gov2
Labour tax rate (flat for all worker households)	0.10	0.20
Capital gains tax rate	0.20	0.10

13 Agent-based simulations as an early-warning system for natural disasters[1]

Asjad Naqvi and Miriam Rehm

Introduction

In the summer of 2010, Pakistan was hit by the worst floods in its history. The floods directly affected 160,000 square kilometers of land area (20% of the total area) along the Indus river and its tributaries, and displaced around 20 million people (11% of the total population of 173 million in 2011: World Bank 2010b). Crop loss was estimated at US$ 500 million, with indirect losses as high as US$ 43 billion (26% of 2010 GDP, World Bank 2010b). The agrarian region around the Indus river, where low-income groups rely on subsistence farming, faced food shortages and rising food prices immediately after the floods. With minimal savings, virtually non-existent social safety nets, and a slow government response, a large proportion of the displaced population suffered secondary effects of the natural disaster, including food insecurity, starvation, and poor health conditions (World Bank 2010b). Despite international aid flows of around US$ 1.52 billion (UN-OCHA 2014), the lack of on-the-ground coordination, disruption of the food supply network, and poor understanding of shock transmission through population displacement resulted in an ineffective policy response.

This issue is not unique to Pakistan. From 1980 to 2011, low-income countries lost on average four times more of their gross domestic product (GDP) and suffered 16 times more deaths than high-income countries as a result of natural disasters, even though the incidence rates are comparable (Guha-Sapir et al. 2014). Studies show that important factors in the higher toll of disasters in low-income regions are the inability of the poorest groups to invest in prevention (Kahn 2005) and hedge against income disruptions (Carter et al. 2007; Naschold et al. 2011). A prompt and comprehensive emergency response is therefore essential in mitigating these losses, but relief work in these regions is often confronted with limited resources and a lack of data and information. In fact, poor responses in low-income regions have been widely documented in the aftermath of natural disasters (Amin and Goldstein 2008; Shen et al. 2010; IPCC 2012).

The economic literature on natural disasters amply discusses their *ex post* economic impact (Okuyama 2007; Toya and Skidmore 2007; Patnaik and Narayanan 2010; Cavallo and Noy 2011). While modeling frameworks that could be used for *ex ante* scenario analysis do exist, many are still limited in their ability to cope with the complex short-run adaptation processes after natural disasters. Cavallo and Noy (2011) note that the modeling of natural disasters suffers from two key shortcomings: first, existing models are ill equipped for an analysis of channels of causality that lead through the complex transition process to post-disaster outcomes. Second, due to the lack of detailed micro-level data, especially in disaster-prone low-income regions, the baseline information is weak. The combination can result in poor policy guidelines.

In order to demonstrate possible avenues for policy analysis in the face of these constraints, this chapter develops a multi-agent modeling framework that we term SHELscape – Simulation Hub for Economic Landscapes. SHELscape is an agent-based model (ABM) of a low-income agrarian region that aims at capturing short-run adjustment processes and secondary spatial spillover effects following disaster-like negative shocks. The decentralized, spatially explicit set-up is designed to analyze how shocks in one part of the environment spill over to the rest of the system. It also permits distributional analysis to identify vulnerable population groups.

The environment is divided into a rural, food-producing region and an urban, "other goods"-producing region (e.g., consumption goods such as clothes or services such as healthcare). All locations are connected through a road network. There are two agent categories, owners and workers. Individual agents' decisions are defined at the micro level. Six modules describe economic activity in the model: production, wage payment, buying, selling, consumption, and migration. Migration of workers and the supply decisions of firms drive wages and prices towards an equilibrium across locations over time.

The model is calibrated to a low-income region of rural agrarian Pakistan that faced severe floods in 2010. While the findings should be interpreted with caution and taken mainly as illustrative, results are broadly in line with empirical evidence from the 2010 floods in the Punjab. The model points to groups that may be vulnerable to negative outcomes such as displacement and starvation, and it traces possible transmission channels which lead to these outcomes. To demonstrate the use of the model as a policy tool, we then conduct two hypothetical policy scenarios, a food and a cash transfer scheme, and test their impact on consumption levels and food prices in the model. Our findings suggest that the cash transfer scheme raises incomes more, but the food transfer scheme has a greater impact on worker welfare if it succeeds in reducing monopoly rents of producers.

The chapter is organized as follows. The next section presents a literature review and a brief discussion of the methodology of computational modeling for natural disasters and briefly describes the model. This is followed by an outline of the calibration and validation of the model and the simulation, and the results. The next section presents policy experiments, followed by the conclusion.

Modeling natural disasters

Literature review

The literature modeling natural disasters focuses on estimating the impacts of natural disasters *ex ante* using input–output (IO) and computational general equilibrium (CGE) models. The simple structure of IO models based on a representation of the productive sector means that they are well equipped to capture regional as well as sectoral distributive effects. Early work thus provided sectoral assessments of direct and indirect effects of natural disasters from IO models (Dacy and Kunreuther 1969; Cochrane 1974; Rose 1981), while more refined representations focused on sectoral loss estimations (Gordon et al. 2004). A shortcoming of traditional IO models is the limited modeling of other sectors, such as households and the government, and their inability to factor in feedback effects on household behavior. While such feedback effects have been captured by recent CGE models (Rose et al. 2007), including incorporating some spatial dimensions (Ueda et al. 2001; Tsuchiya et al. 2007), their focus remains on long-run macroequilibrium with optimizing rational agents. While these are very useful tools to investigate the cases of zero and full adaptation by fully rational economic agents in response to a shock, little research has delved into the wide field of limited substitution between these two extremes, and gone beyond macroeconomic loss estimations. In short, the underlying shortcomings of these methodological approaches to short-run fluctuations have not been entirely overcome; heterogeneity, networks and non-linear feedback effects, and stock-flow consistency remain a challenge to models of natural disasters (Hallegatte 2014).

This chapter argues that multi-agent models extend the spectrum of tools for modeling natural disasters. ABMs have evolved from simple representation of agents following basic rules (Schelling 1978; Holland 1992; Miller and Page 2004) to simple representations of societies (Epstein and Axtell 1996; Gilbert and Terna 2000) to more advanced models that are constructed to replicate complex developed economies, some with a special focus on the financial sector (Lebaron 2002; Alfarano et al. 2008; Dosi et al. 2010; Raberto et al. 2012).

In contrast to ABMs of high-income economies and especially financial markets, low-income economies and particularly natural disaster economics have not received much attention in the literature. Important exceptions focusing on individual aspects of low-income economies include Dean et al. (2000), Angus et al. (2009), Kniveton et al. (2012), and Rehm (2012). However, comparatively little effort has been put into developing a comprehensive model of low-income economies with multiple and heterogeneous markets. While important insights can be gained from the work on high-income economies, the structure of an economy with a large agricultural sector needs to be represented differently. Furthermore, the focus of the analysis is guided by the lack of a functioning social security system: living standards and consumption need to be viewed from a more fundamental survival aspect of access to sufficient food, and as a consequence, how and whether consumption can be smoothed over the shock remains an important research question (Sen 1982; Morduch 1995; Kurosaki and Fafchamps 2002).

ABMs are uniquely well suited for capturing feedback effects, a key aspect of natural disasters. Agents facing highly non-linear environments make adaptive decisions based on their current settings, which may result in non-Pareto optimal choices. Furthermore, since shocks are localized, both their temporal and their spatial dispersion need to be tracked carefully. ABMs excel at dealing with true heterogeneity, and are thus very well suited for the analysis of distributions. Far from a representative agent approach, agent-based modeling makes it possible to generate stable distributions of income and consumption from homogenous agents ('statistical equilibria', see Foley 1994). Finally, simulating outcomes with ABMs makes it possible to provide counter-factual scenarios, run experiments, and provide distributions. It can therefore not only provide theoretical insights, but is suitable for policy analysis under resource and information constraints.

However, agent-based modeling also poses important challenges. On the one hand, the flexibility of ABMs substantially loosens the methodological constraints on the potential research questions compared to, for instance, analytical mathematical models. On the other hand, the discretion in formulating models places the burden of choosing appropriate restrictions for the model on the researcher. In particular for larger models this raises questions regarding the effects of individual assumptions and causality within models (Axtell 2000; Borrill and Tesfatsion 2011).

This chapter takes three hedging steps in formalizing the SHELscape economy to address the above concerns. First, behavioral rules are defined based on the economic literature on low-income economies and empirical evidence from disaster-affected regions. Second, parts of the model relevant to the focus of this chapter, such as consumption smoothing, are developed in more detail, while other aspects are kept to a minimum. Third, the model is calibrated to a flood-affected region in Pakistan and model results are validated using outcomes in the steady state before the 2010 floods.

An agent-based model of a low-income region

The model is set up as a circular-flow semi-closed economy.[2] The environment of the model is divided into two spatially defined location categories, *cities* and *villages*. These locations are interconnected through a road network. There are two agent categories, *owners* and *workers*, endowed with three assets, *labor*, *money*, and *goods*. *Capital* comprises the capital stock required for producing goods, such as land and machinery, and is held by owners. Goods owned by agents include the essential consumption good (food) produced in villages and the tradeable good (e.g., clothes or healthcare) produced in cities. Agent interactions take place at two levels: either within a location (village or city) or across locations (migration and goods exchange).

Production takes place on farm land in villages and in firms in cities, with owners aiming to maximize output in a first instance, and to maximize profits in a second step. Since the primary focus of this chapter is on rural areas and vulnerable populations, we focus the discussion here on large landholdings and landless day laborers. In the short run, land has a certain maximum possible production capacity. In low-income regions, part of the land held by owners is farmed by owners themselves, using their own labor. For the remaining land, owners hire labor at piece rates (Ray 1998; FBS 2010a).

The model aims to replicate a typical rural agrarian labor sector in South Asia. Since labor-saving technological progress has not yet advanced far, the agricultural sector is able to absorb the unskilled labor available in excess (Lewis 1954). This pushes wages towards subsistence levels (Baland et al. 1999; Hossain 2008). There is full employment in the model both because of workers' and employers' incentive structures. In the absence of public insurance mechanisms and social safety nets, workers are forced to search for work in order to sustain their consumption, pushing the implicit reservation wage to zero (Ray 1998). This simplifying assumption is the more appropriate, the more limited societal insurance mechanisms against income shortfalls are. On the other hand, owners maximize output, and have no reason to impose hiring limits. The cost of labor is assumed to be a piece rate, and the falling productivity associated with a larger number of workers on the same plot of land or in the same business drives workers' incomes down.

Agents buy food not just for immediate consumption, but they hold inventories of food – a few days' worth of supply, for instance – to smooth consumption over minor income shocks (Fafchamps et al. 1998; Chaudhuri and Paxson 2002). The decision to purchase food is determined by three parameters: a minimum consumption level which is a calorie-based consumption poverty line, the desired level of food stock agents wish to hold measured in number of days, and the marginal propensity to consume food out of income.

We model firm supply as profit maximization under constraints in a locally monopolistic environment and with limited information. That is, on the supply side firms first produce the maximum output, and then aim at maximizing profits given their output of goods by selling in the market that offers the highest price. On the demand side, individual agents' desired consumption interacts with their savings and market prices to generate local demand. Local goods markets are modeled as an applied adaptive *tâtonnement* process in the spirit of Albin and Foley (1992). Intra-regional trade makes prices gravitate around the reservation price. Local current prices are calculated as the ratio of past demand over past supply. Producers and consumers observe past market prices and adapt their supply and demand decisions accordingly, which leads to direct-feedback loops between supply and demand, and prices.

Wages are driven towards their equilibrium value in the model through worker mobility, analogous to the way trade roughly equilibrates prices. The decision to migrate of each worker depends on the joint probability distribution of real income differentials and distances, where the probability to migrate correlates positively with income, and negatively with distance.

Simulating natural disasters – a food production shock experiment

The model is programmed in NetLogo (Wilensky 1999) and calibrated to represent a stylized low-income region, the Punjab in Pakistan, which faced severe flooding in 2010 (see Introduction). The stylized layout of the region is shown in Figure 13.1. In the southern Punjab, about 75% of the population lives in rural areas, so the model is set up with nine villages and three cities. The road network is sparse; villages are only linked to the nearest city, but all cities are interconnected.

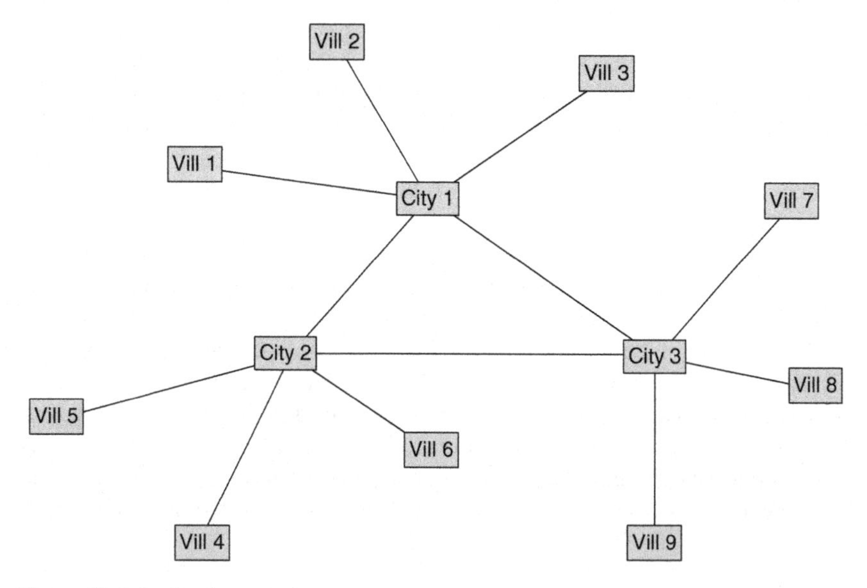

Figure 13.1 Stylized economy

Two central aspects of model calibration are units of time and output. Since the focus of the model is on the very short run, each time step in the model represents a day. Simulations are updated synchronously and 360 time steps represent a year. Furthermore, units of food in the model need to be transformed into empirically measurable quantities so that they can be empirically validated. Here, we use kilograms.

We calibrate parameters to empirical data as far as possible. Table 13.1 gives an overview of key parameter values used in the model.

The marginal propensity to consume food out of income is set to 90% and for other goods to 5%, in accordance with data from the Pakistan Household Expenditure Survey (FBS 2010b). In Pakistan, the average consumption per day is roughly 1.4 kg of food per day, and the average caloric intake is estimated to be about 2,410 kilocalories (FAO 2014). We thus define 1 kg of food as providing roughly 1,730 kcal. We also define this amount as the minimum consumption level, below which agents starve based on Food and Agriculture Organization minimum dietary energy requirements for Pakistan (FAO 2010). Finally, we assume that low-income groups hold 10 days' worth of food stock based on FBS (2010b), and that producers retain about 20% of production based on World Bank (2010a) and FAO (2013).

The initial value of some variables are defined so that important model outputs in the quasi-steady state conform to empirical values. Table 13.2 shows these initialized variables, and Table 13.3 shows that key model outputs are in line with empirical data. According to the Pakistan Agriculture Census of 2010 (FBS

2010a), the share of large land owners in the total population is about 5%, while laborers make up almost 95% of the population. As mentioned above, the population living in rural areas is about 75%. Total food production is estimated at 24 million tonnes in 2010 in Pakistan; divided by the total area of cultivated land of 8,000 square kilometers this gives about 3,000 tons of annual food production per square kilometer (FAO 2014), which translates to roughly 8 kg of food production per day per square kilometer. We thus implicitly assume that the size of landholdings in the model is about 1 square kilometer or 100 hectares. We set owners' capacity to self-produce output to about 1.6 kg, so that the remainder, roughly 80%, corresponds to the empirical value of the share of output produced by workers.

The average food price in 2010 was US$ 0.23 per kg of wheat, a level which is almost identically replicated by the model. The nominal income for rural workers is estimated at an average of US$ 0.22 per day (World Bank 2010b; Kurosaki and Fafchamps 2002), which is close to the model result of US$ 0.25 per day. Since we calibrated the marginal propensity to consume, the savings rate in the model is not far from its empirical value. Finally, in the quasi-steady state, households

Table 13.1 Parameter calibration

Parameter	*Variable*	*Value*	*Source*
Marginal propensity to consume food	$\bar{\alpha}_F$	0.9	FBS (2010b)
Marginal propensity to consume goods	$\bar{\alpha}_G$	0.05	FBS (2010b)
Minimum consumption	$\bar{C}_F$	1 kg (1730 kcal)	FAO (2010)
Days of food stock held*	δ_F	10	FBS (2010b)
Stock hoarded by owners*	$\bar{\beta}$	20%	World Bank (2010a); FAO (2013)

*Authors' assumptions based on referenced sources.

Table 13.2 Initial values of variables

Parameter	*Variable*	*Value*
Number of workers	Σi	1,000
Number of owners	Σh	60
Maximum daily land production capacity	$\bar{x}$	8 kg
Output self-produced by owners	$\bar{\upsilon}$	1.6 kg
Wage rate	λ	1

Table 13.3 Model outputs and empirical data

Variables	*Value*		*Source*
	Model*	Empirical	
Share of workers in population (%)	94.84 (0)	95	FBS (2010c)
Rural population share (%)	74.81 (0.145)	75	FBS (2010c)
Output produced by workers (%)	79.03 (0.43)	80	FAO (2013)
Average food price per unit (US$)	0.231 (0.0006)	0.23	World Bank (2010b)
Average daily income (US$)	0.254 (0.0006)	0.22	FBS (2010b, c)
Percentage income saved (%)	5.5 (0.129)	5	FBS (2010b)
Average daily food stock consumed (kg)	1.51 (0.0014)	1.38	FAO (2014)
Average daily food consumption (kcal)	2,611 (2.28)	2,423	FAO (2014)

* Standard error in brackets. Estimates are averages of ten model runs.

on average consume approximately 2,600 kcal, which is slightly higher than the empirical data of 2,410 kcal (Friedman et al. 2011; FAO 2014).

The 2010 floods in the Punjab are the natural disaster to which the shock in the model is calibrated. They resulted in a loss of food output up to 70% in the most vulnerable regions (World Bank 2010b). In the model, the natural disaster is thus captured as a 70% food production shock in each of the nine villages. Production recovers linearly starting 1 year after the shock; it takes 2 years for output to fully recover. Intuitively, this formulation corresponds to a flooding of farm land, the water receding slowly and land being brought back into production over time. While the season in which the floods occurred might make a difference due to crop cycles, we refrain from taking this aspect into account here since the Punjab produces two crops per year.

Baseline results

The shock propagates through the economy in the following way. First, the sharp decline in agricultural production capacity immediately reduces nominal incomes in villages as output per worker declines. This leads to a drop in consumption. At the same time, the decline in output means that the food supply to markets falls, causing prices to rise. These two effects trigger an adjustment process through the supply and migration procedures. Exports decline as owners increase their supply to the local market, and rising prices allow producers to sell in markets located at a greater distance. As real incomes fall in villages, village workers migrate to cities. This influx of workers in turn results in declining urban incomes, while on the other hand increasing the demand for food and thus further contributing to a rise in prices.

The top row of Figure 13.2 quantifies these effects of the natural disaster on the economy for income and consumption of an average worker, separated out by villages and cities. Income falls precipitously by about 60%, while food consumption also drops, but in a more gradual manner. That is because workers use the coping strategies available to them, essentially using up savings, to mitigate the impact of the natural disaster on their food intake. Nevertheless, average consumption falls well below the minimum consumption line for about half a year.

The next row of Figure 13.2 shows food prices and the percentage of the population living in the affected rural areas. Due to both supply and demand side effects, food prices rise by roughly 55%. The combination of falling incomes and rising prices leads to displacement – the share of the population living in rural areas falls by about 40%. The effects take almost 6 months to plateau due to the adjustment and feedback processes in the ABM, which are neither instantaneous nor non-existent. For the same reason, income and consumption take almost another year to return to their pre-crisis level after production has fully recovered.

Furthermore, the low incomes and high prices have a significant impact on the ability of agents to finance consumption. If income does not cover minimum consumption, agents start running down their savings. This effect is shown by the graphs in the third row of Figure 13.2. Consumption out of savings follows an inverted U-shaped curve: it first increases as income falls and prices rise, and then decreases again as savings run out. Finally, when savings are exhausted, agents fall below the minimum consumption line, as shown by the inverted U-curve of the share in the population that is starving. The comparison of these two graphs illustrates the time lag between consumption out of saving and starvation. Without policy intervention, eventually up to 85% of the landless worker population starve.

Finally, the last row of Figure 13.2 spells out the effects on savings in more detail. The typical worker is unable to save for almost a full year, since the cost of desired consumption is higher than income so workers run down their savings.

Consumption, savings, and starvation

Since the focus of this chapter is on vulnerable populations and starvation, this section explores the factors lying behind the shortfall in food consumption in more detail. The aggregates in Figure 13.2 hide both the dynamics underlying the overall outcome and substantial differences between groups. Distributional outcomes are important in the case of natural disasters. Even with homogeneous agents and productivity levels, the variation from probabilistic decision-making processes results in different levels of income and consumption patterns and thus different levels of vulnerabilities. The ABM points to potential pockets of vulnerabilities – spatially, temporally, and personally – and can thus provide indications for policy targeting.

Figure 13.3 shows the income and consumption distributions for workers in quintiles after the shock. Figure 13.3a demonstrates that the income of all quintiles falls in the aftermath of the natural disaster – no group is insulated from the economic shock. At the same time, prices rise, which increases the cost of the

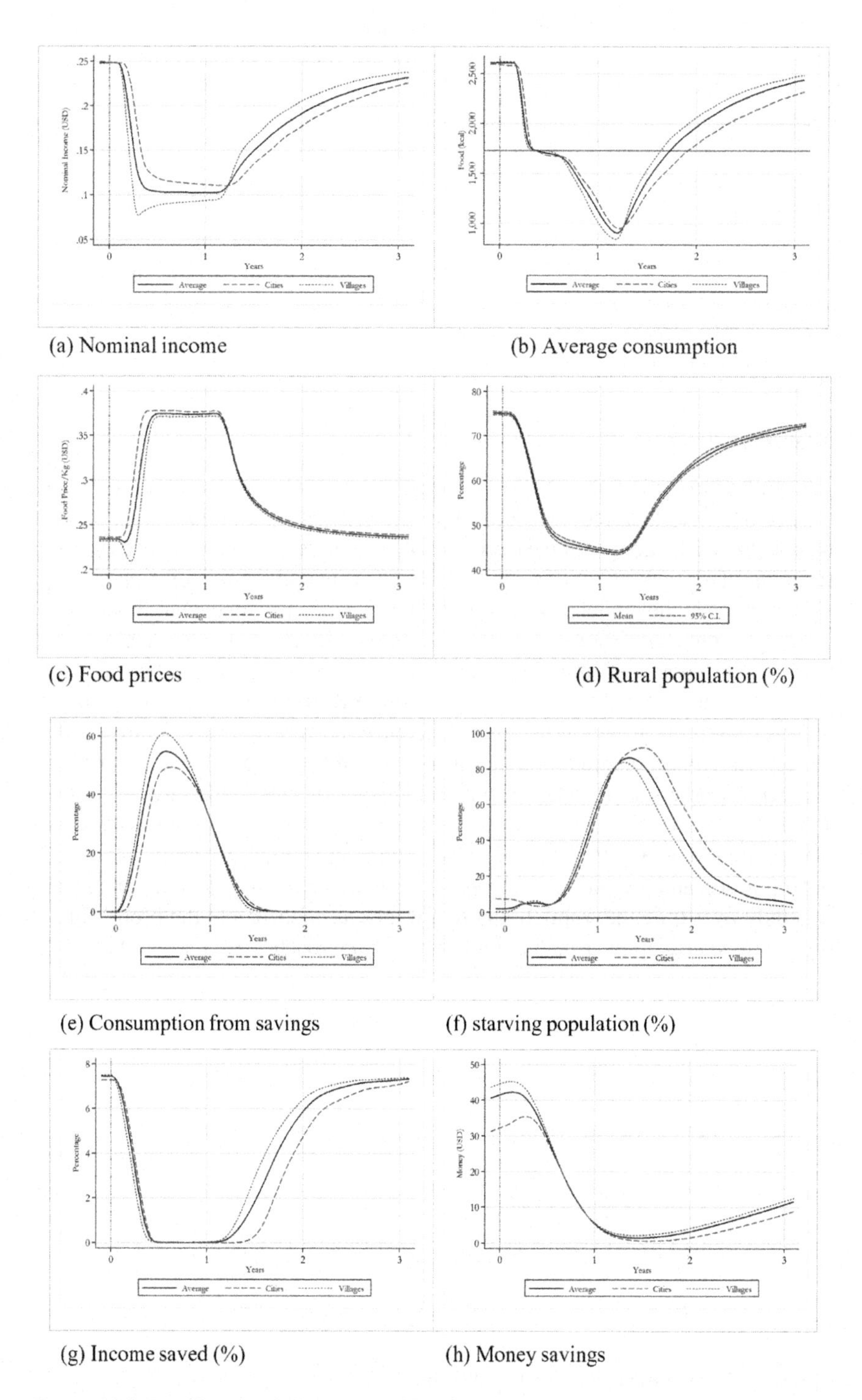

(a) Nominal income

(b) Average consumption

(c) Food prices

(d) Rural population (%)

(e) Consumption from savings

(f) starving population (%)

(g) Income saved (%)

(h) Money savings

Figure 13.2 Baseline simulations

minimum consumption bundle. As a consequence, all five income quintiles fall below the minimum consumption line within 6 months of the natural disaster. Workers in the model therefore resort to financing their consumption for survival out of savings.

Figure 13.3b demonstrates that this consumption out of savings allows all income groups to delay starvation. Only the highest-income quintile, however, is able to stave off starvation until the onset of recovery lifts incomes again. In the case of the second-income quintile, workers' savings allow them to hedge against the income shock for a full year. The next quintiles fall below the minimum consumption line faster. The bottom quintile starves about 7 months after the natural disaster. It takes the longest to recover, and its consumption after the recovery lies just barely above the minimum consumption line.

Migration effects

The main propagation mechanisms underlying these outcomes are migration, i.e., the geographical location decisions of workers, and the evolution of supply networks, that is, the geographical decisions of producers. This section discusses this secondary feedback effect of migration, the next section the one of supply.

Migration in the model primarily functions as a mechanism to equilibrate wages across geographical locations. However, since the adjustment to the natural disaster is not instantaneous, migration decisions can have consequences not intended by the workers: they also lead to a non-uniform distribution of income. Workers migrate based on information about differences in real incomes, and once they reach their new destination, find the employer offering the highest wage. A higher number of workers at any one owner results in lower wages at this particular owner. This in turn pushes down the average real income for that location. This is how secondary migration effects arise: the workers once again look for other employment opportunities, and they sometimes find them in the region they just migrated from. It is only over time that rural–urban real wages normalize, and the probability of finding another employer paying higher wages approaches zero. Even though the

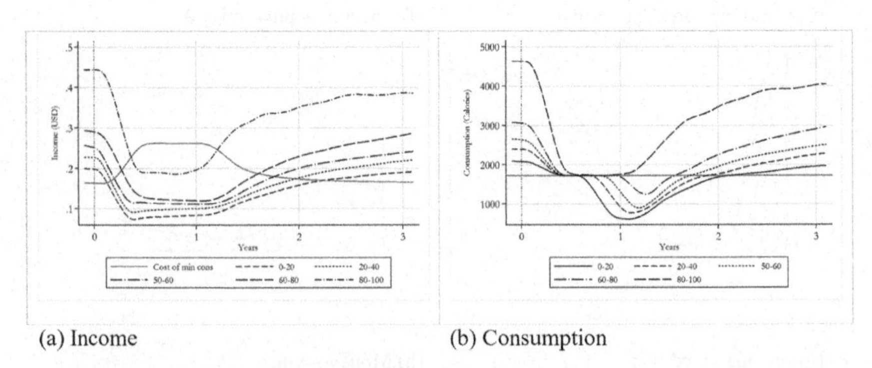

(a) Income (b) Consumption

Figure 13.3 Income and consumption distributions

model is set up with homogeneous agents within the two groups, workers and owners, due to this probabilistic decision-making process and the second-round effects of migration, wages are non-uniform. The resulting statistical equilibrium gives rise to the distributions described in the section on consumption, savings, and starvation, above. This section investigates the migration flows at a more disaggregated level in order to dissect the second-order effects.

Figure 13.4 shows that the migration rate peaks at over 4% of the total worker population about 4 months after the natural disaster. As shown in Figure 13.4, this decreases the share of the population living in rural areas roughly from 75% to 45%. The natural disaster thus induces a major demographic shift in the regional economy as 30% of the total population in the region under study is displaced. When the rural economy recovers, the aggregate migration rate declines and the migration pattern reverses.

These overall urbanization trends obscure non-trivial underlying flows. Figure 13.4 graphs the flows (as a share of total population) for the four possible directions of migration between villages and cities; in a sense, it illustrates the transition matrix between these two possible states. It shows that there are non-negligible inter-regional migration trends besides the dominant rural–urban pattern. The root cause of these migration flows lies in the income incentive structure and the interaction of relative incomes and migration.

The immediate effect of the natural disaster is a large movement of landless workers from the affected villages to cities in the immediate aftermath of the floods because of rapidly declining relative incomes in rural areas. At the same time, parallel to this major tendency, non-negligible secondary migration patterns emerge. Due to overshooting in migration during the first migration wave, the push to urban

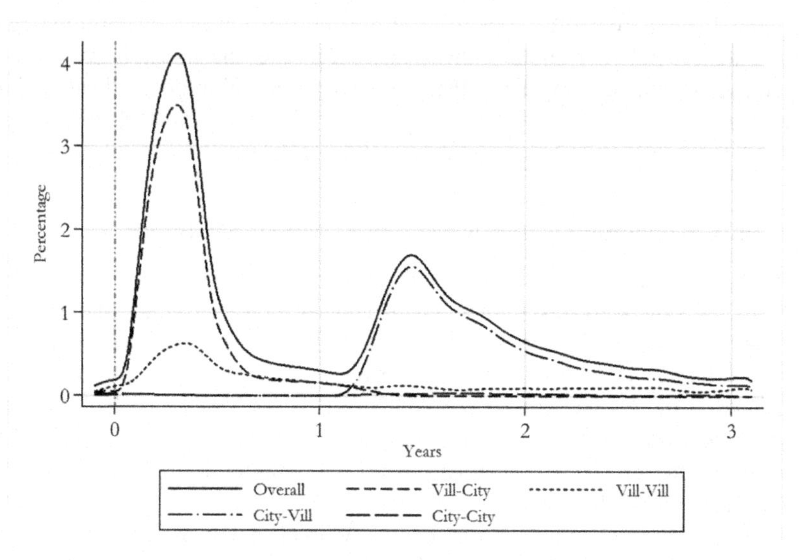

Figure 13.4 Migration transitions

areas creates opportunities in rural areas, where village-to-village migration rises. Similarly, post-recovery we observe minor inter-village and inter-city migration. These take place because the push of a large group of workers into one region creates opportunities in their region of origin; there is over- and undershooting of wages in all locations, until wages settle down around a new quasi-equilibrium.

These migration flows can be visualized spatially in the nine-village, three-city set-up of the model. Before the shock, the model shows the expected pattern – workers mostly migrate to the nearest city for work, with very minor inter-regional migration. After the shock, there is a surge in migration. While the dominant pattern is still rural to urban migration, the severity of the shock leads to high wage differentials and overshooting of migration. This results in multiple migration options, causing the migration network to become denser. Migration thus plays an important role in transmitting the shock from one part of the regional economy across the entire system through its effect on real income.

Supply

This section explores the evolution of supply networks, which equilibrate prices across the region. After the shock, prices increase substantially, as described above. An immediate effect is that supply is diverted from exports to local markets as owners can earn higher profits there. Even though income levels fall, workers tap into savings and migrate, i.e., engage in any coping strategy available to them in order to stave off starvation, so that demand does not plummet as dramatically as incomes do. As a result of the rising prices, suppliers who previously could not sell in local markets because their costs were higher than regional market prices are now entering the local market.

Regarding the evolution of selling networks, before the shock, villages closest to cities benefit from their proximity in the form of lower transportation costs, crowding out sellers from more distant villages. After the shock, however, a fall in output accompanied by a less than commensurate fall in demand causes local market prices to rise. The adjustment processes following the natural disaster give owners in all villages the opportunity to sell in urban markets.

A policy experiment – food versus cash transfer schemes

This section gives an example of how possible policy responses to the natural disaster can be simulated and compared with a non-response baseline counter-factual scenario. The two main policy options discussed intensively in the literature are cash versus in-kind transfer schemes (for reviews see, for example, Dercon and Krishnan 2003; Currie and Firouz 2008). We thus demonstrate here how two hypothetical transfer programs that aim to mitigate the negative impact of the natural disaster on starving populations by providing cash or in-kind assistance can be analyzed in the model.

First, a direct cash transfer program gives workers below the consumption poverty line sufficient income to cover the minimum consumption bundle. Second, a food transfer program buys food from local producers at local market prices and transfers it to starving agents in order to raise their consumption above the minimum consumption level. In effect, this program purchases food from the inventories of owners and thus works as though owners had reduced their stockpiling. In the case of both policies, we assume that these injections are exogenous, such as aid provided by the central government or international agencies, that they are initiated immediately after that shock, and that starving agents receive the full value of the minimum consumption level in cash or in kind. While we make the last assumption for simplicity, relief work in natural disasters does face difficulties in establishing vulnerability due to information asymmetry, incentives to overstate neediness, and high monitoring costs (Zaidi et al. 2008).

The two policies thus take different routes by which they mitigate the effects of the natural disaster. The cash program injects money into the regional system, while the food transfer program has a more fundamental effect on the economic structure. It should be emphasized that these are highly stylized policy interventions, and that at best they can point in the general direction of possible effects.

Figure 13.5 shows consumption in the baseline scenario with no intervention, and for the two policy schemes. Both policy interventions are clearly effective in preventing starvation compared to the baseline scenario.

However, they differ markedly in other model outputs. Figure 13.6 shows the impact of the two programs on real income (Figure 13.6a) and prices (Figure 13.6b), again relative to the baseline scenario. While both transfer

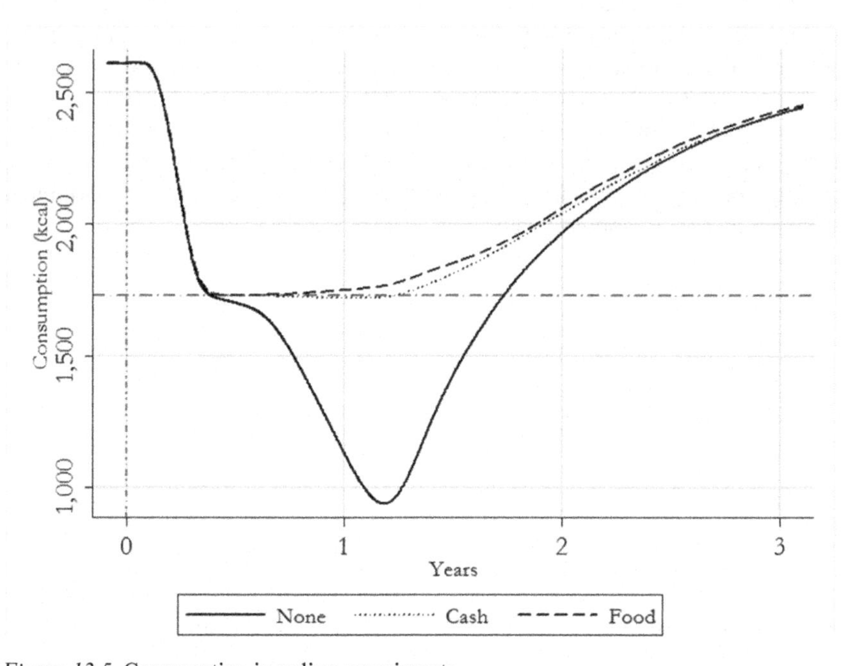

Figure 13.5 Consumption in policy experiments

programs prevent income from dropping as low as in the baseline case, the recovery in the cash transfer program which directly provides income is, unsurprisingly, more rapid and sustained than in the food transfer program.

On the other hand, the food transfer scheme has an interesting impact on prices. As mentioned above, by purchasing additional food stock directly from owners, the government implicitly reduces their hoarding. By reducing demand and increasing supply, this has the effect of pushing down prices across the whole region, which raises average real income in the food transfer scheme. This price effect of in-kind transfers is corroborated by empirical evidence (IFAD 2011).

As a consequence, the two schemes differ in their impact on savings and wealth (Figure 13.7). The cash transfer scheme allows some of the recipient workers to save part of their income. The closer a worker was to the minimum consumption line before the transfer, the more the cash program allows them to save. On the other hand, the food transfer program reduces the cost of the consumption bundle for all workers, thus allowing them to spend less on food items and save more. The higher savings rate under the food transfer program spurs the growth of wealth, and leads to a higher trajectory of money wealth for the average worker. However, it should be noted that, while the savings rates might be high, the savings of workers in absolute terms remain low in the case of the food transfer policy, as well.

The two schemes have different impacts on the distribution of consumption and income. Compared to the baseline scenario, both cash and food transfer schemes substantially reduce consumption inequality (Figure 13.8). That is because the policies are set up to effectively eradicate starvation in the population after the disaster. With the natural disaster pushing the consumption of better-off workers towards the minimum consumption level, and the program successfully lifting workers out of starvation to the minimum consumption level, the Gini coefficient becomes very low. However, it is important to note here that, while consumption inequality is almost negligible in the two transfer schemes, the average consumption level remains near the minimum consumption line, as shown in Figure 13.8a. As the economy recovers, inequality increases due to improving job opportunities from which not all workers profit.

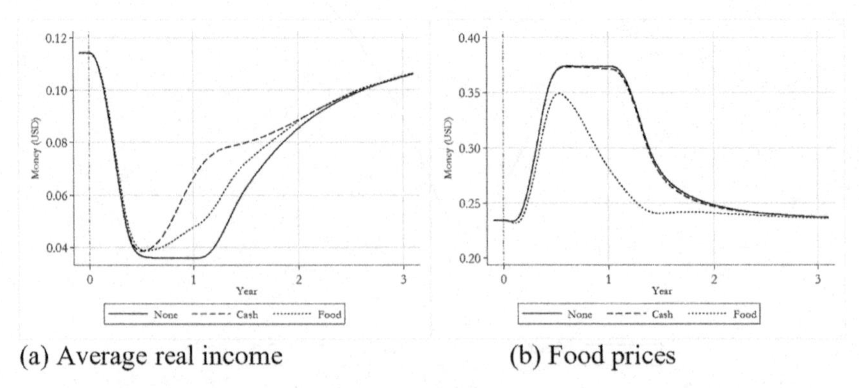

(a) Average real income

(b) Food prices

Figure 13.6 Income and prices in policy experiments

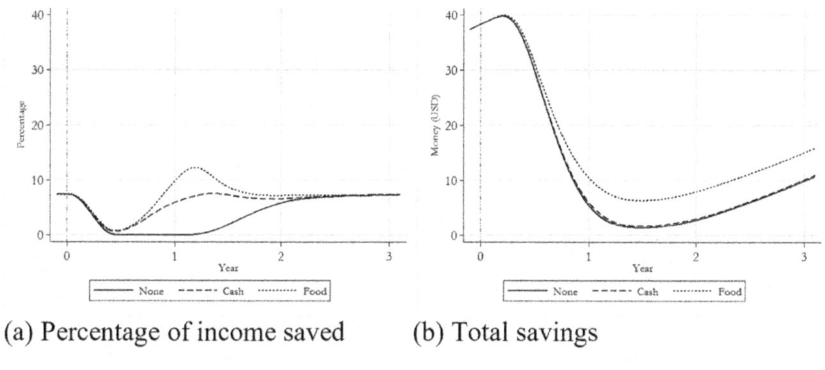

(a) Percentage of income saved (b) Total savings

Figure 13.7 Savings and wealth

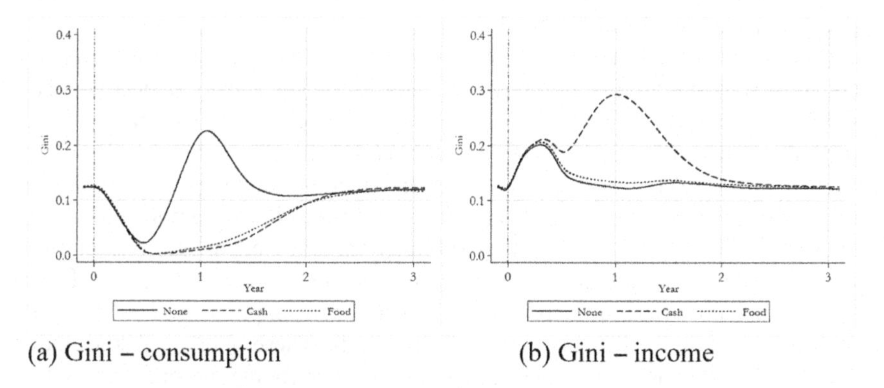

(a) Gini – consumption (b) Gini – income

Figure 13.8 Income and consumption inequality

On the other hand, the income transfer scheme results in a sharp rise in income inequality (Figure 13.8b). This is a result of the way the scheme is formulated: The income in the targeted population rises, while those just above the minimum consumption stay at relatively low income levels. A more differentiated policy which supplements income could alleviate this problem; however we leave a detailed exploration for future research.

Conclusions

This chapter develops, calibrates, and tests policies in a multi-agent model, SHELscape, of a low-income region in order to investigate the impact of natural disasters. It makes several contributions to the modeling of disaster-prone regions. First, it presents a model of low-income regions. Low-income countries face substantially higher losses both of human lives and of GDP than high-income countries following natural disasters despite comparable incidence rates. This disparity is fueled by inadequate social security systems in low-income regions and poor policy responses. The model is set up to capture the essence of low-income regions, such as a large agricultural sector which acts as an employer of last resort, locally monopolistic competition of producers, and a large population of landless workers.

Second, the model comprises decentralized markets, which are integrated into a full economy model with goods and labor markets. It thus goes beyond partial equilibrium analysis to allow for a comprehensive assessment of the various channels in which natural disasters affect the local economy. The model is also defined spatially explicitly, which makes it possible to incorporate distances in decision-making processes and to visualize population displacement.

Third, the model is geared towards analyzing short-run adjustment processes. These highly non-linear transitions are the defining feature of economies in the aftermath of natural disasters. The asynchronous nature of the adaptation to the natural disaster at the individual level gives rise to distributions and vulnerable populations, which the model tracks.

The focus of the chapter is on these landless low-income groups ("workers") and their consumption-smoothing strategies following a natural disaster. The mechanisms which we explore in more detail in this chapter are migration, holding buffer stocks of food, and running down cash savings.

The model is set up with two agent groups (workers and owners) that produce two goods (a consumption good and a tradeable good) in two regions (urban cities and rural villages). Six modules (production, wage payment, consumption, buying, selling, and migration) describe the behavioral rules. Selling their labor, workers acquire money to purchase the essential consumption good, while owners receive labor for the production of the goods. These goods are sold under locally monopolistic competition, generating revenue for the owners. Agents aim to smooth consumption by holding buffer stocks of the consumption good and by consuming out of savings. Migration and supply decisions equilibrate wages and prices, respectively, across the region.

The model is calibrated and validated to the Punjab, a low-income region in Pakistan that was hit by floods in 2010. In the model, the natural disaster is thus captured as a 70% food production shock in rural areas. The shock propagates through the economy in the following way. First, the sharp decline in agricultural production capacity immediately reduces nominal incomes in villages as output per worker declines. At the same time, the decline in output means that the food supply to markets falls, causing prices to rise. This double whammy to real incomes of workers triggers migration waves from villages to cities. The influx of workers in cities in turn results in declining urban incomes, while on the other hand increasing the demand for food and thus further contributing to a rise in prices. The upshot is a stark increase in starvation levels in the population.

Workers' coping strategies, i.e., using up savings and migrating for work, lead to consumption levels dropping more slowly than income levels. Yet, the results for different groups of workers show that, while all income quintiles are hit by the shock, the top quintile is able to hedge against the shock. In contrast, the lowest-income quintile suffers from starvation first, takes the longest to recuperate, and its income and consumption do not fully recover to pre-shock levels.

The dynamic processes underlying these results include feedback effects of migration and supply decisions motivated by wage and price differentials. The adaptive decision making of individuals can lead to over- and undershooting, and it not only generates spillover effects in regions not affected by the disaster, but also minor secondary effects like village-to-village and return migration.

To demonstrate the use of the model, we conducted a policy experiment. We compared a zero-relief baseline scenario to two possible policy programs, a food and a cash transfer scheme. While the policies are highly simplified and our findings should be taken as illustrative, some basic insights can be gleaned from this exercise. Both schemes are effective in reducing starvation rates and consumption inequality; however they differ in the routes by which this is achieved. The cash transfer scheme boosts purchasing power through direct income transfers, resulting in higher incomes, but also a significantly higher level of income inequality. The latter is partly due to the policy formulation. The food transfer scheme, on the other hand, has a region-wide price effect through its reduction of hoarding among producers, and therefore indirectly benefits broad population groups. It thus raises the savings rate, albeit minimally in absolute levels.

These findings naturally lend themselves to policy conclusions. Since our results indicate that feedback effects and failing coping strategies are important for the inequality and poverty following the natural disaster, a timely policy response is crucial for mitigating its effects. Furthermore, policies targeted at vulnerable population groups can go a long way towards reducing the harshest effects of natural disasters. The modeling framework presented in this paper may possibly improve both on the reaction time and the targeting of economic first responders after a large shock. It probabilistically predicts population flows, and points to potential vulnerable groups, supply shortages, and price spikes close to real time, updating at little time and resource cost as information becomes available. However, given the assumptions required in modeling, results should not be interpreted too confidently.

An important avenue for future work is an expansion of the types of shocks. Varying the exogenous shock to include loss of human life, disruption of road networks, and destruction of capital would be a first step. Furthermore, since agent-based modeling lends itself to endogenous shocks, the analysis of slow-onset natural disasters such as climate change is an obvious extension. Refining the consumption-smoothing mechanisms in the model further, for instance by introducing credit markets, could also be a fruitful direction for future research. Finally, the framework can be easily calibrated to Geographical Information System (GIS) data, which would be a natural next step in making the model more readily applicable to real-world policy processes.

Notes

1 An earlier version of this article appeared as Naqvi, A. and Rehm, M.,A multi-agent model of a low-income economy: Simulating the distributional effects of natural disasters. *Journal of Economic Interaction and Coordination*, 9, 2, (2014), pp. 275–309. This paper has been republished with permission of Springer.

2 For a precise and more formal description of the model, see Naqvi and Rehm (2014).

References

Albin, Peter and Duncan Foley, "Decentralized, Dispersed Exchange Without an Auctioneer: A Simulation Study", *Journal of Economic Behavior and Organization* 18(1992), pp. 27–51.

Alfarano, Simone, Lux Thomas and Wagner Friedrich, "Time Variation of Higher Moments in a Financial Market with Heterogeneous Agents: An Analytical Approach", *Journal of Economic Dynamics and Control* 32, 1(2008), pp. 101–136.

Amin, Samia and Markus Goldstein, *Data against Natural Disasters: Establishing Effective Systems for Relief, Recovery and Reconstruction* (Washington, D.C.: The World Bank, 2008).

Angus, D., Brett Parris and B. Hassani-M., "Climate Change Impacts and Adaptation in Bangladesh: An Agent-Based Approach", *18th World IMACS / MODSIM Congress, Cairns, Australia* (2009).

Axtell, Robert, "Why Agents? On the Varied Motivations for Agent Computing in the Social Sciences", Washington, D.C.: Center on Social and Economic Dynamics, Brookings Institute Working Paper No. 17(2000).

Baland, Jean-Marie, Dreze Jean and Leruth Luc, "Daily Wages and Piece Rates in Agrarian Economies", *Journal of Development Economics* 59, 2(1999), pp. 445–461.

Borrill, Paul L. and Tesfatsion, Leigh S. "Agent-Based Modeling: The Right Mathematics for the Social Sciences?", in: Davis, John B. and Hands, D. Wade, eds., *Elgar Companion to Recent Economic Methodology* (Edward Elgar Publishers, Cheltenham, UK, 2011).

Carter, Michael R., Little Peter D., Mogues Tewodaj, Negatu Workneh, "Poverty Traps and Natural Disasters in Ethiopia and Honduras", *World Development* 35, 5(2007), pp. 835–856.

Cavallo, Eduardo and Ilan Noy, "The Economics of Natural Disasters: A Survey", *International Review of Environmental and Resource Economics* 5 (2011), pp. 63–102.

Chaudhuri, Shubham and Paxson Christina, "Smoothing Consumption under Income Seasonality: Buffer Stocks Vs. Credit Markets", Discussion Paper (Columbia University, Department of Economics, New York, 2002).

Cochrane, Harold C., "Predicting the Economic Impact of Earthquakes", in Cochrane, Harold C., Haas, J. Eugene, Bowden, Martyn J. and Kates, Robert W., eds., *Social Science Perspectives on the Coming San Francisco Earthquakes: Economic Impact, Prediction, and Reconstruction* (Boulder, CO, 1974), pp. 1–42.

Currie, Janet and Gahvari Firouz, "Transfers in Cash and In-Kind: Theory Meets the Data", *Journal of Economic Literature* 46, 2(2008), pp. 333–383.

Dacy, Douglas C. and Kunreuther Howard, *The Economics of Natural Disasters* (New York: The Free Press, 1969).

Dean, Jeffrey S., Gumerman George J., Epstein Joshua M., Axtell Robert L., Swedlund Alan C. and Parker Miles . . ., *Understanding Anasazi Culture Change Through Agent-Based Modeling* (Oxford: Oxford University Press, 2000), pp. 179–205.

Dercon, Stefan and Krishnan Pramila, *Food Aid and Informal Insurance* (World Institute for Development Economic Research (UNU-WIDER, Helsinki, Finland, 2003).

Dosi, Giovanni, Fagiolo Giorgio and Roventini Andrea, "Schumpeter Meeting Keynes: A Policy-Friendly Model of Endogenous Growth and Business Cycles", *Journal of Economic Dynamics and Control* 34, 9(2010), pp.1748–1767.

Epstein, Joshua and Robert Axtell, *Growing Artificial Societies: Social Sciences from the Bottom Up* (Cambridge, MA: MIT Press, 1996).

Fafchamps, Marcel, Udry Christopher and Czukas Katherine, "Drought and Saving in West Africa: Are Livestock a Buffer Stock?", *Journal of Development Economics* 55, 2(1998), pp. 273–305.

FAO, *Minimum Dietary Energy Requirement* (FAO, Rome, Italy, 2010).

FAO, *Pakistan: Review of the Wheat Sector and Grain Storage Issues* (Food and Agriculture Organization (FAO), World Bank, Islamabad, Pakistan, 2013).

FAO, *Food and Agriculture Organization Statistical Database* (FAO, Rome, Italy, 2014).

FBS, *Agriculture Census* (Government of Pakistan: Federal Bureau of Statistics, Islamabad, Pakistan, 2010a).

FBS, *Household Integrated Economic Survey* (Government of Pakistan: Federal Bureau of Statistics, Islamabad, Pakistan, 2010b).

FBS, *Labor Force Survey* (Government of Pakistan: Federal Bureau of Statistics, Islamabad, Pakistan, 2010c).

Foley, Duncan K., "A Statistical Equilibrium Theory of Markets", *Journal of Economic Theory* 62, 2(1994), pp. 321–345.

Friedman, Jed, Hong Seo Yeon and Hou Xiaohui, "The Impact of the Food Price Crisis on Consumption and Caloric Availability in Pakistan: Evidence from Repeated Cross-Section.", *World Bank Health, Nutrition and Population (HNP) discussion paper no. 66305.* (World Bank, Washington, D.C., USA, 2011).

Gilbert, N. and P. Terna, "How to Build and Use Agent-Based Models in Social Sciences", *Mind and Society* 1, 1(2000), pp. 57–72.

Gordon, Peter, Moore II James E., Richardson Harry W., Shinozuka Masanobu, An Donghwan and Cho Sungbin, "Earthquake Disaster Mitigation for Urban Transportation Systems: An Integrated Methodology that Builds on the Kobe and Northr . . .", in Okuyama, Yasuhido and Chang, Stephanie E., eds., *Modeling Spatial and Economic Impacts of Disasters* (New York: Springer, 2004), pp. 205–232.

Guha-Sapir, D., Below R. and Hoyois Ph. EM-DAT, *The OFDA/CRED International Disaster Database*. www.emdat.be. (Université Catholique de Louvain. Brussels, Belgium, 2014).

Hallegatte, Stéphane, "Modeling the Role of Inventories and Heterogeneity in the Assessment of the Economic Costs of Natural Disasters", *Risk Analysis* 34, 1(2014), pp. 152–167.

Holland, John H., *Adaptation in Natural and Artificial Systems: An Introductory Analysis with Applications to Biology, Control, and Artificial . . .* (Cambridge, MA: The MIT Press, 1992).

Hossain, Akhand Akhtar, "Rural Labour Market Developments, Agricultural Productivity, and Real Wages in Bangladesh, 1950–2006", *The Pakistan Development Review* 47, 1(2008), pp. 89–114.

IFAD, "Rural Poverty Report 2011" (International Fund for Agriculture Development Policy Report, Rome, Italy, 2011).

IPCC, *Managing the Risks of Extreme Events and Disasters to Advance Climate Change Adaptation* (New York, NY: Cambridge University Press, 2012).

Kahn, Matthew E., "The Death Toll from Natural Disasters: The Role of Income, Geography and Institutions", *Review of Economics and Statistics* 87, 2(2005), pp. 271–284.

Kniveton, Dominic R., Smith Christopher D. and Black Richard, "Emerging Migration Flows in a Changing Climate in Dryland Africa", *Nature Climate Change* 2, 6(2012), pp. 444–447.

Kurosaki, Takashi and Fafchamps, Marcel,"Insurance Market Efficiency and Crop Choices in Pakistan", *Journal of Development Economics* (2002), pp. 419–453.

Lebaron, Blake, "Building the Santa Fe Artificial Stock Market", (Brandeis University, Waltham, MA, USA, 2002), pp. 1117–1147.

Lewis, William A., "Economic Development with Unlimited Supplies of Labour", *Manchester School of Economic and Social Studies* 22(1954), pp. 139–191.

Miller, John H. and Page Scott E., "The Standing Ovation Problem", *Complexity* 9(2004), pp. 8–16.

Morduch, Jonathan, "Income Smoothing and Consumption Smoothing", *Journal of Economic Perspectives* 9, 3(1995), pp. 103–114.

Naschold, Felix, Walker Thomas F., Barrett Christopher B. and Osei Robert, "Idiosyncratic Shocks, Risk Management and Welfare Dynamics in Rural Ghana", *The Agricultural and Applied Economics Association Annual Meeting* (Agricultural and Applied Economics Association, Pittsburgh, PA, USA, 2011).

Naqvi, A. and Rehm, M. A multi-agent model of a low income economy: Simulating the distributional effects of natural disasters. *Journal of Economic Interaction and Coordination*, 9, 2(2014), pp. 275–309.Okuyama, Yasuhido, "Economic Modeling for Disaster Impact Analysis: Past, Present, and Future", *Economic Systems Research* 19, 2(2007), pp. 115–124.

Patnaik, Unmesh and Narayanan K, "Vulnerability and Coping to Disasters: A Study of Household Behaviour in Flood Prone Region of India"(Munich: University Library of Munich, 2010).

Raberto, Marco, Teglio Andrea and Cincotti Silvano, "Debt, Deleveraging and Business Cycles: An Agent-Based Perspective", *Economics: The Open-Access, Open-Assessment E-Journal* 6, 27(2012), pp. 1–49.

Ray, Debraj, *Development Economics* (Princeton University Press, Princeton, 1998).

Rehm, Miriam, "Migration and Remittances: An Agent-Based Model", Working paper 1307 (Department of Economics, New School for Social Reasearch, New York, USA, 2012).

Rose, Adam, "Utility Lifelines and Economic Activity in the Context of Earthquakes", in Isenberg, Jeremy, ed., *Social and Economic Impacts of Earthquakes on Utility Lifelines* (New York: American Society of Civil Engineers, Construction Division, 1981), pp. 107–120.

Rose, Adam, Oladuso Gbadebo and Liao Shu-Yi, "Business Interruption Impacts of a Terrorist Atttack on the Electric Power System of Los Angeles: Customer Resilience to a To . . .", *Risk Analysis* 27, 3(2007), pp. 513–531.

Schelling, Thomas, *Micromotives and Macrobehavior* (New York: W. W. Norton, 1978).

Sen, Amartya, *Poverty and Famines: An Essay on Entitlement and Deprivation* (Oxford: Oxford University Press, 1982).

Shen, Xiaomeng, Downing Thomas E. and Hamza Mohamed, "Tipping Points in Humanitarian Crisis: From Hot Spots to Hot Systems", *UNU-EHS SOURCE 13*(UNU, Bonn, Germany, 2010).

Toya, Hideki and Mark Skidmore, "Economic Development and the Impacts of Natural Disasters", *Economics Letters* 94, 1(2007), pp. 20–25.

Tsuchiya, Satoshi, Tatano Hirokazu and Okada Norio, "Economic Loss Assessment due to Railroad and Highway Disruptions", *Economic Systems Research* 19, 2(2007), pp. 147–162.

Ueda, Takayuki, Koike Atsushi and Iwakami Kazuki, "Economic Damage Assessment of Catastrophes in High Speed Rail Network", http://www.drs.dpri.kyoto-u.ac.jp/us-japan/cd-1/TakaUeda.pdf, Working Paper Kyoto University (Kyoto University, Kyoto, Japan, 2001), pp. 13–19.

UN-OCHA, "Pakistan Floods 2010: Total Humanitarian Assistance per Donor as of May 2014" (UN-OCHA, Islamabad, Pakistan, 2014).

Wilensky, Uri, "NetLogo", *Center for Connected Learning and Computer-Based Modeling. Northwestern University, Evanston, IL.* http://ccl.northwestern.edu/netlogo (1999).

World Bank, *Food Price Increases in South Asia. National Responses and Regional Dimensions* (The World Bank, South Asia Region, Sustainable Development Department, Agriculture and Rural Development Unit, Washington, D.C., USA, 2010a).

World Bank, *Pakistan Floods 2010: Preliminary Damage and Needs Assessment* (World Bank, Asian Development Bank, Government of Pakistan, Washington, D.C., USA, 2010b).

Zaidi, Sarah, Ahsan Kamal, M. A. Ishaque, Hamza Khalil, Ayesha Sehgol, Nishat Shafi and Zara Sharif, *Ruins to Recovery* (Lahore, Pakistan: Lahore University of Management Sciences, 2008).

14 Dealing adequately with the political element in formal modelling

Claudius Gräbner

Introduction

Paul Samuelson once said that he doesn't care who writes a nation's laws, if only he could write its textbooks. This illustrates very well the importance of economics in the public discourse and its political relevance. In contrast to classical economists such as Adam Smith, most economists today usually claim that their science is not normative *per se*, but that there exists a clear distinction between positive and normative economics.

This has an important effect on the role played by economists and their models in the public discourse. Economists are often perceived (and present themselves) as scientists using models that help to understand the world as it is and which do not contain any implicit normative elements. And if economists make explicitly normative statements, these are usually said to rest on sound positive theoretical foundations. For example, if one considers the actual discussions about the Transatlantic Trade and Investment Partnership (TTIP), economists influenced both the public debate and the political decision makers with their reports. The way these reports are written suggests that they apply objective measures to assess the economic impact of the free-trade agreement and that their (normative) suggestion to implement TTIP is based on sound, positive, state-of-the-art measures which do not carry any normative content on their own. But is this view adequate?

This chapter shows that the idea of positive economics is an idealistic, but wrong, conception of science that has been abandoned by much of the social science at the latest at the beginning of the 20th century, but experienced a revival in economics during the last decades. We will study the arguments underlying this development and show the relevance of acknowledging the normative element in economic modelling. By this we will make clear that the quality, reliability and societal usefulness of economic theory can be increased if economists understand the inevitability of normative elements in economic modelling and draw adequate conclusions.

The rest of this chapter is structured as follows: the next section presents theoretical arguments on whether a value-free science of economics can exist and how methodological innovations in the 21st century had an influence on this question. This is followed by an introduction to a framework that shows how formal models can get epistemic meaningfulness, what the different components of a model are and how this relates to the question of positive economic modelling. Subsequently we discuss whether more data-oriented research practice can lead to more positive economics, followed by an application of the theoretical arguments to the current debate about TTIP. Finally the chapter is summarized and conclusions are drawn.

The inevitability of a normative element in economic theory

To what extent can science in general and social science in particular be *value-free* or *positive?* In economics one usually uses the two terms as nearly interchangeable: whenever a theory describes 'what is', it is called *positive.* Whenever the theory describes 'what should be', it is called normative. This dichotomic taxonomy clearly suggests that 'positive' economics has nothing to do with 'normative' judgements, i.e. is value-free, or objective. But how this distinction is to be made in practice is not always clear: is the basic model of perfect competition part of positive or normative economics? It is not particularly concerned with the question of 'what should be done', but its (empirically dubious) assumptions imply the conclusions that any taxes yield a particular 'deadweight loss'. Even if the scepticism against government intervention and the principal optimism towards the market mechanism are not articulated explicitly, it is hard to believe that such a model does not carry normative elements. But here I will not deal with the particular case of the theory of perfect competition – I will rather consider economic theory in general.

But before, recall that the fact of whether a theory can be considered positive (in the sense of *not normative*) has important *political* relevance: value-free results can be expected to play a particularly strong role in public and political discourse. Normative results are always scrutinized more thoroughly because people explicitly question the normative axioms of the results – a potential source of refusal (both in political and scientific debate). In this sense, the question of whether social science can produce *positive* results has immediate consequences for its place in the public political discourse and the way it shapes this discourse. Later, I will consider the economic assessments of TTIP – and it turns out that all these studies contain elements that are allegedly positive, but which in fact result from very subjective choices and have enormous political relevance.

From the point of view of scientific progress and effective debate, to have value-free, or *positive*, theories would be desirable: beyond the increased power in the public discourse, such theories would be uncontroversial and could represent a solid scientific foundation on which normative debates could then be contended. Having a set of positive results would facilitate the discourse among scientists since the common positive beliefs could serve as an effective common language enabling constructive normative debate, even if the scientists had different normative beliefs.

Because of this attractiveness of positive theory, its possible existence had been extensively debated in the social sciences.[1] In particular social economists and institutionalists made important contributions to this subject matter. These include, but are not limited to, the important pragmatist elaborations of Pierce and Dewey, who laid the philosophical groundwork for Veblenian institutionalism, a research programme that has always insisted that economics is a normative science. Gunnar Myrdal (1954) explains comprehensively (in a very influential book) how and why implicit value judgement enter economics through the interdependence of production and distribution, and through its very basic utility theory. And Hans Albert (1963), and later Jakob Kapeller (2013), elaborated on how economists use *axiomatic variation* to safe the results of their models from falsification, illustrating how malleable and open to subjective manipulation economic formalism can be.

So, although this compilation represents only a small subset of the critical literature on the subject matter, it illustrates that for most scholars who are directly concerned with the philosophy of sciences, the debate on whether positive economics can exist was settled some time ago – a fact that is, unfortunately, not known to many economists not working in the areas of the scholars mentioned above. This is noteworthy because an early and decisive part of this debate was conducted by members of the German Economic Association (*Verein für Socialpolitik*) in the so-called *Werturteilsstreit* at the beginning of the 20th century.

In this chapter I will focus on the main results of this early debate and not on the many explicit contributions made by social theorists, mentioned above. The reason is that it is not particularly surprising that institutionalist scholars disagree with more 'mainstream' economists about the epistemological foundations of economics – but it *is* striking that even the conservative scholars formulating an objective and value-free science as the ideal practice have reached the conclusion that this state of affairs is impossible. I will therefore focus on their arguments because if even these scholars acknowledge the unavoidable normativity in economics, we do not need to deal with more elaborated arguments. We only need to check whether recent methodological advances suggest the necessity for a reconsideration of these classical arguments.

One of the main conservative actors in the *Werturteilsstreit* was the economist and sociologist Max Weber. He clearly expressed his belief that an ideal social science would be entirely value-free and would be driven only by the scientist's thirst for knowledge (Weber, 1922a). This is why he is often quoted as an example for scholars arguing for the necessity of positive science. But in his writings he explicitly acknowledged that values and normative beliefs (unfortunately but) *necessarily* enter any analysis through the predispositions and experiences of the researcher (Weber, 1922a, b). This makes researchers from different persuasions hold different interpretations even for the (allegedly) simplest causal relationships between observed 'facts' (Weber, 1922a, p. 151). Even the choice of which questions warrant scientific inquiry is said to be driven partly by subjective idealist beliefs.[2] In his famous essay on the objectivity of the social sciences, he is very explicit:

> It is correct that in our discipline the personal worldviews [*Weltanschauungen*] always bias the scientific argument, and affect the judgement of the importance

> of scientific arguments, even if one tries to identify the simplest causal relationships of facts, always depending on whether the result would relate well to the personal worldviews and ideals, and how it affects the possibility to achieve a personal aim.
>
> (Weber, 1922a, p. 151, translation by CG)

Weber's point of view is helpful for our discussion because it shows that even those who are often considered of advocating a *positive* social science in fact acknowledged a subjective and normative element in the social sciences. This was something Weber also demanded from his fellows, since the most objectionable practice for him was to claim one's research to be absolutely value-free – something that in reality is simply impossible (Weber, 1922b).[3]

Strikingly, today the conventional wisdom in economics (in particular, economic textbooks) has changed completely. Many economists now take the misleading distinction between positive and normative economics as self-evident.

Representative for many, Milton Friedman claims in his famous (and notorious) essay on economic methodology that 'economics can be, and in part is, a positive science' (Friedman, 1953, p. 3). He later explicates that 'economics as a positive science is a body of tentatively accepted generalizations about economic phenomena that can be used to predict the consequences of changes in circumstances'.

Has there been any particular methodological innovation in the 20th century that has finally facilitated a truly positive science of economics? One of the leading economists of this century, Gerard Debreu (1991), describes very well that after World War II economics entered a phase of 'intense mathematization' that profoundly transformed the profession. This mathematization is often considered an objectification of economics since the rules of mathematics as such are usually considered entirely objective.

This view has been explicated most clearly by Debreu himself, who claims that the mathematical form of economic models can be and is completely separated from their economic content. From this 'divorce of form and content' (Debreu, 1986, p. 1265) it follows that every new interpretation of the formal economic models represents a new theory itself and that the mathematical model in its bare form exists *independent of any economic interpretation.*

From this perspective it is clear that economists (who are in this sense pure mathematicians) working on the development of the formal structure of the economic models (which are then essentially purely mathematical models) are concerned only with abstract mathematical objects without any content and thus no normativity at all.

But such arguments ignore the fact that the whole architecture economists use to build their models, in particular the fundamental assumptions (what Debreu (1986, p. 1265) calls the 'primitive concepts' and their 'representation as a mathematical object', the first step of building a mathematical-economic model), always contain at least a grain of subjectivity and normativity. And no matter how 'value-free' a deduction in the resulting mathematical framework as such might be, if the axiom is subjective, so is the conclusion.

Another important reason for why the mathematization of economics cannot eliminate the subjective elements in the theory is the fact that mathematics itself is a very diverse field. Economists use some mathematical tools significantly more than others. It is precisely this choice of the mathematical representation of primitive theoretical concepts (cf. Debreu, 1986) that is led by the subjective epistemological interest (*Erkenntnisinteresse*) of the researcher and often entails additional subjective (and thus potentially normative) elements: to approach a problem from a general equilibrium or an agent-based perspective both represent a mathematical strategy. Yet the implications are very different. Interestingly, Friedman is pretty explicit about this when he argues that 'the ultimate goal of a positive science is the development of a theory' and that such a theory is a "language" designed to promote "systematic and organized methods of reasoning"'. But which kind of language is to be chosen to build a model is still a decision to be made by the researcher and there are a lot of different languages, even within mathematics (see Hanappi, 2008, for more details).

The next section will provide a more precise account of how formal models gain epistemic meaningfulness and how this process illustrates their inherent subjectivity in their specification.

The political element of formal models in economics – an epistemological perspective

Economists regularly use formal models to study economic and social systems. Whoever uses models must, of course, be able to explain how the models generate knowledge about these systems despite the fact that the models are never an exact representation of reality. Unfortunately, economists are often not very explicit about how their models gain this epistemic meaningfulness. But the following framework provides both a philosophically well-grounded and intuitive answer. It is built upon Uskali Mäki's concept of '' (MISS) (Mäki, 2009a, b), which is enriched by the work of Miller and Page (2007) and Gräbner (2015).

According to the MISS approach, all models share two fundamental functions: in the first place they are built to *represent* the target system. This is required as real systems are regularly too complex to be understood directly. One thus reduces their complexity by abstracting away unnecessary details and focusing on particular aspects of reality. The result is a picture of reality that we shall call either *surrogate* or *substitute* models (Mäki, 2009a). A *surrogate* results from an active and reasonable attempt to learn something about reality and is therefore a direct representation of the real-world situation under study. In contrast, we speak of a *substitute* if the act of representing reality was a failure. There are numerous reasons for such a failure: either the researcher was not successful in building a representation, e.g. by choosing a wrong form of representation, or because the researcher was more interested in studying a model for its own sake, and not to learn something about the particular target system. This act is illustrated in Figure 14.1 by the function on the left: taking the target system R at $t = 0$ and reducing its complexity yields the surrogate S_0. We can think of the process of reducing the complexity as a mapping from the target system to the model.

The second function of a model is called *resemblance*. In the course of time the target system changes due to the mechanisms operating within it. These mechanisms are usually not observable and are never directly understandable. What researchers usually do is to build some artificial mechanisms into their surrogate, let them operate within the model and hope that the changes in the model correspond to those in the target system. In serious models, even the mechanisms within the models are not trivial, so one has to study the behaviour of the model, e.g. by simulating the system while altering certain parameters or by deriving mathematical proofs. This process is called model *exploration*. If we can learn something about the real world by the exploration of our model, the model resembles the real world and we have successfully increased our understanding of reality. Understanding here comes from the isolation of particular aspects of the target system.

Note that the act of 'understanding reality' can be interpreted in different ways. One may be interested in how certain variables in the real world change over time. One then wishes to infer facts about the real world. 'How does gross domestic product (GDP) per capita change over time?' would be a typical question. The crucial inference would be from the variable GDP in the model to the variable GDP in the real world. Another motivation for research may be one's interest in the mechanisms operating in the real world. That is, one wishes to infer from the mechanisms built into the model to the mechanisms operating in reality. 'Why does GDP evolve as it usually does?' or 'What are the determinants of income inequality over time?' would be typical questions for this case.

Again, we can illustrate this exercise with Figure 14.1: the mechanisms of the model are represented as the mapping s, the (unknown) mechanisms of the target system are represented via the mapping r. After the model world has evolved from S_0 to S_1 at time $t = 1$, one can then compare the resulting system S_1 with reality R_1 via the mapping h (i.e. comparing the resulting 'facts'). Or, one may assess the plausibility of the mechanisms operating in the model compared with reality, which may or may not lead to a similarity between R_1 and S_1.

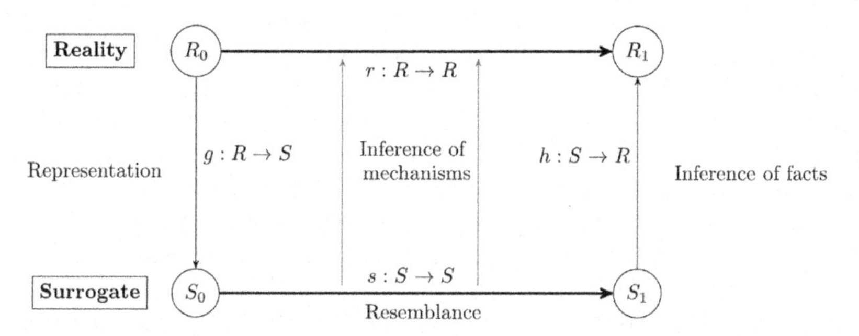

Figure 14.1 The models as isolation and surrogate systems (MISS) concept interpreted as a mapping process (Gräbner, 2015).

Here it becomes clear that different models differ both according to the mechanisms that operate within them (i.e. in their resemblance aspect), but also in the particular way they reduce the complexity of their target system (i.e. their representation aspect, or their complexity reduction function). The two aspects are related: certain mechanisms require a particular form of complexity reduction. If I want to model the dynamics resulting from the interactions among individuals and the emerging institutions, the complexity reduction function must preserve the notion of heterogeneous agents and their interaction structure. If I decide to model my target system using a single representative agent, such a form of resemblance is not possible any more.

This means that we can make a more general statement: it is not only the particular specification and interpretation of a model that is potentially normative. Also the choice of a particular *modelling framework* already explicates such kind of normativity: if a modeller decides to use a modelling framework that makes it impossible to study the consequences of direct interaction among heterogeneous agents then the researcher might not actively decide against modelling this particular element of the target system, but she did so indirectly – with potentially important consequences. In the case of direct interactions, Albin and Foley (1992) showed that if one allows for direct bargaining in a general equilibrium model, then a unique equilibrium emerges, but with different distributional consequences than in the static version with a *tâtonnement* process. We will see in the section dealing with the models assessing the effects of TTIP that exactly this aspect is particularly relevant.

Such aspects of modelling are missed by Debreu's idea of a complete 'divorce of form and content'. To capture all these aspects, Mäki (2009b) suggests a 'functional decomposition approach to modeling'. According to this view, models consist of different components that serve different purposes, and that models are not only constrained by the characteristics of their target system (the so-called *ontological constraints*), but also by the 'modellers' goals and contexts' (Mäki, 2009b, p. 179) – a clearly subjective and potentially normative element that can be explicated further.

Besides the mathematical form of the model, every model has a particular (potentially normative) *purpose* (Giere, 2006; Mäki, 2009b). But models are also addressed to a particular *audience,* usually to persuade it of the value of the model or to change its beliefs. There is also a model *description* and a *comment* on the model: a model in itself is just a bunch of equations or algorithms. For being a representation of reality it needs to be explained and interpreted by the modeller. Here, obvious degrees of freedom and thus room for personal judgements and tendentious descriptions exist – and researchers frequently use this freedom to (implicitly) convey their messages. Again, excellent examples are provided by the studies on the impact of a potential free-trade agreement between the USA and Europe, as discussed below.

Thinking about models in this way is useful because it explicates the degrees of freedom researchers have, and the role played by subjective motives in using these degrees. Before we turn to the examples provided by the TTIP studies, we will make a few comments on the misconception that the degrees of freedom could also be eliminated by empirically derived 'hard facts' and that a positive economics can emerge from empirical, data-driven work.

A positive science cannot be constructed by the retreat to empirical economics

During the last decades, theoretical economics has come under increasing critique. In particular when it comes to applied questions, more and more economists have become sceptical of economic theory. A common reaction is the retreat to less theoretical and more empirical work (Deaton, 2010). The intention is to substitute the imprecise theory for a more objective and scientific study of observed 'facts'.

If it wasn't the 'mathematization of economic theory' that enables a positive science of economics, then could this trend be a potential evasion of the problem of the subjective element in economic theory? If there is no theory, there is no normative element either. This strategy has been articulated most clearly by the advocates of *randomized controlled trials* (RCT) in economics. Banerjee (2007a), for example, calls RCTs 'a new economics' that is able to produce the 'hard facts' that lead to a thorough understanding of development processes and that is required to design reasonable and effective policy measures (Banerjee, 2007b).[4]

Note that, in this argument, the clear distinction between positive economics in the sense of 'what is' and normative economics in the sense of 'what should be' is explicitly blurred since the right policy follows directly from the 'hard facts'. In this sense this statement implicitly acknowledges the failure of such a distinction.

Yet such an inductive and observation-driven strategy will always be unsuccessful in constructing a truly positive science of economics, Firstly, observations can usually be interpreted very differently (see Weber, 1922b, p. 463). Examples in economics abound. For example, there is serious disagreement on whether the spike in Figure 14.2 represents either a speculative bubble (as argued by Richard Thaler in his presidential address at the American Economic Association meeting in 2016, an interpretation that would not be consistent with the standard theory), or simply two successive changes of the risk preferences of people (as argued by Cochrane (2011), an interpretation that is consistent with the standard theory).

Secondly, even the positivist members of the *Wiener Kreis* admitted after the *Protokollsatzdebatte* in the 1940s that even the most basic observations, the so-called protocol statements, cannot be considered fully objective elements.

But a strategy of focusing on empirical data to restore scientific objectivity will not only be unsuccessful in constructing a truly positive economics – it will also harm scientific progress in economics as such (Deaton, 2010). RCTs and other attempts to rely exclusively on the 'data' do not advance understanding at all because, instead of explaining *why* a certain policy was (un)successful, such models focus on *whether* it was (un)successful. Referring to Figure 14.1: they only care about predicting facts, not about the understanding of how the model has resembled the mechanisms of reality. Without a reference on the precise mechanisms underlying the success or failure of the policies, nothing can be gained (Deaton,

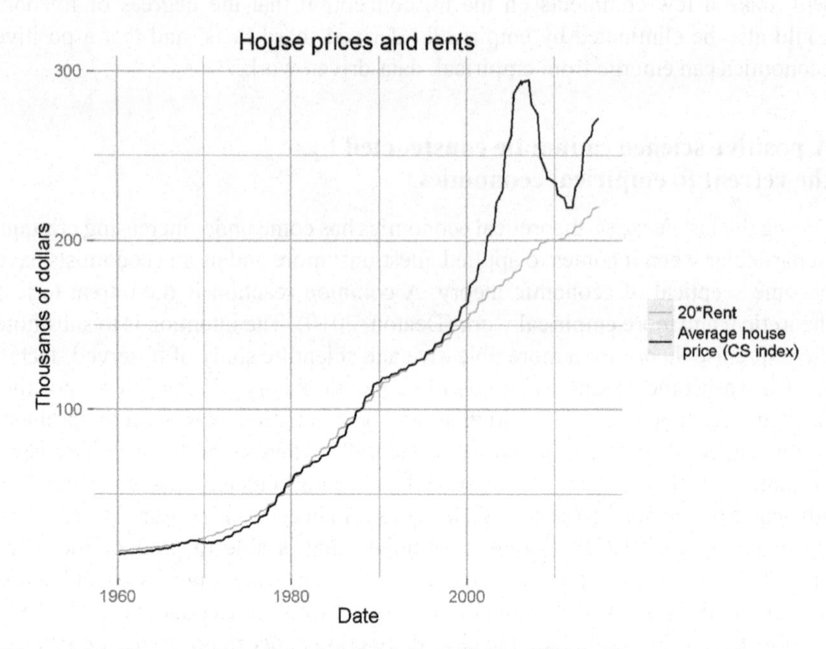

Figure 14.2 The evolution of rents and the Case–Shiller (CS) index measuring house prices. Is the spike a bubble or not?

2010, p. 426). And without reference to causal mechanisms, the results are almost useless for the design of policy measures since the policy implementation always differs from the trial – and since it is not clear *why* the trial was successful or not, nothing can be inferred about the potential success of the policy itself. The same argument applies to the external validity of the experiments: without a reference to the mechanisms that have led to the particular outcome of the study, it is by no means clear whether the results of the experiment can be generalized to other circumstances.

For example, the Mexican project of conditional cash transfer to parents who let their children attend school (called *Progresa*) was evaluated very successfully using RCT. But Levy (2006), the founder of this programme, made very clear that one must not infer the applicability of the programme to other institutional circumstances, since the conditional cash transfer is likely to interfere with other habits, traditions or institutional arrangements such as particular poverty reduction programmes. This relates to the argument of Page (2012) and Gräbner (2015) that mechanisms can have very different effects when operating in the existence of other mechanisms, and that the resulting interaction effects are of great theoretical importance. Of course, to study such interaction effects between different mechanisms one requires particular methods, e.g. agent-based computational models (Gräbner, 2016), which are still underdeveloped in most branches of economics.[5]

Of course, all these arguments in favour of theory-driven explanations apply not only to RCTs and other experimental approaches; they address all theory-free econometric work. Mechanisms are essential for understanding and mechanisms can only be suggested by good economic theory. Deaton (2010) makes his claim for the focus on concrete mechanisms from a very pragmatic perspective. Gräbner (2016) and Gräbner and Kapeller (2015) build upon Bunge (2004) and provide a general ontological and epistemological argument for a focus on mechanisms in providing economic explanations.

The direct consequence for applied economic research is that greater objectivity cannot be attained by focusing on the data alone. Rather, one must study a particular question with different models and theoretical approaches to reach a final conclusion. This is clearly beyond the scope of a single study. Thus, single studies should not sell their models as if they were the scientifically objective answer to a given problem. While this is increasingly common within the academic discourse (particularly in econometrics), the studies addressed to policy makers, reviewed in the next section, are making exactly this mistake.

Illustration: the debate about TTIP

The proceeding elaborations were necessarily very theoretical. Here I will illustrate what has been said on the unavoidable normative character of economic theory by looking at an important example. The discussions about the TTIP agreement between Europe and the USA are of essential political and societal importance and many economists have participated in the debate. Most of them argue in favour of the agreement, pointing to the potential gains of trade suggested by classical and neoclassical theory (Felbermayr and Larch, 2013). I will not enter the discussion about the precise effects of TTIP. Neither will I provide a thorough overview of all the existing studies and meta-studies. This work has already been done (for an excellent critical overview see, e.g. Raza et al., 2014). Instead I will use the most influential studies on TTIP as an example for the theoretical elaborations made above: all these models clearly contain formal models associated with particular comments, interpretation and audience-specific elements – as suggested by the functional decomposition approach discussed above. As such, they also contain subjective and (in this sense) clearly political elements that are, unfortunately, neither admitted nor discussed by the authors of the studies.

The studies thus also serve as an illustration that economic models consist of more than a pure mathematical model, as it was claimed by Debreu (1981). Instead, the mathematical models are inseparable from the author's comments, interpretations and economic ideals. This exercise shows the usefulness of Mäki's functional decomposition approach to modelling and illustrates a practice incompatible with Debreu's thesis of a separation of 'mathematical form and economic content'.

The result is a pseudo-scientific assessment of TTIP – exactly what Max Weber considered the worst case of scientific practice. This is representative of much of current economics and we will see that it is directly related to the narrow toolbox for the assessment of questions such as TTIP: an acknowledgement of the political element in formal modelling would imply the need for a methodologically more pluralistic assessment of policy relevant questions such as TTIP – and this is exactly what is not happening. In the following I will first give an overview of the models used for the TTIP studies, then provide some examples for their implicit political tendency, and finally make a constructive suggestion of how to improve the assessment of important political challenges such as the discussion about TTIP.

Overview of the existing studies and their methodological foundation

While a couple of studies on TTIP exist, some of them have been of particular political relevance (Raza et al., 2014):

1 Berden et al. (2009) was the first study commissioned by the European Commission and it provides the (data) basis for many of the later studies on TTIP.
2 Felbermayr et al. (2013a) is a report for the German Ministry for Economic Affairs also carried out by economists from the IFO institute. It is available only in German.
3 Francois et al. (2013) is a more recent report by the Centre for Economic Policy Research (London, UK) commissioned by the European Commission and the basis for the following assessments of the Commission.
4 Fontagné et al. (2013) provide a report for the French Centre d'Etudes Prospectives et d'Informations Internationales, which is dedicated to producing 'independent, policy-oriented economic research' and which has produced the standard computable general equilibrium (CGE) model for trade analysis called MIRAGE (Modelling International Relationships in Applied General Equilibrium).

There are a couple of important similarities between the studies: all come to a positive conclusion concerning the welfare and employment effects of TTIP and suggest its implementation.[6] Also, all of them use the same type of model, so-called CGE models.[7] Francois et al. (2013) used the CGE model developed by Berden et al. (2009), albeit with an updated version of the original database. The model of Fontagne et al. (2013) is of the same modelling class, uses a very similar database and differs only in details (see Raza et al., 2014, p. 42).

Using the vocabulary of our methodological framework outlined above, the way these models reduce the complexity of the real world is – *by design of the models* – very similar. All of them use representative individuals and neglect heterogeneity of the actors involved; none of them considers uncertainty or negative externalities of abolishing regulations (such as pollution or impact on health) at all. Also the mechanisms considered in the models are very similar since prices dissipate through (by assumption) cleared markets which function through perfect or imperfect competition. This means that the technical design of almost all studies on TTIP is very similar. But the similarity is not limited to the technical design: also the other functional components of the models resemble each other: they address a similar audience (policy makers). They provide very similar descriptions and arguments for motivating the modelling frameworks (which is simply considered 'standard') and particular specifications. The absence of any methodological self-reflection, yet a particular (even verbal) sensitivity analysis concerning more critical assumptions, is also missing from all elaborations. Even the commentaries that are used to relate these elements to each other are similar. All models consider themselves to be objective scientific assessments that in the end suggest a straightforward policy recommendation. This is interesting since one might argue that the choice of the CGE modelling framework is, given its prominent place in economics curricula and its accepted place in the journal landscape, not surprising. But it *is* somehow surprising that all these different economists present and justify their models in such a similar fashion. In particular against the backdrop of the largely critical experiences made with CGE models, e.g. when estimating the effects of the North American Free Trade Agreement (NAFTA, see Raza et al., 2014, chapter 2.3), this is an alarming signal.[8]

Examples for the political elements

A closer inspection of the models reveals that there is a large number of small but significant decisions to be made regarding the closure and parametrization of the models. In the following I will use three simple examples that illustrate the political element in the studies on TTIP. They address decisions made on different levels of specificity: firstly I argue that the choice of the CGE framework is normative as such since its form of complexity reduction excludes certain questions that can be of relevance for welfare assessments, e.g. the distributions of gains and harms of the agreement. The second point is similar but refers to the choice of using static models instead of dynamic ones. The third point does not refer to CGE modelling in general, but to the particular parameterization of the models.

The choice of the modelling framework has normative consequences and the description of the model results does not reflect this. Considering the presentation of the models, it has already been mentioned that authors do not discuss potential disadvantages of CGE modelling. The fact that the way these models reduce the complexity of the real world makes it particularly difficult to study questions of inequality, however, represents a particular political element in the choice of this framework – especially if this disadvantage is not articulated and authors focus instead on describing other, allegedly positive effects of the agreement that can be studied with CGE models. The fact, however, that inequality is an important variable to be discussed in the context of free-trade arrangements is, at least since the experience with NAFTA, very clear (see, e.g. Hanson, 2003, or Abbott, 2004). So a direct reference to this potential disadvantage of the models in the model description of the comments on the results would have improved the analysis significantly. In the current form it is hard to neglect an implicit and intransparent political tendency in these studies.

The model framework and its specification: static model and no adjustment

None of the studies considers the size and distribution of adjustment costs. This is clearly related to the modelling framework employed by the studies: CGE models often assume complete use of factor endowments – therefore all CGE models used do not feature unemployment by assumption. The authors justify this practice with their focus on the long-run effects of the trade agreement (i.e. at least 10 years), but this clearly masks the negative effects of short- and medium-run unemployment. As illustrated by Raza et al. (2014), these adjustment costs are very likely to be distributed unequally, affecting low-skilled and older employees much harder (since they are more likely not to find a new job at all). Again, this drawback refers to the fact that most CGE models are static by construction, and even 'dynamic' versions do not feature a dynamic analysis of the equilibrium adjustment paths.

The formal specification of the models

One crucial decision within the model specification process is the specification or estimation of model elasticities, in particular the *price elasticity of trade*. These parameters specify the sensitivity of exports to changes in the price of the product. Since price decreases have by assumption no negative impact on employment (and thus aggregate income), the higher the price elasticity to trade, the higher the potential gains from a free-trade agreement (Raza et al., 2014, p. 81). Several aspects are noteworthy: firstly, one might have expected to see a careful sensitivity analysis for such a fundamental quantity in the models. This is, however, not the case. Given the proficiency of the authors involved, this is surprising. Secondly, one might have expected the authors to use parameters well informed by the empirical literature. Again, the authors have decided differently: the elasticities used vary between 5% and 7%. Such a value is common for microeconomic studies – for macroeconomic applications, values of 1.5–2.0% are considered realistic (Taylor & von Armin, 2006; Raza et al., 2014). Such choices make it hard to ascribe objectivity to these models – in particular because they do not explain their choice of parameters transparently.

What an economic assessment of TTIP should have looked like

How would a reasonable assessment of TTIP look like if one had accepted the argument presented above that any economic model contains particular subjective (and thus potentially normative) statements, if one had considered the epistemological and methodological framework elaborated above, and if one had been aware of the limitations of empirical work in yielding a truly positive science, outlined above? In the following I will make three very simple and immediate suggestions that – unintentionally – align very well with the research practice of evolutionary political economy as outlined by Hanappi and Scholz-Wäckerle (2015).

Firstly, any policy-relevant study in economics should be transparent and fair concerning the (potentially arbitrary) assumptions one has made. This has already been emphasized by Max Weber and it is as true as ever: in any applied economic model, the modeller has certain degrees of freedom, e.g. by determining the elasticities of the CGE model, whose specification depends partly on their personal worldview. In this case the researcher should just say so. It does not invalidate the model, in particular if the modeller performed at least some rough sensitivity analysis. But it would certainly address the critique of making pseudo-objective science.

Secondly, any policy report must include a section on methodological considerations. By this I do not mean the description of the model, but a clear discussion of what modelling frameworks are principally at disposal, their respective advantages and disadvantages, why one has picked in particular the one that has been used in the study, and what this means for the interpretation of the results.

Thirdly, ideally, extensive policy reports that are meant to form the basis for further political decision making (such as the study by Francois et al. (2013) for the European Commission) should include at least two competing (and distinctive) modelling frameworks. It is striking that there is not a single agent-based model used to analyse the effects of TTIP. Agent-based models would have yet another advantage, thanks to their flexibility that can be used to perform sensitivity analysis for the particular assumptions made in more analytical models. They are also predestined for a dynamic analysis of the TTIP effects, including adjustment costs. This argument does not only relate to the economists who write the report: politicians also should not think they can outsource their political decisions to an objective scientific apparatus. Therefore they should consider different studies and demand a methodological and theoretical pluralism among the reports they base their decision on.

The last two points illustrate an important dilemma economics is currently facing: because it is methodologically extremely narrow, all studies on TTIP use similar complexity reduction functions (Figure 14.1). An adequate assessment would have used different modelling approaches that have fewer results already built in in the assumptions of the model itself. No model will ever fit perfectly, and some degree of uncertainty about the outcome of policy measures will always remain. But this uncertainty could be reduced significantly if the variance of the complexity reduction strategies was larger. The current situation is thus also a direct consequence of the narrow curricula in economics education.

Summary and conclusion

The starting point of the chapter was the question of whether economic modelling can be *positive* in the sense of *non-normative* or *value-free*. I showed that earlier social theorists did not believe in the existence of a positive economics in this sense – even if authors such as Max Weber considered it to be the ideal way of doing economics. We then continued to discuss the methodological trends and innovations in the 21st century and asked whether they enabled a positive economics. We concluded, however, that neither the mathematization of economics nor a trend towards a-theoretical empiricism was able to reverse the original result.

Does the inevitability of a normative element in economic theory pose a threat to economics as a science? I do not think so. The fact that any economic model is to some extent normative does not mean it cannot be a good model that helps to understand the real world – even if such understanding will always remain provisional. But the current crisis shows that good economic analysis is needed more than ever.

But there are a couple of consequences that can be drawn from the elaborations above: firstly, acknowledgement and transparent communication of normative elements in modelling and a transparent discussion of them increases the quality of scientific work. Secondly, flexible modelling techniques that are able to test for the particular consequences of certain complexity reduction strategies are required. Agent-based models immediately come to mind. They are able to test the relevance of assumptions that are inextricably linked to other modelling approaches such as CGE modelling: if one wishes to know whether agent heterogeneity is important, a CGE model does not help, since it cannot produce the counterfactual with heterogeneous agents. Generally, keeping in mind the case study of TTIP, the toolbox of economists seems to be far too narrow.

Therefore, a third conclusion would be a more pluralistic education of economists, including basics in economic methodology and epistemology. This should help them to communicate their research more transparently and engage in productive discussions of economists taking other approaches, instead of masking political elements in modelling and thus doing qualitatively poor pseudo-objective science.

Notes

1 The discussion was particular important for the social sciences because observation of facts and mechanisms is much more difficult than in the natural sciences. But in particular in physics a similar debate took place, with the result that all experiments and the corresponding interpretations always entail a particular subjective – and thus potentially normative – element.
2 What Weber did reject was the possibility of deriving certain normative values or *Weltanschauungen* scientifically. For him, these were ultimately a subjective matter derived from the fundamental ideals and beliefs of individual researchers. He therefore also claimed that scientists should only study the potential effects of particular policy measure. But the ultimate decision of which measures should be taken to achieve a certain aim is said to be beyond the realm of science and scientists should not engage in such discussions as scientists but only as politicians (Weber, 1922a).
3 A debate that was related to the *Werturteilsstreit* was the so-called *Positivismusstreit* (Positivism dispute). But again, in this discourse both conservative thinkers such as Karl Popper and progressive thinkers such as Jürgen Habermas agreed on the existence of a subjective element in the social sciences.
4 This form of argument has already been anticipated and criticized by Weber, who writes: 'I will not discuss, but explicitly acknowledge that particularly the alleged eradication of any practical judgment, in particular of the form that one "let's the facts speak for themselves", suggestively evokes exactly this kind of judgment' (Weber, 1922b, p. 460, translation by CG).
5 Similar arguments have been made by institutionalist economists ever since. But they are often sceptical of identifying general mechanisms in economics at all. I do not

share this pessimism and think that mechanisms with a certain generality can indeed be identified (and classical institutionalists have indeed done this very successfully, e.g. Gunnar Myrdal with his *backwash* and *spread effects,* or his notion of *circular cumulative causation*). The argument is also similar to the elaborations of Pawson and Tilley (1997), who accentuate the importance of the environment in which particular mechanisms operate.

6 Their suggestion in favour of TTIP is clearly a normative statement. All studies, however, base this statement on an allegedly thorough and positive analysis of the effects of the free-trade agreement. This kind of schizophrenia can also be observed in Felbermayr and Larch (2013), a journal article providing answers to the most urgent answers around TTIP. In this context it is striking that, even in the explicitly normative part of the reports, the authors do not discuss the many implicit assumptions inherent in their welfare analysis. In particular, they do not discuss any negative implications of abandoning certain legal rules as a measure to reduce non-tariff trade barriers. To the contrary: lowering the regulation standard as a means of harmonizing the regulatory framework is considered as welfare-enhancing. There is not a word about regulations addressing negative (and welfare-decreasing) negative external effects or protecting the interests of the individuals.

7 One study that is not discussed here, Felbermayr et al. (2013b), takes indeed another approach. It is a report resulting from a study commissioned by the business-friendly Bertelsmann-Stiftung and carried out by economists mainly affiliated with the IFO institute in Munich, Germany. Here the authors try to answer a different question, namely how much liberalization is required to reach a certain positive effect. While the authors use CGE modelling only sparely, the theory underlying their econometric model is very similar to the ones discussed here.

8 An even more dubious practice is that some of the authors of a TTIP study write in another article (Felbermayr and Lerch, 2013) that nearly all studies on TTIP find positive effects – and use this as an argument for the validity of the studies. Not mentioning that all underlying models are very similar and use almost the same data seems to be an (at best unintended) deception.

References

Abbott, M. 2004. The impacts of integration and trade on labor markets: Methodological challenges and consensus findings in the NAFTA context, *Commission for Labor Cooperation Working Papers Series,* December, No. 1.

Albert, H. 1963. Modell-Platonismus – Der neoklassische Stil des o ökonomischen Denkens in kritischer Beleuchtung, in E. Topitsch (ed.), *Logik der Sozialwissenschaften*, Berlin: Kiepenheuer & Witsch, pp. 406–434.

Albin, P., and Foley, D. 1992. Decentralized, dispersed exchange without an auctioneer: A simulation study, in: *Journal of Economic Behavior & Organization,* Vol. 18(1), 27–51.

Banerjee, A. 2007a. *Making Aid Work*, Cambridge, MA: MIT Press.

Banerjee, A. 2007b. Inside the machine: Toward a new development economics, in: *Boston Review,* Vol. 32(2), 12–18.

Berden, K., Francois, J., Thelle, M., Wymenga, P., and Tamminen, S. 2009. Non-Tariff Measures in EU-US Trade and Investment – An Economic Analysis, Final Report for the European Commission. Available at: http://trade.ec.europa.eu/doclib/docs/2009/december/tradoc_145613.pdf (accessed 30 September 2016).

Bunge, M. 2004. How does it work? The search for explanatory mechanisms, in: *Philosophy of the Social Sciences*, Vol. 34(2), 182–210.

Cochrane, J. 2011. Presidential address: Discount rates, in: *The Journal of Finance,* Vol. 66(4), 1047–1108.

Deaton, A. 2010. Instruments, randomization, and learning about development, in: *Journal of Economic Literature*, Vol. 48(2), 424–455.

Debreu, G. 1986. Mathematical form and economic content, in: *Econometrica*, Vol. 54(6), 1259–1270.

Debreu, G. 1991. The mathematization of economic theory, in: *American Economic Review*, Vol. 81(1), 1–7.

Felbermayr, G., and Larch, M. 2013. Transatlantic free trade: Questions and answers from the vantage point of trade theory, in: *CESifo Forum,* Vol. 14(4), 3–17.

Felbermayr, G., Larch, M., Flach, L., Yalcin, E., and Benz, S. 2013a. Dimensionen und Auswirkungen eines Freihandelsabkommens zwischen der EU und den USA. Endbericht zur Studie im Auftrag des Bundesministeriums für Wirtschaft und Technologie. Final report for the Federal Ministry for Economic Affairs and Energy (ifo Institute, Munich).

Felbermayr, G., Heid, B., and Lehwald, S. 2013b. Transatlantic trade and investment partnership (TTIP). Who benefits from a free trade deal? Part 1: macroeconomic effects. Final report for the Bertelsmann Stiftung, Bertelsmann Stiftung, Gütersloh. Available at: http://www.bfna.org/sites/default/files/TTIP-GED%20study%2017June%202013.pdf (accessed 30 September 2016).

Fontagné, L., Gourdon, J., and Jean, S. 2013. Transatlantic trade: Whither partnership, which economic consequences?, in: *Centre d'Etudes Prospectives et d'Informations Internationales, Policy Brief,* No. 1.

Francois, J., Manchin, M., Norberg, H., Pindyuk, O., and Tomberger, P. 2013. Reducing transatlantic barriers to trade and investment: An economic assessment. Report for the European Commission, Centre for Economic Policy Research, London, UK. Available at: http://trade.ec.europa.eu/doclib/docs/2013/march/tradoc_150737.pdf (accessed 30 September 2016).

Friedman, M. 1953. The methodology of positive economics, in: *Essays in Positive Economics,* Chicago, IL: University of Chicago Press, pp. 3–48.

Giere, R. 2006. *Scientific Perspectivism*, Chicago, IL: University of Chicago Press.

Gräbner, C. 2016. Agent-based computational models: A formal heuristic for institutionalist pattern modelling? in: *Journal of Institutional Economics*, Vol. 12(1), 241–261.

Gräbner, C. 2015. Methodology does matter: About implicit assumptions in applied formal modelling. *Mpra Working Paper No. 63003.*

Gräbner, C., and Kapeller, J. 2015. New perspectives on institutionalist pattern modeling: Systemism, complexity, and agent-based modeling. in: *Journal of Economic Issues,* Vol. 49(2), 433–440.

Hanappi, H. 2008. On the nature of knowledge. An evolutionary perspective, *Mpra Working Paper No. 27615.*

Hanappi, H., and Scholz-Wäckerle, M. 2008. Evolutionary political economy: Content and methods. *Forum for Social Economics,* forthcoming.

Hanson, G. 2003. What has happened to wages in Mexico since NAFTA? *NBER Working Papers 9563.*

Kapeller, J. 2013. 'Model-Platonism' in economics: on a classical epistemological critique, in: *Journal of Institutional Economics*, Vol. 9(2), 199–221.

Levy, S. 2006. *Progress Against Poverty: Sustaining Mexico's Progresa-Oportunidades Program,* Washington, WA: Brookings Institution Press.

Mäki, U. 2009a. Missing the world. Models as isolations and credible surrogate systems, in: *Erkenntnis*, Vol. 70(1), 29–43.

Mäki, U. 2009b. Models and truth: The functional decomposition approach. In M. Suárez, M. Rédei, & M. Dorato (Eds.), *EPSA Epistemology and Methodology of Science: Launch of the European Philosophy of Science Association*, Dordrecht: Springer, pp. 177–187.

Miller, J. H., and Page, S. 2007. *Complex Adaptive Systems. An Introduction to Computational Models of Social Life*, Princeton, NJ: Princeton University Press.

Myrdal, G. 1954. *The Political Element in the Development of Economic Theory*, Cambridge, MA: Harvard University Press.Page, S. 2012. Aggregation in agent-based models of economies, in: *The Knowledge Engineering Review*, Vol. 27(2), 151–162.

Pawson, R., and Tilley, N. 1997. *Realistic Evaluation*, London, UK: Sage Publications.

Raza, W., Grumiller, J., Taylor, L., Tröster, B., and von Arnim, R. 2014. An economic assessment of the claimed benefits of the Transatlantic Trade and Investment Partnership (TTIP). In: Scherrer, C., ed. *The Transatlantic Trade and Investment Partnership (TTIP): Implications for Labor*. Munich: Rainer Hampp Verlag, pp. 41–99.

Taylor, L., and von Arnim, R. 2006. *Modelling the Impact of Trade Liberalisation: A Critique of Computable General Equilibrium Models, Report for Oxfam International*. Available at: http://policy-practice.oxfam.org.uk/publications/modelling-the-impact-of-trade-liberalisation-a-critique-of-computable-general-e-112547 (accessed 30 September 2016).

Thaler, R. 2016. Behavioral economics: past, present, and future, in: *American Economic Review*, Vol. 106(7), 1577–1600.

Weber, M. 1922a. Die Objektivität sozialwissenschaftlicher und sozialpolitischer Erkenntnis, in: *Gesammelte Aufsätze zur Wissenschaftslehre*, Tübingen: Mohr Siebeck, pp. 146–214.

Weber, M. 1922b. Der Sinn der "Wertfreiheit" der soziologischen und ökonomischen Wissenschaften, in: *Gesammelte Aufsätze zur Wissenschaftslehre*, Tübingen: Mohr Siebeck, pp. 451–502.

Index